MEMOIRS OF A BRETON PEASANT

Memoirs of a Breton Peasant

JEAN-MARIE DÉGUIGNET

Translated from the French by Linda Asher

Seven Stories Press

NEW YORK I LONDON I TORONTO I MELBOURNE

Seven Stories Press
140 Watts Street
New York, NY 10013
www.sevenstories.com

In Canada: Hushion House, 36 Northline Road, Toronto, Ontario M4B 3E2

In the U.K.: Turnaround Publisher Services Ltd., Unit 3, Olympia Trading Estate,
Coburg Road, Wood Green, London N22 6TZ

In Australia: Palgrave Macmillan, 627 Chapel Street, South Yarra VIC 3141

Library of Congress Cataloging-in-Publication Data

Déguignet, Jean-Marie, 1834–1905.
 [Mémoires d'un paysan bas-breton. English]
 Memoirs of a Breton peasant, 1834-1905 / Jean-Marie Déguignet ;
translated from the French by Linda Asher.—1st ed.
  p. cm.
Includes bibliographical references.
 ISBN 1-58322-616-8 (alk. paper)
1. Déguignet, Jean-Marie, 1834–1905. 2. Peasantry—France—Brittany—
Biography.
3. Poor—France—Brittany—Biography. 4. Soldiers—France—Biography.
5. Farmers—France—Brittany—Biography. 6. Church and state—France.
7. Brittany (France)—Rural conditions. I. Asher, Linda. II. Title.
HD1536.F8 D39713 2004
305.5'633'092—dc22
                                                2003020061

9 8 7 6 5 4 3 2 1

College professors may order examination copies of Seven Stories Press titles for a
free six-month trial period. To order, visit www.sevenstories.com/textbook/, or fax
on school letterhead to (212) 226-1411.

Book design by Cindy LaBreacht

Printed in the U.S.A.

CONTENTS

I
THE BEGGAR BOY
1834–1853

II
THE SOLDIER
1853–1868

III
THE FARMER
1868–1882

IV
PERSECUTED
1882–1905

THE STORY BEHIND THIS STORY

Bernez Rouz, editor

In the late 1970s, it became apparent that the population was growing and changing rapidly in the village of Ergué-Gaberic on the outskirts of Quimper in Brittany. New settlers had come to outnumber the native-born residents, and it seemed urgent to gather what recollections and historical records might preserve the sense and artifacts of the old rural commune. The local historical society, *Arkae*, set out to establish an archive for that purpose.

The easiest way to begin was to find and inventory the few existing studies on the commune or on notable figures who came from it. Researchers turned to "The Bulletin of the Archaeological Society of Finistère" as a major avenue for these first steps into the byways of the collective memory. And there, on page 83 of a grayish, unprepossessing volume of issues from 1963, they came across an article by [historian] Louis Ogès introducing a "humble bouquet of ancestral blossoms sprung from the folk soul of Breton Cornouaille"—fifty pages of tales and legends. Routine enough, it would seem, in that heyday of interest in regional traditions, but the writer of these tales det-

[11]

onated off the page: "The informants made fools of the scholars . . . in exchange for a glass of brandy, those men and women
invented legends out of whole cloth. . . ." That set the tone.
And Ogès went on to say that this sharply opinionated character wrote his whole life story with that same caustic verve—
twenty-six notebooks of a hundred pages each.

Unbelievable! But the delight of the discovery was followed
by long nights of discussion and puzzlement: where had those
sulfurous manuscripts got to?

The quest led us to *La revue de Paris*, a literary magazine
that published work by such well-known writers as Renan,
Loti, Barrès, D'Annunzio. And in the issue of December 1904
there appeared an excerpt of *Mémoires d'un paysan bas-Breton*
by Jean-Marie Déguignet. The folklorist Anatole Le Braz, who
prepared the text, described the author in dithyrambic terms:

It was in 1897, an evening in June.

In comes a man of about sixty years, still very lively
in appearance and manner, fairly small, short-legged
with hulking shoulders, the classic type of the
Quimperois peasant, dressed in the local style and bearing all the external markers of such a man, except for
one detail: instead of the shaven face of his fellows, he
let his tow-colored beard grow freely, and it bristled his
face with its abundant, untended brush. He wore
wooden clogs. His clothes were worn but clean.

I saw in short order that he knew French very well,
and even used it, mostly with a precision of expression
that a good many bourgeois would envy.

There was a certain bitter harshness to his tone.
Great was my surprise to hear a peasant of Lower
Brittany speak with such casual disrespect about beliefs
that may be the most profoundly rooted in the heart of

the race. He saw my amazement, and, levelling upon me the clear gaze of his gray eyes hooded by a canopy of thick brows, he said:

"Ah! well, you see—I am a peasant who has moved about a good deal, whereas the others stayed put."

And the excerpted *Mémoires* tell us that this Déguignet—in turn beggar, cowherd, domestic servant—learned French on his own. As a soldier, he fought in the Crimean campaign; on furlough in Jerusalem, he lost his faith, revolted by the commercial practices around pilgrimage. Promoted to corporal, he took part in the Italian campaign for liberation. Then—nothing more: *La revue de Paris* ceased its publication of the *Mémoires*.

Those one hundred-thirty pages in *La revue de Paris*, largely on his military campaigns, gave us a taste for this wild honey mead. We had those first clues, but the Grail itself remained to be found.

A few soundings of the familial history left us skeptical as to the continued existence of the notebooks, for no one had heard of them. Then a journalist's newspaper appeal for the manuscript bore fruit: the precious writings lay sleeping in a public housing project in Quimper. Thanks to the kindness of Jean-Marie Déguignet's descendants, and the diligence of the municipality of Ergué-Gaberic, forty-three notebooks—nearly 4,000 pages—were photocopied.

The saga of Jean-Marie Déguignet could now be made whole. He left the army after the Italian wars; he looked in vain for work in Brittany; he re-enlisted. His new military career took him to Algeria and then to Mexico to help shore up the ill-fated Emperor Maximilian. Discharged in 1868, he came home to work as a peasant farmer, insurance agent, tobacco-seller; his republican, anticlerical views got him hounded by the church party. He spent his last years destitute in various Quimper slums. There, in the 1890s, he wrote his story, his account of his "ninth-class peasant" life.

But the *Story of My Life* that we have in hand is not the same one represented by *La revue de Paris* text. On page 1467 of the newer manuscript, Jean-Marie Déguignet explains that [back in 1897] Anatole Le Braz paid him one hundred francs for the rights to publish his *Mémoires,* and took away the original writings. Several years later, when neither publication nor money had turned up, Déguignet cries thief, imagines a conspiracy of "the Breton nationalisto-clericocos," and sets about writing his life story all over again. What we have is that new version.

Now, to put it before the public.

As it was for Anatole Le Braz, for Louis Ogès, for the editors at *La revue de Paris,* the task promised to be very arduous. The French idiom of the autodidact Déguignet is remarkable, threaded with Bretonisms, bejeweled with quotations in Latin, Italian, and Spanish; the text is studded with digressions, but rich with vernacular expressions in the man's savory Cornouaille speech. It might mean rewriting the *Mémoires* entirely: 2,584 pages of student notebooks! *La revue de Paris* had given up on the task; it had published only those hundred thirty pages, revised and corrected by Anatole Le Braz. But that reworked version, which might appeal to fans of cheap fiction, would not be useful as a document for demanding readers shaped by the present-day social sciences.

The decision was reached to type up the text bit by bit. Thanks to a long chain of volunteers, the Ergué-Gaberic Municipal Library inherited an accessible version of the twenty-four surviving notebooks of Déguignet's *Mémoires.* Other notebooks of lesser interest on philosophy, politics, sociology, and even mythology remain in manuscript form.

But it soon became apparent that, given the chance, readers were unwilling to read the full text. The author, who was writing in enormously trying circumstances at the turn of the last century—he lived in a hovel on a fern-frond mat—was mentally troubled, obsessed with his persecution; he was angry at the nobility, the parish priests, the politicians, all of them the sources of his misfortunes. He especially resented Anatole Le Braz, who "stole" his manuscripts. His writings are burdened by anticlericalist tirades, by digressions into local or national politics, by diatribes against his enemies, all running off at the pen in indescribable disorder. These circumvolutions, which become unremitting from the ninth notebook on, make the reading an ordeal.

We therefore decided to propose to An Here Publishers this edited text: a running narrative made up of excerpts from the adventures of Citizen Déguignet, one that would make the account coherent and readily accessible without betraying either the spirit or the letter of the original.

For the testimony is still enormously powerful. It is a unique document of rural Breton society in the nineteenth century. Déguignet is not part of that tradition of churchmen, aristocrats, and intellectuals interested in glorifying folkways. De La Villemarque, Souvestre, Luzel, Le Braz, and many others are a million miles away from the concerns of our autodidact. What we have here, for the first time, is the direct testimony of a poor man among poor men: beggar, cowherd, private soldier, sergeant, farmer, shopkeeper, pauper, madman—a fierce destiny in which life's pleasures have little place. These memoirs of a tormented soul challenge afresh a number of preconceived notions about the golden age of rural civilization in Lower Brittany.

Déguignet the soldier is also highly incisive on military life. The Crimean War, the Italian War, the Algerian

Campaign, the Mexican War—in the space of fourteen years he lived through all the expeditions of the Second Empire. Through his experience as corporal and as sergeant, he provides us a scathing look inside the French Army—a wholesome counterpoint to the soothing accounts by the generals and the official historians.

The most disconcerting element in Déguignet is certainly his anticlerical bias. A journey to Jerusalem definitively turned this model catechism pupil away from religion. A priest-eating ogre, his arguments and diatribes may stir a smile these days, but at the time he was writing his life story, Finistère was involved in a virtual religious war. From 1902 to 1905, the secular and anticlericalist policies of the national government were hotly contested in Brittany. Demonstrations against the expulsion of the religious communities, protests against the prohibition of the Breton language in church sermons, made the climate particularly tense. Déguignet, the atheistic republican, could scarcely keep silent in such a debate. He flooded powerful people, officials, and local newspapers with abusive letters—letters he reproduces whole in his text, and of slight interest. But his tangles with the local clergy are vivid, and, if the imprecations are ignored, the text is a flavorful evocation of the difficulty of being a freethinker in a society entirely regulated and controlled by the all-powerful Church.

There remains, finally, the polemic against Anatole Le Braz. The noted writer meets our peasant in Quimper in 1897. The text is a shock to him: "All unsuspecting, I opened the first notebook. It was a revelation. Not until I had read every word could I tear myself away from the powerful, rough appeal of these intimate writings from a Breton man of the people." He offers Déguignet one hundred francs and promises to publish his manuscript. For some reason, not until December 1904 (seven years later!) does *La revue de Paris* print the first of

Déguignet's pages. For seven years, no contact at all, while Le Braz is publishing successful books like *The Legend of Death among Armorican Bretons.* Déguignet is convinced that Le Braz has destroyed his work because of its anticonformist views, or—worse still—that he plundered Déguignet's manuscript to feed his own work: hence the condemnation. The publication of the first pages of his *Mémoires* a few weeks before his death came as a veritable balm to his spirit's sufferings.

Some readers will be startled by the violence of Déguignet's comments on his Breton compatriots. Few come off well. An avenger against conservatism, against the routine, alert to anarchist and revolutionary ideas, he is always out of step with the society of his time. This diary of a tormented soul sometimes reminds one of the *Confessions* of Jean-Jacques Rousseau.* Déguignet may irritate, but his narrative is alive, forever rebounding, and it reads like a true adventure tale. Certainly its finest quality is sincerity, and that is its appeal. No bookshelf devoted to truth can be without Déguignet as an extraordinary witness and critic of "The Waning of Rural France" and the start of the breakdown of traditional Breton society.

—Bernez Rouz

---

*The name "Déguignet" has some linguistic link to the Breton term for "flayed alive."

1er Janvier 1901.

Nous voici au XXᵉ siècle et je vis toujours. Né le 17 juillet 1834 j'aurai bientôt 67 ans. C'est peut être un peu trop vivre quand on ne sert plus à rien. Il est vrai que bien des gens qui n'ont jamais servi à rien sont encore plus vieux que moi et qui supportent leur vieillesse sans se plaindre, ni sans plaindre ceux qui les supportent. Ces gens du reste, dont j'en connais plusieurs ici, ne pensent plus si jamais ils ont pensé, leur moral, leur esprit, leur intelligence ne comptent plus si jamais ils ont compté pour quelque chose dans leur existence. Leur vie d'aujourd'hui n'est qu'une vie purement animale ou même végétale car leur raison et leur sentiment ne sont plus bien que ceux de ces êtres animés ou inanimés. Ce sont des êtres relativement heureux encore. Ceux dont les souleurs physiques ne tourmentent pas trop. C'est de ceux-là que parlent les évangiles. beati pauperes spiritu quoniam regnum cælorum ipsorum est. Et en effet, dans cet état d'anéantissement intellectuel, une pensée cependant leur reste, celle d'être encore heureux dans un autre monde après l'anéantissement du corps. quoique je ne sache pas trop comment il

TRANSLATOR'S NOTE

Occasional words are interpolated for context or clarification, either from the translator or from editors of the French compilation; these are usually bracketed, though phrasing alone sometimes broadens an interpretation. Direct translations, typically from or to the Breton or Latin, appear in parentheses.

—L.A.

Map of Glazig Region

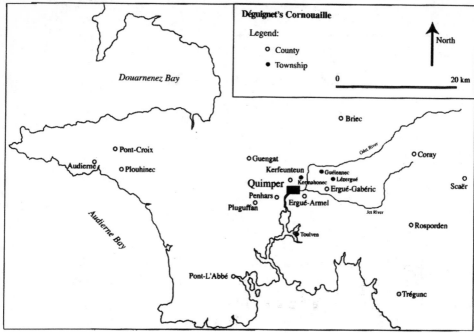

Déguignet's Cornouaille

Legend:
○ County
● Township

North

0   20 km

Douarnenez Bay

○ Briec

Odet River

○ Pont-Croix   ○ Coray

Audierne ○   ○ Plouhinec   ○ Guengat   ● Guéleanec
                                    Kerfeunteun   ● Lézergué   ○ Scaër
                            Quimper   ● Kernahonec   ● Ergué-Gabéric
                                    Penhars   ○
                            Pluguffan   Ergué-Armel   Jet River
                                                        ○ Rosporden
Audierne Bay   ● Toulven

Pont-L'Abbé ○   ○ Trégunc

Copyright © Norbert Bernard 2001

Map of Déguignet's Military Travels

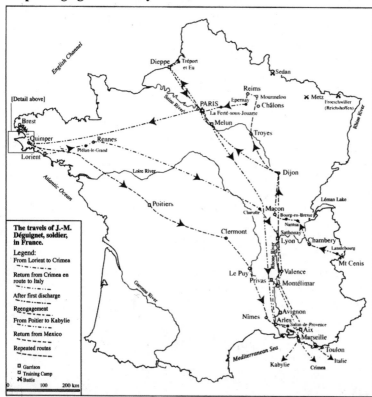

English Channel

Dieppe   Tréport et Eu   ✗ Sedan

Reims
[Detail above]   Epernay   ○ Mourmelon   ✗ Metz
                                                Froeschwiller
Brest   PARIS   Châlons   (Reichshoffen)
        La Ferté-sous-Jouarre
○ Quimper   Melun   Rhine River
        Rennes   Troyes
Lorient   Piélan-le-Grand

Loire River   Dijon

Atlantic Ocean   Léman Lake
        ○ Poitiers
                        Charolle   ○ Macon   Bourg-en-Bresse
                                        Nantua
                Clermont   Sathonay   ○ Chambery
                                        Lyon   Lanslebourg
                                                Mt Cenis
The travels of J.-M.
Déguignet, soldier,   Le Puy   Valence
in France.   Privas   Montélimar

Legend:
From Lorient to Crimea
                        Avignon
Return from Crimea en   Nîmes   Arles   Salon-de-Provence
route to Italy   Aix
                                Marseille
After first discharge   Toulon
                                        Italie
Reengagement   Mediterranean Sea
                        Kabylie   Crimea
From Poitier to Kabylie

Return from Mexico

Repeated routes

□ Garrison
▫ Training Camp
✗ Battle
0   100   200 km

Garonne River

Rhône River

Copyright © Norbert Bernard 2001

LIFE CHRONOLOGY OF
JEAN-MARIE DÉGUIGNET

1834	Geungat	Born at Quilihouarn (July 19)
1844	Ergué-Gabéric	Beggar
1851	Kerfeunteun	Cowherd at Kermanhonec
1854	Kerfeunteun	Domestic at the mayor's farm (January–August)
1854	Lorient	Army induction, 37th Line-Regiment
1855	Marseille	Embarks for Crimea (August)
1855	Sevastopol	Inducted into 26th Line Regiment
1856	Jerusalem	Visit (April)
1856	Marseille	Returns from Crimea (June 15); Barracks Fort at Saint-Jean
1859	Paris	Garrisoned at Popincourt, Charenton, Ivry, Bicetre
1859	Toulon	Embarks for Italy (May 23)
1860	Mont Cenis	Returns to France (June 15)

1861	Ergué-Gabéric	Demobilized; returns to home district
1862	Marseille	Embarks for Algeria (September 21)
1865	Algeria	Embarks for Mexico (August 11)
1867	Vera Cruz	Embarks for France (May 3)
1868	Aix	Sergeant (January 1)
1868	Ergué-Gabéric	Demobilized, back home (September 11)
1868	Ergué-Armel	Farming at Toulven
1883	Pluguffan	Tobacconist
1892	Quimper	Poverty
1897	Quimper	Meets Anatole Le Braz (June)
1902	Quimper	Psychiatric hospital
1904	Paris	Publication in *La revue de Paris* (December 15)
1905	Quimper	Dies (August 29)

AUTHOR'S APOSTROPHE
TO THE READER*

To you, my writings, do I address these words today,
You consolers of my sad old age.
You are my children, luckless children,
Like me in this world, you are ignored.

But what will become of you, alas, after my death?
What is your destiny? What will be your fate?
Are you destined to be devoured
By mice, by rats? Or sold in sheaves

To make up cones at the next-door grocery
For wrapping sugar, pepper, meal?
Whatever may be your fate, it will be no worse
Than mine has been, I tell you that.

If you are eaten by the mice, the rats,
All the better, my good friends; I cannot pity you.
Better for you to be all of you devoured
Than to stay on to be mistreated,

Or than to wait and rot like those old secret books

---

*From *Story of My Life*

[23]

Buried in bundles deep in old cupboards,
Better even than to be printed, published,
And then critiqued and abused by fools,

As the most honest writings always are,
And the most truthful, the most illuminating.
So very often do we see works condemned
For honestly telling honest truths.

I

---◖◗---

THE BEGGAR BOY

1834–1853

Today I begin a project which will be completed I know neither how nor when, if in fact it ever is completed. Still, I shall try it. I know that at my death there will be no one—no kinsman, no friend—to come shed a few tears over my grave, or to say a few words of farewell to my poor corpse. I imagined that, if my writings should happen to fall into the hands of some strangers, they might win me a bit of that kindly feeling I have sought in vain among kin or friends throughout my lifetime. Recently I have read a great many lives, memoirs, confessions by courtiers, political figures, great writers, men who played significant roles in this world; but never except in novels have I read any memoirs or confessions by poor artisans, workingmen, laborers—workhorses, as they are called, and quite justly so, for they bear the heaviest burdens and endure the cruelest hardships. I know that artisans and laborers are in no position to record their lives, as they have neither the education nor the time it would require. Although I belong to that class, having lived my whole life in the heart of it, now—in my present forced leisure—I shall try to write, if not with talent at least with sincerity and openness, how I have lived and thought and reflected within this wretched setting, and how I joined and kept up the terrible struggle for existence.*

---

*The first manuscript notebook of the *Life of Jean-Marie Déguignet* has unfortunately disappeared. We have therefore taken these first two precious pages, edited by Anatole Le Braz, from *La Revue de Paris* of December 15, 1904. This text was somewhat revised at the time by the *Revue*'s editors, who wrote, "We have tried to make a minimal number of changes."

---<o>---

THAT PESTILENT SEWER, THE RUE VILI

I entered the world in very sorry circumstances. I was born just when my father, a tenant farmer, had been completely ruined by a string of poor harvests and livestock deaths. I first saw the light of day on the 29th of July, 1834. Two months later, my parents were obliged to move out of the Kilihouarn-Guengat farm, and, in payment of their back rent, to leave behind everything they owned, right down to items that were the most indispensable to their poor household. They moved to Quimper with a few wormy boards, a bit of straw, an old cracked cauldron, eight bowls, and eight wooden spoons. They found shelter in a miserable hovel in the rue Vili, a street known in Quimper for its poverty and squalor. We lived there for two years, during which time I was constantly sick. On several occasions the holy candle was lighted to guide my way to the next world. I learned all this later, from my mother and from other people who had seen us in that sorry slum.

My father, who knew no other trade than farming, could not find work in town, and we were five children at home, the eldest not even ten years old. He eventually found a *penn-ty* (cottage) to rent at Le Guélennec, in Ergué-Gabéric, and then was able to do day labor for the farmers and earn eight or ten sous a day. In winter he would collect bundles of firewood or brush. We also had a bit of land where we sowed potatoes—those heavy, red, very prolific potatoes, which at the time were the principal sustenance for poor folk and hogs. My brother and sister died there, probably as a result of the misfortunes and privations they had to endure in that pestiferous cesspool, the rue Vili. I remember—for I was five at the time—those sad pale faces that did not change as they passed from life to death. I remember watching my mother pluck huge fleas from my sister's head after she died. My father and mother seemed pleased: they said that we now had two angels in heaven to intercede with God for us. And our household was none the smaller, for I already had another little brother, and a sister came along soon after. The God of Abraham had said, "Be fruitful and multiply." We were multiplying, but we were not very impressive fruit, for at the age of six I was no taller than a riding boot. Still, the fresh country air gave me life and health and a bit of vigor. I would go every day to the neighboring farmers to ask for my supper, and often, when they had stuffed my little stomach with oatmeal mush, they would also give me chunks of black bread and moldy crêpes to take home.

MY THIRD ACCIDENT

[The actual "third accident" is not described in these excerpts, though it is present by allusion throughout the long text. Apparently, a bee from a hive the boy tended stung a nearby horse, which reared and kicked the child in the head and stove in his temple. The unhealed wound accompanied him until adolescence, and the scar throughout

his life, but despite its miseries (suppuration, pain, inflammation, social discomfort) Déguignet came to attribute to it his extraordinary sensibility and intellectual capacity. —L.A.]

... I will have occasion later to discuss the *karr ann ankou*,* and the origins of the legends around the death figure, about which so many contradictory stories are told. But first I must get off the miserable pallet where they say I lingered for four days and four nights in a state that was neither death nor life, at least as concerns my body.

There was still some life and activity going on in my mind. But my poor heartbroken parents could not see that: all they could see was my small body stretched like a corpse on its pallet; only the veins in my neck and a few faint twitches of the lips showed that I was not yet entirely a corpse. On the morning of the fifth day, my mind, which had been scampering deliriously after the bees and elfin *couriquets*,† came back to rest in the lobes of my brain, now no longer in turmoil. I opened my eyes—I had two of them again, as the swelling in my left lid had subsided. I looked about astonished, for while I remembered everything I had seen elsewhere during those four days and nights, I had absolutely no idea what had gone on around me or within me. My mother was gazing at me, and when she saw my eyes, which she had not seen for four days, she asked if I was feeling better; I answered in a very weak voice that I didn't know, since I had no idea what state I'd been in before. All I did know was that I was not in pain, so the worst danger must be past.

---

*The cart of the *ankou*, who is a Breton death figure: skeletal, carrying a scythe, a javelin, sometimes a hammer.

† *Couriquets*, probably a French version of *corrigans*: these were small supernatural figures, elves or fairies like the Irish leprechauns, who looked like little old men; they were not particularly malevolent, but they had secrets and sought to keep humans away from them [LA].

My bandages had been changed at some point, for Monsieur the Weaver* wanted to look at the state of the wound on my temple; he had not seen it at the time of the injury because of all the blood. Family had come to visit me, my mother said, and had brought candy and white bread. The white bread, as far as I recalled, I had not so far tasted. In the course of the day my mother made me a little *"bouët miton-net"* (bread pudding) with the white bread; it was delicious.

But I see that I am lingering too long over the details of that third accident; even though it was to have unexpected and rather extraordinary consequences for me, I should not go on about it forever. Suffice it to say that I recovered in about three weeks, but that it left a large crater-shaped scar on my left temple from which, now and then over several years, there ran a kind of yellowish fluid that caused me a good deal of unpleasantness. My mother and other women attributed the suppuration to the fact that I had never had cradle-cap as an infant; but other people said it was caused by the king's disease, scrofula *(drouck ar roue)*. The term *drouck ar roue* was applied at that time to any suppurating sores appearing on a person's body. The term "king's disease" probably came to Brittany at the time of King Francis I or later; we know that this king—beaten at the Battle of Marignan and prisoner of the king of Spain—died of the disorder. It was then called "the Neapolitan disease," although some claim that it was imported to Europe by Christopher Columbus's crewmen, who had picked it up in Santo Domingo. There were doggerel rhymes about this disease previously unknown in France:

---

*The weaver, otherwise unidentified in these pages, was an influential friend of the family, and often steps into the chronicle as wise aide to Déguignet.

The peasant in his shack with its roof of thatch
Is subject to its laws
And at the Louvre door the guard on watch
Cannot save kings from its jaws.[*]

Whatever the case, when I was young, there was much fuss about *drouck an roue*, and for my own part, I suffered its disagreeable and humiliating effects for a long while.

However, though the oblivious honeybee, whose sting brought on my accident, did cause me so many difficulties and problems, it also contributed to the remarkable development of my mental capacities, a phenomenon which is actually nicely explained by the science of phrenology. History tells of a pope, Clement VI, I think, who as a boy suffered the same accident as I did—or at least had his left temple stove in like mine. And as a result he had one of the great minds of his time. We also know that operating on the skulls of young cretins can turn them into highly intelligent men. But ought I to boast of having intellectual faculties better developed than my brothers and my childhood companions, all of whom remained in a state of complete ignorance? For as I saw them at the time, I see them still today, at least those who have not yet died. In a way, they lived happier lives than I did, but lives exclusively physical and animal, with just two selfish concerns: first to live as luxuriously as possible; and then to die in a state of grace, so as to go upstairs and keep on living even more luxuriously and more delectably.

Meanwhile, if this accidental development of my faculties did not serve to make my fortune, or even an adequate material existence, it has provided me with a good many moments of intellectual and moral pleasure over the course of my trou-

---

[*]From a poem of condolence by François de Malherbe (1555–1628).

bled life. And today still, at the end of this extraordinary life, I take a real pleasure in setting down some honest and precise accounts of them. For since that accident, and doubtless because of it, all the events of my life remain etched into my memory like sounds in a phonograph recording.

After my recovery, I returned to my usual task: going out to beg my daily dinner at the farmsteads, driving cows to pasture in the Stang-Odet valley and back.* The bees had finished swarming and I no longer had to care for them. The six hives had each given us at least one swarm, and three of them two each, so we now had fifteen days' worth. My father was still busy handling chores for the employees at the town paper mill, and then at harvest time he went to work for the farmers. He would contract to cut certain fields of rye or oats, the only grains grown in our area at that time. My mother used to go along to help him. And when the grain was brought in, my father was much in demand for a particular job: setting the sheaves up in rounded stacks called *groac'hel*—*groach'hili* in the plural. My father was a past master in the art of constructing such stacks.

Stacks had to be very well built; because the winnowing was done entirely by flail, it took a long while, and if during that time it should rain heavily on poorly constructed stacks, the water would get inside and everything would be ruined, grain and straw. Therefore most of the neighboring farmers were determined to have my father build their stacks. We ourselves had a good harvest that year, of potatoes, and our little house was full of them, in every corner and under the beds—big red potatoes often weighing over a pound; we had enough to live through the whole winter. At Michaelmas,† my father sold six

---

**Stang is a Cornouaille word for a V-shaped valley.

†September 29, harvest-time and traditional date for new farm leases.

of the heaviest beehives and I got the new clothes I'd been promised—canvas trousers, a *chupen* (jacket), and a hat.

PRAYERS AND CATECHISM

I was nine by then; it was time to think about learning my prayers and catechism. That wasn't hard, since now anything I heard or saw stayed graven in my memory. My mother could read Breton, but only in three books: the catechism, the *Lives of the Saints*, and her missal. It was easy enough for her to teach me what she knew, though she didn't do it alone. There lived nearby a spinster, a *quemenerez* (seamstress) who took on the mission of teaching the village children their prayers and catechism, and even how to read, for those who wanted it. She had her reward, when every Sunday the priest would say a prayer from on high in the pulpit for people who taught children prayers and catechism, but he never mentioned those who taught reading. I learned a lot better at her house, because there I had rivals whom, in my small pride and boyish arrogance, I was determined to outdo, and she supported me marvelously in such impulses with her flattery, constantly holding me up as an example to the others.

A NATURAL HISTORY OF MEN AND WOMEN

Here I should say something about the spinster and about some of the other people who used to come to her house at the same time as we youngsters did; because it has to do with the customs in Brittany that I propose to show from all aspects. The spinster would teach us the prayers and the catechism (she managed to teach reading only to me), but after those first few lessons, which were unquestionably edifying, with the help of other spinster friends, she would give us equally edifying lessons on the natural history of man and woman, including practical training. In our large village there was a poor imbecile who, though not mute, never said a word; he could only emit groans of pain or satisfaction. He was the plaything of all the village children; often he would follow along behind them when they came for their catechism at our good spinster's cottage. Once the catechism and the prayers were done, the spinster and her women friends would start playing with the idiot, and he always let them do what they wanted. With no objection, they would pull down his big breeches and lay him on the ground, then take turns doing to him what Onan did to himself alongside his sister-in-law Tamar and what God had him die for doing. At times when the idiot did not come to the cottage, the old maids would amuse themselves with the children, some of whom were already quite grown-up. All this with no shame or discomfort, like children of nature. And the spinster herself, our teacher, was considered a saintly woman; very often she went to communion. I don't know whether in confession she told the priest about all the lessons she taught us beyond the ones in catechism, or whether the priest approved of her actions—maybe so. Our Breton priests do not see much harm in those little natural matters, no more than they do in drunkenness; they see a good deal more harm in the instruction and the moral and scientific teachings of secular educators.

What the spinster did in her house and outdoors too was fairly common practice, among adults. The women's favorite game was putting the *coz* and the *goaskerez* to the big fellows. This usually happened during the *grandes journées*, when great numbers of hands were gathered for the peak labor season—collecting firewood, or cutting brush, or scorching farmland for planting—and the best men were about. After the midday meal, the men would take a siesta in the cottage gardens around the farmstead or in the passages off the threshing-floor; when the women found one of them off by himself and fast asleep on his back, four or five at a time would surround him and each jump onto an arm or leg so the man couldn't move. The fifth woman would unbutton his breeches and stuff his pouch with earth, or mud, or cow dung; this was called *laka ar c'hoz* (putting the muck in), and it did the victim no great harm. But the other trick was worse. In this one, the woman left free would split the end of a thick stick, then with her two hands she would pry it apart the way you open a trap, and fit it onto the *organis generationis ex pace per hominis.** This was called *lakad ar woaskeres* (putting on pressure). It was done in full daylight and right out in the fields in front of everyone, in front of gangs of children clapping and screaming with laughter. I said before that it was like the state of nature; but I don't believe that our early forebears in the state of nature in the forests indulged in such games. And it wasn't only in Le Guélennec that people played these games and others like them; I have seen them played all through different parts of Lower Brittany.

THOSE CHARACTERS WE USED TO CALL WILD MEN

I began by describing some Breton customs involving women; now I will provide a few portraits of men.

There lived in Le Guélennec an old fellow named Poher, who was actually the father of the idiot boy mentioned above. The older Poher had been struck by lightning and lost movement in his lower back and his right leg. Everyone said it was a well-deserved punishment from heaven, because when he was healthy he was contemptuous of everything—people, God,

---

*Genitals.

the devil, and the elements; he may not have shot arrows at the thunder, as the Gauls did, but he did shoot curses and blasphemies. One day he was on his way home from town in a huge storm, cursing and blaspheming as usual against the thunder, and he was knocked down by a bolt of lightning as he was crossing a hedgerow in front of his house. It was Colossus felled by Jupiter. At the time he was running a farm at Keruel, a short distance from Le Guélennec. From there he moved to the Ty-Glas farm in Le Guélennec. But now that he couldn't work or walk without pain, he had passed along the management to his son, the idiot's older brother. We boys would see the old man someplace every day, leaning upright against a hedgerow, for he could not sit, what with his lower back and right hip stiffened by the lightning.

Whenever we caught sight of him, we would turn back or go the long way around so as not to pass him, he scared us so. He had such a frightening face, great red-rimmed eyes bulging out of his face, long sunken cheeks, an owl's beak of a nose and a wrinkled, receding chin beneath it, and along with all that, a voice that made us tremble. When he saw us going by on our way to gather firewood, or coming back with our little bundles, we always had to hear him shout the same awful curses he would howl at the thunder. The first time I came on him unexpectedly with my load, I was so scared that I dropped the wood and ran off shaking. Lucky for us he couldn't run—he could hardly even drag along in his wide breeches, leaning on a stick with a forked iron tip to keep it from slipping. He would often threaten us with the stick, which was called a *casporn** in Breton. In his wild rage he sometimes threw the casporn at us. But then he would be stuck in place longer than he wanted, because nobody dared

---

*An instrument for cleaning a plowshare.

return his *casporn* to him for fear of getting it in our back the minute the big brute got hold of it. So then he would shout to the idiot son who would go fetch it for him if he was nearby. This wild man always had his rosary in hand, which got him the nickname *Pach Coz*, for he looked just like the pious local landlord, said the old-timers.

That *Pach* used to live at the Mez Anaonic farm, about halfway along the road from Quimper to Coray. At the time, the road was just a terrible sunken lane full of holes and ruts and overrun with bandits and robbers. It was unwise to use that road on nights after a fair; the bandits would work together to seize the cattle and horses from buyers, and the money from the sellers. On such days the *Pach* could also be found at the roadside with his big rosary, sometimes standing, sometimes kneeling, praying loudly and beseeching God to protect the travelers against robbers; he knew practically all the travelers and the merchants. When he saw a person go by who had just sold cattle or horses that day and whose purse he knew was good and full, he would approach them and in a mournful, wheedling voice say, "*Ma Doue beniguet, va zud kez, me meus truez ouzoc'h*" (Blessed Lord—you poor people, how I pity you)! I know you're carrying money, and I also know that there are thieves hereabouts just lying in wait for you. I'm not a rich man, but I am a man who loves God, and in His Holy name I serve mankind. So come to my house; you can sleep there at no charge, and then tomorrow by daylight you can go home safely."

And, indeed, the travelers who did go to his house could see that they were entering the house of a saintly man, with rosaries and crosses everywhere, and images of Christ and the Virgin and crowds of saints. The old saint would give them a good meal and then, after saying some prayers, he would lead them to their beds with the assurance that they could sleep easy. But alas! Not a single one of the travelers who set foot inside Mez Anaonic was ever to tell what they'd seen there. While they were sleeping easy, trusting in the saintly fellow, he was boiling water in a huge copper pot; then, tossing off his clogs and drawing himself up to his Herculean height, he would go to the first traveler, grip his throat with one iron fist and his leg with the other, and proceed to plunge him head first into the pot, already strangled before he got there. And if there were several of them, they all went the same route. Then he would throw all the corpses down a huge deep well and cap it over carefully. The well was only discovered long after the *Pach's* death. In it were found the bony remains of all the victims of that man of God. When I was young, you could still go to Mez Anaonic and see the spot where the well used to be.

Not far from Le Guélennec, in a place called Griffonez, there was another wild man; that was what we called all those growers or farmers who were always chasing us off, whether we were begging food or gathering firewood. The one from Griffonez didn't frighten us as much as the old cripple at Le Guélennec, but he did do us more harm. We could always count on him to strip us of our loads of wood when he caught us; for we were several together—I wasn't the only poor child in that large village. When we saw him coming, this wild man with his long red hair and his forest-animal face, all we could do was throw down our bundles on the spot and take to our heels, because anyone he caught was sure to get a good shaking and a tug on the ears and hair. Whenever he found one of us perched in a tree or up on a pollarded trunk cutting dead branches, he would take up a position at the foot of the tree and shout to the poor fellow to come down: "*Don a rafet an traon a lesse, sarter laër, ma vec'h c'hinget?*" (Are you coming down from there, you damn thief, so I can give you a shake?)

Naturally, the poor fellow was in no hurry to come down. So then the wild man would circle around the tree, staring up like a dog stalking a squirrel; in the end he had to leave, for the boy would never come down while he was there.

On that vast property, though, there was no shortage of firewood, it bordered on the Stang-Odet (the valley of the Odet River) as well, with its enormous spread of virgin forest, though it was impossible at the time to extract timber from it except on a man's back, for there were no trails to get to it. But events came to avenge us poor innocent victims on that rough son of the savage coastal tribe: he lost all his land in the courts, robbed naked by the notaries and the other lawyers; in time I saw him forced to go out scavenging firewood himself.

It would take too long to describe each of those characters we used to term "wild men"; their savagery, their ways of seeing and of behaving were much alike. And I will be talking about several other specific types in the course of these accounts. These wild men were probably descended from the barbaric inhabitants along the seacoasts and the islands who, well into the last century, survived by plundering from the sea. They were practically cannibals; they did not eat human flesh, but they did ruthlessly kill off any shipwrecked castaway trying to reach safety. These barbarians utilized all sorts of strategies to lure the passing ships onto the coast. For instance, they had priestesses do incantations and invoke their gods to send them good booty, and when the gods did not answer their prayers by conjuring a great storm, they would turn to less supernatural means. They would hook a lantern to the end of a pole and have a man walk along the shore at night making the lantern rock and bob like a moving ship; or they would hook the lantern to a cow's horn, and then tie a rope from the horn to a back leg so that she was forced to raise and lower her head as she walked, imitating the pitch of a moving boat.

Sailors on ships approaching from the open sea would see this bobbing light and steer toward it, believing they were following in another ship's wake, and then would crash on the rocks. The barbaric inhabitants were waiting there with long hooked poles; they would pull in the barrels, chests, and other objects that came floating to shore, and would kill the poor castaways trying to land. "To each his own," these savages would say. "The sea gets the corpses and we get the loot." And the inland savages I described earlier talked and thought the same way: they would have liked to see us all destitute, useless, flung into the sea or buried underground, so as to keep all the goods of the earth for themselves.

Still, it must be acknowledged that there was a reason for this deplorable state of affairs, as much for the coastal and island folk as for the farmers inland. If these barbarians on the Sein and Ouessant Islands and the neighboring coasts plundered the seas, it was because there was no other way to make a living down on those arid cliffs. Even today, all the many denizens of those rocks live exclusively from the sea, from fishing. If the fish should disappear, or if the transport of the catch were to be disrupted for any reason at all, what would these people do? They would be absolutely forced to resume their ancestral profession.

HORSE-MOVERS AND WOLF-KILLERS

And now, if farmers and landowners in the interior were so hard-hearted and so cruel toward the poor, it was because they were literally swamped by them at the time, not only by the usual beggars but also by plunderers, thieves, and real bandits. The farmers were always having something stolen—grain from their barns, farming tools, hay and straw from the stacks, cattle and horses from the fields or stables—and with no chance of catching the thieves. For stealing cattle and horses, there was a well-organized syndicate with headquarters in a forest at the juncture of the three counties of Lower Brittany—Morbihan, Côtes-du-Nord, and Finistère. The organization had agents everywhere, called movers *(an diblasserien kesec)*. These people sometimes did some doctoring, too, for beggary took many forms at the time. Some traveled the countryside on nags looking for old ironwork, others for rags, *pilhou* in Breton; some scavenged for *étoupes* (hemp or linen fiber scrap) to sell for caulking material; and others journeyed about with stuffed wolf-skins. These last were not begging for charity; they demanded a reward for having freed the area of a wolf, and for risking their life to capture it. Some of them would come through several times with the same skin. I witnessed a rather amusing scene with one such fellow: I saw a crowd of the village children following him from farm to farm as he went with his wolf-pelt to claim his reward, I walked along with the troop, and we came to the last farmstead, the *Ty-glas* (blue house) so-called because the whole farmhouse was covered with blue-slate tiles, a rare thing in those days. At the door, the man with the wolf-hide found himself nose to nose with Farmer le Poher, the older son of the crippled wildman, who resembled his father in every way except that his face was less terrifying. The visitor set down his stuffed wolf on the doorstep, but Le Poher told him, "*Saper matin*, you've been by here before with this skin, I recognize it *(kers da bourmen gant ar c'hohen coz-se)*. Get your ass out of here with this old hide, I'm not giving you a thing! *(Mes digas din crohen eur pilloyer ha me rai mern vad dit!)* But send me the hide of a rag-picking beggar, and then I'll give you a good meal."

All the urchins shouted with laughter; yes, but not the man with the wolf-skin. Because in those times and even today still, Breton beggars have a decisive and dreadful retort to fling at people who refuse them what they ask, or who seem to laugh at them; and that dreadful retort rarely missed its mark then. It was the curse of God called down on the farm and on all it contained—house, people, land, and livestock. The curse was the Breton translation of this passage in the Gospel:

> And whomsoever shall not receive you, nor hear your words, when you depart out of that house or city, shake off the dust of your feet as a sign of malediction. Verily I say unto you, it shall be more tolerable for the land of Sodom and Gomorrah in the day of judgment than for that city. (Matthew 10:14–15)

This was approximately the response of our man with the wolf-skin when Le Poher ejected him so ignominiously. No sooner was he out the door then he turned and, stretching his hands toward the farmer, pronounced these dreadful words:

"Me denn malos doue varnit et var tout ar pez a teus." (I hereby call down God's curse upon you and upon everything you own.)

Then, setting his wolf-skin back on his shoulder, he departed, muttering still more curses. Le Poher, despite his confidence and his swashbuckling style, was taken aback for a moment by the weight of these dreadful imprecations, and watched wordlessly as the wolf-man moved off. Fortunately, the farmer's wife, who was busy cooking the stew for dinner, had heard none of it. If she had, she would certainly have run after the man crying, *"O Jesu, Maria, itron varia ar Guerzeot beniguet, nign zo tud kolet, deud an dro ma den mad!* (Jesus, Mary, Our Lady of Kerdevot, we're lost!) Come back, my good man, I'll give you something! In the name of God, lift your curse from us!"

Such a curse weighs for a long time on those it was aimed at; any misfortune that may later befall the farm, its dwellers, or its livestock is laid to it. And the person who provoked the curse by his hard-heartedness regrets it bitterly. Let the slightest misfortune touch a farm under such a curse, and the beggar who leveled it rejoices and proclaims far and wide that he's the one who made it happen.

The cattle and horse "movers" often came from among the scavengers for iron, rags, and fiber; they were familiar with all the farms and knew where the good cattle were; they would go by night to steal them and drive them off to a prearranged location, where other characters waited to drive them along to the next lap. It is understandable that with such things going on, the farmers were not entirely wrong to be harsh to the beggars, to the point of wishing, like Gourmelen,* to pack them all up and put them in the hayloft to dry out over the winter.

I have now come up to the end of 1843, when for the third time I had barely escaped Atropos' terrible shears, and, by which time, I had learned my prayers, my catechism, and how to read the Breton language—which is to say, the entire range of pedagogical, theological, philosophical, and psychological knowledge being taught at the time in our Breton countryside. I had no further need to seek out the prayer-and-catechism lady, for I already knew as much as she did. I could have done with a few more of her lessons in natural history, but I thought I knew enough on the subject as it was.

---

*Perhaps Hyacinthe Gourmelen, author of an 1848 treatise on "Social and Religious Reform."

STORIES AND LEGENDS
The beggar's trade

In the spring of 1844, an old goodwife from the neighborhood came to tell my mother that she would do better to send me out to make the rounds of the whole commune with a beggar's pouch than to let me simply beg for my daily meal around Le Guélennec—that I would bring in much more provender for the household. My mother agreed to it.

This goodwife was a professional beggar; she undertook to teach me the trade. She showed my mother how to sew me a double-pouched beggar's sack: it mustn't be too long or it would hinder my walking, nor too short or it would slip off my shoulders. But it could be made to measure, since I was right there. My mother did make it, and when it was done she tried it on me; it fit like a glove. She attached a cord to the corner of the rear sack; the other end tied, to the front sack, kept the double pouch from sliding off my shoulder.

Two days later, I went out with my teacher for the first lesson. The goodwife informed me that the profession I was about to begin was the most honorable, the noblest in the world, for God himself had practiced it and so had our greatest saints. What an honor, what glory, to be able at the age of nine to walk in the steps of God and the Saints! If at the time I had known our French laws, I could have given my teacher a few lessons on the topic of this honorable, noble profession, as I propose to do here when the time comes. My debut was not bad. Because my teacher and guide was known and welcome everywhere, I was made welcome too. I was so small, so thin, so sorry-looking that the good farmwives took pity on me, not so much to soothe my misery as to do a good deed in the eyes of their Lord. Their charity always had a self-interested purpose; it was never given for the sake of humankind—an idea unknown among Bretons—but solely for the sake of God. When those women gave me two liards' worth of ground oats or buckwheat flour, the customary donation at the time, it was because they were convinced that they would get it back a hundredfold. As the gospel says: they knew that a prayer recited by me, this puny, humble child, would earn them as much as a hundred prayers rattled off mechanically by some old beggar woman.

So my first rounds were excellent. For three days running—the time it took to cover the whole commune—I brought home the double-pouch full of oat and buckwheat flour. Meanwhile, it was soon clear that my guide added other equally lucrative trades to her job as professional mendicant. First, she was the living, walking newspaper of the commune, where she knew everything and everybody; then besides, she acted as matchmaker, in Breton a *bas vanel*.* So when she visited a farmstead where there were young folks to be married off, she was extremely welcome; she was sometimes even invited to take a seat at the table and served the traditional bread and lard, the highest honor that could be paid a stranger at that time in our parts.

Finally, after five or six weeks of apprenticeship, thinking I knew the trade fairly well and feeling that the old gossip lingered too long at some farms, I decided to go out on my own to accomplish my weekly rounds quicker—it was customary to visit each farm only once a week.

Unfortunately, it was a bad idea to go about alone, especially at my age, weak and timid as I was. There was a vast population of beggars of all ages, real bandits who, if they ran across some solitary wretch with his sack full, thought nothing

---

*Literally, a stick or branch of broom.

of emptying it into their own, and tugging the poor devil's ears besides. They did it to me three or four different times and I had to go home empty-handed, and then be scolded besides by my mother, who thought I'd been playing instead of begging. Yes, there were then a dozen characters in town who were supposedly beggars but who were actually just thieves. Two of them in particular, who had robbed me several times, were a couple of real scoundrels of the worst kind. There wasn't one hanging crime, not a single trick deserving of the scaffold, that they didn't pull on the farmers, and on everybody else too, once in a while. These two thieves wasted no time saying a prayer at the door, in fact, they didn't even know any prayers.

When they discovered there were only women in a house, which often happened in the country—the men being nearly always out in the fields—they would walk boldly in and settle down at the table, commanding the poor terrified women to give them food or watch out for the *penbas* (a clublike walking-stick). And it was not wise to object or argue with these rascals, for while they might not know their prayers, they did on the other hand have the whole pornographic, hooligocratic, scatologic Breton lexicon at their fingertips. Even Lord Seymour—the notorious Milord l'Arsouille, king of hooligans, who was still alive in those days—would have been taken by that pair of Breton bandits. When they found nobody home at a farm, they would go right in anyhow, by the door or by the window or by the roof. If they were hungry they ate, if not, they filled up their sacks and left—never failing to deposit on the dining table what pigs deposit along the rim of their trough. And when they came across tailors and seamstresses sewing at a farmstead, they gave those workers an earful. And if they found out—and they nearly always did find out—what road the tailors would be taking to go home in the evening, they carefully smeared excrement on any fences the tailors would have to clamber over. So these workers would get home with their good clothes in a fine state, and smelling of you-know-what.

And, toward evening, when the bandits walked a narrow, much-used trail, they would lay sticks across the path, or knot two branches of broom or thorn across it. People coming through after them, in the dark, would catch their legs in the obstacles and topple headfirst onto the path, often hurting themselves badly. And when the pair found some stream that people had to cross by a plank or beam (highways, roads, and bridges were still unknown in those parts), after getting across themselves, they would go to great effort to pull the beam over to their side, leaving only a small stretch of it supported on the far bank. When someone came along and stepped onto it, the beam would slip into the water and take the poor traveler down with it. Well, there wasn't a low trick these two beggar-thieves left untried. And they were not the only ones. I mention only these two because I had personal experience with them and their dirty schemes.

Still, in the end I did find myself a companion, who was about my age but had at least twice my weight and twice my strength. We began to do the weekly rounds together, avoiding the bandits as best we could. Humble and timid both of us, we got along very well, and when we had finished our begging circuit, three days a week, we would go together to look for firewood and, in springtime, to collect goat turds and dried cow manure to sell for people to burn down into ash. Such ash was much in demand by farmers for laying down with buckwheat seed, back when the animal charcoal and natural phosphates, so useful in agriculture, were still unknown in our area.

Potato death

That year 1844 was another quite good one for my family. The bees had increased as they had the year before, and the potatoes gave a good yield in that bit of rough land that had cost my father so much sweat to clear. But alas, for the potatoes it was the last year, the next season they were to disappear forever— at least, that strain of big red potatoes, which was all we knew at that time. If that had been the only strain existent on our little planet, it would have meant "goodbye potatoes" forever.

I have no special incident to report from my life as a poor beggar boy in the years '44 and '45, so, I will proceed immediately to the potato death that occurred in July of '45. Everyone knows what a disaster, what terrible famine that sudden death of the potatoes caused the Irish as well as us poor peasants in Lower Brittany, for we had nothing else to live on but potatoes and black bread. Ah, what stories, what tales, what legends were born then, on the subject of that black disease that carried off—in one blow, in a single season—a whole breed of potato.

The first idea we had, we poor folks, was to blame the scourge on the rich; then the rich flung it back onto the poor, onto the farmhands, saying it was because they were always cursing the potatoes; the farmhands especially, because they had to eat them too often—two and three and four times a day in summer, when there were four daily meals. There were songs satirizing certain farmers on the subject:

Da lein e vez dec'huites
Da vern e vez patates
Da vern vian, des pommes de terre
E da gouan, avalou douar.

(At lunch, and at dinner, and at snack, and at supper,
　　Potatoes! always potatoes!)

The potatoes were baptized with all sorts of different names: for instance, *dec'huites* was the Quimper area's patois for the very small potatoes used for pig fodder.

So, the rich folk claimed it was such blasphemies and curses against the fat tubers that eventually drew down the rage of the Most Holy, who did just the opposite of his Father in the Garden of Eden, condemning two people to death for eating an apple; here it was the "earth-apples" themselves, the *pommes de terre*, that were condemned to death, and with no progeny left behind them.

Now that the potatoes, the servants, and the Good Lord himself stood indicted, it was the devil's turn for blame. The disease began by attacking the leaves of the plant; it was black as charcoal, therefore it could only have come from the Ruler of the Dark Empire. The stench of the leaves could only be the smell of hell broiling. The broiled and roasted leaves, the tubers' stewy mush, were the very image of the damned in the fiery furnace. What won the case for partisans of the devil theory was a story that came from Leuhan, a hamlet between Coray and Chateauneuf—an actual-fact story, supposedly, that confirmed the Diabolists' views in every respect.

The legend of the black cat (*ar has du*)

To make the Leuhan story clear, it is indispensable to recount the legend of the Black Cat (*ar has du*). Although this is one of Lower Brittany's most curious legends, I have not seen it reported anywhere by researchers in such material. This Black Cat is the devil himself, who takes that form to provide people with all the money they want, but on certain conditions. First, the cat must be fed on wheat porridge like a baby, and like a baby, must have a wet nurse to suckle from. The cat contracts to work for a certain term, and when the term is up, the soul of the contracting party or parties belongs to the cat by right. But the contracting party almost always manages to get rid of the cat before the term expires. In fact, there used to be a special fair at Gourin for Black Cats; and you sometimes still hear a Breton insult that refers to it, applied to a person who is never satisfied with himself or with other people: "*Kers da foar ann diaoul da C'hourin.*" (Oh, off with you to the devil's fair at Gourin.) The line is a vestige from the Black Cat fair. But things were done differently there from other fairs, the buyer—the cat's taker—got a sum of money along with the animal and instructions on its upkeep and feeding. The happiest person at these market fairs was always the seller, of course. By now he was rolling in money brought in by the Black Cat, and his soul he had sold to the cat reverted back to him, since he'd managed to rid himself of the animal before the deadline.

So: In the year of grace 1845, a married couple in Leuhan had acquired a Black Cat for just a few months, because the animal was quick to fill a house with gold and silver, especially for people who knew how to tend and pamper it nicely. The cat was in good hands. The wife was young, she was nursing her first infant. The Black Cat ate wheat porridge like the baby, and the woman gave it first turn at her breast. And so the drawers quickly filled up with fine gold coins from every land, which the cat fetched from the vast hoards at the bottom of the sea where there is so much of it.

A man here in Quimper, originally from Leuhan, told me only recently that his father, who lived near that couple, had seen the cat go by his house one morning before dawn carrying a white valise on its back, bulging at both sides, and he could tell it was full of gold coins. But the contract term was nearly up, and the young pair were starting to worry. The seller had told them that unless they handed on the animal before the deadline, the cat would carry the two of them straight back with him to hell. Yes, but how were they to get rid of it now? The Black Cat Fair was held only once a year, around Christmas, and the contract, set by the couple themselves, was to end in July. Now they were sorry they had not made it for a year and a day, as people usually did. For it was always on that extra day that the devil got tricked, if not before. Finally, not knowing what to do, and foreseeing disaster, the husband told the wife to go see what the priest could suggest.

So the wife went to confess to the elderly rector of Leuhan, and she explained the terrible situation she and her husband were in. The rector thought for a moment, and told her that indeed their problem was very serious, but that there might still be a way out of the impasse they had so clumsily got themselves into; they would just have to exorcise the cat, this black devil. But the devil is cunning, or anyhow he used to be: in the Garden of Eden he had tricked the old Eternal Father by slipping into a serpent's body, and later on he tricked the Son by hiding in the guts of Judas Iscariot. But the Leuhan rector planned to be more cunning than those two were, and more cunning than the devil himself. The high priests of Jerusalem had promised Judas a fee in silver if he would deliver to them the Son of Man; here the Leuhan woman promised the rector a handsome sum in gold for delivering her from Satan's son. And the good rector promised to do it.

The old fellow had already performed exorcisms on the souls of a good many rich peasants. But such simple, ignorant souls as these fell easily into the rector's snares. It would probably be a different story with the devil, the most cunning of all. So the rector joined forces with his colleagues in the neighborhood to plan more drastic measures. There was a goodly fee to be gained, and he would share it with any colleagues who came to his aid. But there was no time to lose, for the fateful date was nigh. One night, then, he gathered his colleagues together in his study, and after a copious meal, they girded themselves with all the instruments necessary for the extraordinary exorcism and walked to the farm where the Black Cat lived. The unhappy couple were crouched by the hearth, weeping and praying; they believed they were doomed. But when they saw the priests come in they rose to their feet. These men had certainly come to save them. They told the priests that the Black Cat had gone off to the sea as usual, and would not be back until morning, a few hours before daybreak.

"That is well," the old rector told them. "Now you go to bed. We will keep watch through the night. Tomorrow you will hear noise, screams and horrendous curses, but no one should stir. Be sure to tell all your servants."

The nights are short in July; to be back in the house two hours before daybreak, the Black Cat would have to return at around one o'clock. It was actually a little before that hour that the couple, half paralyzed in their cupboard bed,* saw the priests don their white surplices and each take his stole in hand, then slip quietly from the house, locking the door firmly behind them. A moment later, as the rector had warned, the people in the house, shaking in their beds, did indeed hear noise and horrendous screams that went on and on; then suddenly there came a horrendous thunderclap that shook the house and still harder the wretches inside it. Then, nothing more.

As day broke, the priests came back into the house rubbing their hands and laughing. The old rector told the couple they could get up without fear and make the priests a good breakfast; they had certainly earned it. The job was a tough one, but Paulic† had been captured in time, cast out and forced to

---

*Traditional Breton "box beds" are enclosed behind shutters.

†Little Paul, a Breton nickname for the devil.

return empty-handed to his dark empire. As he left, though, in rage and fury at having been caught, he let go a horrendous fart that shook the very earth and blew all the priests into the ditch. When they came up, their faces and their white surplices were black as coal and the air was so noxious that they could barely breathe. But now it was all over.

The couple were pleased and happy; they gave the priests a grand meal and fine gold coins. But alas, two days later, the potato vines began to turn black throughout the land, and the priests and the Black Cat couple knew where that came from. Having missed his prey, Paulic the devil was taking revenge by poisoning the potatoes. The story spread fast throughout the countryside, and then people knew whom to blame for this horrendous catastrophe.

The experts, or those who pass for such, sought the source of the disease for a long time. This is it. So strongly did the local people believe in that story from Leuhan that the potato disease has always kept that name among our peasants: every year when the leaves begin to turn black, they say: "*Coued e ann diaoul var an avalou douar a dare*" (There's the devil falling onto the potatoes again.) The sickness actually does "fall," since it is in the air and not in the tubers as many people still believe. It is a simple microscopic black mold, generated by moisture and heat like all molds. In this case, the potatoes are destroyed by black mold and the oats by red mold.*

The scientists who worked out how to make rain should also work out how to keep it from falling on the potato and oat fields during June and July, and then neither the potatoes nor the oats would be stricken by mold.

Or the Breton peasants, my confreres, who attribute all

---

*Potatoes are afflicted by mildew, *Philophtora infestans* or *peronospora*, and oats by rust, a cryptogamic fungus.

things and all powers to their God, should ask him to hold back the rains during those two months, and then neither the black devil nor the red devil would come to poison their potatoes or their oats.

In olden times, this God was able to keep the rain from falling for seven years, the Bible tells us, so why shouldn't He be able to stop it for a mere two months in our present day?

I had often heard tell of the famous Black Cat, but people mentioned it mainly in connection with the terrible potato disease. They cited many people who had once had possession of that gold mine, or had it now. Anyone who got rich rather abruptly had the cat or still did. A neighbor of ours in Le Guélennec was said to have it just then, because all at once the man went from being a very small farmer to being a big cattle dealer. But that did not last for long. He was taken into custody and all his cattle sold off, as well as his farming equipment and household furnishings. Tongues started wagging: some said he had amassed all the money he needed with the cat, and had set up the arrest as a sham, to deflect the suspicion that he had sold out to the Devil. Some said that to rid himself of the cat he was forced to sell everything else he owned along with it. Still others said his wife had not been good enough at feeding and coddling the cat, so it never brought them in anything at all.

Whatever the story, that man, like all ruined growers, went to live in Quimper, and he became an ordinary day laborer. Later on, though, all his children did become rich, and people who had known the father made a point of saying that the wealth came from the Black Cat, *ar has du*. That Black Cat is not dead yet. There is talk of people who have possession of it even today. I may have occasion to speak of it elsewhere.

So we were ruined that year; Paulic killed off all our potatoes like everyone else's. How were we to live now? How could we get enough bread and crêpes for four people, on the eight sous a day our father earned when he found work and the bit of bad flour I brought in three times a week? For the rich farmers had also been hard hit by the terrible scourge and were only giving out scanty alms. Many even gave nothing at all now, for they had just enough bran and bad flour to feed the pigs that they used to feed only potatoes.

There was poverty that year in our countryside, and we were not the worst off. The bread-seekers (a Breton term for beggars) had doubled, while the number of donors had fallen. However, the people on the coast who grew another strain of potato were not so hard tried. They did not lose everything, and the following spring there were again seed potatoes to be bought in Quimper, but at prices too high for us. My father sowed rye on the land he had cleared, to make use of the fertilizer he had spread there, along with rotted potatoes for additional fertilizer.

MY FIRST COMMUNION

On the next Michaelmas we moved out of the Ty-Forn house and went to live in a small cottage that was next door, so to speak, to the house of the fellow whom people called the man with the Black Cat *(potr ar has du)*. That year I made my First Communion.

Breton priests were very strict on these matters at the time: they would never give the sacrament to children under the age of twelve, and then only when they really knew their catechism and their prayers. And three consecutive ceremonies were required, so it was not uncommon to see young people already old enough to marry who had not yet got past the level of children, for there were always some rejected for not knowing their catechism, and sent back to try again the following year.

People said of them that they had donkey's ears *(diouscouarn ann azen)*. As for me, I couldn't be refused my communion on grounds of ignorance, for I already knew my complete catechism better than the priest himself did. So I was not obliged to go into town for the daily catechism class during the two weeks of preparatory exams, except for the three last days, the retreat period when you had to spend the whole day in church saying prayers, singing hymns, and confessing.

Confession was an easy matter for us back then. Our priests took care of it themselves, probably to speed things up; those priests are known to have a complete catalog of sins, the way pharmacists have a catalog of poisons. The priests would run the catalog past our ears through the grill of the confession booth, asking the questions and then answering themselves as they went:

"You did this, didn't you, oh yes my child; you saw that, didn't you? You touched that, didn't you? You felt something nice, a little pleasure, looking at it, did you?" and on and on, so that the confession took place without a word from us except for the *confiteor deo omnipotenti* at the beginning and the penance at the end.

I did see, though, that the catalog of sins was quite long, and that of the questions he asked us, many had more to do with natural history, with anatomy and physiology, than with theology. During the three days of the retreat, the priest served a meal at noon to the poorest students; I was among them.

For those three days, priests from the vicinity were always called in to help with the confessions and to do all the preparatory instruction; and, each one had his particular role, like in a theater. One was responsible for teaching catechism, another the chanting, another gave the sermons, and then there was an instructor of horrendous pictures that showed the damned in hell being impaled on forks and pikes by black devils with cow's horns and long tails; in other scenes, the devils were pictured as pigs, toads, serpents, and other animals circling around somebody's heart and trying to get inside it to chase out the good angel, and there was one where the devils finally did invade the heart as the good angel ran out in tears.[*] And these priests discussed the whole thing with a pointer stick, tapping on the pictures, like fairground entertainers in front of their stalls. And you'd hear weeping, and screaming, and moaning among the poor little terrified listeners while the instructor, swollen with pride and a nice wine, would be snickering.

When a priest showed us these terrifying pictures of devils and hell, I wondered how poor little fellows like myself, who never asked to be born and have had ten times more suffering than pleasure from life, could be consigned to eternal torments for having one moment of pride, or yearning, or lust, things that Nature forces us to feel; I saw right away that there were too many contradictions between those eternal torments and a God we were told was good, excellent, magnanimous, and all-powerful *(eun Doue mad, karantezus, truezus ac oll galloudec)*.

Still, I emerged from my First Communion with full battlefield honors; I was held up as an example of learning and wisdom, humble and docile as befit my status of poor beggar; and because I could read Breton, the priest made me a gift of a little missal that gave me great pleasure. Indeed, until then the only reading I had done was in my teacher's two-sous spelling book and in the catechism, which were in Breton only. But the little missal had the Breton text translated almost word for word from the Latin on the facing page. I realized

---

[*]The famous *taolennoù* (mission pictures) devised in the eighteenth century by Father Maunoir.

instantly that I could learn Latin from it, since I learn all sorts of things so easily. It didn't take me long to learn all the Latin in the book—without rules, of course, but neither does Breton have any rules, either for talking or for writing. Every canton, and even every commune, speaks the language differently, and it is impossible to say who is speaking most correctly. The rare writers who write it do the same: each of them writes it and spells it in his own way. I have heard supposed experts, though, argue that Breton is a "mother tongue." It would certainly be a very odd mother, since it has produced no daughters or sons—as odd as Joachim's daughter [Mary], who bore a child without being a mother, or anyhow without losing her virginity.

MY FOURTH MORTAL ACCIDENT

That year, when we moved, I suffered a fourth accident that nearly carried me off into the next world. This time I even spent several minutes there. . . .

In early October, a few days after Michaelmas, we had settled into a small house beside the one belonging to the man with the Black Cat. As I was on my way to gather firewood one afternoon, by myself this time, I wandered into a place called Stang-Viannic, a valley full of big trees, chestnuts and nearby tall *penngos dero* (pollarded oaks); for so close to Le Guélennec, it was futile to look for firewood anywhere but in the mature, tall pollard trunks, which not everyone could climb. I found a chestnut tree with several dead branches, more than I could carry; it was a thick tree, at least twenty feet tall. No matter; I'm used to climbing trees, so I stuck my pruning knife into the branch-bundling rope wrapped as a belt around my waist, and like a squirrel I climbed up to the topmost limbs and start cutting as I moved down. At the last dead branch, the thickest, I did roughly what the miller's helper in the folktale does, not exactly, though, because rather than straddle the branch I meant to cut, I sat on a different one. But because this was a bit far from the dead branch, I had to lean forward to reach it and to keep my balance I was gripping another small branch with my left hand. Just then a goodwife came along on her way from Penanec'h to Le Guélennec, and she said something on the order of what the old beggar said to the miller-boy: *"Potr paour te gouéo an traon a lese!"* (Poor boy, you're going to fall off there!)

I just answered: *"O! na ring ket."* (Oh no, I won't.)

Then she went on her way. But if she had stayed just five minutes longer she would have seen her prophecy come true. For, seeing that my dead branch was about to give way, I slashed at it harder and harder to separate it fully from the tree; to manage it, I leaned over a little more and strained harder at the small supporting branch, and just as the dead branch came away the small one snapped, and all four of us tumbled down—the two branches, my pruning knife, and me. I do believe I hit the ground first. I cannot be sure, though, for after that last blow with the pruning knife I didn't see or hear another thing. This time I was dead for sure. I must have lain there about a quarter of an hour before I could feel myself reviving; and then, even though I could tell I wasn't dead, I did not dare move. I lay flat on my back and stayed that way for a long time, staring at the sky. If anyone had come along at that moment and asked what I was doing, I might have answered like the miller's helper ["I'm dead"]. What surprised me was that I was feeling some indescribable well-being, something like what you feel lying on the grass after a swim. When I finally came to my senses and realized what had happened, I stood up shaking my arms, stretching my legs, feeling along my ribs; nothing broken, no pain any-where. I went back to trimming my wood and making up a bundle, and then I went home as if nothing had happened. Neither my mother nor anyone else at Le Guélennec ever heard about the incident, although it had sent me into the next world for a good quarter-hour.

Thus I reached the year 1848; I was nearly fourteen years old, and I looked to be only ten, I was still so small and puny. My parents always said that the blow from falling on my head had stunted my growth. But for me it was not my stunted growth that upset me the most, it was the wound on my temple that never healed. And everyone said it never would heal. Plenty of witches and wizards had told my mother that they could cure me if we wanted; but the great weaver thought (and my father and mother agreed) that it was better to let it heal on its own, for if it were to be cured suddenly, the evil would move to some other spot that was probably even more dangerous. So I should resign myself to bearing that hideous wound for perhaps the rest of my life.

THE REVOLUTION OF 1848

[In June], revolution suddenly broke out, without our hear-ing a word about it from anyone beforehand, and yet no sooner did it become known in our area than all the old peo-ple—and my father first among them—claimed to have seen signs in the sky that clearly foretold this event. It's always thus, actually. Whenever an extraordinary event occurs, all old Bretons declare that they saw warning signs about it before-hand. For big political events—revolution, war—the signs appeared in the sky; for accidental deaths and suicides, the signs and portents had appeared at the place where the death would occur. But until it did occur, no one mentioned them. Similarly, all these old fellows who claimed to have seen signs predicting the revolution of 1848 had never said a word about it even as late as twenty-four hours beforehand. Now the tongues were all wagging on the subject, and on what consequences the revolution might have.

There were still some old people around who had known the previous revolution, the big one, *ar révolution vras,* and who remembered the name Robespierre. The memory alone struck fear in them, as much as the memories of the *Chouans** and the foot-burners, *ann domerien.* There were still three or four rich men in the commune who had reason to remember those foot-burning fellows; they still bore significant scars on their legs, and higher up too. They'd had their legs grilled by resin torches and their buttocks roasted on crêpe pans to make them tell where they hid their wealth. Those people especially struck fear into the others, but when word came that the government had suppressed the revolution, things quieted down. And when word came that Prince Napoleon had been named President of the Republic—ah, well then, all the old folks cheered. France was saved, and Brittany along with it.

Some time after the revolution, we happened to be passing by the house of the mayor, who at the time lived very near to Le Guélennec. We were half a dozen or so. We stopped to look at a great plaster statue with a big pipe in his mouth set in the middle of the town's threshing-floor. The mayor, a stout peasant who liked a good laugh, saw us standing there looking at the statue and came out to ask if we knew who it was. Heavens, no! None of us had ever seen the person.

"What!" he said, "You're all from Le Guélennec and you don't recognize *An Téo Philippe?*"

---

*Royalist rebels in Brittany.

On second look I did see that the figure was a good likeness of a heavy local man we called Fat Philippe.

"He does look like our Téo, right?" said the mayor, "And this one's name is Philippe too . . . Louis-Philippe. He was king of France but he ran out like a *bramer coz* (old fart). The Parisians wanted to kill him, but they didn't manage to. Well, my children," he went on, "let's see if you're any better at it than the Parisians—you go collect some rocks and throw them at him, and the first one to break his pipe will get a reward."

You can imagine how the stones rained down thick and fast on poor Philippe, not only on his pipe but also on his head, and all the rest of his body was smashed in less than five minutes, while the mayor stood there clutching his sides with laughter. This is what people do with fallen heroes, kings as well as anyone else. Yet the mayor had been a fervent partisan of Philippe—he himself had ordered the statue made for his office—and then he was perhaps the first of all the mayors in France to put him out the door and have him mutilated.

AT THE QUIMPER HOSPICE

That day the mayor, who had seen my wound over the years, noticed it again and asked if I would be interested in going to the hospice, where he was sure they could cure the ugly thing.

"Yes indeed," I told him. "I would be happy to go."

"Well," he said, "Just tell your father or your mother to come see me and you'll soon be in."

When I told my mother that, she made something of a face, and when my father came home at night he shook his head. . . .

In going to the hospice, I had two ideas in mind: first, the idea that they would cure me of that horrible, troublesome wound; and then the idea that perhaps I could learn a little French there. But as to that I was immediately disappointed, for the only patients there were Bretons—peasants like me, fishermen from the coast, and laborers. These last did know a little French, but they almost never spoke.

On the other hand, it was possible to learn some Breton tales and legends. It was all one heard. At that time, with no education, the peasants, laborers, and fishermen had no other topics to talk about, they were the sole matter for conversation, for chatting wherever a few people found themselves together with nothing else to do. But I, who already knew all those tales and legends from my father and mother, and especially from the great weaver, I learned only one thing there in the hospice: I learned that legends—about ghosts and elves and *couriquets*, about forest-and-water sprites, night-washerwomen* and night-screamers, about childbirth and death and spells—legends were the same everywhere, at least throughout the Finistère, for the hospice had people from all over the *département*. There were fishermen from everywhere along the coast, injured laborers from the mines and quarries of Poullaouen, ragpickers *(pilloyers)* from the Arreé mountains, and old paupers from just about every region.

Some old men there had served under Napoleon I, and while they may not have known the history of that destroyer of peoples, kings, and empires, they did know all the legends about him current in Brittany at the time. These legends became all the more interesting now when the talk everywhere was about his nephew,† who might possibly do as he had. It was something to hear those old folks talk about the extraordinary, supernatural things they claimed they had seen: time and again

---

*Harbingers of death.

†Louis Napoleon. He was chief of state in the Second Republic, then king and, after a coup, Emperor.

they saw the man with the bicorne hat fly through the air on his white horse to go reconnoiter the enemy's position. They had seen him toss a set of playing cards into the air and instantly an imaginary army materialized before the enemy, who spent its whole supply of munitions against it to no avail.

Unbeknownst to all, he went off to Egypt leading an army and fleet he assembled magically around him. And down there in Egypt, when the soldiers were disheartened by exhaustion, heat, and thirst, with the tip of his sword he would show them fine cities and great clearwater lakes that never were, but that would lift the soldiers' spirits. From there, returning to France, he made himself invisible—himself and the boat he sailed on. But on this point the old men disagreed sharply. Some maintained that he had gone right through the English fleet like a thunderbolt, scattering their ships to clear himself a path, and the English never saw a thing. Others said he had flown through the air over their heads, and only came back down onto the water when he was far past them.

But among all these legends the old men told, I found the one about Moscow strangest of all. They said that during a great fire that devoured the entire city and its inhabitants, the man in the hat was seen battling an angel in the air right above the city, and that the angel ultimately threw his adversary down into the flames. That was the sign that portended his later misfortunes. And the cause of all those misfortunes was that the Emperor had cast off his wife to take another woman. The Good Lord was angered by that, and had sent an angel to bring him down, since men could not. But on the subject of Moscow, there arose discussions and arguments that went on far longer than the telling of legends.

I have said that hardly any language other than Breton was spoken in the hospice. But yes, when those old men started quarreling, they would do it in French, probably calling up the trooper's vocabulary of the time, which was very rough.

I would listen to these French-language disputes, trying to retain a few of the words. The argument would begin with a few Breton words, one man saying another had never so much as farted in Moscow, that he didn't even know where it was. "Oh no, never, of course not," the other would retort, "and I suppose you were there instead of me?" Then would begin the stream, in French, of that wonderful soldier vocabulary that I later had the pleasure of hearing for fourteen years, consisting of many words that either do not figure in our big French dictionaries or, when they do, appear with no indication of all the meanings they carry for the lower classes.

But when it came to local lore, there was none of that wrangling. Those legends, or rather accounts—for they were always real-life stories—were about personal incidents that every man would tell and that no one would want to dispute. In those times, everyone had seen ghosts, miserable souls caught in some swamp, or in a nook of some old house, or in a hollow tree trunk, or out on a moor; everyone had seen fairies, night-washerwomen, night-screamers, and the elfin *couriquets*; and each claimed to have had a struggle to get free of them, as we shall see in due course.

I was never too bored at the hospice. Since I was not basically sick, I could go everywhere in the wards and the courtyard. The head nurse often called on me to help him with housekeeping, waxing, or scrubbing, or polishing, and he would give me bits of bread and meat for my trouble, for the ward-sisters' daily rations were very meager. The doctor kept lancing my wound with his infernal pencil, each day going closer and closer to the core.*

---

*Probably cauterization by a silver-nitrate stick.

After about three weeks, it was all burned away and had completely stopped suppurating. Yes, but it was not healed, because for days afterward it gave me more pain than I had ever felt, and a great lump grew to fill out the cavity in my temple that convinced me I would never be cured of this hideous wound. However, the doctor seemed not to think the situation as desperate as I did. He had them put unguent on it and bandage my head the way the weaver had when the accident first happened. I suffered horribly for three more days and nights, and then suddenly the lump burst, and out of it came a good half-liter of yellowish pus—I thought it was my whole brain running out. The doctor said then that it was all over, that I had nothing further to fear from the problem. I was very glad; it had certainly given me enough trouble over the past five years, from insults and sarcasm, even more than from physical misery.

I still had a broad scar on my temple, though, and the skull fracture never did seal properly. And I believe it was because of that gap that all my life I have had an extraordinary faculty for comprehension, for feeling, and even for concepts. But that accidental faculty also deprived me of the primal instinct that nature provides to all creatures, even seemingly inanimate ones: the instinct for self-preservation, for thinking only of oneself, as the Bretons say: "*Pep hini evinthan e c'hunan, e Doue vit an oll.*" (Every man for himself and God for all.) That maxim, so simple and natural though hardly philanthropic, I have never known or practiced, and there again, as in other regards, I have found myself at odds with my fellow man. The central lobe of my brain, the organ that governs that natural instinct, must have been destroyed in the terrible blow to my skull.

After I healed, I was kept on for another two weeks at the hospice, where I had no complaints, thanks to the chief nurse and the ward-sister who gave me things to do; then I was set free. But alas, what was I to do with my freedom but take up my beggar's pouch again, run my three circuits a week as before, and on the other days gather wood or help my father when he worked in the marketplace?

THE IDLER-KINGS OF LOWER BRITTANY

"In Lower Brittany," said a researcher of Breton folklore, "the poor are the idler-kings of the land. Their kingdom comes by divine right; they are venerated like close kin to God, people consider themselves bound to give them shelter, and are careful not to mistreat them. They approach you with a *paternoster* and leave you with a blessing, and you're indebted to them."*

I do not know who told the researcher that—probably one of those women who told him so much other conflicting nonsense which he then published as Breton lore.

It is true that at the time I did consider begging to be a divine institution, my father and mother had told me so often, and in the little book the rector gave me at my First Communion—a book I had already learned by heart, both the Latin and the Breton—I saw that Jesus and his comrades had practiced the same trade I did, not exactly the way my regular companion and I did it, but roughly like the two rascals I mentioned before. He didn't stand around mumbling *paternosters* at doorways, not Him; He'd walk right in and sit down at the table and get himself served a meal, not only in friends' houses but even in the house of his enemies, at the tables of Pharisees, of pagans, and of low-lifes. That is clear in the Gospels, particularly in Luke; Chapters 5, 7, 10, 19, and 22. And when He sent out His seventy disciples to make the rounds, He would tell them:

---

*All the folklorists of the nineteenth century speak of the semi-sacred status of beggars; see Souvestre, de la Villemarque, Sebillot. Déguignet's derogatory references to folklorists frequently target Anatole Le Braz, whom he long suspected of misusing his memoirs, until they were published in 1905.

Go your ways . . .
Carry neither purse, nor scrip, nor shoes; and salute no
man by the way.
And into whatsoever house ye enter, . . .
. . . remain, eating and drinking such things as they
give . . .
And into whatsoever city ye enter, and they receive you,
eat such things as are set before you . . .
But into whatsoever city ye enter, and they receive you
not, go your ways out into the streets, and say,
Even the very dust of your city . . . we do wipe off against
you; notwithstanding, be ye sure of this, that the kingdom of God is come nigh unto you.
But I say unto you, that it shall be more tolerable in that
day for Sodom, than for that city. (Luke 10:4–12)

Once, they were refused drink and food in a town in Samaria,
and they told the Master to call down the fire of heaven on the
town, as the fierce Eli had called it down onto the two captains
of Achazia and their hundred men.

The rogues in my township, whom I already mentioned,
did the same thing when they were refused something. Six
farms are still living under the curse of those thugs. You still
hear it said about those farms:

Leston vian, Leston vras,
Guili vian, Guili vras,
Keruel et Penec'h,
Mar ve ann tan en ho c'huec'h.

(May fire catch in all six places.)

That is, they too called fire down on those six farms
because they were not always given what they asked there. As

that Breton lore expert says, those beggars might consider themselves—and be considered by others—close kin to God. But they did not leave their clients with a blessing; if they collected nothing, they left them with the most dreadful curses; and with mockery and obscene gestures when they did get something. They were feared like the plague, but they certainly were not venerated, no more than their Lord was venerated when he plied the same trade: He was run out of everywhere, even out of His own village and the bosom of His family, run out by stoning, and He deserved it.

I knew another one of those "idler-kings of Lower Brittany," who took himself the title not of "Idler King" but "King of the Beggars." Nor was it an empty title, for he was actually the champion of them all in style, in cunning, and in strength. This one would have ranked as Grand Master, and possibly even become king, in the famous Paris *Cour des Miracles* that Victor Hugo described so well in *Notre Dame de Paris*. Where poor Gringoire would not find a single job, this Breton beggar would have found ten. He could fabricate fake wounds on his arms and legs, make himself crippled, lame, one-armed, legless, blind; and when it came to whining and moaning, he could give lessons to Hilkia's son Jeremiah, of the *Lamentations*. This fellow was certainly the master or, as he said, the king in the category, but he was not alone. On days of *pardons* [religious processions or pilgrimages] in our chapels, the roads leading to them were lined on either side with beggars wailing and moaning, some displaying real wounds and mutilations, others showing off perfectly fake ones, worked up and applied that morning behind the hedgerow. A curious and discerning observer could have seen some character fighting with kicks and punches in the evening who that very morning had been missing an arm and displaying a hideously swollen leg covered with rotten flesh.

These were the sort of Breton beggars who might be called, as our learned man did, the "idler-kings of Lower Brittany," and in this they were in perfect accord with their God, who ranked vagabondage and beggary at the top of the social order, and who forbade working. But not all Breton beggars of the time were like those fellows. Most of them were merely beggars by accident like me, forced to it for want of work and of bread. For my part, I was far from being a king, and I was no idler either, for working was my greatest pleasure; when my father had work in the marketplace, rather than spending three days on my begging rounds, I did my best to finish them off in two so I could go help him out for the rest of the week.

TERRIBLE AND CRUEL NOBLEMEN

At that time, we finally left Le Guélennec and went to live close to town, in the great chateau [manor house] of Lez-Ergué. Like all farmsteads back then, it had three small cottages for day laborers. The owner of the chateau would let a little *penn-ty* in exchange for a certain number of days of work, so many during the sowing and so many during the harvest. The seigneurial chateau, which since the revolution had come into the hands of a simple countryman, was the subject of many legends. The last seigneur of the manor, a man named de Lamarche, was said to be the most terrible and cruel of the many terrible and cruel seigneurs the poor Bretons had known.[*]

Visitors can still see where he used to hang his *villeins* out of hatred, anger, or pleasure. Nearby stood the ruins of an old

---

[*]In 1790, the elder La Marche, seventy years old, and his son, thirty-five, lived alone on their estate with only one servant and a sharecropper. The two La Marches emigrated to Guadeloupe. The manor became the property of the state during the French Revolution, and was sold in 1808.

church where this seigneur would have Mass said every Sunday and require all the neighboring peasants to attend under pain of death.* Halfway through the Mass, he would ride in on his horse and command the priest to give the animal communion, then he would go around the church, causing his horse to stomp on the prostrate parishioners, who could neither move aside nor object. He kept a great number of pigeons, which would ravage all the sowings and harvests thereabouts, and no one could complain on pain of instant hanging. In the end, by dint of his pigeon-keeping, he broke his own neck falling through the floor from the chateau's second story. I was often shown where he fell through, and the story went that no one ever managed to repair the floor at the western end of that second story; the planks would not stay in place. I don't know if it has been floored over since then, but in my time it was not, and no one would try because it was also said that anyone who dared would break his neck too, the minute he laid his first plank. This seigneur broke his neck so badly that his head went rolling away to the far end of the room he fell into, and afterwards he could be seen walking there like Mac-Gloire in *The Devil's Pills*† searching about for that crowning ornament to his carcass. My father, great clairvoyant that he was, claimed to have seen the man several times. And the specter had other business there besides searching for his head: he was guarding a hidden treasure, and his penance would not be over until the day he could pass that treasure on to some mortal. And the treasure, everyone knew it existed, but nobody knew exactly where it was. Some

---

*The Chapel of St. Joachim was built around 1650, by Guy Auret, Lord of Lezergué and of Missirien. In 1660, he published an extended edition of Albert Le Grand's *Life of the Saints*.

†A celebrated melodrama by Anicet Bourgeois (1867).

said it was under the chateau stairway; others thought it must be at the bottom of the pond, because someone had seen an extraordinary huge eel there, who was none other than the seigneur himself, who assumed that shape in the daytime, the better to watch over his treasure; still others said that it must be underneath the pigeon-cote, a huge round tower built entirely of chiseled stone, which would have stood till the end of the world if it hadn't been demolished. Back then, they said that certain gentlemen, who looked to be foreign, had come to ask the proprietor for permission to dig for the treasure, offering him a large sum of money before starting and then a share of the treasure. But the proprietor would not allow it. Later, I was told that his son-in-law eventually did find the treasure, by tearing down the huge pigeon-cote, and that the discovery was the cause of his death, for he died suddenly a short time later.

However, others—scandalmongers, probably—said that the son-in-law's treasure came not from the pigeon-cote but straight from Notre Dame de Kerdévot, at whose church the gentleman was treasurer; since this Dame needed neither a treasure nor a treasurer for her own account, the Monsieur could safely transfer the whole thing right into his own cashbox. It goes without saying that I vouch for none of this. These are probably just new legends to add to the old ones about that chateau.

THE MIDSUMMER NIGHT'S FESTIVAL

When I read accounts by these researchers of Breton lore, I am more and more convinced that they have seen none of what they report, and that they have been fooled and taken in by the old rascals and drunken biddies about everything and everywhere. I see nothing in their accounts that matches reality. For instance, one of them, speaking of St. John's Day celebration, says that the peasants gather around a fire at night to say prayers of thanks, and that this is called *tantad.**

No, that is not the way it went. On the contrary, this was one of the greatest celebrations among Breton peasants: everyone in a village would come, from the oldest to the newborn babes. There would be two separate bonfires, and thus two different nighttime festivals, not one; the first was not called *tantad* but *Tan San Yan*, in honor of whom it was lighted for, and the other, four or five days later, was the *Tan San Per*.

And those nighttime festivities often lasted from just after sundown until midnight. Cartloads of brush, brambles, and thorn were burned; and every inhabitant, adult or child, poor or rich, had to throw on a bundle of sticks or an armload of bramble as he arrived, on pain of a fine or of having a finger chopped off. The festival was announced by rifle shots and then enormous bangs on great copper tubs, and someone would blow on a *corn boud.*†

And they would play a kind of music I have never heard played anywhere else. A tub with some water in the bottom was set upon a tripod; two long, sturdy prairie reeds were laid across the tub, and held firmly against the rim. A woman skilled at milking cows would grip the reeds, pull them taut and slide her fingers along them, exactly as if she were pulling at a cow's teats. Then, as it happens with spirit mediums but probably better, the tub would start to vibrate and dance about on the tripod. Two or three other women or children held keys hung from strings, and they would touch them to the

---

*Tantad, the customary name for big festive bonfires. Déguignet is making a specious distinction between St. John's and St. Peter's bonfires.

†A deep-toned horn.

inside of the tub. The keys were of different sizes, and they gave off different pitches as they trembled against the rim of the vibrating basin. The whole thing made an extraordinary music that sounded from one end of a commune to the other, especially when in the bigger villages they would use several tubs of different sizes and thickness.

No, never have I heard anything like that music, and I've heard a good many kinds. The god Triton, Neptune's bugler, could never make such a sound. And Joshua's seven high priests with their seven ram's horns, what were they in comparison? Even if they did—so it's said—knock down the walls of Jericho with their din.

While the women played music, and a few old huntsmen fired off gunshots, the young fellows tried their skill at fire-jumping, a fairly dangerous game as there were always some who burned their feet. It involved leaping over the fire, which was several meters broad, and when the flame was at its highest. And while these fellows were playing around the fire, there would be a few lovebirds courting a little way off. When the supply of brush was all burned up, a prayer of thanks brought the festival to an end. After the prayers, people would walk three times around the fire, and then the ash was put up for auction. It sometimes sold quite dear, that ash, because everyone wanted it, at least the farmers did, for land spread with the ash was considered certain to yield good buckwheat. And that was how the *Tan San Yan* and *Tan San Per* festivals were celebrated.

One of those muddlers of Breton lore, having published several volumes of nonsense he got from shameless old gossips, told me one day that he planned to publish another big book on the legends about life. That being the case, I advised him to go look up a certain fellow, a poor idiot who tends the cows at the insane asylum. That boy will give him enough for a hundred volumes if he wants. He'll tell him how children come into the world and how they're there for the gathering by anyone who wants them. If this writer had come among us back when I was a child, he would have found plenty of such stories. But these days, I doubt whether, even among the very youngest children out in the backwoods, he would find anyone to tell him how they'd been found bare-naked in a bush or under a cabbage leaf. For money, though, he'll always find some biddies to tell him, on that subject as they already have on others, any nonsense and rubbish he wants, since such nonsense and rubbish seem to amuse scholars no end.

EXTRAORDINARY VISITORS

But to return to my situation: After the old sinner [of a land-lord] died and his wicked soul was sent off to Yeun-Helez in the Arrée Mountains, things went much better at the farm.[*] The mistress was a fine woman, charitable to all. She always gave alms, and took in the poor folk who asked for shelter. From every corner of the *département* came *stouperezets, potret ann ouarn coz*, old sailors, and so on. . . .[†] All these people would pay for their lodgings with stories and legends, and that showed me that these tales and legends were the same everywhere, the sole differences being in the way they were told. Only the old seafarers brought us anything new. They really did tell us some great ones. They had all seen amazing things: fish fluttering through the air like birds, snakes miles long, furry men with dogs' heads, fearsome giants with just a single eye in the center of the forehead; black and yellow and red

---

[*]Yeun-Helez: marshland in Brittany's central highlands, the Monts d'Arrée.

[†]*Stouperezets* and *potret ann ourarn coz:* scavengers for flax- and hemp-fiber scrap, and for scrap iron.

men; and enormous cities, and trees that touched the sky as well as the mountains. All of them had been to the end of the world, and so close to the sun they could almost touch it as it rose from its bed in the morning or sank back at night, for they had been to both sides and to both ends.

And I, just like everyone else, believed it all. I might already have begun to doubt the existence of devils, ghosts, and elves, but matters of nature I could not question. Back then, still to my mind, the earth did not turn on its own axis, and it could not be round and, since I could see the rising and setting sun skim the earth, people who were way out at the horizon could probably touch the sun as it went down into its bed and came up out of it. Those sailors could certainly have sailed that far; looking at the sun rising at the horizon, it doesn't seem so very distant.

But the strangest lodger I saw come through in those days was a peasant, still young, quite nicely turned out, carrying a thick book under his arm. He intrigued me. Who the devil could the fellow be, traveling about that way with a big book under his arm? He did not stop to mumble prayers at the door, that one; he came right to the table where we were already having supper and asked almost commandingly if he could sleep there. The mistress, who never refused anyone, said yes, and invited him to sit down at the table to eat with us. He immediately told us that he was an alumnus of the Pont-Croix seminary, where he had studied all the sciences, and that he was traveling now in order to teach others what he knew. All that learning was written down in the big book he was carrying with him. He could give anyone whatever instruction he might desire, and at low cost. He would teach incantations for making the devil come when he was wanted and leave when he was not; for dealing with the Black Cat and not being tricked by him; for healing every sickness—and for inflicting them on enemies; for attracting the girl you want; for drawing a good number in a lottery; for always winning fights and games—in short, he was a great professor of the occult sciences.

When we had finished eating, he took his book and set it on the table, and tapping on it he said:"Yes, it is all in here, but you've got to know more than your *paternoster* to read it and understand it."

As he talked, he opened the cover, and because I was right beside him, I caught a glimpse of some large red letters at the top of the first page that formed two words I understood, even though I had not been to the seminary. I clearly saw *Albertus Magnus*, the Latin I had managed to learn from my little missal was adequate to know that those words meant *Alber Braz* in Breton, and *Albert Le Grand* in French.*

But that got me nowhere, I knew no more about Albertus Magnus than I knew about the *dominus magnus*.†

The mistress saw me staring at the big book, and she said, "Here's a boy who would love to get his nose into your book." "Oh, yes," the fellow said. "Then the child must know how to read." "He certainly does, you'll see."

She handed me the *Lives of the Saints*, which I read every evening, and I began reading out loud the life of that day's saint. When I finished, the traveler in occult sciences said, "Good heavens, he reads like a regular notary!"

My father didn't know what to make of the fellow, and had kept silent while the man went on about all his knowledge. Now Papa said, "Let Jean-Marie have a look inside your book,

---

*Albertus Magnus: monk, philosopher, and alchemist in the 12th century. For his knowledge in the natural sciences he was reputed to be a magician. His name was given to books of sorcery and spells.

†The Lord Almighty.

just to see; I wager he'll read that as well as he does the *Lives of the Saints.*" "Oh, no," the traveler said, "this is Greek in here."

And I'd seen two Latin words! But I didn't know if there were differences between Latin and Greek.

This strange mendicant was given permission to come sleep with us in the *ty-diavez* (outbuilding), and there he went on talking with the servants, trying to sell them his spells. But those poor folks were not rich enough to pay the price the abracadabra-peddler was asking. One of them did yearn to get hold of the *ann ol yeoten,* * a mysterious herb that you see glowing at night in certain meadows, but that always fades away as you draw near. A person who possesses the herb can never be hoodwinked. The only problem is that no one has ever managed to possess it, and no one ever will. The servant did pay forty sous—all he had—to the peddler of infallible charms for the trick to finding the mysterious herb, but the poor fellow died before he ever found it.

I later heard that this so-called student from the Pont-Croix seminary had worked a number of schemes, quite cruel ones, on many people naive enough to believe in his bottomless knowledge. At the Pont en Pleuven mill, he took four hundred francs from a poor blacksmith by selling him an old black cat, telling him it would bring him all the money he wanted. The blacksmith had often heard tell of the Black Cats who could supply gold and silver, and he believed this was one of those. But this cat was a real flesh-and-blood animal that the sorcerer had stolen from some farm; it didn't go out collecting silver or gold. The blacksmith was told that to make the cat bring in treasure, it had to be whipped. So one day the blacksmith started thrashing the cat, but the cat clawed at him, and

---

*The golden herb is said to help its owner find treasure or lost objects, and to talk with birds. It has never been identified.

someone told him to put it into a sack. Once it was in the sack, the blacksmith took a stick and gave the poor animal a real beating, to the point where when he opened the sack to let it go fetch the treasure, it was dead. And again, at Kervoalic, in Ergué-Armel, the traveler swindled another farmer of seven or eight hundred francs. To this one, he had promised millions, but to be shared among all the people in the household, for they would have to work together to bring in those millions. This scheme required burning a goat alive on a major road as dead bodies were carried past for burial. The goat was to be laid in a ring of gorse and thorn brush that would be set afire, and as the goat burned, all the farm folk, men and women both, were to circle around it, naked as worms, shouting: "Million, million!" This was executed to the letter: the only thing missing from the program was the millions. The poor imbecile farmer was out the costs, and on top of it he and his people had to suffer everyone's jeers and mockery afterward. I knew those poor fools, some of whom are still alive, in fact. As for the crafty sorcerer, apparently nobody ever saw him again after that one.

AT DEATH'S DOOR FOR THE FIFTH TIME

At Kervelen, the farm where I tended the cows, there was a large courtyard at whose far end long grass always grew, in winter as well as summer. That was because of a spring that kept a constant temperature—which is to say it seemed warmer in winter than summer because of the contrast with the air temperature. To harvest the grass, you had to walk knee-deep into the water. There was a plank there that you could stand on to avoid that, yes; but the plank hampered the work, and your feet still got wet. So I always ignored it and waded right into the water. But [one time] I stayed in for over an hour, with my face and upper body drenched in sweat while my feet and legs were deep in the cold water. I ended by catching a fever. My father had left the Lez-Ergué chateau and gone back to stay in our old house at Le Guélennec, but he still came to work at our place most of the time. He happened to be with us when the fever took me, and sensing immediately that it was going to be very bad for me, he carried me home and put me in my mother's care. So there I was, thrown back onto the pallet where death had visited me once before.

As my father foresaw, the fever did grow terrible, so terrible that after a few days I was considered done for. The curé was called in to give me extreme unction, my marching orders to the eternal kingdom. So this time it was really all over. After the curé left, the old biddies who considered me already a corpse, and who thought that I could no longer see or hear a thing, gave free rein to their usual babble. But although I could neither move nor speak, I could hear very well. One of them was saying she was convinced that a certain someone would soon come past her door: she had heard *Karik Ann Ankou* go by. Another said she had heard a coffin being nailed shut, another had heard the little bell, still others claimed to have heard death-watch chants and prayers for forgiveness. In short, they had all heard something foretelling that I would soon be leaving the village flat on my back and feet first. Because of their chatter, when night came I saw everything the women had mentioned: I saw the specter of the *Ankou,* the specter of a specter with his scythe, scowling at me from the foot of my cot. All night long I watched my own funeral ceremonies, never feeling the slightest fear. On the contrary, I was pleased; I had gotten a certificate of good behavior and my marching orders to heaven: *Ite, anima sancta, ad regnum eternum!* (Depart, holy soul, for the eternal kingdom!) For at the time I was a believer. People told me that everyone, Bretons included, went to the celestial Jerusalem of Jesus so well described by his cousin John. Only much later, as I leafed back and forth through all the rosters of the elect, did I see that there were no Bretons in that wondrous city.

Anyhow, those goodwives were mistaken, or the *Ankou* had misled them; I did not die, although I lingered several days in a state where it was unclear whether I was dead or alive. In the age of the famous Cardinal Mazarin, it once happened that some people declared that the cardinal had died, but others said he was still alive: "Well," someone said, "I maintain that he is neither one nor the other." I think they could have said the same about me. Myself, I didn't know where I really was, on earth or in the grave. However, I did emerge from that state that was neither death nor life, and I saw that I was still in the world, body and soul. Soon I began to drink, eat, speak, and move. But then, ah misery—I was stricken with a dreadful paralysis that made me regret that death had not carried me off. Both feet were twisted almost entirely backwards; they were practically no longer underneath my legs. When my mother saw the hideous sight, she could not help uttering her usual laments, *Ma Doue Beniguet, Itronn a Guerzeot!* (Blessed God, Holy Mother of Kerdévot!) and she began to weep, no doubt recalling the bad omens that preceded my birth. And I wept too, for I saw myself deprived of my most important limbs for the rest of my life. Ah, if only death had taken me! Almost all the old biddies and the witches, when they saw my feet, said I had the *Hurlou,*[*] as Bretons call any disorder of the feet and legs, except an injury. There is even a special saint for curing such disorders, as there is for everything else, and his name is the same as the disease: Saint Hurlou.

---

[*]The gout.

So they started praying to him for help. One of the women was determined to carry out the procedure customary in such cases. It involved scraping the roof of my mouth with a razor and rubbing the wound with coarse salt, then making a wreath from a privet branch and hanging it in the fireplace, when the wreath dried out the sickness would be cured. I let them operate on me without a whimper, though the razor hurt terribly, but in my misery, I would have let my head be cut off without a peep. However, my friend the weaver was still nearby, and when he heard about my terrible state, he came to see. He looked at my feet and frowned sadly, which hurt me as much as the old witch's razor had. However, he did try moving them, to force them back into their natural position; it was futile. He told the women to boil up some mallow blossoms, to hold my feet in the tinctured water for as long as possible, and then apply the flowers to my feet as a poultice. All that was done, and the next day the weaver came back early in the morning and began manipulating my feet. It hurt terribly but I did not complain. When he felt my feet beginning to give, he took some lard and began to rub, press, twist, and pull at my toes. He would stop now and then to let me catch my breath, then set to work again, repeating over and over, *dont a rint!* (they'll get there!). And he did eventually bring my feet into their normal position; we only hoped they wouldn't turn back again. To avoid a relapse, the weaver bound both feet with strong cloth strips and told me not to try standing up until he said to. I stayed still for two weeks, as much because of my feet as of the general weakness of my whole body, which was like a skeleton. When I was nearly recovered, I went out with my father to do day labor or to help him on his jobs when he had some; then I finally found a position as farmhand/servant at the Griffonez farm, with one of those wild men I have described.

A PROFESSOR OF AGRICULTURE

I was seventeen by then, but still small and weak. Field work was arduous in that period, when all labor was done by hand and with heavy rudimentary tools. *Durus uterque labor. Laudato ingénia rura. Exignum colito.* (Virgil: Every form of labor is hard. Praise the countryman's ingenuity. Stick to the small.)

During that time, a gentleman came to Kerfeunteun as professor of agriculture, to teach Bretons new farming skills.[*] But the peasants had little interest then in learning agriculture or anything else. The old ways—nothing else would do. A few elderly farmers would come by the professor's place to look at the new-style tools, which they had never seen, and to watch the farmhands work. But they would go off shrugging their shoulders and saying that they could give that professor a few lessons. Of course they could see that he had some fine meadows, nicely drained and irrigated, and fields of clover and fat cabbages and rutabagas; but all that cost more than it was worth, and Breton cattle didn't need those things to live on, any more than men needed white bread, meat, and vegetables, all of which were then unknown in our countryside. In short, the peasants wanted no truck with any agricultural lessons from this gentleman. Maybe if he'd been a peasant! But a high-hatted gentleman who didn't know how to speak Breton—how could he be a farmer? Please! The peasants could not allow that a man from the city might know how to cut brush, turn over a clump of earth, scythe, harvest, load manure into a cart, rake out ditches, dig a furrow with a front-loading wooden plow—still the same kind Tryptolemus[†]

---

[*]Clément-François Olive, professor of agriculture at the Likès school at Quimper; at the time it was an agricultural institute run by the Church.

[†]In Greek mythology, the original priest of Demeter, the wheat goddess. She supplied him with a plow and seed to instruct mankind in agriculture.

used—which by their lights were the sole requirements for being a good farmer. They had no use for agricultural science. You do not do agriculture with books.

Sundays, when I went to nine-o'clock mass in Quimper, I passed by Kermahonec Kerfeunteun where the agriculture professor lived. I would stand a long time looking at the farm implements that I had never seen before and whose names I didn't even know. I would look at the fields of clover, of rutabagas, heavy cabbages, and other forage crops unknown to me.

One time, seeing the door to the stable open, I decided to look at the cows I'd heard such marvelous things about—that each of them gave as much milk and butter as a half-dozen of the scrawny little local cows which were never fed anything but what they found to graze on outdoors in summer, and a little dry straw in winter. I did see that these cows were much bigger than ours, very fat and sleek; they were standing in front of a rack and a trough, things unheard of in our Breton stables. There was an old man caring for them, a day laborer who had often seen me go by. He was filling in as cowherd temporarily, for the regular man had left; he asked if I would like to take on the job. Oh, yes, absolutely, I was glad to work for a professor of agriculture. I never even wondered whether I could handle the duties, all I thought about was the fine things I saw there. Right then the good man said to go with him to find the owners (*ann dud chentil*).*

But when I saw the master, *ann Autrou*, I was almost frightened. The man had a full beard, a thing we were unused to seeing, and a not too friendly manner, and on top of it, he didn't know a word of Breton. But his lady was there, and this *itronn* knew our language very well. Although the gentleman could not speak to me, he gave me to understand that I suited

---

*Breton for "gentleman," a term for the nobility but also applied to bourgeois.

him quite well. So I was accepted right off, and I promised to be there the following morning; as to wages, I was told that would be settled later on, when I was trained and familiar with all my duties. The wages, anyhow, hardly concerned me; then, nor at anytime in my life, money held no temptation for me as long as I was given food and a few clothes to cover me—that was all I asked. The next morning, I was at Kermahonec and at the stable door before anyone was up. As the *potr saout* (cowherd), I was to sleep in the stable, for such were Monsieur's orders: a cowherd must sleep with his animals to watch over them night and day. That requirement had already caused two or three cowherds to leave, for the stable was far from the house, and goblins would come and disturb the boys' sleep. When the day laborer woke up and found me there, he started my theoretical and practical training right away. I saw that I would have a lot to do but it would not be beyond me. I soon learned everything involving my department—for on that farm, things worked as they do in an orderly government—each person, man or woman, ran his own ministry.

The gentleman taught agricultural subjects at the Likès school in Quimper, and every week his students would come for practical training at the farm. They were assigned to all the different sorts of work done there, some to the plowing, others to manual tasks with the farmhands, others to me for learning to tend the cows and supposedly to help me. But it was more like pestering me, because those student workers, who were all rich boys, had no interest in learning to tend cows; all they thought about was playing, which rather than easing my task, slowed it down. They did do me one useful service, though. From them I learned a good many French words, the words I needed most for understanding the Monsieur as best I could in my work. And also, those students were always leaving pieces of paper everywhere; I would collect them all, and try to decipher something from the handwriting, which was brand new to me. Unfortunately the written characters looked nothing like printed characters; it was all Greek to me. One day, I found a larger sheet than usual with the whole alphabet on it. That discovery gave me more pleasure than finding a casket of gold. Since I was obliged to go with the cows when they were put out to pasture, now I could use the time to study the sheets of paper that always filled my pocket. As soon as I learned the alphabet I was easily able to read them. They were all just notes on agricultural things.

WE WOULD HAVE ORGIES

On this model farm, things were managed along religious lines. The mistress (*an intronn*) would come to us every evening to say prayers. Each Sunday, everyone went to Mass; she had built a small chapel to the Virgin, where we all had to go every evening through the month of May, and on Sundays and annual feast days to sing hymns and say our rosaries and our *oremuses*. And yet despite that, never anywhere, in any country the world over, in any social milieu, have I seen people living so fully in a state of nature.

I have already described the Le Guélennec people, but they were only playing vulgar games with nature. Here, people did more than play: they lived out nature to the fullest, as animals do, without the slightest discomfort or self-consciousness. In the Georgics, Virgil speaks of love among animals as similar to love among humans. And, indeed, here I saw that there was no difference, except that men became more aroused than animals. Every day I would see such love scenes being enacted on the threshing floor, in the cottage gardens, in the barns, and in the stable. The big housemaid, who went nearly every Sunday to confession and communion, I would find afternoons in a barn rolling in the hay with all the menservants; and the same was true for the rest of them. Evenings, after the mistress had recited the prayers and gone back upstairs, we would have orgies the like of which I have only read about in books. They say that in America, where there are so many novel things, there is a Free Love Association; here too, love was free and unashamed, with all the refinements that men are better at bringing to lovemaking than animals are. These people did fear God, though, and hell and purgatory, ghosts and goblins, and they knew their prayers and their catechism, which the mistress (*an intronn*) reminded them of every day as well.

Now, Breton prayers say there is no sin more damnable than lust: *Eur peched vil, pehini hervez San Paul, ne glefet beza hanavet et touesk ar gristenien.* (The vilest sin, which Saint Paul says should be unknown among Christians)—although Paul and his companions used and abused it themselves.

Yet the mistress and master, who practiced the Christian religion and made their servants do so, neglected the first principles of that religion: unselfishness and charity. Paupers and beggars never entered their house. They considered such shabby folk to be lazy people, unwilling to work and eager to live off others. Back in Ergué-Gabéric I had known several people, among the ones I called "wild men," who also wanted nothing to do with beggars, but all of them had wives who were very charitable. Here, though, both master and mistress had the same contempt for beggars.

SUPERSTITIONS

We had an elderly day laborer lodging at the farm. He was a veteran of Louis Philippe's army, but he had learned nothing at all in the service, not even how to speak French. On the other hand, neither had he forgotten any of the superstitions of his countryside. He was from Briec, a great area for legends and superstitions; he was always talking about goblins, gnomes, ghosts, and spirits, and he always insisted he had seen every single thing he described. For instance, he said he had known two loose girls who were condemned to hell to serve as mares to the devil; he had seen them cantering about in that form, always with handsome horsemen mounted on their backs. One day, one of the mares was brought to a blacksmith shop for reshoeing. The farrier and his helpers were surprised to see that this fine mare had the pretty feet of a woman; and she told the farrier to stuff rags between her feet and the iron horseshoes. But when he heard her voice and understood who she was, he said, "Oh, sure, I should put rags under your feet, you slut! I'm going to put some red-hot shoes on you, that's what!" And so he did, to the damned damsel's screams. But as she left, she told the farrier that she would remember him, and indeed she did: the cruel, inhuman fellow had nothing but misfortune and misery for the rest of his days, and they say he went to hell besides.

This old soldier had seen several persons undergo exorcism—one in particular, a former seigneur, who had needed eighteen priests to hold him down. He had seen the priests running off, one after the other, and they'd all told him to get away too, as fast as he could; but he hadn't gone a hundred paces before he was knocked over by something like a lightning bolt, and a hideous stink enveloped him. He could not pick himself up until the next morning. On several occasions, too, he had had to do battle with goblins and werewolves, who were plentiful at the time. Many nights he had danced with gnomes. And no one around him had ever died without first seeing a vision of their burial. He had been apprenticed to the greatest sorcerer in Briec; unfortunately, though, he did not have the qualities needed for the job. In fact, that great sorcerer, who brought about anything the soldier and other peo-

ple asked for, finally died without passing along all his enormous knowledge to anyone, for he'd found no one capable to
receive it. That was a great misfortune. A man still living in
Quimper told me he had known that great sorcerer, who had
helped him to draw a good number for the military draft, and
gave him the number beforehand; if his father hadn't stood
in the way, he would have got all the great man's knowledge,
as he alone was deemed capable and worthy to receive it.

Some people say that, nowadays all these beliefs are dead
and gone. Not at all: the beliefs are just as lively today as when
I was young, but what's missing are the sorcerers, who have
nearly all died without leaving successors, and the doctors
and gendarmes are quite hard on the ones who are left. The
belief in exorcism has not disappeared, either; but exorcists
have. If priests these days only exorcise a few unknown souls,
it's because they make more by sending rich souls to purgatory
than by sending them to Yeun Helez; sending a soul to hell
would earn them a fee only once, whereas by sending it to purgatory they get paid annually, monthly, weekly, even daily, and
so on, *usque ad eternam die* (unto eternity).

GWERZ DE KÊR-IS (THE BALLAD OF KÊR-IS)

While I was at Kermahonec, a new *guers*[*] came out, about the
famous city of Ys. Such songs were in fashion at the time;
every chapel had one, telling of the endless number of miracles its particular patron saint had worked.

One of our housemaids had bought a copy of this new *guers*
on a trip to town to sell the butter. Those good-natured girls
enjoyed everything—mass, confession, hymns, sermons, songs,
guers, and easy lovemaking.

---

[*] *Guers*, a ballad or lament. This one, *Ar Roue Gralon ha Kearis* (King Gradlon
and the City of Ys), was composed in 1850 by Olivier Souvestre. It was quite
successful.

I had already heard about the marvelous city of Ys. At the time, there was a Breton proverb: *Abaoue eo beunzet Is, n'eus ker ebet evel Paris.* (Ever since the city of Ys was flooded, there is no city left equal to Paris.) Because, for elderly Bretons, the syllable "par" means "exactly equal to," so the word "PAR-IS" simply means "equal to Ys." No Breton peasant questioned the long-ago existence of that city, which had been engulfed by the sea for the sins of King Gradlon's daughter and her companions in debauchery.

Those debaucheries, and the catastrophe they brought on, are the subjects of this *guers.*[*]

The glorious city of Ys lay at the edge of the sea, protected by mighty dikes. It was ruled by old King Gradlon; his daughter, Ahès, led the young folk of the town in endless orgies and dissipation, and the Lord determined to destroy the city for its wicked ways. He sent the devil, called Paulic in Breton lore, to do his bidding. Disguised as a handsome, gorgeously attired prince, Paulic was so seductive to Ahès that to please him she stole into her sleeping father's chamber and stole the golden key he wore always around his neck—the key to the floodgates in the dike. No sooner did Paulic have the key in hand that he went and opened the gates, and the waters rushed in while the princess and her dissolute companions went on dancing their bacchante dances in her orgy-palace. As the waters rose, the monk Guénolé, also on the Almighty's orders, came galloping to wake the good king and urge him to mount his own horse and flee the oncoming seas. Riding through the streets of his beloved Ys, the king sees his daughter fleeing the angry waves; he takes her up behind him. But his horse slows down abruptly, even as the turbulent waters go on rising. Guénolé sees that the king will be drowned along with all the rest of the city, and he cries "*Taol en diaoul er mour!*" (Throw the devil into the sea!) Finally, seeing

---

[*]This segment is partly recast in translation. [L.A.]

doom approach, old Gradlon pushes his daughter into the waves—and they instantly fall calm. His horse, freed of its diabolical burden, takes a single great leap and lands at Quimper, just as Mohammed's mare leapt from Mecca to Jerusalem. King Gradlon built a palace on the spot where his horse landed. And because the hermit Chorentin (or Kaour, or Kaourentin) had first made him welcome there, the king later gave him the palace, to be made into a church. And there where the palace had stood rose the great cathedral of Saint Corentin; at its crest, between the two towers, rides King Gradlon astride his horse, with his eyes fixed on the ocean as if he hoped to see his City of Ys rise again from beneath the waves.

Another legend says that Gradlon's horse came down not at Quimper but at Rumengol;[*] natives there point out the rock where he landed and where his hooves struck their deep prints—just as in the temple of Omar in Jerusalem, true believers are shown the rock cleaved by Mohammed and his white mare. Where Gradlon and his horse are said to have landed, the king commanded a chapel to be built to honor the Mother of God, Our Lady of Rumengol, who has the power to save anyone who trusts in her, says the *guers*:

> "*Ann neb en em roi d'ann Itronn Varia Rumengol*
> *Birviken, james ne yello da goll.*"
> (*He who worships the Lady of Rumengol*
> *Will never be lost.*)

That Lady of Rumengol is these days locked in a disastrous competition with the Lady of Kerdévot, ever since the railroad started carrying pilgrims to Rumengol at reduced fares.

---

[*]Rumengol, in the township of Faou in the center of Finistère, is a great site of pilgrimage.

The self-styled mythology experts, the researchers of tales and legends, have quibbled endlessly over the famous city of Ys, over how to classify the story or legend. According to one, it belongs among tales like *Sleeping Beauty;* another calls Ys a spellbound city; and another says it is an underwater home for sailors who have drowned. "A day will come," says one scholar, "when the city of Ys will emerge from the seas, and the cities we know today will in turn fall to ruin." This person is speaking from the standpoint of geological science, which holds that not only cities but also peoples, and whole continents, have been engulfed while other continents were rising from the deep.

Another of these harvesters of legends, this one a Breton, locates the engulfed city on the Channel coast near Tréguier, whereas the other legends all place it on the opposite coast, in Cornouaille near Douarnenez. A village there still bears the princess' name: Poul Dahut. In the legends, Gradlon's daughter is variously named Ahès, Dahès, and Dahut.

The differing legends should have caused some embarrassment to the manufacturers of Breton saints, if those black charlatans were people with the slightest concern for—I won't say "truth," they do not care about that—but even a modicum of good sense. Indeed, according to those saint-makers, King Gradlon was supposed to be simultaneously at Corisopetensis with his friend Chorentin (Kaour, Kaourentin, or Corentin) and at Landevenec with the person who saved him from the catastrophe of Ys: Gringolé, Gringalois, or Guénolé.

Those early manufacturers of Breton saints all speak of the famous King Gradlon but they say nothing about his lovely capital city Leuxobie, or Ys, whereas modern writers on the saints' lives do mention it, which proves that the legend is not as old as certain manufacturers or collectors of Breton lore contend. As further proof, all the tales describe the city of Ys as a Christian town, when we know from history that not all the people living on those coasts had yet been Christianized by the last century. The Ys legend is, like most Breton legends, an invention of the priests. Having already fabricated saints just for Brittany, and fables and legends suited to such saints and to the narrow ideas of impoverished Bretons, these priests were now trying to round off their Breton Genesis with a cataclysm of the sort found in the Genesis stories of all peoples, and the best they could come up with was to copy Chapter 19 of the Hebrew Genesis. For the story of Ys is an exact replica of the fable of Sodom and Gomorrah. Those two cities were flooded because of their citizens' debauchery, and the same was true of the city of Ys. In the first fable, old Lot was warned and saved by an angel; in the Breton fable, old Gradlon was also warned and saved by an emissary from God, Saint Guénolé. There Edith, Lot's wife, was turned into a pillar of salt [as punishment for having looked back on Sodom's destruction]; here Ahès, Gradlon's daughter, was turned into a mermaid. Lot went to live in a cave with his two daughters; old Gradlon also went off to live in a cave, with young Kaourentin, and they fed on fishes that came flying of their own will onto the skewer or into the pot. According to Benjamin Jonos [a 12th century writer], who saw Lot's wife in the twelfth century, she was not completely dead; when animals licked at her and thereby made her smaller, she turned back into her old shape and resumed her monthly periods like other women, though she probably did not enjoy that much. Gradlon's daughter, though, has a fine time with her liberation into a mermaid: like the mythological Sirens, she delights in playing tricks on mariners along the coast. They often report hearing her sing, and her lovely voice casts a spell that makes them lose their heads and their way; they see her on the rocks combing out her beautiful golden locks.

I have heard old fishermen from Douarnenez claim they saw her several times, and were bewitched and drawn off course by her songs. There is still an old woman living here, a direct descendant of the barbarians on the Île de Sein, who has often told me the story of that lovely princess with the golden hair and the fish's tail. With her songs and her frolics, she foretold good weather and bad—but for the islanders, "bad weather" was clear nights and calm wind; "good weather" was dark and stormy nights, when ships would crash on the rocks, which was providential for these island barbarians who lived exclusively off the wreckage from the sea.

The *guers* about Ker Ys was bought for my sake; of all the servants at Kermahonec, I was the only one who could read. I was thus called upon to sing it to the others, and very often, because it delighted them, especially the women, who wanted to learn it by heart. That *guers*, as I said before, is simply a rhymed version of the catastrophic legend of Ys.

I have told other stories in which the devil, Paulic, was always being tricked and made a fool of by the peasants. In the Ys legend, it was Paulic duping and exploiting all the rich young folk of the city, along with the princess herself; true, in this case Paulic was acting in the name and on the orders of the Eternal One, as he had the other time, when he was sent to punish Job.

LEARNING TO WRITE

Now I return to my cows. It was no sinecure, the job of cowherd on that model farm. The masters considered their cowherd the most important and useful of their employees, and with good reason, for whatever money they earned from the farm came from the cows; they sold nothing but milk and

butter. So all their concern centered on the cows and consequently on the cow keeper, especially the latter, on whom
depended the production of milk and butter through the
feed and the care he gave his animals. My work was rather
hard, and always the same; in summer and autumn I had to
mow clover and grass for the animals, transport it from the
field to the farmyard and distribute it in the feeding racks,
clean and arrange the bedding litter while my cows were still
inside the stable, because once they went out I had to follow
and watch over them; in winter, I had to gather the cabbages,
cut the root vegetables, cabbages, turnips, and rutabagas, give
the animals warm water and pull straw down from the great
hayricks, which was the hardest and slowest work of all. And
on top of that, I still had the schoolboys coming to pester me
once and sometimes twice a week on the pretext of learning
to tend the cows, but actually only to play or to spoil my own
work. One day a boy dropped his satchel, which was full of
writing samples and a few blank sheets of paper with a pencil.
That find pleased me enormously. I decided that now I was
going to learn to write. I couldn't wait to find a spare moment
to see if I could form letters like the ones in those samples.

As soon as I was alone in the pasture with my cows, I took
up my pencil and a blank sheet and began to draw letters, but
I soon saw that learning to write would be harder for me than
it had been to read. My head was quick to learn anything it
heard and saw, but my hand didn't have the same abilities; it
was used to wielding heavy tools and not very apt at wielding
a pencil. I managed to form some As and Bs, but clumsily, tearing holes in the paper; I did better tracing them in earth or
sand with my fingers or my whip-handle. Still, I wasn't discouraged; whenever I was out with my cows and was sure no
one could see me, I would again set about forming as best I
could the letters of the alphabet, big and small; then I would

scratch out the words "cow," "bull," "horse," "hay," "straw," "cabbage," and other farming words that I could read among the examples. But I was furious at not managing to form a single letter like the ones I was seeing on the sheet.

Despite all the precautions I took to avoid being caught at this occupation, which was not part of my job, I was found out there by my Mistress's old mother, who sometimes took a walk in the fields to pass the time. I had just finished scribbling over a whole side of a sheet of paper, but as usual I was dissatisfied with my work. One of the cows came to stand and chew its cud beside me; looking at the animal, it occurred to me to try to draw it on the clean side of the sheet. I was happier over that; I thought the finished sketch looked a lot more like the cow than my writing looked like the samples. I was considering my drawing and touching it up when suddenly I heard a voice behind me: *"Ha ha e guiche e mer e tiwoal ar zaout!* (So that's how you watch the cows!) I nearly jumped into the air as if a snake had bitten me. The first cannonball that ever shot past me and nearly knocked me over, later on, frightened me less than the voice of that old *intronn.*

Death has never frightened me, but I have always been extremely sensitive to the mildest reproach, especially when the reproach is barely or not at all deserved. The old woman didn't exactly mean to reproach me, but I felt it anyhow, and I was vexed at being caught doing something that did not number among my responsibilities. I quickly gathered up my paper and pencil, stuffed everything into my pocket, and set about counting my cows.

"Oh," said the old woman, "I know perfectly well all your cows are here, but how come I gave you such a fright? I was told you weren't skittish."

"No, Madame," I said, "I'm not skittish; it's because I was caught doing something that's not my job."

"I see no harm," she said, "in a cowherd entertaining himself while his cows graze or chew. But show me the nice work you were doing there."

Of course I had to hand her my paper. When she had studied the scribblings and the sketch, she asked me at what school I had learned all that. It was no use telling her I had never been to any school, she kept insisting that a person doesn't learn to read, write, and draw without some kind of schooling.

"I'm going to show this to my son-in-law," she said. "He's a professor; I wager he'll say the same thing."

"Well then, Madame," I said, "you're going to get me dismissed as unfit for tending cows."

"Don't worry about a thing," she said. "My son-in-law and my daughter are very pleased with you, they'll be still more so when they see this."

Monsieur and Madame thought it extraordinary that I had learned to read and write without a teacher, and wished that I had the means to go to school—I would certainly have done something worthwhile. But that was impossible for me in those times. There were no schools except for the rich. And I really think it may be just as well, for a poor wretch with some learning is doubly wretched, unless he is a great philosopher. Still, I went on scribbling when I got a chance, but I was careful not to let anyone catch me at it ever again.

A REGULAR DOMESTIC SERVANT

The mayor of Kerfeunteun lived quite near the model farm at the time, but he was not friends with the professor. Now and then as I grazed my cows along the Brest road, he would come and chat with me, asking how I fed the cows and what I did for them in the stable, what the household help was fed, and all sorts of things; he felt all that was well and good for someone who was being paid to farm, but that if the peasants did as my master did, they would all soon be out begging for their bread. That was what all the peasants said, actually.

One day, the mayor asked me if I liked my situation as cowherd, which was, actually, a veritable slavery: I could never leave the place, not Sundays nor feast-days. I replied with the Breton proverb: *Laec'h ma stag ar c'haor, e red dei puri.* (The goat must browse where it is tethered.)

"Sometimes," he said, "the goat snaps its rope and goes to browse someplace else."

Then he went off. Some time later, as the end of the year drew near, I started to reflect on what the mayor had said about the goat and my slave condition. One Sunday evening, I hurried to finish my work and, when everything was in order and I was sure no one was watching, I galloped cross-country to the mayor's house. As soon as he saw me, he said, "I'll wager you've snapped your rope."

"Not completely," I said. "But I remembered what you said the other day."

The mayor understood, and we made an arrangement quickly, for I had no time to lose. On the first of January, I would go to his house, no longer as a cowherd but as a regular domestic. I was back at the farm in time for supper and no one had noticed my absence. But now I still had to let the master know that I had committed myself somewhere else. The best thing was to tell everyone in the kitchen; that way he would soon find out. I therefore announced after supper that I had just contracted for another position. So the next morning I expected a scolding from Monsieur and Madame, and perhaps an immediate discharge; but I was wrong. Monsieur and Madame did come to talk to me the next morning, she as interpreter since the master knew not a word of Breton; but they spoke very nicely, asking why I was leaving, saying they had had some good things in mind for me, that they were planning to raise my pay, and so on. I told them I felt I was too old now to remain a cowherd, and that in any case I would not go back on my word. In the end, when they saw clearly that I would not be staying, they asked me to find them a good replacement. Well, finding someone good was not so easy. The thing is, a great many qualities go into being a good cowherd for this master; first, you couldn't be lazy or slow-moving, you had to learn quickly and thoroughly his method of tending the cows, which was exactly the opposite of the peasants' method; you needed the strength to resist being influenced and ordered about by the housemaids, or by the other servants, who had nothing to do with the dairy-farming department; but for that, the cowherd had to really know his business and keep things constantly in good order; he could not be too friendly with Morpheus, the god of sleep, and he could not be thinking about festivals, *pardons* and games, nor actually about any free moments. But where to find an eighteen- or twenty-year-old Breton peasant of that caliber? It was hard enough back then, and still harder these days!

But still, I had no complaints about the time I spent on that Kermahonec farm. We were well fed there, and because my work was more a matter of quickness than of strength, my body had developed and grown strong. Now I had just one thing in mind—whether I would qualify for military service. That was the only way I could expect to get out of Brittany, to travel, to see other things and to learn. For I was increasingly devoured by the desire to learn what I did not know, and there were plenty of things I still did not know at the time, since I had no idea even what world I was living in, did not know its name, or its shape, or its size.

OBSERVING THE MOON

I wondered about a great many other questions as well, with no way to answer them. I was told that Paradise was up above and Hell down below in a realm of shadows. But Hell could not be always in the shadows, because I saw the sun slip beneath the earth every day, and since Hell was down there, the sun must go through it; then Paradise would become the shadowy place, since the Scriptures speak of only a single sun, and this sun clearly cannot be lighting Paradise since it lies up there beneath the sky-ceiling along with the moon and the stars. On the subject of the moon and the stars, I had made an astronomical discovery, which did still more to increase my confusion and further agitate my unquiet mind. One is told that it was the shepherds in the East, Chaldeans or others, who made the first astronomical discoveries, although Voltaire and other learned men have disputed that, saying no such thing as astronomer-shepherds or philosopher-shepherds have ever been known. Astrologers they might have been, for astrology did exist a good many centuries before astronomy, as alchemy did before chemistry. Whatever the case, it was while I was a shepherd that I made my own first astronomical discovery. And they say Newton was a farmer when he discovered the laws of gravity—a real discovery, that one. Mine was only a discovery already discovered by thousands of individuals before me. But I didn't know that at the time.

Breton peasants say that those patches of shade we see on the moon are a peasant, a brush-thief, whom Dame Moon swallowed one night with his whole load of stolen brushwood. And indeed, for anyone who has ever seen an old Breton peasant of that period with a load of brush on his back, those shadows on the moon do look exactly like that. One evening, I was contemplating the old fellow as I used to contemplate anything I heard about that came within my view. Observing the moon with its little man, I also observed a large star very close to it on the left, and I saw that the star was drawing closer to the moon; then, after a moment, it disappeared. Where had it gone? Had it been swallowed by the moon like the brush-thief, or had it burrowed into the sky ceiling? Another mystery for me. I was watching all this through the window from my bed in the stable. I finally fell asleep, and immediately had dreams about that moon and star. I could not tell exactly how long I slept, but when I woke, by leaning a bit in the bed I could still see the moon, and I was very surprised to see the large star now to the right of the moon. But then how had the star traveled—through the body of the moon, or behind it, piercing the sky? Another mystery. And then on the following night, I saw that the star was now distant from the moon, and it looked to be moving still farther off in that direction, on the opposite side. So then it followed that neither star nor moon could be attached to the sky's ceiling, as all ignorant people believe, since each moved independently along its own path.

And the moon—why and how did it wear down every month? And again, why were there long and short days, and winters and summers, and where did the wind, and thunder, and rain, and hail, and snow come from? I knew that ignorant people have an answer to all such questions—one answer, always the same: It's God's doing, it's not for humans to understand; in fact it's impious, sacrilegious, to try to understand such mysteries.

Bretons even have a fable on the subject to mock the learned men: One day, one of those savants was pondering on the seashore and he saw a little child carrying water in a shell to a small hole; the savant, hoping to plumb the mystery of the Trinity, asked the child what he was doing.

"I'm trying to put all the water in the ocean into this little hole," the child answered.

"Oh," said the savant, "that's folly, my child, you'll never succeed."

"Still," said the child, "I'll get the ocean into this little hole with my seashell sooner than you'll solve your problem." And from that day on, the savant stopped trying to comprehend any mystery, and counseled others to do the same.

This is yet another fable concocted by the priests, who have always sought, and continue to seek, every possible way to quash the flight of the human spirit. Despite all that, I could not keep my spirit from soaring, I could not keep my brain from taking in the impressions of natural phenomena that my eyes saw or my ears heard. I was quite aware that the prayers, the catechism, and the priests in the confessional booth were telling me to close my eyes when I saw vile things, to stop my ears from hearing vile remarks. And I often reflected on the priests' advice, the catechism lessons—none of which I had forgotten—and the adjurations of the prayers I still said morning and night. Unfortunately, my mind found as much matter for scrutiny in those lessons, in those prayers, as in the phenomena of nature.

LEARNING FRENCH

Another *potr-saout* was finally found to take my place and, on the first of January 1854, I took up service as a domestic with the mayor of Kerfeunteun. He came himself to snatch me, so to speak, out of my cowbarn, for without him it was nearly certain that I would not yet have left Kermahonec.

Now in the mayor's house, I was no longer so completely a slave; I had only to do what the other domestics did, and when the day was done I was no longer responsible for the livestock, and on Sundays, I was free the whole day. I used the time to study, for I had bought a little French-Breton vocabulary book* and I would carry it off every Sunday to a hiding place in the stable, if it was cold out, or to a spot in the meadow if the weather was fine. I did not want anyone to know I was studying. The mayor subscribed to a French-language newspaper, which he left lying about the house. When he was done with it, I would pick it up and try with the help of my manual to make out what I could of it. Unfortunately, that was not easy. With the little sheets I had found and gathered up at Kermahonec, I had managed to understand a good deal, because they only spoke of agricultural matters. But that was not what the mayor's newspaper discussed. At every word I had to turn to my vocabulary book and, unfortunately, often I would not find the word I wanted, for the Breton language is so old and so meager that it does not contain half the words that occur these days in all the great modern languages. So I could not manage to understand much in the newspaper, though it must have been interesting, for war had been declared between France and Russia, and the mayor told us about it every day.

This peasant-mayor loved to talk and show off his knowledge; he was not one of that race of wild men, several of whom I've mentioned. He belonged rather to that category of chaffing, joking countrymen who have an answer for everything, but always contrariwise, with no regard for common sense, or reason, or truth. Such fellows enjoy a fine reputation; people may call them banterers, jokers, or yarn spinners, but they are all decent characters, and even though you may not believe them, at least their talk is entertaining and it makes a person laugh. They are preferable to those sav-

---

*One such was published in Quimper in 1808.

ages whose only speech is like a snarling dog about to bite, or those sly, hypocritical peasants who are so numerous, and so dangerous.

The mayor had a niece living in the house who had lost both her father and her mother; she was considered to be the richest heiress in these parts, at least for a peasant. She was fifteen or sixteen at the time, a madcap, and the mayor left her completely free to go her own way. She could not read or write, though she sometimes went to school, when she felt like it. She didn't go to a school where a person would learn reading, writing, and a bit of correct behavior, but she did attend—with others pretty much like herself—a school where they must have done natural history, anatomy, and physiology, for in those matters she was very well versed. On the farm, when she had nothing else to do, she would entertain herself by pulling all kinds of pranks and mischief on everyone, especially on me, who was the youngest of the household help and the most forbearing; who didn't even dare complain when she hurt me, or when she put ant-eggs into my soup, or those flower petals that arouse a person or make him belch *per basso.**

The mischievous little miss was the first to spot me reading the newspaper. It was a Sunday in the spring, and I had found the paper on the kitchen table. I put it into my pocket with my dictionary, and went off to hide in an oat field to read it, for by now I had come to understand many words and even whole phrases. I was busy studying away in my hideout, leaning against the hedgerow, when all of a sudden a clump of sod hits me on the head and, at the same time, the mad girl tumbles onto my back, rolling me into the ditch with my newspaper. Then, when she'd picked herself up: "Well, well, so Monsieur knows how to read! And that's how you spend your Sundays.

---

*Out the bottom.

I've been trying to find out for a long time, because I never see you anywhere on Sundays."

"Yes," I told her, "I do know how to read. Unfortunately I don't understand much of what I'm reading here in this paper—it's in French—but I have hopes of getting to understand it; I've got a little book here that's already taught me a lot. Ah," I said, "if only I could go to school like you, I would soon learn French and probably lots of other things."

"Well, I would have learned, too," she says, "if I wanted to, but what good would it do me? I know enough as it is, since I can speak two languages. I see plenty of fine young ladies in town who go to school every day and they don't know as much as I do."

Then she told me that she was quite rich, that she had no need for learning, or for a skill to earn her living by. If she had known any Molière she could have said what Chrysale told Belise in *Les Femmes Savantes*—that a woman always knows enough

"When her mental capacity finally reaches

To knowing the difference 'tween doublet and breeches."

And she could have added that she knew more; that her own mind reached above the doublet, the *chupen*, and below the breeches, the *bragou*.

It was dinner time, and I walked back to the house with her. She had nothing more pressing to do than to tell her uncle that she'd found the little gentleman reading his master's newspaper like the fine gentlemen of the town. The uncle, who was a goodhearted tease, and who knew his niece was a fine little tease and talker herself, paid no attention to her story, but because by now I was fairly comfortable with the uncle, I told him that it wasn't the first time I had picked up his paper to read, that I had long since learned to read Breton and Latin, and that back at Kermahonec, thanks to the pages the schoolboys left about, I had even learned to write a little.

"Well!" he said, "You might know more than I do, with my fifteen years of schooling. Here, read me something from the newspaper."

I did not have to be asked twice. I started reading rather fluently from the paper, which by the way I had already read and re-read ten times. But I made the uncle laugh, and sometimes the niece too, who knew enough French to hear that I was pronouncing the words wrong, for I was reading the French the way I read Breton and Latin: pronouncing every letter: I would say "meeneestress,"for *ministres,* "homm-es" for *hommes,* and so on. But when I had finished reading the article and my two listeners had finished laughing, the mayor gave me a brief lesson on my mistakes; he told me that in French the *e* is never pronounced unless there is a mark over it, and neither are final consonants like *d, t, s, x, b, c, p, g.*

"But in that case," I said, "the French are even more foolish than Bretons; why put so many letters down on the page if they're not used?"

So then he began to explain that the French language had rules that had to be followed in speaking and writing, and that the rules were all to be found in a book called *Grammar,* but that learning the rules took a lot of time, intelligence, patience, and determination.

"Well," I said, "then I can never learn French."

"Sure you can," he said, "if you go into the service, you'll learn barracks French. But learning proper French as it's written and spoken in the educated world, you'll never manage that; it's too late now for you to learn grammar. And besides, grammar isn't enough by itself; a person has to read other books, bigger and harder ones, to really know French. Look at me, I spent fifteen years in school and I barely know it."

"So then," I said, "nobody knows French."

"Oh, very few Frenchmen know French."

"But what's that 'barracks French' you mentioned earlier?"

"It's a kind of French you'll pick up very quickly if you go into the army; it comes with the job, like the language you learned at Kermahonec—enough to manage the cows. I know men here in Quimper who were in the army for thirty years and don't know any more French now than they knew after a few months in the barracks."

"Well then, I'm sunk. I have no other way to learn it, and I've been dying to know it for a long time, not for the language itself, but in the hope of using it to solve certain problems that torment me day and night."

"Tormenting yourself makes no sense. You'll never solve those problems. There are plenty of learned folks in the world who haven't managed to do that."

THE BRETON SAINTS

From that day on, the mayor enjoyed quizzing me on my little store of learning. When he discovered that I could recite the evening prayers, which I had always done wherever I'd lived, except at Kermahonec where the mistress took care of them herself, he immediately handed over those holy duties, which are supposed to be carried out by the youngest person in the house capable of it. So I was appointed master of ceremonies in the house of the village mayor. I also had to read aloud from *The Lives of the Saints*, and I enjoyed doing it more there than I had elsewhere, because the mayor allowed me some commentary and critiques on the saints, particularly on the Breton saints.

The mayor, although a practicing Catholic, had a touch of the philosopher about him, and, since it was his nature to scoff, he even allowed some scoffing on matters concerning the Good Lord. I startled him, and the others, one day when

I asked him why our Breton saints were not in Paradise. He burst into laughter and said, "But you must be out of your mind to ask why the saints aren't in Paradise—where do you think they are, in Hell?"

"I don't know," I answered, "but they're certainly not in the Christians' Paradise; just look at the Roman calendar, you won't see a single Breton name on it."

"Ha ha," he said, "it would be strange if the greatest saints in the world were not recognized in Rome or in heaven. I'll show you where they are."

He took up a Roman calendar, expecting to find a Breton saint right off. But search as he might from start to finish, he never found one. He looked at another calendar: not there either.

"Well now, well now," he said, "isn't that something."

But since he never could bear to be without an answer, he said, "Oh, it's because our saints didn't know French and didn't much care for those grand folks. That's why they weren't put in with the others; the Good Lord probably made a special section for them."

This is an example of how little attention Bretons pay to what they see and hear. Here was a mayor, an educated man who had been reading the saints' lives for years and years, and he did not even know which saints were Breton, nor their status compared to other saints. And when I asked him why we had no female Breton saint:"What do you mean, no female saints? They're all over the place!"

"Yes, there are plenty of female saints, but they're all foreigners—not one of them comes from Brittany. You've read the lives of the saints so often, and you've never noticed that! It proves that you don't pay much attention to what you read—about as little as do the people who listen to you talk."

And the mayor burrows through the calendars and through the *Lives of the Saints* and finds not a single female saint born in Brittany.

"Well now, *gast avat**—it gets stranger and stranger! And yet they have Breton names."

"Yes," I say, "they were given those Breton names. Anna—who's the oldest of them all, since she was Jesus' grandmother, and who was made the patron saint of our province—Anna has a Breton name here. But she was very far away from here, since she comes from the same country as her daughter Mary. Barba, another old saint, also has a Breton name, but she came from the same country as Anna; Catell—Catherine—got a Breton name too, even though she was Spanish; and the same is true for all the rest of them. The female saint who was born closest to Brittany is *Saint Marc'harit* (Margaret), from England, where the earliest and the greatest saints of Brittany came from, like Malo, Paol, Gildas, and others."

The mayor was dumbstruck. What?—Brittany did not have a single female saint, such a Catholic country! And none of the Breton saints—such great, famous saints—none of them were known in Rome?

After that, we had discussions almost every day on the subject, because every day I read out the life of one or another saint. Each time I finished my reading, he would ask, "Well, what have you got to say about that one?"

Now that I knew the mayor well, and knew that he rather enjoyed a little scoffing, even about the saints, and never took offense, I did not hesitate to talk freely about my whole way of thinking. I told him I found it rather odd that the priests urged us to follow the example of these saints and that none of them did so. And, besides, if we did follow the saints' example,

---

*Breton expletive—roughly "I'll be damned!"

the human race would have ceased to exist long ago, since all of them died bachelors and none of them ever did a lick of manual labor.

"But you know very well," he said, "that the Gospels tell us to seek the Kingdom of Heaven above all else, without a thought for the rest."

"I did see that in my little book, and I know all our saints followed those principles. But if everyone else had done the same, there wouldn't be many people in the Kingdom of Heaven."

One day the mayor said, "Where the devil do you get all these ideas and thoughts? They're so strange for a Breton who's never been to school."

I showed him my left temple, which still bore the scar of the cranial fracture a simple bumblebee had caused, and I pointed out the flattening and broadening of my upper skull. "There it is," I told him, "the hole that all the ideas and thoughts enter my head through; and because my brain was enlarged by the shock, they have room to lodge there."

"Really!" he said. "And you think that's what gives you these unusual thoughts and curious ideas that never occurred to me even though I've had fifteen years of schooling?"

"Yes, I'm sure of it now; besides, the reason why seems quite simple to me: the brain is the seat of ideas, thoughts, and reflections, but those ideas and thoughts and reflections are not innate; if they were, we would all have the same intelligence and knowledge with no need for school. The brain is only a warehouse for receiving and storing thoughts and ideas, which all come from outside but which can only get into the warehouse, as you know, if the skull is young and soft; but since mine has a gap in it, they can probably keep coming in all the time."

The mayor laughed with that chaffing laugh, skeptical but good-natured as ever.

THE FIRST TELEGRAPH LINE

The first telegraph line had just been strung between Quimper and Brest, and it passed close to our farm.* This was something new for my mind to puzzle over, my mind that could never see a thing without trying immediately to understand the purpose, the why, what mathematicians would call the x. There was talk too about the railroad coming soon to Quimper. Thinking that the mayor might know about such matters, I asked him one day how the telegraph and the railroad worked. Because he had an answer for everything whether or not he knew about it, he said the steel wire strung from Brest to Quimper was for carrying news: the news was written on a bit of paper and inserted into the wire; blowing on it at one end sent it along instantly to the other end.

"But I saw the workers cutting the wire," I said, "and it wasn't hollow."

"No," he said, "the paper hollows it out as it goes."

I had to be satisfied with that. I could see that despite his fifteen years of schooling, the mayor understood no more about telegraphy than I did. At the time I did not know, even by name, any of the sciences that have brought men to so many modern discoveries, but by dint of research I managed to solve the puzzle in a way that was both more scientific and closer to reality than the mayor. Several times I climbed up a pole and, with a hand on the top and an ear pressed to the wire, I listened to hear if I couldn't catch some sound. When the weather was calm and I wasn't touching the wire, I heard nothing, but when there was a wind or I tapped on the wire with my hand, I could hear a kind of hum moving along the

---

*The electric telegraph was invented in 1844 by the American, Samuel F. B. Morse. Construction began on the Nantes–Quimper–Brest link as of 1852, and the service reached Quimper in April 1853. (Alain Le Grand: *Quimper, a Century of History*.)

wire and dying out in the distance. So then I thought, now I know. A man in Quimper taps a hammer at his end of the wire and the strokes reverberate along the line as far as Brest; by tapping in pre-arranged patterns, the operators can spell out words. Well! *tonnerre de brest!*—when, some years later, I saw a dial-telegraph operating in a railway station, I thought, "Look at that! My idea wasn't so stupid, or so far off the mark!"

But as to the railway, the mayor said it was a system made entirely of iron railing—the bottom, the two side walls, and the top; that it was like a long metal tube with linked cars inside it; a fire would be lit in the last car, and all of them would be propelled forward as if there were a fire under their rear end (*an tan en o reor*).

That explanation I found no more satisfactory than the other. But whereas on the telegraph I had come to a fairly correct answer, in the case of the railway, I had no guideline to consult, no clue to provide me any idea on the subject—which did not stop my brain from laboring over the problem, and building all sorts of iron railways in the air.

AT THE RECRUITMENT OFFICE

It was harvest time. There was much talk about the war.[†]

I was not yet tall enough to be a soldier, but I thought that under the circumstances they would not be looking too closely. I was burning with desire, not to be a soldier but to leave the area to learn things, and I had no other way of leaving but to join the army.

---

[*]Local expletive, originally referring to sound from cannon blast in nearby city of Brest to signal a prison escape. The expression is famous from the *Tintin* comics.

[†]The Crimean War, 1854–1856: Russia against a coalition of Turkey, France, Great Britain, and Piedmont.

The harvest was completed early that year; we had finished by August fifteenth. I could go off now without fear; nobody could say I was leaving to avoid the hard work of the harvest. The day after the August Fifteenth holiday—the Emperor's birthday, but also Assumption Day and the great annual Quimper festival—I went into town without telling anyone, and looked up a veteran of the old Imperial Army, a man named Robic. He could always be found in the square at Saint-Corentin Cathedral, always ready for a drink, but also to give a hand to anyone who asked. I asked him where to find out if I could qualify for the army.

"Ah, you want to sign up," Robic said.

"Yes, if they'll take me."

"Oh yes, yes, I'm sure they will at this point, you'll see. I'll take you to the recruiting station later."

After I'd bought a drink for the old soldier of the old Empire, he took me over to the station. I wasn't very confident; despite all my efforts to look like a warrior, I was still shy, almost shaking, the deplorable effect of long habits as a beggar and a low-level servant. Fortunately, I was not made to wait long, for as soon as Robic said a few words, I was gripped by the arm and taken to stand beneath the measuring bar. I knew very well that I didn't meet the height requirement, and thought I would be rejected out of hand.* But no, on the contrary, they said I would make a very good soldier. I had no idea yet what kind of soldier I would be, but I was certainly pleased that they considered me right for the army—just when I was seeing so many men departing in tears, and others going so far as to mutilate themselves in order to be unfit for service. All I had still to do was fetch my birth certificate, and I brought it to the office that very afternoon; I was told

---

*Regulation height was about five feet.

that the following morning at ten o'clock I would be issued my marching orders. No one was bothering with formalities by then; they hadn't even had me undress. Since I was to pick up my orders the next morning and would probably have to set out immediately, I went that evening to see my family—for the last time; for alas, I was never to see them again, my mother and father at least.*

Early the next morning I was back at Saint-Corentin Square, where Robic was waiting, for he was thirsty. Now I had to go inform my employer, the mayor, that I was a soldier and must leave immediately. Meanwhile, Robic would see about finding someone to buy my belongings. Knowing that the mayor would not believe me when I said I had just signed up, I wanted to have my orders in hand to show him. As I had been told, at ten o'clock the papers were ready. I was assigned to the Thirty-seventh Line Regiment stationed presently at Lorient and was to report there in only three days' time.

When I reached the mayor's farm, carrying my orders in my pocket, people were in the midst of eating their lunchtime mush. They had just been talking about me, for I was never known to be absent longer than a half-day. I told them that I was a soldier now, and everyone burst into laughter, the mayor along with the rest, because they knew very well that I was not big enough, but when I showed the mayor my orders, the laughing stopped. It was really true, I was a soldier. In those days it was the custom that domestic servants who quit their jobs in August were not entitled to claim any of their pay for the year. The mayor pointed that out. But I answered that the harvest was completed and, anyhow, if he did not want to give me anything, it did not matter now; I would have food on my

---

*J.-M. Déguignet's father, François-Marie, died on February 29, 1856, and his mother, Françoise-Marie Le Quéré, on January 25, 1857.

plate and new clothes. I did not stop to eat, and I went and collected my belongings to bring back to Robic. Luckily the crazy *peneres** was out of the house.

I was told she had gone into town to look for me.

I quickly finished gathering up my things; I packed them onto my back and went to see if Robic had found someone to buy them for any price at all. He had found an old second-hand dealer who gave me fifty francs for the whole bundle. My clothes were worth easily twice that, but I had no time to argue. Besides, I thought fifty francs would be more than enough to get me to the base and, afterwards, what need would I have for money? Robic had told me what to do when I got there: If I could put forty francs into the company fund right off, that would be a good start; and then I would also have to buy drinks all around to mark my entry into the squadron, or risk a poor welcome. I reckoned my fifty francs would suffice for all of that. I told Robic that the mayor had refused me my back pay because I was quitting in August.

"Oh no, *tonnerre de Brest!*" said the old soldier. "I can't believe it! What?—you sign up as a volunteer to go serve the endangered homeland, and someone pulls a low trick like that on you? Oh no, no, no—you come with me, we'll find that gent and you'll see."

But as we were talking, the mayor arrived in the square and headed straight toward us.

"What is this?" he says to me. "You left just like that, without even coming in to say *kenavo* (goodbye) and without collecting what I owed you?"

"You told me I had no right to any pay—what was I going to collect, since that's the custom?"

"I was joking. Would I want to let a young volunteer go off that way without a sou?"

---

*Heiress.

So he led us into a big tavern where he gave me my wages and then bought us coffee, the first in my life, and told me that when I got to Sevastopol,* if I was sent there, I should write him and he would find a way to send me a little more money as I needed it. I promised him, and we parted good friends.

My poor old Robic had drunk so much that he couldn't stand up. He went off to lie down, promising to meet me the next morning to walk me some of the way. For my part, I went to sleep at the house of an aged uncle who had also served under "the old man," and who kept a boarding house at a place called Stang-ar-C'hoat, on land that was part of the mayor's property. I had told Robic he would find me there. I was barefoot, and expected to walk that way from Quimper to Lorient, but so as not to enter the barracks barefoot I had bought myself an old pair of shoes. The next morning I was up at dawn, for I wanted to leave early; I meant to do a trial march the first day. I had always heard veterans say that the hardest part of the military was the marches. When Robic did not turn up, I went to the square to see if he was somewhere there; he was not, so I walked into the cathedral porch and, kneeling down in a corner, I fervently recited two *paters* and two *aves*. Then I set out directly along the rue Neuve to pick up the highway to Rosporden, where we had seen so many conscripts walking some time earlier, nearly all of them in tears.

When I reached Kergonan, ten kilometers out of Quimper, I stopped for a moment. From there I could look back on the whole Quimper region; I could see all of Ergué-Gabéric and most of the farms I had so often visited asking for alms, and the cemetery I nearly went into more than once, and which my parents would soon enter. Seeing in an instant the entire history of my life, still so young but already much tried, I

*Russian port on the Black Sea, site of the crucial battle of the Crimean War.

could not help shedding tears. These will be the last I will shed at the sight of my home territory, I reflected. Then, wiping my cheeks with my cuff—for I had not yet seen handkerchiefs—I set out again on my journey, with my old shoes tucked under my arm.

II

---◄○►---

THE SOLDIER
1853–1868

THIS BARRACKS LOOKED LESS CHEERFUL

I could have slept at Rosporden, which is an official stopover point, but I wanted to do a double distance the first day to put my legs and feet to the test. After eating two sous worth of brown bread and drinking a mug of cider at that first stop, I went back on the road toward the second, and reached Quimperlé when it was still quite early. There, I went to the town hall to ask for a housing voucher. The man I spoke to looked me over from head to foot and said, "What—you're a soldier? You can't be! You're not old enough or big enough!" He said it in French, but I understood him perfectly well. I answered in Breton, telling him to look at my marching orders, where he would find all my particulars. When he had taken a good look at everything, me and my orders both, he ended up giving me the voucher. If I had known then what I learned later on, I would have answered the gentleman: "I am young, it is true, but in a man well born, worth lies not in the number of his years."*

---

*Corneille, Pierre; *Le Cid*; Act II, Scene 2.

[121]

The voucher was addressed to someone who ran a tavern and inn; I could read well enough to understand everything that was on the slip. On entering the bar, I recited in Breton:

"You usually have paying clients; I'm sending you one who will not pay, not for his bed anyhow," and I handed the slip to the proprietress, who looked at me the way the man at the town hall had.

These people probably thought I was traveling with false papers; they could not believe I was a soldier, as I looked even shorter for being barefoot. They finally gave me a bed anyhow, and I ate supper with the help, and the next day when I asked the proprietor what I owed for my supper, he would not take any payment. In fact, he gave me another hefty drink as I left.

I wanted to start off early, so as to have time to look around Lorient before signing in at the barracks. Robic had warned me to tidy up before entering the barracks, or I would be called a filthy Breton, a Breton pig. Before reaching Lorient, I washed my feet and legs, hands and face as clean as possible, then I put on my old shoes to enter the town. At the city gate I saw sentry soldiers. Fearing that they would recognize me as a recruit and rush me right over to the barracks, I took advantage of a traffic jam to slip past the sentry-post without being noticed.

I went down the first street I saw, crossed several squares, turned and twisted through more streets, and ended up at the port. There I stood considering the ships, especially the large ones, and right off another problem came to mind—How could such large, heavy structures stay on top of the water like that when a simple grain of sand sinks of its own weight? But for the moment it was useless for me to try to solve this problem. I settled for storing it in my mnemonic warehouse along with so many others, until such time as I could examine it with full knowledge of the facts. If ever chance should permit me to acquire such knowledge.

After I had looked over much of the town, I stepped into a cabaret where food and drink were served. I had to remember to eat something before signing into the barracks, for I was not entitled to anything there yet. When I had eaten a hearty peasant meal, I went out to look around again before signing in. Now the wharf and all the squares were filled with small squads of soldiers carrying out exercises. It was clear that they too were new arrivals, some were still wearing their peasant smocks and cotton breeches as they drilled. "That will be you, tomorrow," I said to myself, and I went around to all the squares, listening to the commands and watching how the sergeants and corporals treated their pupils. For Robic had told me that these instructors were usually cruel and rough toward the young recruits, especially toward Bretons, who could not understand the [French] commands or the reprimands. And I did see several of them being shoved about and shaken by the shoulders, their feet pushed into position by a rifle butt, their noses tugged to force their heads around to the right direction. It all gave me the shudders.

But now I had to make up my mind to go in. I walked toward the barracks that looked less cheerful now than in my dreams.

TU FARAÏ UN BOUNN SOUDART (YOU'LL MAKE A GOOD SOLDIER)

I had my orders in hand, and on arriving at the door I presented them to a sergeant, who looked at them for a moment and then called an orderly from the adjutant's office. This fellow took me to the chief officer to have me registered and formally enrolled in the Thirty-seventh Line Regiment. There the orderly was given a note and told to take me to the sergeant major of the Second Company of the Third Battalion.

On the way over, the orderly kept talking to me and I did not understand a word he was saying. *Tonnerre*, I thought—so French is not the same everywhere; back in Quimper I understood a good many words and here I can't understand any. Eventually, though, I did understand what my escort wanted when he said "*Noun pagas pao l'agouteur?*"(Aren't you going to stand us to a drink?) For fear I might still miss it, he tipped up his right hand and elbow. So I took him into a bar and told the mistress, in Breton, to serve my guide a nice glass. She gave him one for four sous, and I had a mug of cider myself. After he drank it, the old soldier smacked his lips and put a hand on my shoulder, saying, "*Bounn camarade, toi, tu faraï un bounn soudart, vaï.*" (Pal, you're going to make a fine soldier, don't worry.)

Finally he led me to my sergeant major. This man was himself a tiny little fellow, hardly any taller than I was and also without a whisker of a beard. But he spoke a different idiom from the orderly, though not the way the Frenchmen of Quimper do, either. As Robic had said, the first thing this officer did was ask me for money, saying that contributing forty francs at the start to the company pool would gain me two advantages; first, I would earn a deduction every trimester, and second, I would be well thought of by the officers and non-coms in my company. I had no objection; on the contrary, I handed over the forty francs with pleasure. I would have no further use for money now. After that, the sergeant major himself accompanied me to my squadron—the last one, of course; at the time, men were assigned within companies by order of height, so I would have to be last in mine. My squad was billeted alone in a small separate room. The sergeant-major took me to the corporal and told him: "Here's a young man I recommend particularly to you; I am sure this one will make a good little soldier."

Such were the early fruits of my forty francs. Now I still had another obligation to fulfill, to buy my way in here; again I got help from my bunkmate, a poor Breton himself who knew no more French than I did, for he had been in the service for only six months. But he did know the barracks' customs. He went down to the canteen with me, and after we each had a glass of wine, we carried up six liters of brandy, for I wanted to give some to the whole unit. I meant to be a good prince, since I was still rich and saw no other use for my money; I knew that from now on I would be fed, laundered, dressed, and housed at government expense. A moment later, the quartermaster came for me, to go to the warehouse to outfit me and to collect all my soldier's baggage: knapsack, gun and gear. When I had brought it all back to my bunk, I was frightened—what would I do with so many things? Luckily my bunkmate and even the squad corporal came to my aid. They folded my clothes, set up my knapsack, fitted each item into its proper place, and taught me how to make up my cot. Then they said that my kit wasn't yet complete: I still had to buy various little knick-knacks and, if I could manage it, an extra pair of trousers for the drills, otherwise I would have to wear the same ones every day, and at review and on Sundays I would be reprimanded for the state of my trousers. Just then an old drummer came by selling a pair for five francs. I did not quibble, and that very afternoon I was able to step out of the barracks dressed in proper military garb, accompanied by my corporal and my bunkmate, who had taken on the task of selling off my civilian clothes. They were certainly not worth much; he got only forty francs for everything, a sum that was quickly used up and more besides, for I was eager to treat my new friends and pay them back for the help they were giving me and would probably give me in the future. Because in the military, if money doesn't buy everything it does elsewhere, it still buys a great deal. I have known a few rich youths to join up on a whim and then do hardly any of a soldier's actual job. They would pay someone to keep their things in order, to cover their duties, and even to stand guard for them. They would eat in the canteen or go into town to eat, and they were given leave whenever they wanted. It's not too rough, being that kind of soldier. Yet these days, when everyone is fairly well obligated to put in some time in the army, there must still be some soldiers like that.

ALL I HEARD WAS FOUL LANGUAGE

The first night in the barracks was a sad one for me, accustomed as I was to sleeping in stacks of straw and hay, in stables or closet-beds. My military cot felt very narrow, and whenever I started to fall asleep I felt as if I was rolling off a cliff; I couldn't sleep for two minutes straight. If my mate hadn't said it was forbidden to get up before the drummer beat reveille, I would have done so much earlier. But at the first tap of the drumstick, I leapt to the floor, and as Robic had warned me to do, I rushed to the pump and gave my face and hands a good wash for fear of being dragged under it by four men and a corporal, as I heard sometimes happened. Before all the men in my room were awake, I was ready for the training exercise, the thing that concerned me most now. I intended to put my whole will and intelligence to it. I feared only one thing—that one of those brutal instructors would abuse me too harshly, or rough me up as I had seen happen; for although I have spent my whole life among crude, brutal people, I have always been very sensitive to crudeness and brutality. So I was determined to do all I could to avoid contact with the old instructors, who were very free with such behavior. I was not expected to handle my rifle before learning a soldier's positions and the proper way to march with it, but I did have to carry it on to the drill ground, so as soon as my bunkmate woke, I asked him to show me the way to carry the rifle on the shoulder. That was quickly done, and I set out for my first drill carrying my rifle like a seasoned soldier. As I was the only newcomer, I was handed over to an old corporal who started off by having me take up the position of a soldier without a weapon—a position my mate had already showed me back in the room—then turn my head to the right and to the left, and then, finally, launch into the basic marching step. In the end, I was satisfied with my first day of drill; I had heard my instructor tell another soldier, "That kid will catch up to the others quick if he keeps on at this rate."

And, in fact, it did not take me long. After a few days I was already in the most advanced platoon of troops executing maneuvers without weapons, having skipped ahead of men who were there long before I was. And when they started on maneuvers with the rifle, I already knew all the moves my comrade had been glad to show me in the barracks, whenever I had a few moments free. I quickly moved along through the platoons until I reached the most advanced one, and I joined the battalion with that group in just under a month. Before the end of October, I was already ranked with the experienced soldiers.

But I had not joined the army just to be a soldier; I enlisted mainly to educate myself, for I had no other way to do that. Unfortunately, I soon saw that I was in no position for learning literature or the sciences in this milieu, where almost no one knew how to read or even speak a word of proper French. All I heard on every side was crude talk, or Bretons speaking patois among themselves, even though they didn't understand each other because the Breton spoken in Finistère and in Morbihan are as different as Italian and Spanish; or Germans,

Gascons, Auvergnats, and Parisians who just spoke the argot of their own districts. And, besides, there was not a single book in the barracks, except for training manuals, of which each sergeant and each corporal had his own. When my corporal was out, I picked up his to read, and quickly memorized everything in it, most of which I already knew from hearing it repeated ten times a day on the drill field. But nearby there was a Jesuit center to which our colonel was said to belong. I was told that every evening they gave lessons in reading and writing to young soldiers eager for education. But special permission was needed. I readily obtained it, and went to see what they taught in that institute for the children of Jesus. Again I was disappointed. They taught only the Gospels and prayers and hymns, and they prepared soldiers for communion. I had already learned all that long ago.

YOU ASKED FOR IT, SO NOW MARCH OR DIE DOING IT!

A few days after I moved into the battalion, they called for volunteers to go to Sevastopol. I came forward, but I was too young—not a chance I could go. A while later, though, toward the end of the year 1854, we heard that the entire regiment was soon to leave for there. And indeed, on the first of January 1855, we set out, in abominable weather. Those who were too old, the injured, and the constitutionally frail were left behind at the base in Lorient; they wanted to leave me behind as well. But I told the captain that I had not volunteered for service to stand about doing nothing in the base camps. They let me go along. Lots of old soldiers in my company laughed and scoffed, saying that I wouldn't get far, that they'd soon see me back in Lorient. First thing, I was assigned to the advance party—the adjutant, all the quartermasters, and two men from each company—that went ahead to arrange the housing and food for the regiment. The advance party usually marched very fast. Snow fell continuously throughout the march, so it was doubly arduous. That first day out I began to think my mates' predictions would come true; I had to stiffen myself against the pain and fatigue. I told myself, "You asked for it, so now march, or die doing it." On top of it, my mate got drunk on arrival, and never turned up at the depot where I was to spend the night guarding the baggage; he was carrying my pay and my rations with him, so I had to do without food. The next morning, though, it was his turn to set out with the advance party. He came by early to bring me my ration of bread and my ten sous, telling me that the night before he had drunk just two brandies and completely lost his head. He'd had no idea where he was, and he hadn't eaten any supper either. He was early now, so he went off to get a flask of brandy for us to drink with our bread, the first bread ration of the journey. For the second lap of the journey, those of us who had spent the night guarding the baggage were allowed to load our own kits into the wagons. That gave me a chance to recover a little from the exhaustion of the previous day, and I handled the third lap almost like an old trooper.

At Grand-Plélan, a way station before Rennes, we were forced to stop for two days. The snow had fallen steadily since we started out and a freeze followed. The roads were like very thick mirrors. A drummer trying to beat the call-to-arms that morning had slipped and rolled into a ravine, breaking an arm.

We were billeted at farms, some of them quite far from town; everyone gathered in the town, in the morning, to set off again. But confronted with the impossibility of keeping a footing on the road, the colonel ordered us to return to our lodgings until further orders. Too bad for the landlords, who were probably not all pleased, except for the barkeeps of the town. Not until two days later, toward ten in the morning, did we hear the drummers and buglers calling us in from all quarters. The weather had changed and the thaw would soon turn the icy roads into muddy roads. It was noon when we set out for Rennes, and we arrived very late that night, smeared with mud to the top of our heads. Many men fell out along the way. My mate, who along with everyone else had laughed at me back in Lorient, saying I wouldn't last more than two laps of the march, missed the roll-call himself, as did many others. It was standard practice that any man whose mate fell behind should go to headquarters at the town hall and leave his billet address so the latecomer would know where to go when he reached town.

The city of Rennes presented an indescribable spectacle that night. The local inhabitants had evidently been warned we would arrive late; they were all awake and running through the streets with lanterns, looking for their assigned guests. Once we had got our billet vouchers, people snatched them from our hands every minute to see the assignments. Mine was to a gardener, which made me think he was probably some distance away, as gardeners do not live in city centers. When I had gone to the headquarters and left my address for my lagging bunkmate, I set about looking for my gardener as well. Out in the town square it was impossible to hear or make out a thing; people were trying to explain to several soldiers at a time how to get to their housing, and ended by not explaining anything to anyone. Seeing this hullabaloo, I crossed the square heading randomly for the edge of town, knowing that my billet would be somewhere out there. However, before going down any street, I needed to know the general location of the area where my landlord lived. I saw a young man running from group to group with his lantern, looking at their vouchers; before I had time to speak to him he snatched mine from my hand, and uttered a cry of satisfaction: "Here's the fellow I've been looking for so long! Come quickly, you'll be at my house—but where's your mate?"

"He's still on the road," I said, "and I don't know when he'll get here; he'll be coming with the luggage wagons, and it's not certain the wagons will get here tonight, with the road as bad as it is."

I followed the young man, who was the gardener's son. At the house everyone was still awake, and they hadn't eaten, they were waiting for the guests. When they saw me come in, they cried out in surprise, and my arrival was probably not the only reason. There I stood in the middle of their sitting room looking like some supernatural being. I was totally covered with yellowish mud, to the point where one couldn't make out the red of my pants or the blue of my greatcoat; really, there was nothing human about me, except perhaps the face, and what a face—a timid child's face, half hidden by the headgear we wore at the time—an enormous shako like a butter churn. With the shako, the load on my knapsack piled to the height of the huge headpiece, my equipment hanging about my hips, my long rifle as tall as I was, I must absolutely have looked like some mythological apparition among these people who seemed to belong to an elegant world, as the expression goes. Some neighbors and relatives, with no soldiers to put up, had apparently come to see the ones billeted with the gardener, who of course had expected to have two of us. They wanted to look at these poor soldiers setting off for a faraway war, who would never see their homeland again. I was treated like one of their own. I was made to take off my coat and my shoes and put on some sort of robe and slippers, but despite all the attentions and despite their eagerness to sit me down at the table for the supper that had doubtless been waiting a long while, I took up my rifle to clean it, wipe it down, and grease it before the dampness coating it should turn to rust. As to cleaning the mud on my clothes, I would have time in the morning, for we had been told that because of the late hour and our great fatigue from that day, we would not start out the next morning until ten o'clock. However, despite all the consideration and care lavished on me by these people, young and old, I would certainly have preferred to be alone in the kitchen eating just a chunk of bacon with my bread ration and a glass of rotgut. I was really too uncomfortable there, in a society not my own, that spoke a language I did not know. To all their questions—and the Goddess Echo knows, they asked me hundreds—I could only respond by a "yes" or "no." So it was a great deliverance for me when the youngster who had found me in the town square returned to lead me to my bed. After I left the room, those people must have thought, "If France has only soldiers like that to defend her, she's not going to do awfully well." So I reflected as I lay down, and I think I was not mistaken. But I wasn't in the bed for five minutes before I had to get out or suffocate. It was a feather bed, a thing unknown to me, and far too warm. I pulled off the sheets and the blanket and spread them on the floor, and I slept there like a happy man, dreaming as always of past, present, and future events in my life.

Although we were not to leave before ten in the morning, I was up as early as the servants of the house, which is to say around five o'clock. I went down to the kitchen to clean up my clothes while the cook prepared the breakfast. There I felt a bit more at ease, with the cook who was of my own class and who, I saw, was not much better at proper French than I was. When the son awoke, he also came into the kitchen, and had me eat breakfast with him. The weather seemed better that day, but there was such a heavy fog that it was hard to tell if it was day or night. Toward a quarter past nine, I heard the drummers and the buglers calling us to the square; I was ready. I had so neatly cleaned my uniform, my equipment, and my weapons that I looked like a soldier on his way to review, and I was quite cheerful as well, for I had drunk some good wine, some coffee, and good cognac, and I was carrying a nice chunk of roast in my mess kit for the night. But it was clear that not everyone had been as lucky as I was; I saw some sad faces in my company, and I heard complaints from many who had got very bad lodgings, they said. But I looked in vain for my bunkmate. Later, the corporal told me he had gone into the hospital that morning, dangerously ill.

So I was alone now, no more bunkmate; and I was none the worse. It would be pointless to relate here the stories of all the stages along the way from Rennes to Lyons, for I would be telling pretty much the same story over and over. Being alone, so small, so young, and looking so bashful, I was received everywhere as an unfortunate child to be pitied; but I liked it much better when I was billeted with peasants or workers than with the rich.

AT THE SATHONAY CAMP

We reached Lyons in early February, having crossed the whole of France from west to southeast. We had left Lorient in snowy weather, and we were still all covered in snow as we entered Lyons, that great city, which at the time had the honor of being governed by the overrated Marshal Castellane.* He, of course, came out to review the troops, and kept us standing for over an hour on Bellecour Square, despite the snow falling on us since morning. Another regiment, the Sixty-fourth, also reached Lyons that day, by a different route. On the mar-

*Castellane (1788–1862), known for his severity and eccentricity.

shal's order, the colonel of that regiment was arrested immediately upon his arrival for having his soldiers travel in white
gaiters—or rather, in canvas gaiters; for our own gaiters,
though made of leather, were as white as theirs, given that we
were white all over.

When the old fool finished with his review, we were led to
an old barracks, or rather into the underground caverns
beneath Fourvière, where icy water oozed through the rocks.
Barely were we settled there on our miserable damp cots when
someone shouted: "Everybody up for the distribution!" What
distribution? we wondered, for we had already been issued
our daily rations. But we found out soon enough that it was
the distribution of encampment materials, the real furniture
of war, which comprised a tent, a half-blanket, a pole, a rope
and three stakes for each man, and for the squad; a mess-pot,
a bowl, a water-flask, a shovel, a pick-axe, a hatchet, and a
coffee-grinder. When we had all the gear in hand, we went
back to our bunk in horror, because we had to put all of it into
our packs, and arrange it all properly, and have everything
ready for the next morning's departure. But there were a couple of old soldiers among us who already had their gear, and
who showed the rest of us how to fit it into the pack. This took
a long time, for four or five men were needed to roll up each
soldier's blanket and tent. We'd had to buy candle-stubs to see
our way to untangling the mess. We did not even have the time
to eat. And eat what, anyhow? All we had was our dry bread
rations. We were consigned to this hole; no way could we go
out and buy a bit of cheese. Actually, there was a canteen
within this miserable hole, but it was impossible to get near it.
Fortunately, I still had a good portion of the meat I'd been
given at my Villefranche billet. When I finished arranging my
pack, I set to eating that on the camp bed, while half the men
were still struggling and cursing over their baggage without

managing to finish up. We barely slept that night. We were not very sure where we were going the next day, although we had been told to be prepared. I still thought we would be continuing to the embarkation port for Sevastopol. I was wrong.

In the morning, we were told that we were going to the Sathenay camp, four or five kilometers from Lyons, a camp that Castellane had recently set up to train soldiers in all the miseries of war. We arrived there, four regiments at almost the same time, in dreadful weather. Wind and snow. We were put up in rudimentary barracks, open-walled, with the wind and snow blowing in from all sides, and for bedding only the camp cot, an old mattress stuffed with crumbled straw-dust, and a long canvas sack to crawl into like a snail into its shell; for warmth we huddled against one another. But we were given one good thing we were not accustomed to: coffee—which was served every morning before we set to work, because in that place, we had to work every day like a real road gang, either in the camp or on the roads being developed to link the camp to the city. Not a minute of rest. One day we would go to the worksite, the next to maneuvers, or on long marches with all our battle gear on our backs. And every Sunday we had to go to Mass, wearing our packs of course, like Castellane. A soldier, his rifle, and his pack were supposed to form a single unit, like a cavalryman with his horse. Castellane himself set the prime example, for he never took off his clothes, it was said, and since he was so very humpbacked he seemed always to be carrying his pack, and quite a heavy pack at that—from behind, his head was invisible. Mass was celebrated beneath an open chapel at the upper end of the camp, with the regiments arrayed before it in battle order; the choirboys were the grenadiers and artillery men, who would announce the phases of the service by cannon shots. The rest of us were made to perform drill maneuvers throughout the Mass, present arms, shoulder arms, slope arms, at rest, kneel, etc. I do not know if the Good Lord attended that Mass; if He did, He would have heard a fine lot of prayers, rosaries, litanies, and orisons of a sort He was not used to hearing in church. But He would also have heard four regimental bands and the brasses from the infantry, the cavalry, and the artillery; if He cares at all for military music, He would have had a grand time at a low price.

There was a good deal of complaining in that miserable camp, people saying that the troops already at the walls of Sevastopol were better off than we were, and wondering why we hadn't gone there directly, as we had been told when we left Lorient. However, after two months we returned to Lyons and the soldiers there went to replace us at the camp. But that, as we said among ourselves, was just exchanging a yellow misery for a black misery; at the camp we had lived constantly in mud or in yellow dust, whereas in Lyons we would be living in the fog off the two rivers, the factory smoke, and the wharves always filthy with coal dust.

A VOLUNTEER FOR THE CRIMEA

We had been at the camp two months when they called for volunteers to go to the Crimea. Each company was to supply twenty men if possible; otherwise, lots would be drawn to determine who was to go. Well, a curious thing: I'd been hearing all the soldiers complaining and storming about the miseries of Lyons and the Sathonay camp, how they'd rather be at Sevastopol; but now that volunteers were being sought to go over there, nobody spoke up. Our sergeant major stood there in the middle of the shed with notebook and pencil in hand, ready to take names, doubtless believing that he would collect more than the quota. I was the first to step forward—I, the least, the smallest, and the youngest of the company. After me, a few more came forward. Finally he gathered about half the quota. After that, he made out lottery tickets for all the others. Too bad now for the men who would draw the unlucky numbers—thus the list was filled.

It was urgent, for the order had reached the camp that evening, and we were to leave the following day. We had to hurry to the storeroom and turn in our tunics and our shakoes, which were useless on the battlefield. Early the next day we were ready. We were told then that we would be joining the Twenty-sixth Line Regiment which, we heard, had just been almost totally annihilated in an engagement near the Malakoff Tower.* So they were sending us quickly; we would take a train from Lyons.

However, before we left the base, the colonel arranged to say farewell in a very moving speech; he wept like an old codger, telling us he regretted not being assigned the honor of leading us to victory himself. He called us his children: "I know, my children," he said in closing, "that there are many among you who have had a number of penalties, but I am certain you will wipe them clean on those fields of Honor and Glory." In that, the good fellow was not mistaken, for many of us left our bones to bleach down beneath the earth of Chersonesus,† beneath the Black Sea, and beneath the earth of old Istanbul; thus were penalties and the penalized wiped out together.

We embarked at Lyons. It was the first time I had ever set foot in a train. We were piled in like peddler's goods, pell-mell with our packs and our clumsy battle gear. We could not move, so that we arrived the following day in Marseille in worse shape than if we had done a long march with packs on our

*A famous fortified tower at Sevastopol, the site of terrible battles and finally of a French victory.

†The ancient Greek city at that location.

backs. When the train stopped, we climbed down with our baggage and were ordered to cross the city amid a crowd of people from every nation and all colors, shouting all sorts of cheers: "Long live the army! Long live France! Long live the emperor! Long live the brave soldiers who will be the victors at Sevastopol!" et cetera. We reached the port, where two ships were already waiting for us; they were English ships, one steam, one sail. Those of us from the Thirty-seventh were put on the latter, but it was attached to the steamship by two long cables to pull us along behind it. The sun was about to set when we left the port, saluted by thousands of shouts uttered by the people jammed onto the wharf, waving their hats and their handkerchiefs; from deck we responded with the same shouts, waving our caps. Soon the cries no longer reached us, though we could still see the swarming crowd of townspeople, nearly vanishing and finally fading into the blue steam along with the city of Marseille itself. The sun had just dropped into the sea as well, and all we could still see was the water and the sky with brilliant stars shining in its far reaches. The gentle rocking of the ship almost made me believe that it was the sky and the stars that were rocking. We had been left with our tents and blankets, and each man was free to go and settle himself wherever he wanted to sleep.

We were truly well treated by those good Englishmen; they left us free to settle in where we wished, and in going about their own activities they always fretted about injuring us. We were served four meals a day, coffee with rum in the morning, then three other meals—meat, white biscuits better than bread, and wine each time. I have often heard ill spoken of the English, but nowhere have I ever come across better people. I have traveled three times on their ships, and I saw a good deal of them at Sevastopol; I was always made welcome like one of their own.

MALTA

The next morning we arrived at the Island of Malta and docked there. The English were at home here. As soon as the ships stopped, we were surrounded by a swarm of tiny boats, all of them filled with the most tempting fruits. The male and female vendors called to us in every tongue except Breton— I never heard that. Large boats soon arrived and forced the small ones to pull away. The new ones were stacked with provisions for us and the crew; we loaded them all day long. The steamship took on coal as well. While the Englishmen worked, the soldiers swam all in a tangle with the young natives, who were playing in the water and smoking cigarettes there as if they were on a lawn. When we tossed coins into the water, they would dive after them and come up soon with the coin in hand. They were real amphibians. People bathed in Papa Adam's garb, and neither the men nor the women paid any more attention to that primeval outfit than to the finest modern dress. Toward evening, everything was ready, and we weighed anchor to leave. The soldiers had gone back to their lotto games, settled in groups on deck; you could hear the military terms for all the lotto balls, each given its own very meaningful name that made even the English laugh.

IS SÉBAÎSTOUPOUL!

At last we came within sight of Constantinople, a perfectly magical view. The city looked like a forest of larches and spruces and sycamores and other green, yellow, and blue trees, dotted with columns whiter than snow; and I could clearly see two cities, or rather two magical forests—one on land with its head high and the other in the sea, upside down. As we moved into the port, a boat with four or five men on board sailed out past our ship, but as soon as we had gone by,

I saw it overturn and disappear in the turbulent wakes of our two ships. We had already lost two men en route, and now we were causing the loss of four or five more—at least so I supposed, for, search as I might the spot where the boat had disappeared, I saw nothing on the water. I do not know if our skippers noticed; in any case they sailed on as if they had not seen a thing. We expected to stop briefly in Constantinople. But no, we kept moving at a steady rate. Meanwhile, we were sailing past wharves swarming with motley crowds. Shouts, hurrahs, cheers reached our ears quite distinctly. We could see hats and handkerchiefs waving, turbans and fezzes, and soldiers at drill raised their rifles high into the air. From our end, we answered by waving our uniform caps and shouting "Long live France! Long live Turkey!" Many men were crying "We'll take Sevastopol!"

But we scarcely had time to parley, for our skippers were moving full speed ahead; they were probably anxious to cross the Bosporus before night. The sun was setting when we emerged from that narrows no broader than a river. We were now in the Black Sea, which actually did look black to me after the blue waters of the Mediterranean, the Dardanelles, and the Sea of Marmara. Before entering it, the English seamen had lengthened and doubled the cables attaching us to the steamship. I soon understood why. The Black Sea was terrible. It heaved up in enormous rolling mountains and then deep ravines, and those rolling mountains shook our ships hard. If the cables had not been so solid they would have snapped, as they had already snapped earlier at Malta; and from such an abrupt split, amid these liquid mountains, our two ships would have certainly both gone down. Also, the men had put more distance between the ships for fear that a blast of wind would fling ours onto the steamer. The spectacle seemed horrifying to many of my companions, who had never seen the sea in a

fury, but for me it was only amusing. I had gone back to my little corner to spend the last night, and from there, seated, with
my arm hooked through the ladder, I watched the movement
of the two ships. At times the steamer would disappear behind
a mountain and at times our own would be perched atop one
of those mountains, set to dash down onto the other into the
hollow below. But when I looked up at the sky and the stars,
it seemed to me that it was they who were rocking. I saw the
constellations scattered from one horizon to the other. Then,
eventually, I fell asleep in that position. But I did not sleep for
long, for soon I was wakened by shouts and hurrahs right
beside me. What was happening now? These were not cries of
fear or distress. I rubbed my eyes and saw my mates all standing on deck facing toward the bow of the ship. Gazing that
way, I saw, ahead on the left, fiery lines cutting through the air
like meteors, crisscrossing in great arcs. I asked the
Englishmen if that was Sevastopol.

"Ao yes," they answered, "*Is Sébaîstoupoul!*"

THE TERRAIN WAS STREWN WITH SHELLS

So here we were, within sight of that famous city we had been
talking about for so long, which according to some had been
conquered long ago while others declared that it never would
be, that it was impregnable. As we approached, we could better make out those great red arcs that were none other than
the trails traced by bombshells heading for the city and crossing with bombshells coming from it. Then we saw reddish
smoke rising from mortars, monsters shooting those enormous shells. I had often seen this sight in childhood dreams,
when I heard the *vieux de la vieille* (the old veterans) telling
about the wars of Napoleon I's Empire, and even now I could
have mistaken this for a dream since I heard no sound. When

day came, we could no longer see the red trajectories traced by the cannonballs, but there were enormous masses of reddish smoke rising into the air. Finally, toward three in the afternoon, we made out the land. We were served our supper; it was not time for it yet, but we had to be ready to disembark as soon as we made port. Not the port of Sevastopol but the port of Kamiech, a village—a city—entirely in wood, which mercantile companies from every land built to drain the pennies of poor troops by selling them nearly worthless things at high prices. Our packs and rifles were returned to us from where they were stored deep in the hold during the crossing. When our ships pulled in, we already had our packs on our backs; great flat barges were waiting to take us to land, because the ships had to anchor at some distance from the pier. Even before reaching the pier, we saw officers, noncoms, and corporals from our new regiment waiting to take us to the camp. All were wearing tattered, torn uniforms and crushed, twisted kepis on their heads. By comparison, we were fine-looking soldiers, in our brand-new uniforms, our gear and our rifles all gleaming with wax and polish. As we disembarked, we were to form up by battalion and company as we had been in the Thirty-seventh, and our sergeants called the roll. No one was missing. When the roll call was done, we set out. We reached the heights and, in the distance, stretching out of sight, we saw rows of tents, and on a plateau to our right, an enormous telegraph tower whose windmill-like wings spun back and forth in all directions, forming enormous letters. We crossed over embankments and trenches and redoubts that had been used at the start of the siege; everywhere the terrain was strewn with shells, bullets, biscayen shot cases, chunks of cartridge pouches and belts, and shreds of sheet and canvas in all colors. Back beyond the tents hung the thick smoke of mortars and big cannon; we could feel the earth shake beneath our feet. The cannonade went on and on. It was dark when we reached the camp. Nonetheless, all the wreckage left from the Twenty-sixth Regiment was there waiting for us on the battlefield. We were swiftly organized into new battalions and companies. As in the Thirty-seventh, again I ended up in the Third Battalion and the Second Company, and of course the eighth squad. Six of us went into that squad, which had only four men left including the corporal, and of the four, one was wounded. And these men had been out here only two months, brought in like us to replenish the regiment, which was decimated again in late June as it had been a month before our arrival. These fellows told us stories about the great feats they had accomplished since they arrived, and their close scrapes with death. Then they told us we would likely be making another attempt to take the Malakoff Tower, the key to Sevastopol, the very next day, which was September 8—Mrs. Joseph's [Mary's] feast day. The plan was supposed to be secret, but over the past few days a vague rumor had been circulating that Marshal Pélissier had set that day to try a last attack.* So we were arriving just in time to join the party. But while we were listening closely to our new comrades, the ground continued to shake, and dreadful noises sounded from the direction of Sevastopol. Our comrades told us that this had been going on night and day for three days. Our cannoneers were trying to breach the fortifications to let our infantry troops through on the day of the assault.

---

*Aimable-Jean-Jacques Pélissier (1794–1864) Marshal of France, later Duke of Malakoff, commander of First Army Corps in the Crimea.

THE BATTLE OF SEVASTOPOL

The Russians fired the first cannon shot, whose shell flew right over us, and was soon followed by others and then still others coming from every quarter. After a few minutes, it became a veritable thunder roll. We went into the trench, marching single file, bent over, rifles low. We moved only slowly, in fits and starts. Between times, we would lie against the parapet for shelter against the volleys of grapeshot flying like hail above our heads, and also to make room for the stretcher-bearers picking up the wounded, and for the sappers setting up rope ladders for climbing the trench walls if necessary. There were constant shouts of "Watch out for the bomb!" At the cry, everyone would look up into the air, for the big shells were perfectly visible, you could see them trace their great curves, and predict where they would fall. So those bombs were not very dangerous for us, and half of them never burst anyhow. We had the proof before us, the terrain was strewn with unexploded bombs. This was not true of ours, which had destroyed and burned all the buildings in the city, and when one fell at the Malakoff Tower, it caused horrifying carnage; the Russians, who were grouped en masse and unable to defend themselves, were literally torn apart, huge sacks were filled with the body parts that porters collected to take to the cemetery. Later, when peace was made and we had become the best of friends with the Russians, I heard their officers describing the hideous carnage our bombs had wreaked upon them, especially at the Malakoff Tower.

Meanwhile, we continued to move forward slowly, bent double at some spots; even the support-stakes were so low that we had to crawl on all fours to avoid being swept by the gunshot. Anytime we stopped for a moment, we were splattered with earth, gravel, and stones thrown up by the cannonballs, biscayen shotcases, and grapeshot hitting the parapet. During one halt, an argument started between the old-timers and the newcomers among us. Some of the self-styled old-timers had taken to mocking the new fellows a little, saying that we should be damn scared. But they got a sharp response from the newcomers, among whom there were several soldiers more experienced than they, men who had seen battle before they did and in far more dangerous conditions than these. Because with the Russians, you risked only death or a glorious injury; but [in Algeria] with the Arabs and the Kabyles, you risked a long, hideous torture if you should fall into their hands alive. So the supposed old-timers, who had been here for just a few weeks, were swiftly silenced by the newcomers.

Now the fusillade had begun as well. Our captain said: "Well, the attack is about to start, we'll get our turn soon, main thing is, don't be afraid, boys; follow me, I'll guide you."

Several of the newcomers answered, "Never fear, captain— we didn't volunteer to come out here and then quake before the enemy."

"Thanks, men," said the captain. "I can count on you."

The fusillade grew denser and denser but it was covered by the terrible thunder of the cannon and the enormous mortars. We were actually very close to one of those monstrous bomb throwers, and it made us jump each time it went off. But now began the procession of the wounded. They would pass by carrying their left arms in their right hands, others shuffling along leaning on their rifles, others lying on stretchers, all of them leaving trails of blood behind them. An old captain passed with one arm shattered at the shoulder; two men were following behind him with a stretcher, but the old man insisted on walking, at least as long as he could manage. He stopped to shake hands with our captain, who offered him a drink from his canteen. When the captain asked what he thought of the business, the old man hunched his shoulders and kept repeating: "Like June 18th—a pointless massacre, what can I say." But the poor fellow could not stay longer to talk, for he was losing blood. After he left, I heard our captain, in a fury, talking to himself: "Always the same mistakes, the same bad moves; they'll get us all slaughtered here, down to the last one. What are we doing here, more exposed than any-one else to death—to a stupid death? Why not just throw the whole bunch of us en masse at the tower and at the city, instead of leaving us here to be killed off one by one like on June 18th?"

But the captain was interrupted in his angry tirade by the arrival of a company of Piedmontese chasseurs. They could not get through the trenches, obstructed as they were by us and by the wounded coming back from the front; at a sprint, the chasseurs vaulted over them, leaving the dead and wounded behind; we could see their plumed hats arcing between the two trench-lines. If they were trying to move up to join in the attack, they certainly did not all get there. We had advanced a small distance. Suddenly the fusillade almost ceased from our side, and soon we heard the bugle sound the charge—a call that crazed any veteran who knew it. I was no veteran myself as yet, but I had already been part of several attacks—at Lyons, at the Sathonay training camp—to the sound of that bugle call. And so, hearing it, I gripped my rifle in my hands, ready to dash forward. But it couldn't be done; other battalions stood between us and the front line. Still, like many other comrades, I kept my rifle firmly in my clenched hands without regard for the shells raining down on us. I stood head high and eyes fixed on the comrades moving up, bayonets ready in front. Our hearts were beating hard. I felt my own nearly bursting, and my breath came short. Suddenly, a tremendous cheer went up all at once from thousands of French, English, Piedmontese, and from all the civilians clustered up by the telegraph. We had caught sight of the French flag flying at the top of the Malakoff Tower. It was over. Sevastopol was ours.

SCURVY, DYSENTERY, AND TYPHUS

We had, so to speak, finished with the Russians, but we were soon invaded by another enemy—in fact, several of them more terrible than the Russians and against whom our bullets and bayonets were useless. These dreadful enemies, always close on the heels of campaigning armies, especially armies that are badly clothed and nourished, were scurvy, dysentery and typhus. Three enemies at once allied against us, and we were utterly defenseless against them. Until then, despite my small size and my youth, I had weathered all of a soldier's hardships and miseries, but with these terrible invisible enemies, my courage and my will could not fight. Do what I might to withstand the scourge, I was forced to succumb.

Meanwhile, many comrades had already left for Sevastopol and Kamiech before me, for that was where all the sick were being sent. Every morning a mule train left, with each animal carrying two victims hung to its flanks in a kind of iron chair called a *cacolet*; behind each chair hung the sick man's pack and gun.

One fine morning, it was my turn to be hoisted into the "bobber." There were field hospitals along the road between Baidar and Kamiech, where patients would stop to spend the night, and the dead and dying were dropped there. I was abandoned in one of those, about halfway along the route. I was condemned to die there. I lay for two days writhing on a wretched straw mat on the ground. But someone saw that I was not dying, and picked me up to take me farther, on to Kamiech this time, where there were huge sheds with camp beds and straw mattresses. There was one shed in particular where, after a quick examination, they would put almost all the newcomers from the plague area, and most of the men who entered there left it only to go into the ditch.

I was admitted right away, and I just missed being killed there the first night. In the middle of the night, a poor wretch in a fit of madness got up, seized his gun with its bayonet, and began brandishing it all around the hut; eventually he came and thrust the bayonet into my mat just a hairsbreadth from my side. Luckily, he had struck hard, and the bayonet went through the cot so deeply that he could not pull it out. At the sound of his thuds and screams, the nurse woke up; he seized the poor fellow and laid him back on his mattress, where he breathed his last. The next morning, very early, four men came into the shed with stretchers; I saw the nurse point his finger at the mattresses where corpses lay. Immediately these men on fatigue duty set about taking up the corpses by the feet and loading them on the litters, then carried them out the far end of the shed. I did not know where they were taking them. They carried off about a dozen. I watched all that impassively, for despite my extreme weakness, I was still mentally intact; I saw and heard everything going on around me.

The doctor came in to make his rounds in the shed, looking at the mats just vacated; glancing briefly at other wretches who were nearly ready to go and join their mates in the big ditch; stopping a moment to consider the new arrivals and palpate them a little. He gets to me, feels my pulse, looks at my tongue, sits me up on my cot, taps along my back, puts his ear to it; then he orders me rice tea and some kind of potion. I have no idea what it was, but I drank it all down. I went on like that for four days, watching comrades die around me. On the fourth day, the doctor ordered me moved into another shed. There they started feeding me broth, and herb tea with wine, and bitter potions; then fried eggs, and finally bread and meat, so that by the end of a week I was on my feet—saved, the victor over three enemies. Actually, I was among other winners there; they had all had come through the same danger. These were the strong men, the invincible constitutions against whom all the scourges, all the Fates themselves, could not prevail. And, curiously, we were almost all the youngest.

MY LEARNED TEACHER

My bunkmate was a young corporal about my age, a voluntary recruit like me, but better favored than I from the standpoint of fortune and schooling. He had done all his classes, he told me. I did not know what that meant. It was a pedagogical term, and unfamiliar to me. In military terms, I too had done all my classes, from soldier school to battalion school to combat school.

This corporal, though, did not speak the same language as the other soldiers. He used expressions I was not familiar with; he often made allusions to facts of history and famous warriors that meant nothing to anyone in that camp, I'm sure. As his bunkmate, or rather his mattress-neighbor, I asked him to tell me about the history he referred to, and those great warriors he mentioned. This young man—my superior—was happy to do it, and he soon became my teacher. When I told him I could write and read a little, he had me buy paper, pens, and ink, which could then be found in Kamiech. And so now I was at school, the thing I had so longed for ever since I was a child. We had no books, but my teacher needed none. He began by explaining the principal rules of grammar and the basic ideas of arithmetic. Once I started I would work the whole day through, so easily did I grasp the lessons. I was so pleased, so happy, so full of enthusiasm and determination, and I learned—thanks to my incredible memory—so fast that my young teacher really thought I had been mocking him when I said I never had any schooling. But when I showed him my service booklet he could see what most soldiers' files noted at the time: "cannot read or write." So he went on with, I think, as much pleasure as I did to instruct me in all subjects. Evenings, when I could not see well enough to scribble, he would discuss history, ranging a bit everywhere, from the Egyptians, the Persians, the Greeks, the Romans, the Carthaginians, the Gauls, the Franks, up to the history of Napoleon the Great and even Napoleon the Lesser, whose life and adventures he knew all about. To show him that my memory never failed me, I would recite back the next morning everything he had taught me the night before.

But what I most wanted to know about were questions that had been wracking my brain ever since childhood: whether the earth really did turn, how it turned, and what were its shape and size; how railroads worked, and the telegraph, and how ships could stay up on the surface of the water; what was lightning, thunder, the rainbow. My learned teacher quickly taught me all of that, in a clear and intelligible way that my restless, inquiring mind grasped immediately. I even wondered why I hadn't long ago worked out the explanations myself for such simple things, things you see every day, that you smell and touch. It is true, I do know old road workers who have spent forty years outside in wind and rain and hail and snow, in lightning and thunder, without knowing where these natural phenomena come from or what produces them; for them, all those meteors come from heaven, all of them fabricated by the Good Lord.

Yet as to metaphysical and theological questions, my teacher said that was all nothing but fairytales, fables, nonsense made up by swindlers to take advantage of the idiots. I had been almost convinced of that for some time, but without the necessary information I had no way to think about things.

Time never hung heavy in the field hospital; the days, especially, I always found too short, for every day I had some new problem to solve, and sometimes the night caught me before I'd finished. We were completely well now, my young teacher and I, but the doctor was in no hurry to send us back to our regiments. What was the point, after all? Our regiments were doing no more down in the Baidar Plain than we were doing at Kamiech. The war was over. The armistice was signed in Paris, February 25, 1856.

TWO GOOD ENEMIES

One day, we decided to see the far end of the town, and we went down on the embankment. But we had scarcely gotten there when we saw two Russian soldiers coming our way. We wanted to leave immediately. We were unarmed, and we thought these men meant to take us prisoner, for although there were rumors that peace had been negotiated, it was not yet officially announced to us. But before we could get away, one of the Russians called out in very good French, telling us to wait a moment, that we had nothing to fear. We stopped instantly, and the two men came up to us, hands out for a warm clasp, calling us their good friends. We saw that they were officers, although their uniforms differed little from those of ordinary soldiers. The one who had called to us, who spoke French so well, promptly began a conversation with my corporal. He said that hostilities were suspended, and that the peace treaty, if it wasn't yet signed, must be on the verge; all the European diplomats were gathered in Paris for the purpose. Then he recounted the main events of the terrible siege. In the course of it, he said that he had often had occasion to shake hands and share a cigar with Frenchmen during the brief cease-fires agreed to after a battle for collecting the dead and wounded. But that only occurred between Russians and French; they never fraternized with the Turks or the English. And seeing that he had found in my young teacher a man capable of understanding him, he told him that our emperor had committed a grave error in sending his army over here: first for supporting the Turks—fanatical, barbarous Muslims, Semites who destroyed one of the loveliest parts of Europe to the detriment of the Aryan civilization; and then for helping the English, who would reap the greatest benefit from this war. But what can you expect? he said in closing, monarchs' interests are not the same as the peoples' interests.

I listened so attentively to this conversation that I retained it practically word for word. But it did not keep me from reflecting, as I listened, on matters of the human mind. For here I was hearing a foreigner—a man who lived many hundreds of leagues away from France—speaking the language of Voltaire so well, whereas in France I had never yet encountered anyone who spoke it except for my young teacher, and him I had met by chance out here.

But despite the pleasure we were having with these two good enemies, we had to leave them, for it was time we returned to our field hospital. Again we shook hands with the Russians, and quickly made our way back to Kamiech, where we arrived just in time for supper without anyone noticing our absence.

That evening, stretched out on our mattresses, we talked for a long while about our adventure in Sevastopol. The corporal said the Russian officer was a true gentleman and a good citizen, and above all highly educated. He had told the corporal that if [our commander] Canrobert* had been as

---

*Certain Canrobert, Marshal of France (1809–1895). Chief of the French Expeditionary Force in the Crimea, he was wounded at the battle of the Alma, 20 September 1854.

shrewd, and as good a soldier, as people said, he would have taken Sevastopol easily the day of the Battle of Inkermann.*

On that morning, he said, the Russians had all left the city at five o'clock, planning to surround the allies, but the night was so dark that the two Russian corps assigned to carry out the maneuver lost their way in the ravine and instead fell upon each other. Each group believed that the troops they had encountered were Allied soldiers, and they killed each other by rifle fire. Meanwhile, though, another Russian group attacked the English in their encampment; they woke with a start and fought back in their underwear. The French army had also prepared for battle, but they were waiting quietly in Kamiech at the ready while the English were getting themselves slaughtered in their camp and the two battling Russian groups were struggling to get out of their tangle. If the French army had advanced right then, it would certainly have crushed all the Russians in the ravine, or forced them to surrender, and Sevastopol would have been taken while it was still worth taking—when it was still virgin. After that fiasco, Canrobert, blamed by the English whom he had allowed to be decimated, and both blamed and mocked by the French, claimed illness and left, like his predecessor Saint-Arnaud, who died in the Black Sea. Foret, who replaced him, was a traitor. Pélissier, the great broiler of women and children† who succeeded the traitor, eventually had the honor of capturing not Sevastopol but its ruins, which the Russians had been planning to abandon soon in any case, reckoning that it would be foolish to stay and get themselves killed over those sorry ruins.

---

*November 5, 1854, when the Russians were beaten by the French and English.

†Déguignet is referring to an episode in the Algerian campaign in which General Pélissier killed off a whole tribe by setting fire to caves where the villagers had taken refuge.

THE WHIRLWIND

One day, looking down from atop those mountains, we witnessed a strange phenomenon that wreaked havoc on Constantinople and on two of our field hospitals, and must have caused a real disaster farther away. It was an enormous whirlwind coming from the direction of Asian Turkey which, as it passed over the Sea of Marmara, gathered up great quantities of water and formed a huge globe that moved along spinning on its axis like an enormous top. Carrying that mass of water, the twister covered an area of at least five hundred meters around, and it knocked over and sucked up everything in its path. There was dust, hay, straw, lumber, old clothes, and hordes of unidentifiable things spinning in the air and forming a circle around the liquid globe, like a ring around a tiny Saturn. Two of our field hospitals in its path, with very few people in them at the time, had several of their dormitory sheds demolished. In the hospital nearest to us, we saw sick or convalescent men and white-clad Sisters rushing out of a shed when they heard it crack apart, but they were instantly snatched up by the whirlwind, tossed and tumbled like bundles of rags. Despite the horror of the scene, we couldn't help laughing, especially at the sight of the Sisters rolling in a tangle with the soldiers.

The corporal, although perfectly knowledgeable about the cause of the phenomenon, had never seen one before, aside from the small eddies you see everywhere, raising dust and sometimes even little piles of straw and hay. The Bretons call such things *guerven*,[*] and believe they are produced, like storms, by the souls of the wicked rich.

---

[*]Probably from the Cornouaille *korvent,* for hurricane, gale, whirlwind.

THE HORRIBLE BLACK PLAGUE

A few days later, another call came asking for men—not scribes this time, they knew very well there were none—but sturdy, fearless men to nurse plague victims in the Remichiflik field hospital, where many of the stricken patients and auxiliary nurses were presently going in, but all, or nearly all, were coming out in the oxcarts driven by Turk [cemetery] porters, the *arabagias*. But no matter—volunteers were found. For among soldiers, while some characters can always be found to do the most horrid, criminal tasks, there are also those forever ready to sacrifice themselves for the hardest but noblest and most sublime virtues. Several such were found among us. When I went to sign up, the sergeant taking names looked at me for a moment, uncertain; then he enrolled me anyhow, but with a gesture that said: You poor child, you can write your will right now. In the end there were fifteen from our camp willing to meet their death—the most hideous death I was ever to see, though I have seen all kinds. And we had to leave immediately; it was urgent because help was short over there.

So we did leave immediately, and we reached the field hospital shortly before night. An old gray-bearded sergeant came right over to assign each person his task. But first he asked if there was anyone who could read and write; as no one else spoke up, he came to me and said, "You, son—you know how to read and write, I'm sure of it."

"Yes," I said, "I do know a little, but not enough to work in an office."

"That's fine, that's fine," he said, "Go over and find the postmaster—you can work it out with him."

I hurried to the hut he indicated. There I found another old sergeant sitting before huge piles of letters, who told me immediately that my job would be to deliver letters to patients in the field hospital. Letter delivery wouldn't be hard, since I could read; unfortunately, I soon saw that my task consisted not in delivering letters but simply in calling out the names, for most of these letters were addressed to people long dead. Almost all the letters had been sent to the regiment, but by the time they arrived the addressees had gone into the hospital. The postmaster would write on the envelope: "Admitted to such and such a field hospital." But when the letter followed him there, the man had been sent on to another hospital, and then another, so the letters had been chasing after their target for weeks and months, and when they finally reached the place where the man was, it was too late. That was true for almost all the letters that arrived at our hospital. If the addressee was not yet dead, he wasn't far from it. Most of the wretches afflicted with that dreadful *typhus morbus* could no longer see or hear. So the letters sent on to our hospital simply stopped there, the addressees being buried or about to be.

There were mounds of letters, and all of them held money orders or gold coins. For out in the Crimea, a person sometimes had to wait a very long time to cash a money order; to avoid the problem, soldiers asking for money from home would tell their families to send it in ten- or twenty-franc coins concealed under a large wax seal. Thus whenever you saw a letter sealed with wax, you could be sure there was a gold coin underneath.

My job was no sinecure, far from it, but I was much better off than I would be caring for the sick, all of them struck with a disease for which there was no remedy. No sooner were they stricken than they began to decay, so to speak, their guts ravaged by armies of microbes. I slept in the same hut as the sergeant postmaster, and I could go to the kitchen when I wanted, drink and eat generally whatever I wanted—there were always meals ready for poor souls who no longer needed anything. The sickness struck so abruptly that you might see a man chatting and laughing with his friends one minute and a few minutes later find him lying unconscious on a mat and already smelling of rot.

One morning, I had a letter for the man who worked in the amphitheater—the "packer," as he was called; the amphitheater was another big shed set back some hundred meters behind the main part of the hospital, and you would see loaded stretchers being carried into it by two men. When I arrived with my letter I found a fellow built like a strongman, in undershirt and shorts with his sleeves rolled up to his shoulders, in the process of "packing" his lugubrious merchandise. The moment he saw me he said, "Ha—a letter for me, right? I was expecting it. Open it right away and read it to me—I can't read."

I opened the letter, which held a thirty-franc money order. That was all he wanted; the letter scarcely interested him. He had some rum there with him; he tossed back a good glassful and handed me one, and told me he had to drink it often; it was the only thing that could fend off the plague. He had no time to chat, though, for the corpses were coming in from all sides and the cart was at the door. But it didn't take long to pack a corpse. The crates stood alongside, made of four planks and two end pieces. He would grip a corpse by an arm and a leg, toss it into the box, and tack on the lid; it took him under two minutes to pack each one. As fast as he packed them, the *arabagias* would load them into the cart, stacked like ordinary crates of goods. Our packer came by at night to get money from the postmaster, and he asked us to join him for a hot grog at the establishment of an Armenian trader who had set up business behind the field hospital, selling the convalescents and nurses whatever they might desire to drink or eat. He also changed money, and did other things as well. For a twenty-franc gold coin he would give as much as twenty-five francs worth of any country's cheap coins, as long as the money was currency in Constantinople. Every evening his vast shed was full of soldiers. You would see them in groups of ten or twelve, sitting Turkish-style around great basins of blazing cognac or rum, chatting and laughing and singing, not giving a fig for typhus or any other plague from the devil. I took to going there every night with the postmaster, the packer, and other workers. Once you were in the place you had no need to worry about typhus; it would not dare come near so many fires as were lit there every night.

Meanwhile the terrible scourge began to slacken, mainly for two good reasons. First, no more patients were being sent in from the Crimea, and those who had come before us, or with us or even after us, had nearly all died; the plague was no longer finding new victims.

And second, a fire entirely destroyed the big military hospital at Ahoutpacha, which stood on a hill across from us. That dreadful fire went a long way to stanching the horrible black plague, by cleansing the air of the infectious organisms, just as the fire at Varna in 1854 had put a stop to the cholera that threatened the complete annihilation of the first French army to land in Turkey.

JERUSALEM PILGRIMAGE

The three of us boarded a steamer out of Odessa that was carrying a load of pilgrims to the Holy Land.* The Jerusalem pilgrimage is required of all Russian Orthodox, like the one to Mecca for Muslim believers.

---

*The Armenian merchant whom Déguignet met in Constantinople proposed that he and another friend accompany him to his home in Jerusalem.

The ship was overflowing with pilgrims from all parts of Russia, people who did not seem very rich. They were poorly dressed, unclean, with long filthy hair. If the men had been wearing broad-brimmed hats, I would have taken them for Bretons from the Arrée Mountains. My French companion and I were dressed in European style, and we looked a bit like two aristocrats taking in the Grand Tour.

We disembarked at Beirut, and a little beyond there, at Jaffa, we found a carriage, a wagon rather, waiting for us. The pilgrims, too, could select whatever means of transport suited them. There were donkeys, mules, horses, and various sorts of light carts that could be hitched from either end. Our own had been ordered and readied in advance; it was not one of those for hire. Only the three of us climbed in. The Armenian wanted to set out quickly, for the road would soon be crowded, and we would be blinded by the dust.

At Jaffa, guides still show faithful or credulous believers the house of Simon the tanner, where the famous Peter had his vision of an enormous tablecloth dropping from the sky bearing all sorts of roasted game. We could have driven directly from Jaffa to Jerusalem, but our own good guide wanted to lay over in Ramallah, where most pilgrims do indeed stop for the night, as the highway to Jerusalem was not yet very safe. Bands of ugly customers were prowling about with pistols and daggers in their leather belts; they looked much like Mary's elder son Joachim and his bandit companions. There were plenty of Turkish police (*zaptiyeh*) stationed along the way to guard the highways, but these strange gendarmes frightened travelers as much as the bandits they were assigned to watch out for.

Ramallah is only a poor village, but it has a great convent or rather, great hostelry, which the good Franciscan monks established there to exploit the pilgrims. In the convent there is still a little bed that Bonaparte slept on one night during his

Egyptian expedition. The monks who provided him that hospitality were all slaughtered the next day, which did not keep their successors from displaying the historic bed with pride. Ramallah is the former Arimathea, the birthplace of Joseph and of Nicodemus, those two great Jews of the Pharisee sect whom John, the fourth Evangelist—or Fourth Liar—stupidly invited to help embalm and shroud his Dear Master. Also born near Ramallah were the two thieves, the two lesser bandits, who were crucified along with the great bandit of Nazareth. The Christians even built a church at the spot in honor of those two felons, who probably deserved the honor as much as did the pig-snatcher of Gennesaret and all his companions in whose honor millions of churches have been built.

We did sleep at Ramallah, not in the monks' hostelry but in the house of a Jew whom our Armenian friend knew. The next day, we set out early to avoid the traffic, the heat, and the dust. Until Ramallah and a little beyond it, the countryside was beautiful; green mountains, trees, shrubbery, gardens, wheat fields: this was Galilee, our guide told us. But soon we entered Judea, the land given to the children of Judah by the savage Joshua when, aided by the Lord Eternal, he destroyed thirty-one kingdoms and their kings at the famous battle at Gibeon. The God of Abraham cast down great rocks from heaven to crush those who tried to flee, and halted the sun and the moon to give Joshua the time he needed to exterminate those peoples down to the very last person. In the redistribution of those thirty-one kingdoms, as arranged among the nine tribes of the children of Israel, the descendants of Judah—to whom the dying Jacob had promised the eternal damnation of the other tribes and indeed of all the nations of the earth—certainly drew the worst lot. For there is no sorrier land than Judea: nothing but scorched mountains, spent volcanoes that from a distance look like reddish molehills. And on top of that, a heavy, reddish atmosphere that is very oppressive. It is indeed the "land of desolation and abomination" that the prophet describes. [The writer] Ernest Renan said that the sight of those desolate mountains and the heaviness of the atmosphere disturbs the minds of pilgrims, and makes them see things in Jerusalem not as they are, but as they are supposed to see them, with the eyes of blind faith. Which is the reason that even in our own day, nonsense and absurdities just as crude as those in the Bible and the New Testament are still being written by pilgrims, even supposedly learned ones, about this land.

We were finally coming within sight of Jerusalem. The Armenian slowed our pace so as to show us, from high on the hillside, the major monuments of the city, then pointed out the spot where the pilgrims stop and dismount from horse or carriage to kiss the earth and sing the famous hymn *Stantes erant pedes nostri in altrui tuis, Jerusalem.** It is probably from that point on that madness seizes the pilgrims, as it did King David, who leapt and danced and stripped naked like a madman, to the great consternation of his wife Michal.

Some Russian pilgrims drew up behind us, and the Armenian pointed to a large building on the heights: "That is the convent where all those poor Russian muzhiks will be living during their stay here. They will be lodged each according to his fortune. Many of them have worked for ten, fifteen, twenty years to amass the cost of this trip, and all the savings that cost them so much labor and privation will wind up in the hands of the monks. The Catholics have their own convent or guesthouse over there, farther out, on the Mount of Olives; they will go there, and get their pockets emptied by the Franciscan fathers; and we Armenians—we have our own

---

*"Our feet stand upon thy threshold, O Jerusalem." (2 Samuel, 6:13–16)

monk-profiteers out on Mount Zion. Here, priests and monks are all businessmen, merchants, saloon keepers, mercenaries, those are their only occupations and their only concerns."

We entered the city; as we went, I noted taverns and hotels with signs in every language. We reached our host's house, where the whole family, who spoke French better than we did, welcomed us along with the master, our guide, as if we were their own. Probably because they had been expecting us, a great dinner was promptly served, the grandest, the most luxurious I have had in all my life. We were obliged to taste at least twelve different dishes. But delicious as they were, I felt there were ten too many, as I was accustomed to no more than a single dish, two at the very most. We were served wine from Jericho, that land so celebrated in Jewish legend, but they also insisted we try French wines, Bordeaux and Champagne. The master told us, laughing, that he certainly ought to treat us well since it was we—the French and Turkish soldiers—who had earned it all for him. He might as well have said, "You, my friends, are the ones I stole all this from."

After the sumptuous dinner, which for my part lasted far too long, our host provided us with a guide, an excellent cicerone to take us wherever we desired. I knew Biblical Jerusalem, and I told our good "chichironney," as the Italians say it, that I was especially eager to see the famous Mount of Olives where on March 22 in the year 33, twelve Galilean bandits and their chieftain were arrested at midnight as they were sleeping off their wine. We set out in that direction. But it was hard to walk through those streets so crowded with tourists, all of them being followed, or rather pursued, by a crowd of ragamuffins, children, and even several older fellows, practically forcing them to buy all sorts of trinkets; handkerchiefs decorated with various scenes from the Passion, paintings and engravings, rosaries made of chips from the True Cross, little chunks of wood from the same source, bits of cloth taken from the crucified Chieftain's red robe, pebbles from the Gethsemane grotto, et cetera. . . . Fortunately, our guide, who knew the scams as well as the characters who were now operating them, saw to keeping them away from us, although we must have looked like fine prey, well-dressed as we were. Thus we managed to elude the grasp of these fraudulent merchants, crossed the Cedron stream, and finally reached the famous Garden of Olives, which I would sooner have called a kitchen garden. For the Franciscans, who built a great house there to profit by the naive Catholic pilgrims, have spent their leisure time turning the Garden of Olives into a common vegetable plot. Still, they make a point of maintaining four or five olive trees to display to the faithful, persuading them that these are the very same trees beneath which Jesus and his companions often slept. And not far from there, the pilgrims are shown the famous summer grotto of Gethsemane, and, nearby, some red stains that the poor idiots rush to kiss, weeping like calves, in the belief that they are kissing their Lord's true blood, whereas they are kissing only a few patches of vermilion stain spread there and constantly freshened up by the good Franciscan monks. Our guide, whom the Armenian had informed that we were not pilgrims, was happy to tell us about the swindles worked by the idiot-exploiting monks. But he need not have bothered telling me, for ever since the excellent lessons I'd gotten from my corporal at Kamiech, I no longer saw things through a blinding, stupefying faith. To me it was quite clear that those red stains were a compound of mercuric oxide, sulfur, and oil—otherwise known as cinnabar or vermilion—laid down that morning before the pilgrims arrived. And if the fat monk there had not been so busy handing out little olive twigs and stones to the simpletons who had come to kiss the red paint, I would certainly have discussed it with him, for I know the Gospels by heart. For instance: the Gospels say that "Jesus, being in an agony, prayed more earnestly: and his sweat was as it were great clots of blood falling down to the ground" (Luke 22:44). But for anyone who can read and assess what he reads, it is easy to gather that those rather sizeable "clots" were clots of bread and meat and other victuals stained red by wine, and that they emerged not from the sweating pores of the skin but unquestionably from the bandit's gullet. And his companions the same, for they had all been found lying face down on the ground—that is to say, they had just given back what they had swilled too much of at their great banquet in Jerusalem, which went on till midnight. The fat monk kept looking at us, longing to give us some olive twigs and a few stones in hopes of taking in a few small coins. But he could see we were not true believers, as we had not kissed his vermilion stains, and he also saw we were with a guide he probably knew.

In any case we did not stay long there, contemplating this shameful commerce, this profanation of nature, good sense, and reason. I had turned to look in the other direction, to see if I could catch sight of Bethany, for we were near the road to it: the little village where the Galilean bandits often went to carry on their Pantagruelesque partying with Madeleine, Martha, her sister Mary, Joan, Susannah, and other lovely low-class courtesans who trailed everywhere after those partying bandits. But it was growing dark, and we had to start back to our lodgings, walking through streets and squares where our guide pointed out houses that the shysters told naive believers were the houses they longed to see: the houses of Pontius Pilate, of Herod, of Ann, of Caiphus, and so on. And the Via Dolorosa, or the Way of the Cross, that runs from Pilate's house to the Church of the Holy Sepulchre, which was built on the spot where the three bandits were crucified on 23

March, in the year 33, from noon to three o'clock—convicted of the most fearsome crimes, by all the institutions of justice in the land: the Jewish Council, or Sanhedrin; Herod the Tetrarch of Galilee; and Pontius Pilate, governor for Emperor Tiberius.

So in a short time we had seen almost everything in Jerusalem that was shown to the faithful, but with the difference that, for my own part, I was seeing those things for what they were now, whereas the faithful saw them for what they were in biblical times, probably unaware that Jerusalem had been completely destroyed and razed several times over since that period, and that not a stone was left that was there back then, except perhaps for a few old chunks of wall on Mount Zion that the Jews go up and kiss, weeping and beating their breasts, in the belief that these are still the remnants of the marvelous palace of Soliman, or Solomon, just the way the Christians kissing those stains of vermilion paint believe they are kissing the blood of their God.

When we reached the house, supper was ready, and for me it was like the first—far too copious and too long. My companion and I would certainly have been happier to eat a slice of bread and some cheese, sitting on the grass, drinking a bottle of bad wine. After supper, we were led to a room that resembled those fairyland chambers from the thousand-and-one nights. A bed had been readied for each of us. But the beds were too soft; we used only the coverlets, and lay down on the rug with our handsome frockcoats for pillows. . . .

The next day, when we had lunched, our host told us that since we knew the city fairly well now, the two of us might go out on our own if that was our pleasure. But I'm not sure what pleasure we would have gotten from hearing ragamuffins hawking their fraudulent holy trinkets in every language, or from seeing the Russian muzhiks, whose great Easter holiday it was, dragging themselves on their knees from the supposed house of Pilate to the Holy Sepulchre, weeping, kissing the earth, the stones, and parts of the houses. We did go, though, following along after these poor fools, not knowing whether to laugh or cry for them. . . .

There was actually a Turkish guard corps at the very door of that great Christian temple [the Holy Sepulchre]. And they stood there like the guards I had seen in Lyons at Marshal Castellane's door. But, actually, these Turkish soldiers were not there to guard Jesus' person, or his supposed tomb; they were there to keep order among the priests of the different Christian sects who exploited the tomb, each outdoing the next.

There are twenty-one altars in the temple, with twenty-one priests singing the praises of the murderer David's son, in twenty-one different ways. And, of course, all those priests, like proper charlatans, are jealous of one another; they quarrel, threaten, and often come to blows. So then the Turkish Guard pulls the rascals apart and stand them back to back. Despite the horde of pilgrims already filling the temple and others coming in, some on foot and others crawling on their knees, we too wanted to have a look at the inside of that huge casino where idiot believers are robbed worse than in our Paris casinos. We slipped among the poor fools who never saw a thing, like those idols the great bandit King David describes in his stupid psalms and that Catholics sing in church every Sunday and feast day: *os habent et non loquent tui, oculos habent et non vidunt, aures habent et non audient, nares habent et non odorabunt.*[*]

---

[*]Psalm 115: "They have mouths, but they do not speak: eyes have they, but they see not: they have ears, but they hear not: noses have they, but they smell not."

Still, though their eyes, their ears, and their noses went unused there, they were a step ahead of the idols the great murderer speaks of, for they did use their feet, their hands, and even their tongues, to lick the paint, the dust, and all the stones of Jerusalem. When we came to a certain part of the temple, we saw them again, kissing and licking the edges of a hole said to represent the hole where the Cross had stood, and others licking a marble table already well worn by the lips and tongues of the faithful. It was allegedly the table on which, John says, Joseph and Nicodemus packed up the traitor's corpse with fifty kilos of fairly aromatic herbs. . . .

I also looked at that small octagonal chapel-like booth set in the center of the temple, which we had been told about. The booth—a regular magician's box—is where the great Greek patriarch, the temple's chief cleric, calls down the Holy Spirit during the Russian Easter celebrations. The spirit descended upon the apostles as seven tongues of fire—from heaven, of course. But here it simply descends from a match-tip along a thin sulfured wick. When the fire is lit, the great magician opens the small windows pierced all around the booth, and the faithful rush to light their candles from the celestial fire, then they rub their foreheads with the candles, probably to force in what's missing. The women also rub their breasts, and—we are told—lower down too. But what struck me most in that great bazaar of charlatans was a Christ (a rather ugly one), a Saint John, and a Mater Dolorosa that looked exactly like—and were arranged in the same poses as—the ones I had seen so often in the church at Ergué-Gabéric where I made my First Communion.

We did not stay very long, actually, in that den of thieves; it was suffocating. Moving through the streets was torture; you could not take a step without being bombarded by the trinket-sellers and alms-seekers. We decided to stop at an inn to pass the time before returning to the house for dinner. In the evening we went to see Mount Zion, the Armenian convent, and the Temple of Omar, in which the Muhammadan priests exploit their faithful the same way as the Christian priests do, except they are less divided among themselves. Then we went down onto the famous Valley of Jehoshaphat, where all Christians are supposed to go one day to be judged by the criminal of criminals. They would be uncomfortable in that little vale, for even if they were to go there in the form of tiny ants, there would not be room for all of them. Meanwhile, we wanted to leave something of ourselves behind in the famous valley named for the fifth king of Judah, and that "something" is described thus in the gospel of Matthew by Joachim's little son, a direct descendant of Jehoshaphat: "Do not ye yet understand, that whatsoever entereth in at the mouth goeth into the belly, and is cast out into the draught?" (Matthew 15:17)

"At least," said my companion, "when I get home, and anybody mentions the Valley of Jehoshaphat, I'll be able to say I shat in it."

I was very eager to leave Jerusalem the next day, as I had seen enough of it, but our host told us we should wait at least another day for the steamer out of Beirut that could take us back to Constantinople. Seeing that we were not much enjoying our visit to Jerusalem, the Armenian arranged to have us taken the next morning to the little town of Bethany so much celebrated in the Gospels, where Jesus often went for bacchic celebrations with the spoils from his robberies. Well, we had a nice little party there ourselves—our host had given the driver the wherewithal. Only we did not have quite the orgy those biblical bandits did. Simon the Leper and his daughters Martha and Mary, those intimate friends of the Galileans' gang leader, were no longer available. We spent a good part of the day with our driver, a great bon vivant, who like all the other rascals of the place had harvested a good many of the piastres that the Christian ninnies scatter there to honor the greatest malefactor, the greatest criminal known to history.

That was our best day in that miserable country. I have seen many countries since, and if I had the means to travel I would be delighted to see them again, but I would never want to see Jerusalem again. The next day we were driven back to Beirut, where we found a steamer ready to leave, and it carried us back to Constantinople two days before our furlough was up.

OUR TURN TO EMBARK

The troops from Sevastopol had already begun moving out some time earlier. We went to the Bosporus to watch them go by, constantly asking the passing soldiers if there were still many men to come; for though we were not unhappy in Constantinople, we too were eager to return to France. Finally it was our turn to embark. We were the last remnants of the Grand Army, but there were some important remnants with us. We had all the quartermasters-general, the chief administrative officers, the chief medical people, and the paymasters-general. To honor all that great top brass, a new steamship had been sent out to pick them up, the one recently baptized the *Imperial Prince*—for a prince had been born in France just as the peace treaty was being negotiated: the poor prince who would later die in Zululand fighting for the English.*

The ship named for him very nearly died itself, a long time before he did, in that terrible Gulf of Lion where so many

---

*Eugène-Louis-Jean-Joseph Napoléon, the only son of Napoléon III and Empress Eugénie (1856–1879).

ships went down. In fact, as we entered the Gulf, we were caught in a dreadful storm that lasted more than twenty-four hours, during which time we were at the mercy of the waves, for with its large paddle-wheels the ship was impossible to control in those heaving mountains running every which way. Sometimes the ship would dive and slide beneath a mountain; other times it flipped onto its side, with one of the wheels turning completely underwater and the other turning in space. One moment the coast was visibly very close, the next, suddenly, we were flung several miles out. Some civilian passengers who were on deck with us were carried off without our even noticing. We soldiers were all clinging to the rails, to the ropes, to anything we could find to hang on to. I had clutched on to a rope very near the helmsmen. They were four old salts under the command of an officer who did all he could with the wheel, but despite their efforts, the wheel was steering nothing at all at that moment.

The only one truly steering our ship in those hours was old Africus, a son of Atreus—the father of the winds, whom the Arabs call Simoun and the Italians call Sirocco. So when the captain ordered some action or other, I would hear those old seamen mutter, "What's the use? Doing what we're doing and doing nothing at all amounts to the same thing."

And one of them, the oldest, said, "It's all over, forget it, we'll soon be joining the *Semillante.*"

I understood that. We were, indeed, in the vicinity where, a few months earlier, that ship had gone down with all hands and goods, on its way back from over there just as we were now, carrying a load of soldiers, among whom were some men from the class of forty-seven, who had done over a year of extra duty at Sevastopol. I did not know what people were doing or saying in the salons below, where all the big brass were, but on deck I saw only sad, haggard faces.

There were men praying, even aloud; others were weeping, others seemed destroyed. The singers, the jokers, the punsters, the men with the gibes and the filthy talk—everyone was transfigured. The storm did finally abate, and though the liquid mountains went on rolling, but less furiously for a long time after, our ship could make some progress. We were even able to unlash ourselves and go to the storeroom to ask for food, for we had not eaten or drunk a thing for nearly twenty-four hours. We were served double rations. After that, faces went back to normal. Later, toward nightfall, we passed Toulon, and the next morning we disembarked at Marseille. As soon as we were settled in Fort Saint-Jean, some men went off to thank Notre Dame de la Garde for saving them from the furies of Neptune and Aeolus. Others, greater numbers, having already forgotten the danger, went off to make sacrifice to Bacchus, and even to the bacchantes.

MARSHAL DE CASTELLANE

Castellane could not stand light infantrymen, so we were never assigned to guard his post; he always used grenadiers. One day, in fact, during an exercise, a bullet-extractor* hit the old rascal in his plumed hat and shaved him—not his hair, he had none, but his white-leather skull, and the shot came from a company of light infantrymen. He, of course, asked who was the fine marksman with such good aim; if the man would just step forward he would decorate him on the spot. But the fine marksman refrained from showing himself. All knapsacks were searched, but each one still held its bullet-extractor. Here in Ergué-Armel I met a man named Rospart who had served with Louis Philippe and the 1848 Republic; he told me

---

*An instrument for pulling a bullet from a wound or from the barrel of a rifle from the front; no longer in use with modern rifles.

he had been in that very company and knew well the fellow who had done the deed, the whole company knew, but there was not a chance anyone would ever turn him in.

What they regretted, all those troops in the Lyons army, was that the rifleman had aimed a few millimeters too high. And the soldiers weren't the only ones who regretted it; so did the officers. For if that old maniac made life hard for the troops, who in his view should not last any longer than their overcoats, he would ride the officers harder yet, on the slightest pretext and often on no pretext at all. The old bastard, with all his tricks, his cruelties, his mad ways, went so far as to put on a civilian hat, pull a loose smock over the marshal's uniform that he never took off day or night, and with a fake beard and wig went into the officers' taverns; there he would buy drinks left and right and slander "the damn hunchback," "the old bastard"—and, of course, the officers fell right into his basket, into the trap.

Then the "old bastard" would whip off the big smock, resume his natural voice, and say, "And here he is, gentlemen!—the old bastard, the damn hunchback, the old madman, the old skunk! So, gentlemen, you don't care for Castellane? Well then, you just go right along to his "pension" up at Fort Sainte-Foy, and see how you like the fare there."

At the time, the name "Pension Castellane" applied to a certain building at Fort Sainte-Foy where penalized officers were locked up, where they were fed practically like common soldiers, and slept on camp beds in their fatigue-duty coats. But if Castellane made the military men miserable, he was no kinder to the civilians; on his watch, the city of Lyons was constantly under a near state of siege. We were not like French soldiers garrisoned in a city of France; we were like an invading army holding the city and its inhabitants under the threat of bombardment at the slightest hint of revolt. All the surrounding forts had armed cannon aimed at the city, and we non-commissioned officers and corporals were trained to use them. Soldiers were absolutely forbidden to fraternize with civilians, on pain of imprisonment. If the Emperor were to be assassinated, as rumor hinted, and the Lyonnais should show the faintest stirring in response, as was likely, the old bastard would not have hesitated to carry out his threats to crush them. So there was great delight when, in the spring of that year 1858, we received orders to leave Lyons and its dreadful Caesar and tyrant.

NAPOLEON III AT CHÂLONS

The Emperor was traveling in Brittany with his lovely lady of Spain, "the Andalusian redhead."* After visiting Brittany and Normandy to show the Bretons and the Normans that he had not been assassinated,† he came to the camp at Châlons to review the end of our maneuvers. There I had the honor of seeing that sad figure, Napoleon the Lesser, who bore no resemblance to the Bonapartes, from whom in fact he was not descended: Victor Hugo tells us he was the natural child of a Dutch admiral named Varuel. Here the handsome imperial couple, Lord and Lady "Badinguet,"‡ were quite at home among their military family, with no one in civilian dress permitted to approach the camp. The lovely Eugénie de Montijo was often seen walking alone through the camp like any ordinary working-girl, stopping into the kitchens to chat with the

---

*Eugénie Marie de Montijo de Guzmàn, married Napoleon III in 1853.

†In an attempt by Felix Orsini, an Italian nationalist, in August 1858.

‡"Badinguet," a derisive nickname for the emperor, Napoleon III. It was said to come from the caption of a lithograph by Gavarni, the satirical illustrator of the newspaper *Charivari*, or from the name of the stonemason whose clothes he borrowed to escape from the fort at Ham in 1846.

scullery workers and pretending to have a bit of their meal with them. Other times, she would go about on horseback surrounded by her hundred guards, those gorgeous men—the handsomest in France—whom she had selected to make up her male seraglio.

The day of the great final review was a hard one for us light infantrymen and grenadiers. After carrying our knapsacks from four in the morning till three in the afternoon, we barely had time to eat a mouthful before we had to load the sacks on our backs again to march to Rheims, where their majesties were to go the next day [for the coronation ceremony]. The road was very beautiful, decorated along both sides; we marched through one triumphal arch after another. We reached Rheims very late at night, and were left parked in the barracks courtyard, streaming with sweat and completely white with dust. The city was teeming with people, and the civilians had to do as we did—sleep out in the open. There was no time for us soldiers to rest, actually, for we had to prepare to line the avenue for the entrance of the imperial majesties, who were to arrive early in the morning. Charles VII was led into Rheims by Joan of Arc in full armor; our little Lord Badinguet arrived led by Eugénie de Montijo in crinolines. But the rumor was that she too was wearing armor, as a corset, and so was her husband. For ever since Orsini's assassination attempt, they did not feel very secure anywhere but among soldiers. And this was why they no longer took a step without an escort of several platoons, and a double file of foot-soldiers lining the highways and the streets, besides the thousands of secret agents and others who were everywhere in all sorts of disguises, rooting about and spying. When the imperial pair arrived, they went directly to the cathedral and were received at the door by the cardinal bishop, who must surely have made references to Charles VII "the victorious" and Joan of

Arc, and especially to the savage barbarian Clovis, the founder of the Frankish monarchy, which he founded upon treason, perjury, and blood, the blood of his own family, his nephews and his children, all of whom he murdered. For that he was favorably received by Saint Rémy and by Mary's elder son, who sent down from heaven a dove with a little vial of oil for anointing the murderer's head, just as his own father, the fierce Jehovah, sent a dove to his son, the thief, traitor, and coward, on the day he forswore his god and his family, and also betrayed his nation. That little vial of oil later served to anoint all Clovis's successors down to Louis XVI, on whose head it was shattered. Such that when the Corsican bandit—the uncle of our little Lord Badinguet—was to be anointed, the man had to call for another flask. But this time it came not from heaven—at least, not directly; it came from Rome, which is after all the main branch office of the Christian heaven, and it was brought by the crucified bandit's chief vicar,[*] whom the Corsican bandit had sent gendarmes to fetch. Because I was stationed near to the cathedral portal, I was musing on all these things as the drama was playing out inside.

We stayed two days thus at Rheims, knapsacks constantly on our backs day and night, forming up along the streets where the majesties were due to pass by on their way to the prefecture, the town hall, and elsewhere during the day, and at night to balls and the theater; first the sacred performance, then the profane. After attending the ceremonies at the Catholic temple as a pious churchwoman, in the evenings, the lovely Eugénie, dressed as a veritable bacchante and nearly nude, would join in the bacchanales at the Temple of Terpsichore and Bacchus with a company of young bacchantes, more of them than used to attend Dionysus himself on his

---

[*]The Pope.

great journeys. Unfortunately for those lovely bacchantes, their sole escorts were a few old hairless Silenuses, aging marshals, prefects, and mayors. The women could not have had much fun with those old fogies, especially the generals and marshals, who could only speak the rough language of the barracks and camps.

When it was all over, we returned to the camp, where we were informed that we would be leaving the next day but, as usual, for some destination unknown, at least to us little soldier-boys . . .

LONG LIVE ITALY! LONG LIVE FRANCE!

It was the early spring of 1859, and rumors of war were rife for some time. It was said that the Italians were already fighting the Austrians, and almost on our own borders. This was a good opportunity for little Lord Badinguet, who could live and reign only by force and the prestige of his army, which at the time was reputed to be the world's best; we had conquered the great army of Czar Nicholas, before whom the conqueror of the pyramids had been forced to beat a retreat . . .

. . . And then that very evening at rollcall, we were notified that our regiment was to be confined to barracks the next morning, that we must collect our parade uniforms, tunics, shakoes, and other items of no use in action, and turn them in to the quartermaster's storeroom. Ah, what shouts of joy and delight greeted that announcement—shouts of "Long Live Italy! Long Live France!" . . .

. . . By three o'clock our packs were on our backs, and a quarter-hour later we were marching toward Paris amid a crowd of people lining both sides of the highway, shouting,

"Long Live Italy!" "Long Live France!" "Long Live the Twenty-sixth Line Infantry!" and waving their handkerchiefs, their hats, fronds, and flowers; some of them had torn whole plants up from gardens. The "old fellows from the old war," limping and one-armed men wearing their St. Helena's medals,* followed us, shouting and weeping. Our band was playing the *Marseillaise* and some civilians followed behind it singing, although in that period it was a seditious song; under other circumstances, singing it would have got them sent to Devil's Island, but for the moment it was permitted. Once again I was designated to escort the flag carried by a lieutenant, that sorry flag all in shreds and with its staff wired together. All along the route, bunches of flowers and laurel fell about our heads. We finally marched into Paris by the Fontainebleau gate, our first entrance into the capital.

The crowd was still growing, and we could hardly pass through it. The shouts, the waving handkerchiefs and hats, the flowers, and the laurel branches came raining down ever heavier. We finally reached the Gare de Lyon; in ten minutes we were settled into the cars and almost immediately our train left. Now it was the soldiers' turn to shout and sing the *Marseillaise* and other revolutionary and battle songs. But suddenly the train stopped and somebody shouted, "Everyone out, weapons and bags!"

What was happening? We had no idea. Once we were all out and our packs on our backs, we walked along the right side of the track and through a railway station without managing to see which station it was. But outside and on the highway, we learned that we were at Melun. We were taken to an old barracks, where we spent the night on half-rotted old

---

*A medal awarded to all veterans of battles from 1792 to 1815, during the French Revolution and the First Empire.

straw mats. The next day, we were informed that we had set out before our turn; it was only a sham embarkation. They had wanted to do a trial run, to see how much time it would take a regiment to embark without mishap. So we stayed on at Melun, doing combat exercises. We were trained in a new method of encampment, in small tents. The delay irritated many of the men, but several were pleased, for it allowed them to write their families to say a last farewell, and to ask for a little money to celebrate the departure for Italy and . . . for the next world. I, who had no more family to speak of, wrote to no one. But I did go off the next morning to a bookshop to buy a French-Italian grammar. I wanted to know a bit of the local language when I got there, if only to ask for food and drink. But when I consulted the book I saw that the language was much easier to learn than French. The Italian language is just a midpoint between Latin and French: all the words invariably end in vowels, the masculine singular in *o* and the plural in *i*, the feminine singular in *a* and the plural in *e*, and the pronunciation is very easy too, all the words being pronounced with the tip of the tongue and the lips, unlike the Anglo-Saxon languages, which are pronounced with the throat; which proves that these languages were transmitted to mankind by wild beasts, whereas the Latin ones came from birds.

VIVA NOSTRI LIBERATORI!*

On reaching Toulon, we only had time to shake the dust from our coats and have a quick bite before we embarked again, this time on water. Still, before we boarded ship, we did have time to meet the division general who would be in command.

---

*Properly: *"Viva i nostri liberatori!"*

It was General Ulrich. He gave us a speech that had a bit of everything in it: ancient history, modern history and advanced weaponry, legions, geography, and even meteorology, for he explained how to protect ourselves against the abrupt changes of temperature that we would encounter; then he ended by saying that we could trust in him as he trusted in us. "Remember, you will be fighting on terrain where at every step you will come upon the glorious traces of your fathers; be worthy of them." But already, barges were waiting to take us aboard, and soon we were settled on the ship, crammed together like sardines. On all sides we could see other ships loaded like our own, and barges bringing still more; everywhere we could see a seething mass of scarlet képis. Shouts and singing resounded on land and on the water. Some were shouting farewell to France; for many of them it was farewell forever. Our ship set off along with several others. We sailed straight into the setting sun as it was about to vanish on the horizon, and meanwhile we could see other ships, also loaded with troops coming from Marseille and Africa, heading straight north.

Where the devil were they taking us? Going to Sevastopol we had sailed in this same direction. I was fairly familiar with geography, and I was sure that Italy lay over to the left of Toulon—that is, at the north end of the Mediterranean—and [yet] we continued to sail toward the setting sun. But night came, and every man looked for any way he could find to sleep. People slept on top of one another. The following morning I saw the sun rising behind us, so we were still heading west. There was no land in sight by now. However, at around three in the afternoon we saw on the left a pretty bluish band on the horizon, and we were drawing ever nearer to it. Suddenly, we saw a kind of forest of masts topped with waving tricolor flags, and behind the forest something like a city, but from bottom to top, and even to the tops of the clock towers, its structures were entirely hidden behind flags and garlands and other multicolor hangings. We could already hear the bells of all the churches, and cannon shots announcing our arrival. What city was this? Genoa, said some; others said Naples, and some people even said it was Venice. But I was certain it was none of those cities. We had long since passed Genoa and we were still far from Naples; we were farther still from Venice. But the ship soon halted, not far from the pier, and was instantly accosted by great barges onto which we descended by company. At the pier we jumped off one by one, caught as we landed by two girls, or rather two angels, who were trembling with joy and reaching out for us; then we marched between files of these angels, their hands full of flowers and cigars. The very earth was covered with flowers and leaves. The bells rang full force, and bands playing the *Marseillaise* and shouts of "*Viva la Francia! Viva l'Italia! Viva Napoleone! Viva Vittorio Emmanuele! Viva gli soldati! Viva [i] nostri liberatori!*" came from thousands of voices all along our path. We were pelted with flowers and laurels like grapeshot— probably a foretaste of the same thing in iron and lead. We were led outside the city into an enormous orchard and we set up camp on the grass. I learned then that we were in Livorno, in the duchy of Tuscany.

But we had no time to rest there in our camp, sweet as it was. The citizens of the town, all of them dressed as volunteer soldiers, came to take us by the hand and drag us into the cafés, the restaurants and inns, and other places where the wines and liqueurs, coffee and local drinks were served—as much as we wanted, amid shouts and songs in all languages. Everyone was talking at once, each in his own tongue, but they all understood anyhow. For the Tuscans, what was spoken was the love of liberty—love has no language—and the rest of us happily fell into the same enthusiasm, or rather the same delirium; for what was in the hearts of these folk was a true delirium, for homeland and freedom. King Victor Emmanuel came to deliver the Tuscans a heated call to arms—to chase out the foreigners, the Austrians, who had looted and tyrannized them for so long. He called them to the great union of all the peoples of Italy; he invited them to join their efforts to those of the Piedmont soldiers and the brave, invincible soldiers of the great ally nation, France, emancipator of oppressed peoples.

That appeal was posted everywhere, and every citizen carried a copy in his pocket. I was given one, and I read it easily and understood it as well as if it had been written in French. So I concluded that I knew Italian somewhat, except for learning conversational usage. In fact, I also understood the Tuscans' shouts and songs, but I did not quite dare to thrust myself into their conversations, lest I say something foolish. I just kept still, as I had in face of the French language when I first arrived in the army; I would not speak except when I was certain, or when it was absolutely required. We were cautioned, though, not to wander too far or too long away from the camp, for we might take up arms at any moment.

TRIUMPHAL ENTRANCE

Every day we traveled amid these tumultuous crowds, to the sound of bands and bells, and covered with dust and flowers, till we reached Florence, the duchy's lovely capital city, which the Austrian duke had just fled with his guard and with no effort to defend his territory. There we set up camp in a great meadow, directly in front of the ducal palace. We had thus taken the finest, richest part of the peninsula without firing a shot. The day after our arrival, I was assigned orderly duty at the residence of the division general, who had moved into one of the loveliest houses on the great square. From my post on the reception floor of that house, I witnessed the last tumultuous, delirious scene of the Tuscans—or rather, of the Tuscan women, for all I saw anywhere was women, especially young girls lining up, as they had elsewhere, along both sides of the main street and the square; the other women stood on balconies festooned in multicolored banners, holding baskets of flowers and wreaths. All the church bells pealed full force, blending with the voice of the cannon and the endless cries of *Viva la Francia, Viva l'Italia, Viva Napoleone, Viva Vittorio Emmanuele, Viva gli soldati francesi e piemontesi, nostri liberatori!* But soon I heard a still louder cheer: *Viva il principe Napoleone!* And it was indeed Prince Jerome Napoleon, whom we called Prince "Plomb-Plomb," making his triumphal entrance into the Tuscan capital, which later on was briefly the capital of all Italy.* From the casement window where I stood, I saw him proceeding on his white horse, the length of the main street; but he could barely be seen through the veritable rain of flowers and crowns that literally inundated him.

A cloud of those half-nude young angels, shouting and quivering and stamping their feet, fluttered around his horse, clung to the bridle, the stirrups, the feet, and the cloak of the horse and the prince both. Several of them had their petticoats torn away and destroyed by the horse's hooves. It did not matter: never was there a spectacle so grand, so moving. Storytellers inventing tales of marvels never imagined anything like this,

*Jerome Napoleon, son of Napoleon III's brother Jerome, who commanded the Fifth Army Corps in Italy. His nickname, "Plomb-Plomb," came from the Plombières peace agreements struck between Italy's leader Cavour and Napoleon III. The treaty set up a defensive military alliance against Austria, and also provided for the prince's marriage with Clotilde, the daughter of King Victor Emmanuel of Italy.

and the fantastical and marvelous descriptions of various paradises given out by poets, theologians, fabulists, and impostors have never come close to the real, natural spectacle I had the honor to witness at that moment, both as a foreign spectator and as a philosopher. History tells of the triumphal entrances of other times, particularly in Roman history. Those Roman generals coming home after a conquest made their triumphal entrances into Rome beneath enormous *arcs de triomphe*, which they ordered and paid for with the money they took from those they had conquered. Their hands were filled with gold for distributing to the populace cheering them, but those hands were red with the blood of the peoples they had crushed and plundered; and the princes and grandees of those vanquished peoples walked in chains behind the chariot of the triumphant generals. Here, there was none of that. The Tuscan people had risen up spontaneously at our approach, with cries of "Long live freedom" and "Down with foreign tyrants," and their cries had sufficed to send the tyrants packing. So the prince could enter into Florence with his hands white and clean of human blood. And, from the window where I stood, I gazed out at the spectacle and compared it with the one I had seen in Rheims the year before. There, our little Lord Badinguet could only walk between files of rifles, sabres, and bayonets, with cuirassiers before and behind him as he went; and here, his cousin "Plomb-Plomb" walked unarmed, in a white cloak, amid a mass of young girls whose only weapon was their lovely dark eyes. "Plomb-Plomb" must have been proud of that day, perhaps prouder than his cousin who a few days later made his entrance into the capital of Lombardy, but after he had caused the shedding of barrelsful of blood. It is true—a man's glory has always been measured by the quantity of blood he has shed. Peaceful conquests garner no glory.

We lay over for a few days at Florence. I took advantage of

the stay to visit the lovely city, with its structures all made of marble, even to the stones of the streets. One day I went to a bookseller's to buy a map of the theater of war, and to try to learn from him just what our situation was. The bookseller happened to be a very learned man, concerned with politics and social issues. He gave me a map without charge, then told me the history of the war, which Cavour and Garibaldi had instigated. They were the first to call for independence and the union of all the peoples of the peninsula, and those calls had echoed from the Alps to the Adriatic. But Austria had responded with threats of oppression, and moved its army on to Piedmont territory; and in such circumstances, instead of attaining independence, Italy was about to fall entirely under Austria's yoke. Given that state of affairs, the Emperor of the French could not but intervene, for his own borders were under threat. The shrewd diplomat Cavour had foreseen the whole thing. When the Austrians learned that the French were involved, they threw all their forces toward Genoa and the Alps, expecting that the French would surely come that way. They never gave a thought to the duchies, which rose up at the cries of *Viva l'Italia independente, fuero i tedeschi!* (Long live independent Italy, out with the Germans!) The [Austrian] Duke of Tuscany had asked Emperor Franz Josef to send him troops, first to contain the revolution and ultimately to defend his duchy if it should be invaded by a French army. But when he learned that we were coming, he took flight. Meanwhile, Franz Josef did send an army to the area, but too late. A part of that army was actually at the duchy's borders, where a corps of republican volunteer troops was keeping watch on it. The old bookseller was well informed on all those matters, better probably than the generals commanding us. What troubled him was the outcome of this war, for which Tuscany would be sacrificing everything, its gold and its sons. Emperor

Napoleon had indeed said that he wanted to see Italy free from the Alps to the Adriatic, but Emperor Franz Josef had employed much the same language with the opposite meaning. Both of them were Christian, Catholic emperors; how could they, or would they, seek to dethrone the pope, whom the populace considered to be Italy's true king, and who ruled all Christians in the name of the King of kings? And especially as this pope was the intimate friend of Napoleon III, and godfather to the imperial prince! "No matter," concluded the old bookseller, "Right now we are still tasting real happiness, intoxicated with freedom—all our tyrants have vanished." And I was very pleased, myself, to learn what our situation was, there amid this delirious population.

GREAT BATTLE, GREAT VICTORY

It was the end of May, and some other army corps who had disembarked at Genoa and gone through the Alps had not done a thing so far, whereas we, just one division, had already conquered the finest and richest province of Italy, without losing a single man. But a few days later, a great piece of news reached Florence in the evening and turned the city and the population upside down. It was the news of the first great battle, which took place at Magenta and was won by the French Army, on the fourth of June; and immediately we received the order to set out again, this time in forced march, heading for the banks of the River Po, through the towns of Lucca, Massa, Pietra Santa, Pontremoli; then we crossed the Apennines and, with our weapons always at the ready or on the right shoulder, entered yet another capital, the capital of the duchy of Parma, whose duchess had fled as well. There we again set up camp in the vast parkland of the duchess's palace, and stayed there for two days, awaiting reinforcements coming from France through Genoa. Indeed, all the soldiers on provisional leave after returning from the Crimea had been recalled, but because they missed joining us in France, they were sent by fast trains to catch up as we advanced on Parma. They found some vacancies in our ranks, for on that terrible forced march from Florence to the banks of the Po we had already lost a good many men, not from enemy fire but from the fire of the sun, which was overwhelming.

Now that we had conquered the entire right bank of the Po from Leghorn and Florence to Parma and Bologna, we had to move to the left bank. That would have been difficult, perhaps impossible, if a section of our army corps that disembarked with us at Genoa were not already over on that bank. For the Po is a very broad, very fast river, and the Austrians had blown up all the bridges and destroyed all the ferries and boats located on its banks. Prince Jerome Napoleon, our poor "Plomb-Plomb," looked like the Old Man* physically but had none of his genius; he was rather at a loss, not knowing how to get us across to the other side of the great river without bridges or boats, for the war ministry had decided not to provide the prince with a pontoon squad, thinking he would have no need of them to cross the Apennine mountains. However, General d'Autmart, a veteran of North Africa and the Crimea, who was commanding the left-bank division, told the prince that we would move across to the other side within the next forty-eight hours. The old general doubtless recalled what Lord Raglan once said at Sevastopol to an English officer whom he had ordered to send him eight cannon immediately. The officer replied that it was materially impossible. "That is not the issue," said the general, "The issue is getting eight cannon over here

---

*Napoleon I.

immediately." Whereupon a different young officer simply said, "General, you shall have them," and he got them.

Apparently, General d'Autmart had said the same thing to the engineering corps officers who told him it was impossible to get us across the river, as we had no bridges or boats or the material for constructing them.

"I am not asking you about a bridge or a boat," replied the general, "I am telling you that the prince and his whole army must be across the Po within forty-eight hours."

And it was done: "Where there's a will there's a way," goes the English saying.

Everyone was assigned to the bridge, and while work proceeded at both ends to construct two bridgeheads, other squads went searching along the riverbanks, and succeeded in uncovering boats hidden by the shoreline residents. They fabricated a kind of broad raft from them, and in less than forty-eight hours we were all reunited on the left bank of the river, at Casal Majore, a pretty little town, but without one living soul to be seen. The inhabitants had run off, expecting there would be a battle there. But the Austrians had no more interest in fighting. Italian deserters, who slipped away from their companies whenever they could, told us that. Since the defeat at Magenta, where they had been promised a sure victory, Josef's soldiers were completely demoralized, discouraged. Now we were no longer using the roads, we were marching across the fields, the meadows, the orchards, like hunters chasing game. No more *"viva"* now, no more flowers or cigars. The inhabitants scattered as we approached, and when we questioned them about the Austrians who were still fleeing before us, they did not answer. These poor folks could not figure out whom to side with. What they were to be in a few days—French, or Italian, or Lombard, or Austrian—they had no idea; their fate was still in the hands of the god of armies.

It was June 24th, and since morning we had been marching in sweltering heat. On our left, far off, we could hear the dull roar of cannon, and people said "things are heating up." Things certainly were heating up, the sun especially, and we kept marching along with no obstacle. Toward four in the afternoon, we were assailed and stopped, not by the Austrians but by the most terrifying storm you ever saw. It was Jupiter trying to mix up his lightning bolts with the gunpowder. That was how he overthrew the giants who tried to scale the heights of heaven back then. Those fellows were buried beneath the rocks they had piled up for their project. As for us, we narrowly escaped being buried beneath water; never did I see so much water fall in so little time. We were literally inundated, and night had come. We rushed to higher ground, to the hillocks, and we spent the night standing or squatting. We ate nothing, for it was impossible to make a fire.

The next morning they read us these words that roughly echoed Caesar's: "Great battle, great victory, details tomorrow—Solferino June 24" signed *Napoleon, Emperor.* Caesar told the Senate *"Veni, vidi, vici,"* using the first person, whereas our generalissimo *imperator* used the impersonal, and probably on purpose; he could not claim this victory in which he'd had no part, not for himself and not for any of his generals, who were blissfully unaware of it all, as the saying goes. What he could have said, for example—and correctly—was "our rank-and-file troops have carried off another victory, thanks to their spirit and the irresistible power of their bayonets." Everyone who saw that campaign and who spoke impartially said as much, and they spoke the truth. The line about "lions commanded by jackasses," which I believe was born at Sevastopol, was often repeated to us here, after the suspension of hostilities by the Austrian, Piedmontese, and Garibaldian officers. But while the lions were winning battles with unnecessary bloodshed, the jackasses were being cheered and collecting congratulations, rewards, promotions, and titles. MacMahon had spent the whole day of June fourth uselessly moving his army along, and only reached Magenta when it was all over; and he was dubbed Duke of Magenta.* So then, after the battle of June 24th, we wondered why Canrobert was not named "Duke of Solferino"; he had worn his army out running it back and forth on the plain behind the combatants. All he got was praise for canny maneuvering because he arrived at six in the evening to join the Piedmontese when they had already finished dislodging the enemy from San Martino and put them to rout. And, of course, our Prince "Plomb-Plomb" also got a big share—perhaps more deservedly than the other fellow—of imperial congratulations; a nice fistful of rhetorical flowers after having been deluged with real flowers. According to the imperial accolades, "Plomb-Plomb's" corps had actually done the best work. First, a segment of this corps had distinguished itself earlier back at Palestro, under the very eyes and the orders of King Victor Emmanuel, where the king, too, had acted with distinction, so much so that our comrades in that division named him "Corporal in the First Company of the First Battalion, Third Zouaves." It was our prince's foresight, vigilance, and tactics that brought success at Solferino; having already conquered two great provinces, he also arrived in time to repulse an Austrian corps coming in from Mantua to attack the French Emperor's army broadside or even from the rear. That was Prince "Plomb-Plomb's" contribution and, by the way, each of us was also invited to take some small part of the credit. And for "Plomb-Plomb" it was not over, for a few days later, he was assigned to negotiate the armistice and the preliminaries of peace.

---

*Marie-Edmé-Patrice, comte de MacMahon (1808–1893). Marshal of France; victor at Malakoff in 1855 and at Magenta in 1859.

After the terrible day of June 24, the Austrians completely evacuated Lombardy and moved into Veneto, where they were, so to speak, blocked on one side by the Garibaldians and the Piedmontese, and on another by five French corps containing them from Lake Garda to Mantua, while another army corps was in the Adriatic set to enter into Venice. Such was the position of the allied armies by July 6th, who after June 24th had crossed the Mincio at several different points. On the evening of the 7th, we were told of a big battle for the next day, which caused us to remark that this time, for once, the big chiefs had worked out some plans. We were to ready arms at three in the morning, with no knapsacks, only cartridges, biscuits, and coffee-making equipment. We would be less encumbered for fighting and especially for charging with the bayonet, the terrible and irresistible weapon we were using then. At three in the morning we were on our way, having drunk a very stiff coffee, for it might be our last. We were cheerful and full of energy; only the second lieutenant was not laughing—the rascal feared for his hide. He knew he was not much liked in our company, and he had heard that at Solferino some French officers were found on the battlefield with bullets in their backs. First, we climbed a big hill through fields and orchards; going through farms and villages, we saw the poor folks fleeing in every direction, women with babies in their arms and other children trailing behind in tears, men carrying loads of linens and other household goods. For they must have thought that on their return they would find their houses in ashes, or razed by shells. When we had scaled the hill, we light-infantrymen and grenadiers were deployed as sharpshooters.

From the top of the hill we could see Verona, where Josef's headquarters were located; Peschiera on our left, almost behind us, where fifty thousand Austrians were still blockaded; and across from us, Villafranca, where a few minutes later, on a green baize conference table, the fate of the Italians was to be decided. Before us, across a small ravine, we could see white-clad horsemen, some of them posted as sentries, others pacing back and forth as if waiting for something. We too were waiting for something—a command, a gesture, a shout—some signal to start us moving. We were a few hundred meters from Villafranca and we were thinking, "Now that fine city will soon belong to us." Nice little lunch on a skewer, men were saying, with a meaningful wave of the bayonet. But nothing was moving; a solemn silence hovered over the hills where nonetheless there were over two hundred thousand creatures endowed with the power of speech. But all words were stilled by the emotion of the great spectacle that lay before us, and in the expectation of what was to occur on that enormous stage. Horsemen galloped full-speed along the Verona road, raising clouds of dust.

Finally, toward eight in the morning, the sharpshooters were called back in. We formed into files and columns. Then we were permitted to rest or take a walk. On the Verona road, we could now see light carriages escorted by platoons of horsemen. What did it all mean? We did not know. At noon we returned to our camp at Vallegio, and some time later we were told that there was to be a weeklong cease-fire. So we had nothing to do for a week but wander about and swim in the Mincio. But, before the week was out, we learned that the peace treaty had been concluded, to the great stupefaction of the allied army and the whole of Italy. We ourselves were not told the terms of the peace signed by the two emperors. It was none of our business. As we remarked; we had marched nicely, hunted nicely, and cooked a nice lot of eggs, but we had no right to see or hear how the omelet was to be fried and eaten.

THE AGREEMENTS BETWEEN THE TWO IMPERIAL ROGUES

After a day, though, somewhat by indiscretion but without much thought about the peace agreements Josef and Badinguet had reached at Villafranca,[*] I went for a stroll beneath the trees along the banks of the Mincio, where there was no one else for the moment. I sat down on a clump of brush to smoke a cigar from a supply still left to me since Tuscany. A moment later, a Piedmontese officer and a civilian appeared, talking animatedly and paying me no attention, any more than I looked to be paying attention to them.

"Now this is a sorry business," said the civilian, who might also have been an officer, in mufti. "We were promised a liberated Italy from the Alps to the Adriatic, and now here the country is being left to the worst of the tyrants. Our good king Victor Emmanuel, who was supposed to be king of Italy, is still only the little king of Piedmont alone. Lombardy is ceded to Napoleon III, the Veneto to the pope with the support of the Austrian soldiers, just as he holds Romagna with the sweat of the French soldiers. The duchies that rose up to the calls for Italian unification and liberty have been handed right back to their former tyrants, who will take revenge on the rebels. It's an absolute betrayal; we've been betrayed and robbed."

But the two men were far off by now, and I could no longer catch more than a few words, among them the name of Garibaldi, the most famous of all Italians. He must have been in a fury just then against *il traditore Napoleone* (the traitor Napoleon), who had publicly declared that he would liberate the whole of Italy from the yoke of foreigners and instead was now abandoning her, in a worse state than ever, to the yoke of

---

[*]Small town near Verona, where preliminary peace agreements were signed by the Austrian Emperor Franz Josef and Napoleon III, 1859.

those same foreigners—those detested *tedeschi* against whom all true Italians had risen up to the cries of "Death to the *tedeschi* tyrants!" And to top it off, he imposes himself as a tyrant too, taking Lombardy under his own iron yoke (though it's true he did give it back to Victor Emmanuel in exchange for Nice and Savoy), and putting the Venetians under the most dreadful, pernicious tyranny in the world: the pope's.

Thus do kings and emperors keep their word. I recalled then what the old Florentine bookseller had said about the pope, Badinguet's colleague and crony—that the two had earlier conspired against Louis Philippe and the king of Naples. Then, after the sorry performance by the two emperors at Villafranca, our little lord Badinguet had vanished without a word, and returned incognito to Paris with nobody aware by what means or route. He no longer wished to show his face to the Italians, on whom he had just played such a villainous trick. When he arrived in Italy, he had been welcomed by the enthusiastic shouts of an entire people, who trusted in his words; but if he showed himself to that same populace as he left, he would have heard another sort of shouting, and instead of the flowers and wreaths that covered him on his entrance, he would have been covered in whistles, mud, and boiled potatoes. We learned something more about the whole business a few days later. The pie may well have been sliced up at Villafranca among the two emperors, and Pius IX, and their friends the dukes, but there was still the portion to be worked out between Badinguet and Victor Emmanuel. As Béranger's song went, "You poor cattle, you'll be going helplessly from a yoke that is heavy to one that's inhuman."* And that was absolutely true: Joseph had handed the Lombards over to

---

*Pierre Jean de Béranger, a prominent Parisian poet and singer (1780–1857) who celebrated the Napoleonic legend.

Louis N. the way a landowner hands over cattle to a tenant farmer, in consideration of certain agreements. But those Lombard cattle had expected to be liberated from all foreign tyrants, and made great sacrifices for that liberation; they had absolutely no wish to be French. So Badinguet proposed to Victor that he would give him the Lombards if Victor gave him the Niçois and the Savoyards. But Savoy was the very kernel, the cradle, the jewel in the crown of the kings of Sardinia and Piedmont. And Garibaldi, the great Italian patriot, who sacrificed his entire life for an independent and unified Italy, had no intention of letting Savoy be severed from Nice, the land of his birth.

And there was even a canton in Savoy that refused to be either French or Italian, claiming that it belonged by right to Switzerland. For these reasons the settlement did not go smoothly, and we had to stay another year in Lombardy, where we were quite unpopular. When, after the two imperial rascals finally worked out their arrangements, we left the Veneto to move into a garrison at Bergamo, we crossed through the whole of Lombardy, villages and towns, as if we were crossing a desert. The inhabitants hid at our approach; they now regretted the cheers, the wreaths, and the flowers they'd lavished on us. It was certainly not our fault, sorry slaves that we were, and yet we were the ones to suffer the effects.

DEMOBILIZATION AT TRÉPORT

Some time later, I returned to Tréport: the Third Battalion was assigned to occupy Ville d'Eu and Tréport, and we, in the first two companies, were to occupy the small barracks where I had been promoted to a non-commissioned officer while we were at Dieppe. Under the watchful eye of the colonel, our officers had by necessity been fairly well behaved; the colonel would severely reprimand our second lieutenant at every drill for his idiocy and at every parade review for his untidy outfit. But now at Tréport those gentlemen were in charge; no more colonel or commandant. Our sergeant major, the bastard, was named warrant officer—commonly called the barracks' watchdog—and this fellow really was a dog. The second lieutenant, the wretch, the ferocious idiot, had no funds to pay for lodgings in town, so he came to sleep at the barracks alongside the dog—which meant we had a dog and a jackal guarding us. The wretch resented me especially, because during maneuvers back in Dieppe I had several times put him in his place, a place he didn't know. He was all the angrier because so far he had not found an excuse to punish me; I was too careful, knowing what wild beasts I had surrounding me. Now he was in a hurry to find some good reason to give me a serious penalty—demotion, if possible—for he knew my term was nearly up and that I had already given notice of my intention to leave the service. So one day when I was on sentry duty at the barracks door and this fellow came walking by, I saluted him the first time he passed, according to regulations; but when he kept passing by again and again, I was no longer obliged to salute him, and I even went and sat down. Whereupon the wretch came over to me: "So, that's how you do your job, is it, sergeant? Just wait! I'll teach you!"

"You, teach me anything?" I said, "You're too stupid. You've been looking a long time for an excuse to punish me, here's a good one."

And he starts to shout: "Guard! Seize this man and lock him up!"

The rat would have liked to see me struggle against the guard, and against the warrant officer who rushed over at the sound of his friend's shouts. But before the guard had time to lay hands on me, I had thrown down my shako and my belt and run straight to the prison door. The corporal on duty came and opened the door for me. There I was in prison, and with a reason he could present to the military court: insulting a superior. A sorry excuse for a superior, to be sure, since I had once heard the commandant tell him that whoever had made him an officer would be answerable before God—but still, he was one nonetheless, to the misery of the soldiers and the dishonor of the officer corps. Word was sent to the company first lieutenant, the big Jesuit, and he came to see me in jail.

"Well, here's a pretty kettle of fish," he said. "So do you want to go to the penitentiary?"

"Even there," I replied, "I'd probably be better off than in your company. Here I am with seven years of service, and not a single penalty so far. Promotions to corporal, corporal of infantry, and sergeant: always on merit, for my good work and my exemplary conduct—and now in your company it would seem I'm a good-for-nothing. Send me up for court-martial, since you say I brought it on; your second-lieutenant and your sergeant will come along with me, and we'll see what happens there."

"Yes, but that's just what I don't want," he said, "and why I've come to tell you to get back to your position. I'll take care of this business."

I therefore returned to my sentry post while the lieutenant went to the sergeant major and called in the second lieutenant. There the three rascals probably calculated the consequences to themselves of citing me for a court-martial offense; they were well aware that first the commandant and ultimately the colonel would learn of the arrest and would certainly call for an inquiry before proceeding further, especially for a non-commissioned officer who had regularly been promoted on merit and had never incurred the least penalty. So after calculating and considering, they decided to give me just four days of detention at the military police station for negligence of duties. And that was all; it was not too high a price to pay for the pleasure of calling that stupid lout an idiot.

Meanwhile, the date for my discharge was drawing near, and I began to wonder what I would to do. If they had left me a corporal of light infantry, sure, I would not have hesitated to re-enlist. Now, in the circumstances and at my present rank, I could not. At Tréport there were a good many customs officers, most of whom I knew. They told me that if I wanted, I could join them. But the profession did not hold much attraction for me. Those men seemed too unhappy: of course, they were all married, but they were responsible for blocking the smuggling traffic; in order to feed their families they had to become smugglers themselves, and work beyond their regular hours. I felt it was not as good a profession as the military. Youngsters in town, whom I had taught dancing, sword-stick, and fencing, were urging me to stay on there—I could earn a good living, they said, especially in summer during the bathing season. But I had learned all those skills to amuse myself and to keep warm during the winters; I had never expected to earn a livelihood by them, that didn't suit me. So when the ultimate moment arrived, I was a little uncertain as to where I should retire to. In my own region, in Brittany, I had no real ties now. But as the proverb goes: "Woe to him who is born in a bad place, for he will always return there."

I WAS DISCHARGED TO ERGUÉ-GABÉRIC

I did not disprove the proverb: I took my discharge to Ergué-Gabéric, in the canton of Quimper, Finistère, where I had been raised and where my parents died. I still had a brother and sister there, and a few aunts and uncles, but all of them in dire poverty. I was discharged on August 23, 1861. On the morning of the 24th, I boarded the stagecoach to Dieppe, after shaking hands with all my colleagues and friends, and laying my curse on Second Lieutenant Gautier and Sergeant Major Lafont. At Dieppe, just as I was about to board the train, I found myself face to face with the colonel, who asked me why I was leaving the service, whether I had some better means of livelihood at home than in the army. I told him I had no livelihood anywhere, and then I explained why I was obliged to take my discharge—under threat of being sent to a penal colony some day by the stupidity and malevolence of that second lieutenant and his sidekick, the sergeant major. The colonel scolded me for not having informed him of this state of affairs; he would have transferred me to a different company. Now it was too late: I was discharged, and I wanted to go back to my Brittany, with no idea what I would do there.

I stopped in Paris to see the great capital once again. Finally, back at home, I went to seek lodgings at the home of an old uncle, a former gendarme who lived at Le Guélennec in Ergué-Gabéric. This man, who had never seen me before, was astonished that I was a non-commissioned officer and still more astonished that I had not stayed on in the army at such a high rank. But I told him that it was precisely because I was a non-com that I had left, that I preferred reverting to a farmworker over being a non-com in that situation. I went next to see the mayor, an old peasant who passed for very learned; he was as full of pride and vanity as of ignorance.* He too seemed amazed that I was a non-commissioned officer, for in the past he had so often seen me in rags at his door with my hand out. No one from the commune with any sort of rank at all had ever come to see him, and he too asked me why I had not stayed in. I gave the same reasons I was giving everyone who asked why

---

*Michel Feunteun de Gongallic.

I had left the army despite such favorable circumstances, and I told him I wanted to be a farmhand again, if I could find anyone willing to hire me. He began to laugh, saying I was no longer farmer material. Anyhow, I went around to see several other farmers, who all gave me the same answer, shaking their heads, believing I was making fun of them. Some describe the Breton as straightforward and trusting, but he is the least straightforward, the least trusting character in the world. The only thing he trusts or believes in is God. Because he is used to hypocrisy, to lying and scoffing himself, he thinks everyone else does the same thing. When I had gone through the whole commune in vain, I went back to the old uncle, who scoffed like all the rest and would not believe a word I said, for he was just as Breton as the others, despite having spent several years in Paris in the municipal guard.

I finally went back to see Professor Olive at Kermahonec in Kerfeunteun, for whom I had worked two years as cowherd. My reception there was even worse; he absolutely refused to recognize me. It took his wife, his elder son, and ultimately my documents, to convince him that it was really I, his former *"potr saout,"* and then at last he admitted me—even to his table, overwhelming me with congratulations. But when I mentioned coming back to work on the farm, he burst into laughter. So it was clear that it would be impossible for me to find work in the countryside. I went into Quimper, where I looked up a postman I knew. I asked him if there was any way to join that service. He said I could go see the director, who would probably put me on a list, but unless I had a patron, I might wait a very long time. I had no patron, and I could not wait a long time with no livelihood meanwhile; so it would be pointless to try that path.

At the time, the railroad line from Quimper to Landerneau was under construction. I spoke to various supervisors there, who told me that there would soon be need for a great many employees, both at the Quimper station and all along the line, but that they already had twice as many requests as prospective jobs. No hope there either. Finally I walked along the rails watching the pickax crews, and I asked three or four foremen, but they received me much as the farmers had, looking at my sergeant's braid and my hands and then shaking their heads, telling me they needed road-diggers, not penpushers. It did no good to tell them that I was a local peasant and a real road-digger; they refused to understand. So that was it. Here I was at twenty-six—a non-commissioned officer, full of sap and health, strong, energetic, with courage and will, capable of a whole variety of trades or jobs—forced to throw myself into the river or simply die of hunger.

I WAS OFF TO SEE A NEW COUNTRY

My uncle told me to take my time, I was sure to find something eventually. But I could not wait; I did not want to be a burden to the good fellow, who didn't have too much for himself. Moreover, I had no civilian clothes, and it was time I quit my military uniform, which I no longer had the right to wear. I had to make some decisions quickly. Just two paths were left to me: suicide or the army. I had only ten francs left of my savings from the army discharge payment. And to re-enlist, I would have to go to Brest, for recruitment and administration were located there at the time. I took my ten francs and my documents, and I set out on foot for Brest with a slight hope that, before I went to the recruitment center, I would find some hole for shelter in town. I did the twenty-one leagues at one go, and on arriving I walked over the whole city again before looking for lodgings. In fact, I intended to go outside the town and find somewhere to sleep in the fields, fearing I would not have enough money to pay for both supper and a bed. But at Lambézellec, on my way out of town to the open fields, I met another sergeant who was in roughly the same situation as I was, except that his purse was somewhat fuller. This fellow had been staying in Lambézellec for several days; he would soon be going to Le Havre to set sail for the Americas—for Paraguay, which was fighting a war with Uruguay at the time. He said he had been offered seven thousand francs and second lieutenant rank in the Paraguayan army on arrival. He urged me to join him. But that was impossible for me, as I hadn't a sou left, and I could not go on forever wearing a uniform I was no longer entitled to. And besides, I did not really understand the arrangement: how could you be an officer in a country where you didn't speak a word of the language? The whole thing seemed rather unclear. I stayed overnight with him, but the next morning I returned to Brest determined to go to the recruitment center. The offices were not yet open, though, so I strolled around the arsenal, where so many workers find employment. I asked to speak to a chief or director, to see whether I could find some sort of job in there. But I was told that I would have to put the request in writing, show a certificate, and get an official stamp on my written request.

Before he even finished I saluted and left; I had heard enough. Crossing over the great bridge that had only been completed a short while before, I looked at the sea and I could not help but muse, and tell myself, if by some chance I were to be refused for military service, this was the path I would take. Plunging into eternity from the heights of this bridge—that would be the only course left to me. But now I had to go to the recruitment office.

There, though, and in contrast to the usual behavior of bureaucrats, I was received rather well, and as soon as I declared my desire to re-enlist, they asked for my papers and, immediately, what regiment I wished to join. I asked for a North Africa regiment; I was told that the Sixty-third Line Regiment had just shipped out for the colony and therefore had some chance of staying there for several years. So I took that regiment. It was promptly done. From the recruiting office I went to the administration where I was given a money order for a thousand francs; I went immediately to cash it at the pay-master's, and that very evening I boarded a steamer for Châteaulin with a roll of a thousand francs in my pocket. I felt happier and more contented than the happiest king in the world. Now I was assured of a living for another seven years, and of all sorts of work. I was off to see a new country. I would be entering the Sixty-third as a common soldier, I would have no more responsibilities, I would have to answer only for my own self. As a common soldier, I was never penalized, never received even a word of reprimand; quite the opposite, I was more often cited as an example to my comrades. What more could I want? To be happy on this little globe, it's enough to have food and physical and moral occupations that suit one's own temperament and one's intellectual and moral faculties. I deposited nine hundred francs at the Savings Bank in Quimper, and I left my bankbook with the old uncle, whom I gave a few coins besides to pay for the several nights he had given me shelter; then I left for Poitiers, the Sixty-third's depot.

I RECITED DANTE'S LINES TO HIM . . .

We had a rather long way to go from Poitiers to Marseille, crossing through the Limousin, Auvergne, and Provence.[*]

---

[*]Déguignet and three other experienced men were selected to go ahead as supply masters. They were to set up accommodations for a hundred troops who had volunteered for North Africa.

But the four of us made the trip in a highly agreeable style, like tourists rather than like soldiers. We usually ate together. My mate, who was both butcher and cook, took care of the daily meals and acquitted himself admirably well, to the great satisfaction of all. At Clermont, the lieutenant told me he was very pleased with me.

"It's going well," he said, "and not a single complaint so far, neither from the men nor from the civil authorities of the towns we've come through."

"I very much hope there won't be any," I replied.

He invited me to dine that evening with the sergeants in one of Clermont's big hotels. At the dinner, which was not an official one even though it was attended by an officer, a non-commissioned officer, and an ex-officer, for the first time in my life I had the honor of speaking freely with a French officer. I had already held conversations with Russian and Italian officers. This one, in fact, was of Italian origin, and when he learned that I knew the language of Tasso and Garibaldi, that was the language we spoke throughout the evening, scarcely aware of the sergeant, who did not understand us. In any case, whatever language we might have spoken, the poor sergeant would not have done much better, for the topic or rather the topics of our conversation went too far and too high for him. By way of distraction, meanwhile, he kept pouring himself glasses of wine and cognac, and when he had had enough, he asked permission to retire. The two of us stayed on, the officer and the lowly foot soldier, and for a very long time, because the lieutenant, who had completed his studies, wanted to see just how much learning a poor unschooled Breton might acquire. Meanwhile, the fellow who'd completed all his schooling nearly lost his Latin that night, with a fellow who'd never done any at all. Every two minutes he would bang on the table and say again: "No, but really, it's too much, it's unbelievable! And

Italian, which is my own native tongue—the one I always write my parents in—you speak it better than I do!"

We really did talk about everything—history, science, metaphysics, philosophy, poetry. I recited him the most famous verses of Dante, of Tasso, of Leopardi, of Hugo, of Alfred de Musset; Musset's brother Paul had been a close friend of his family, he told me. In the end I said, "I can understand that you would be surprised by my knowledge and by my philosophical ideas. You officers can't, you haven't the time to think about anything but the sciences of war—for instance, how your predecessors went about killing men—and how to perfect their techniques so as to become even more skillful at killing the greatest possible number in the shortest possible time. All your attention, your whole mind, and intellect must be confined to that. It's a bit the opposite of what they teach in medical school: doctors must learn to kill people according to certain procedures—infinitely variable ones at that—but one person at a time, and as slowly as possible."

"Touché! Well done!" said the lieutenant "and now it's time to drop the curtain."

"Yes," I said, "it is time. You can still take a nap before leaving; as for me, I'm going to hitch on my backpack and set out, for I do believe my comrades must already be waiting for me."

And indeed, when I reached my lodgings, my mate was ready and had begun to worry about me. We slung on our sacks and went out to the road where the two others sat waiting for us.

THE ARABS CAUGHT SIGHT OF ME AND CRIED OUT IN TERROR

It was the second time I had the honor of embarking at Marseille. We sailed to Stora, the port of Philippeville at the time, where we had a terrible time disembarking, for the weather was bad. From Stora,* six of us sailed on to Collo, where our company was posted.† On our arrival at Collo, the whole company came to meet us at the port with the captain at their head, for in that remote spot, it was an event when the postal boat stopped to deliver someone or something.

The company commander was an old fellow with a gray beard, who bore the name of the most renowned charlatan there ever was in France, and perhaps in the whole world: the illustrious Mangin. The captain was no charlatan like his namesake, but he could have been his accompanist, for he was a musician, a melomaniac violinist. With nothing else to do in this hole, he spent his time scraping at the strings of his violin. The lieutenant did pathology and studied horse anatomy, for he hoped to enter the gendarmerie. The second lieutenant was a former sergeant major promoted after the China campaign, with eighteen years of service, just as ignorant as my second lieutenant from the Twenty-sixth, but less of a wretch—less stupid and less nasty, probably because of his age. The sergeant major was a poor bugger already half-dead from the dreadful climate, which was unsuited to his frail constitution. In fact, no one in that company seemed much concerned with us, which did not trouble me because that way no one noticed that I had once been a non-com myself.

As I had nothing to do there, I would go walking in the surrounding countryside, along the sea where there were still some Roman ruins, as there are throughout North Africa. Often I would stop to consider the great mountain peak, like a volcano with its sloping base stretching out on two sides to the edge of the sea, for Collo stands on a very narrow spit. The

*Skikda today.
†El-Qoli today.

Arabs say that everyone who climbed to the top stayed there for good—they were devoured by a monster that never left the summit. Several times I had wanted to climb it, but the other men said it was quite dangerous. First of all, it was almost impossible even to reach the base because of the chasms and the inextricable tangle of brush, and then probably still more impossible to get to the top, which looked smooth as a sugarloaf. And then, who knows whether that monster the Arabs describe doesn't actually live up there? Oh, I said, when it comes to monsters, fabulous or mythological beasts, they don't scare me. And it's not very likely there are any real animals up there, either. One day I asked who wanted to come with me to the top. No one did. So I set off alone with my rifle, some brandy in my flask, a little bowl, sugar, and coffee in my pouch. An Arab who spoke a bit of French had already showed me a way to get easily to the foot of the sugarloaf, but then he said I had better not go any farther than that. I thought: I'll see when I get there. I reached the base quite easily. There I stopped to examine the enormous mass that looked so small from afar. After a brief rest, for I was sweating, I looked for a place to begin the ascent. I had strapped my rifle across my body to leave both hands free to grip the rocks, and I started out—moving to the right, then to the left, turning this way and that, but always climbing upward. And, after about a quarter of an hour, I reached the summit, which was broad enough to build a castle on. I saw no beast, fantastic or otherwise, but it was damn cold up there. I had gathered some firewood at the foot of the breadloaf and put it into my sack, and now I hurriedly lit a fire in a hollow in the rock and set my bowl on it; I tossed in the brandy and the water, the sugar and the coffee pell-mell, and when the whole thing warmed up I gulped it down in a rush and hurried to descend, for the cold was taking hold of me. When I was down, I stopped for a moment to smoke a cigarette, but I was back at the camp in time for supper. Everyone asked what I had seen up there. They knew I had been up on the summit because they had seen the smoke from my fire. The Arabs had caught sight of me just then and cried out in terror, seeing the smoke on that peak where no human being could go. I could certainly have told those people all kinds of incredible things, as so many fakers, liars, and impostors would have done, since I was back from a place where, according to the Arabs, no one else had ever returned from, a place of fable; but I have never been able to tell things any other way but just as I saw them. Since all I saw up there was naked rock, I could not say I'd seen anything else, but they looked astonished when I told them it was damn cold there. I could have given them the scientific explanation for that meteorological phenomenon, as I had done back on the Apennines and on Mont-Cenis, but I knew too well the futility, and even the danger, of talking science to ignorant folk.

Some nights, we went hunting boar in a woodland called the Monkey Forest, though every sort of African wild animal lived there, from the lion king to the jackal. The officers let us hunt because they benefited nicely from it, always picking off the best meat. One night a half-dozen of us went out. But we had scarcely begun to lie in wait, at the edge of a clearing where the boar usually came to eat wild onions, when the terrifying roar of a lion sounded nearby. Instantly, panic seized my companions, and they went tearing off. I left too, but the other men were already far ahead. I walked slowly, staring all around me. Suddenly, ten meters to my left, I spotted the two candle-like eyes of the king of the forest. The animal had seen me, and stopped. I did not; I kept walking slowly with my eyes fixed on the beast, holding my rifle in both hands, ready to fire and to charge with the bayonet in case it attacked. But I did not want to attack. I had heard that a lion never harms a man unless the man attacks him first. When I was some distance past him, I saw the animal move majestically on his way, pacing slowly, his long tail slapping at his flanks, which meant: "Don't give me any trouble, if you please, my little man, or I will chomp you up."

Yet I thought then of the famous Gérard, the lion-killer who used to go out alone to hunt those terrible wild beasts. He had killed many, but he wound up as their victim after all.

I reached camp long after the others. They had all assumed that I had been devoured. When I recounted the adventure, a few of them said that I must sure as hell be a sorcerer, and they swore they would never go boar hunting again.

NOW I WAS A SCHOOLMASTER

At the end of Collo Point there was a lighthouse. I often went walking out there. The keeper was an old seaman with war medals. I often chatted with him, for he too had fought in the Crimean campaign. One day he asked if I would give his little girl some lessons, for he himself did not know how to read or write and his wife had no time, or rather was unwilling, to take on the boring business. I told the old sailor that I would happily come and teach his daughter, but that I would need permission from the captain.

"*Oh, trôun de ler,*" he said, "you'll get all the permissions you want, your captain and I are great friends, we come from the same parts. And besides, you know," he said, "I'm the mayor of Collo."

He told his wife, who acted as his secretary, to give me a note for Captain Mangin. The captain read it and told me I could go out to the lighthouse whenever I liked, and stay as long as I liked; in a word, I was totally free.

So now I was a schoolmaster—but a poor one, for I had no

power over my pupil, who was very capricious and headstrong. She would rather sing and dance than do grammar and arithmetic or, when she saw a ship go by in the distance, she would take up a big spyglass and stare at the passengers. The mother knew her own daughter and had quite a sensible philosophy about her: "She wants to learn to sing and dance, let her. You can't force people to learn things they don't want to learn. And if she knows how to sing and dance, then some day when her cupboard is bare maybe she can do some singing and dancing in front of it." And the mother went back to reading her Alexandre Dumas and Eugène Sue novels, which she adored.

The old seaman spent his time clearing terrain to plant a garden, which he could make as large as he wanted; there was plenty of land. I would go and dig with him, which suited me much better than the job of teacher. He had an Arab day laborer with him, who spoke French fairly well. With that fellow, if time had allowed, I would have been quick to learn Arabic—quicker than my pupil would learn French grammar—and the more easily because the sound of Arabic is like the Breton sound, and the words in both languages have the same endings. But on my way back from the lighthouse, I came across another schoolmaster sitting on the grass like a Breton tailor, with his pupils in a circle around him. The pupils were holding their notebooks on their knees and writing from right to left at the teacher's dictation, their reed pens squeaking. It was an Arab school, probably the local village school, but I consider it better-run than all our French schools and others. Because this teacher held his classes in all sorts of settings, in the sunshine when the weather was cool, in the shade when it was too hot, at the seashore, in the woods, on the lawn, and on the rocks—that is to say, in freedom, and in the presence of nature. But our own schoolchildren are closed up, winter and summer, in narrow little cubbyholes surrounded by walls, where all they see and study is words and phrases, which makes them ignorant, useless graduates, dangerous to themselves and even more dangerous to society. Locking birds into cages is no way to teach them to fly and to get themselves food. And, as if to mock the public, in our country we give the title "free school" to these things that are completely sealed off and surrounded by high walls. To decree compulsory education in conditions like that, as the tendency is these days, means to decree compulsory misery for many unlucky children, or charlatanism and deceit for many others.

Meanwhile, things were about to change for us. Up to that time, we had seen nothing of the real life of a soldier in Africa—that is, the marches in the bush, the rocks, the mountains, the battles, the hunger, the thirst, and the dangers at every moment.

We would soon come to know that life, and live it for a long time. The revolt started near Tebessa. All the troops in the province were mustered on the enormous Tebessa plain, later so much discussed for its rich phosphate deposits. When the army was assembled, we set out for the region of the rebelling tribes. For fifteen days we walked, this way and that, to the borders of Tunisia, across which our enemies withdrew when they saw they were in danger.

Meanwhile, several tribes surrendered, and to prove their complete submission they invited us to a meal of the famous *Kouskoussou*, the great Arab national dish, which consists of goat meat cooked with cracked barley. The meal must have cost the tribes dear: to serve a great feast to a whole division, not to mention the *goum* [our Arab horsemen support]—that is, to feed some ten thousand mouths.

Afterwards, we followed the same zigzagging route back to Tebessa.

LONG EXPEDITION

We set out, keeping close to the Tunisian border, behind which the enemy had withdrawn to stay clear of our pursuit. To guard against any surprises from them, who tend to play hide-and-seek, we always marched and camped in square formation with the luggage and the artillery in the middle—a difficult and exhausting march, especially in country split by ravines, irregular and thick with bush, we had to reconnoiter. It was, as I told my artist friend in the regiment, a miniature of Philip of Macedon's phalanx formation. Of course in miniature, since those phalanxes marched eight serried ranks abreast, veritable moving walls, whereas we were marching only five abreast. It would not have been too difficult for seasoned, daring cavalry to penetrate our square. It's true we also had the protection of great numbers of Arab horsemen, the *goum*, who volunteered to help us battle their brothers and who formed a great mobile defense cordon around us. These nimble horsemen also served as scouts and spies.

We did not move fast in that formation, and we often stopped for several days at certain places. Thus it took us weeks to get from Tebessa to La Calle, the end point of the expedition. There the expeditionary force was dissolved, and each regiment was to report to the garrison it was assigned. But though we had not suffered many losses in the course of that long expedition, we did have a number of men sick from terrible exhaustion and burning heat, from drinking bad water, either brackish or poisoned from flowing over oleander roots. The invalids stayed behind at La Calle, to be sent on to the hospitals at Bône and Philippeville. The rest of us returned to Constantine, where we had started from. We had left many sick behind at La Calle, but at Constantine there were more. All the usual plagues that attack troops after wars—fevers, dysentery, cholera, typhus, and others—fell upon us like vermin on beggars. Fortunately, our own squad was assigned to occupy a small post above Constantine, at the location of the spring that supplies water to the town. Up on those heights, with the pure air and excellent water, the evil cholera and typhus microbes spared us. Such organisms hate purity; they are the same race as Jesuits and ignorant monks. The keeper of the spring was our commander; he set us to work clearing land to plant vegetable gardens and nurseries.

THE FIERCE MOUNTAIN MEN OF KABYLIA

When we came down from the mountains to Constantine, we found the regiment set to leave again, this time for Sétif,[*] opposite from Tebessa—that is, looking into and very close to Great Kabylia, near those fearsome mountain men who are said to be neither Moors nor Arabs although they had adopted Islam, and who had never been subjugated by any of the conquerors of West Africa.

"So what race do these Kabyles belong to?" a friend asked as we were en route to Sétif. That, I replied, nobody can work out, just as no one knows or ever will know what race we Bretons are, aside from a general membership, like the Kabyles, in the white race. But where did the Bretons come from before Brittany, speaking this language unlike any other in the world, a language with no detectable father or mother, nor sons or daughters either? The Bretons, like the Kabyles, have never bent to the conquerors who governed and administered them. They took nothing from the Romans who administered them for so long, not even a word of their tongue; nor are they willing to learn anything from the French

---

[*]Stif.

who've been administering them for four hundred years. "Bretons forever" is their cry. All the usual Breton newspapers published by priests carry bold-type headlines *"Doue e Va Bro"* (God and my Brittany)—and nothing more. These races are like untamed forest animals; they will not give in to reason, they listen only to the black and white charlatans who promise them incredible and impossible things in the next world.

But we would soon be tangling with the fierce mountain men of Kabylia. Some French colonists had already been plundered, burned out, and murdered, and others were forced to abandon their farms and return to Sétif. The marabouts were preaching Holy War everywhere. They came from Mecca where they consulted with the great prophet, who told them the time had come to oust the infidels; they had only to rise up en masse and the *roumi*, those Christian dogs, would flee in terror and drown in the sea like the hogs of Gennesaret. All the Kabyles believed their marabouts, and they did rise up to push the *roumi* into the sea, or to slash their throats in the mountains. They were so sure of their mission that a grand caïd of Boussoda, a retired officer of the French infantry with decorations and a pension, was among the first to go off to lead the movement—not before pinning all his medals onto his horse's tail.

We were soon ordered to leave Sétif and go set up camp on a mountain facing the Kabyles to observe them, but we did not have enough forces to launch an attack in those very dangerous mountains, gorges, and defiles. We had to wait for reinforcements. We stayed there as observers until spring. A few leagues away to our right was another observation post with infantry and cavalry. That was Takétoun, where there was a fort or blockhouse. One night a *roumi* came to tell us that the Takétoun garrison had been encircled by the Kabyles, and already half our men had been slaughtered. Immediately we were ordered to break camp and set out. But to reach Takétoun, we had to go down into the gorges, into the long narrow defiles where we were blocked as well. Very soon—in front of us, to our right and left and behind us—there were nothing but Kabyles shouting wild triumphant cries from every side, for they expected to slaughter us all. We could only advance by shooting and striking out with bayonets and rifle-butts. Fortunately for us, these Kabyles were unarmed—they had only one rifle for every three or four men—and the prophet, who had promised his help, had apparently not yet turned up. The unarmed men did try to pelt us with stones, but although they were very strong and might have been descended from the same savage race as David, they did not have the strength or stone-throwing skills of Goliath's conqueror. There was a tragicomic scene between a Kabyle and one of our corporals: the corporal had charged the Kabyle to gut him with his bayonet, but the latter had parried the blow by seizing the bayonet and the muzzle of the rifle. And the two of them went on shooting and shoving until the corporal was beaten, forced to let go his rifle and get out fast or take his own bayonet in his backside. Nobody was available to go to the poor corporal's aid, as each of us was fighting off several enemies and trying to evade the boulders these present-day giants were rolling down on us from the mountaintops—although, again, with less power and skill than when the Eternal Father did the same thing on Gibeon.

Still, despite so many difficulties, and the fact that we had eaten nothing all day, we managed to reach Takétoun at nightfall—and get ourselves blockaded in along with the poor folks who had been caught under siege since the day before. No sooner were we stopped than a veritable ring of steel and fire formed around us, and shells started falling from every side. We did have a meal, though, of which our stomachs were in sore need. But we ate it amid a tremendous racket of explosions and screams in every language from those wild-animal Kabyles. Despite their haste to carry away their dead and wounded that day, they had to leave a good many behind. Just before supper, two of them were dragged to the middle of our encampment. One was swiftly put out of his misery by two bullets in the head, but the other was left to the vengeance of a gunner, who entertained himself for a long while by working over the man's body with his stirrups, then crushing his head with his boots till it was reduced to mash. It was horrible. But the soldier claimed he was avenging several of our comrades who had been martyred the day before. After the meal, our company was assigned to go occupy an advance post six or seven hundred meters ahead of the camp, in the most dangerous position of all, and for us even more dangerous because we had no idea where we were, and knew nothing about the local topography. Our two officers were at a loss. They held their own, though, and even did well, considering their rank. Toward midnight, we were attacked by the Kabyles and nearly surrounded. At the first shots and the wild cries of the attackers, panic seized some of the more fearful men, and they ran back to the camp, leaving behind their knapsacks and even, some of them, their rifles. But the rest held firm, and on our own initiative we rapidly formed up into a small square. Those who had fled alerted the camp; our commander came to our aid with the light-infantry company and brought back the runaways. Now we took the offensive, and managed to force the Kabyles back to the far side of the mountain. Then silence fell all around, and the fires the Kabyles had started everywhere were put out. At daybreak, not one of the enemy was to be seen. The Kabyles had gone to hide in the rocks of their mountains. We had lost five men, only two of whom were found—in the ravine, entirely naked, with their bodies slashed by knives. The night before, on a small rise somewhat ahead of that position, the Kabyles had ambushed another company from the garrison and slaughtered nearly all of them. Several of those wretches fell into the hands of the fanatical barbarians and were put through the most hideous martyrdom. Great pools of blackened blood still stained the ground where they were martyred. A squadron of chasseurs, camped nearby, also lost several men and had to join us in the fort, abandoning their encampment and their gear. We stayed there awaiting reinforcements, which were quick to come. Soon a whole army corps had gathered before those terrible Bas-Bords mountains, the Kabyles' main refuge, where they believed themselves safe from any attack. When we were at full strength we moved down onto the plain, to where the Kabyles usually mustered to attack Takétoun. We searched several villages, but all of them had been deserted by the inhabitants. The able-bodied men were fighting the infidel *roumis*. The women, children, and old folks had gone up into the mountains, and the warriors were hidden among their crags, watching for us. We made several expeditions into the gorges without much trouble. But one day we moved deep into a ravine, and there our regiment—our battalion particularly—was caught in a highly perilous position for a long time. With our backs to a stream, we were facing a mass of Kabyles hidden in the bush and the rocks, pelting us with projectiles with no response from us. It was as if we were set up as targets for our enemies. If the Kabyles had been armed like us, they would have shot us all down. As it was, though, we had only a few wounded. The quartermaster of our battalion's third company, who was standing to the right of his company—that is, beside me, who was the last of ours—took a bullet in his side that pierced right through his belt. We carried him to the mule-litters; we thought he was dead. But he did not die of the wound, for I later saw him on crutches at Philippeville. He had been awarded a medal, and was awaiting a pension before leaving for home. That day had cost the Kabyles dearly, though. Our gunners had set up their mountain artillery on a plateau behind us, and from there they sent shells over our heads into the massed Kabyle troops, every shot devastating them. We could hear them calling on Mohammed and Allah. But those sorry gods were like all their kind—mute, deaf, and blind.

One morning some days later, we were startled to find that the whole [French] colony had vanished from Takétoun, before daylight, without a sign. Only our company was left at that location—that is, at the very place we passed through on the night we arrived at Takétoun. Farther on, one company of the Sixty-sixth was also left behind; and in the fort, a squadron of chasseurs, the very group that was itself surprised by the enemy at the same time as the company from the Sixty-sixth. Left us behind, and after we had undergone such a dreadful night! Was it to punish us for that whole episode that we were being abandoned, sacrificed? We thought so, and said so to each other. That was the sort of war game Bonaparte had used so marvelously, sacrificing a few companies is a small price to win a great victory. But in such a case, Napoleon would ask for volunteers, and he always got them. And our general too, if he had asked, would have got as many as he might want. Instead he selected us out automatically. However, our two captains and the squadron commander met together that morning to plan a joint defense. Nearby there was an old house; it was decided that our group would be stationed inside it at night. The men from the Sixty-sixth in a kind of redoubt at the far end of the fort, and the chasseurs would stay on in the fort, but ready to come in with support wherever there was a serious threat. We worked the whole day on fortifying our house, and entered it only at nightfall. But for a long time we had been watching the Kabyles gathering in the ravine across from us. The night was surely going to be rough, for the Kabyles could see that despite their marabouts' promises, Mohammed was not stepping in to help them, and they were resolved to fight as desperate men, knowing that they could expect no mercy if they were captured. We too were determined, if we had to die, not to sell our lives cheap. This time we did not have to worry that some men would run away like the first night, because the captain had assigned each man his combat post, and placed us, the hardened old-timers, at the two exits, as much to keep the assailants out as to keep the fearful in. Like the first time, the attackers did not arrive till midnight, screaming like wild animals. At the two ends of the house, we had built a kind of bastion of huge rocks from which we could fire at them head on and sideways. Under our volleys they pulled back from time to time, but they kept returning. From the fort the chasseurs were cheering us on: "Courage, boys, we're right here, don't be afraid!"

There were some men among us, though, who were terribly afraid, so much so that they hadn't the courage to load their guns. There were probably several who had already made out their wills; what we had most to fear was that with battering rams and heavy rocks the Kabyles would manage to smash through the house walls. They had certainly thought of that themselves and even tried it, but in vain. Then, finally, dawn broke, and like all forest animals, our assailants disappeared with the darkness. No matter, they had given us another terrible night. The commander of the chasseurs came to see us early the next morning. He congratulated us and shook the captain's hand. We had suffered no damage. The men who had trembled all night long seemed to be the merriest now—the glad return to the things of this world. But their gaiety did not last long.

By eight in the morning, the Kabyles were regrouping at the same spot. Their numbers were visibly growing; dirty white burnooses seemed to sprout up from the earth, and the horsemen pulled away from the horde and came to scrutinize us from a hundred meters away, sending over a few rocks as they advanced. Having had no success at night, they may have thought that daytime would work better for them. Mohammed must have been asleep when they called on him at midnight. Most of the comrades billeted over in the captain's house came up to the fort with the commander of chasseurs, who was now our commander as well. My old friend and I were sitting in front of the house, chatting and contemplating the spectacle before our eyes, and also trying to make out the whereabouts of the column whose leader, General Desveaux, must have a plan for encircling the Kabyles someplace.* Irritated by the horsemen coming up practically under our noses to stare at us and to fling a few rocks at us as they did, we went to fetch our guns and cartridges to give the insolent pups an answer. Others joined us and, following orders, as riflemen we marched off toward the ravine on the other side; the men of the Sixty-sixth did the same.

FROM ALGIERS TO VERA CRUZ

[*Ferdinand Joseph Maximilian, Archduke of Austria, was installed as Emperor of Mexico in 1864 by Napoleon III. The French sent an "expeditionary force" to support the regime and the sizeable French interests in the country, against the indigenous republican movement.*

---

*General Desveaux (1810–1884) was commander of the garrison at Constantine, and Lieutenant Governor of Algeria in 1865.

Faced with resistance there and at home, in 1867, Napoleon III
dropped his support for the venture, and Maximilian was executed by
Mexican republican troops. He was thus "Emperor Maximilian the
First and Last."]

At the close of the Kabylia campaign, our regiment was to
return to France and rest on its laurels—a well deserved rest,
everyone said. But as preparations proceeded for the return
to our country, an urgent order arrived from Paris to seek volunteers from the whole army of Africa, the most seasoned,
hard-boiled old hands, to go to Mexico where things were
starting to go badly for the French. Of course, I was among the
first on the list, not out of some ugly excessive love for war-
making, for I had already seen more than enough slaughter,
but out of a love for faraway journeys, for new countries, and
new adventures. My friend the scholar signed up, too, which
allowed us to talk a lot about philosophy during the long
crossing from Algiers to Vera Cruz.

THREE THOUSAND LEAGUES FROM FRANCE

[Déguignet is garrisoned at Durango, some 350 miles north of Mexico
City, in the foothills of the Sierra Madre.]

A library in this remote area—that surprised me. Yet I hesitated to go in, for I knew that this was a region of real liberals, republicans, and [as a soldier of the French forces
supporting the imposed Emperor Maximilian] I would surely
be unwelcome. Still, the word "library" held so much appeal
for me that I decided to go and see it at the risk of getting
myself killed. But when I entered there were only two people,
whose mild faces were reassuring. A middle-aged man was
leafing through an old manuscript. Another, the librarian, was
lounging on a sofa, peacefully smoking a cigarette. Very
politely, I went over to him and, presuming that a librarian

must know French, I addressed him in that language. He answered in Castilian that he spoke no French. In his own language, I asked if I might consult a work on Mexican history, which such a rich library must surely have.

"Yes," he said, "there is one, and actually it is just about all we have in Castilian, everything else is in French."

He showed me the whole collection and I saw that, in fact, there were only French books there—all the authors were arranged in sections, from Rabelais to Victor Hugo. The volumes were right where they had been ever since they arrived, closed up in vitrines, no one having touched them since. I just stood there, astonished at so large a library here in this nearly unknown area, three thousand leagues from France, and containing all the works of the French writers, here where they were no use to anyone or anything.

The librarian then handed me what he called a history of Mexico, in Castilian, but I could see that the only truly historical element in it was the account of the revolution—that is, the Mexicans' revolt against their tyrants, the Spanish, their exploiters and oppressors, whom they routed from their land the way their neighbors to the north, the Americans, had routed the English. The rest of the book was merely fables and absurd legends—that is, whatever the lying Jesuits felt like writing about this land and its people, some time after the conquest, when they had destroyed all the buildings and documents that might have been useful for writing the history. This *History of Mexico* resembled the *History of France* by the Jesuit Loriquet, which was also on the shelves.[*]

I went back to the library almost every day when I was not on duty. There I could read a newspaper, the only one allowed

---

[*]Jean-Nicolas Loriquet (1767–1845), author of a history of France for young people.

to appear in the country—the official paper of the empire of poor Lord *Maximiliano primero y ultimo*. Its title was "The Telegraph." *El Telegrafo*, doubtless because a telegraph line had just been set up between Mexico City and Durango. But the line did not often work, as it was constantly being cut at various points by bands of chinacos* and liberals. Of course, the paper published nothing but lies, like the French newspapers at that time, about Mexican affairs. No one could know better than I the truth about [our] infamous expedition, [what its supporters in France called] "The finest idea of this Reign."

I never saw anyone else in that library but the librarian and the same fellow I found there on my first visit. The other visitor had already told me a bit about Mexican history, but he did not seem eager to become involved in long discussions. He did watch me, without being obvious; he would glance over at the books I read. But once he understood, as a good physiognomist, whom he was dealing with, he engaged openly in conversation with me, and one evening as we left the library he invited me back to his house. There, seated on piles of books and newspapers, and sipping some *aguardiente*, he told me his story. He was a professor of languages, but, as he belonged to the Liberal Party and was actually a close friend of Juarez, he had had to leave Mexico City with the Republican Army as did all the important liberals; their possessions were impounded by Forey's clerical government. At first he stayed at Zacatecas, where all the French soldiers were to be buried. But when Juarez decided to go to the United States with his army and wait for more auspicious times, the professor moved to Durango, where he lived, poor and philosophical, but in the certainty that he would soon return to Mexico City with his friend Juarez when the French evacuated the capital and the

---

*Mexican guerrillas.

rest of the country. And he knew that would not be long. He was getting secret communications from the United States, where the war between the North and the South had just ended very happily, to the benefit of the slaves. Union makes strength, goes the proverb; up there, strength made Union. Now that those two great republics had become one, it would not allow an emperor to set up at its doorstep.

I had finally again found a man I could talk to, and talk pleasurably and in several languages, for my new friend knew many. He spoke French, Italian, Spanish—three languages in which I could converse with him; he also spoke English, and the two main dialects still spoken in certain parts of Mexico: Aztec and Mixtec. However, I knew one language that this learned linguist did not: Breton, and he found this language quite intriguing because it has no kin among the known human tongues, neither father, nor mother, nor sons, nor daughters.

In any case, I spent pleasant hours thereafter in that little cottage, which my friend called "Uncle Tom's Cabin" after the great philanthropic novel that had stirred all humane hearts in North America, and even in Europe, against the rich slave-owners, and was the major cause of the terrible war between the libertarians* and the partisans of slavery, which had just ended after four years of terrible battle. Our chats, always moistened with a few *copitas de aguardiente* or *mescal,* ranged through all the human sciences and all issues—political, social, philosophical, metaphysical, and religious. And we would make up verses about all sorts of subjects, but especially about the crimes and criminals of the moment. One day, *l'amigo Salvarez*—that was his name—handed me a card bearing his name and that of the President of the Republic, Juarez, saying the card might come in handy one day. "For," he said,

---

*Déguignet's term for the abolitionists.

"if ever you should fall into the hands of the liberal republicans, and you should happen to speak Spanish to them, you're sure to be hanged instantly, for you speak the language with an accent that will lead them to mistake you for a Spaniard. Now, while right now we hate the French, because of your Emperor's cowardice and stupidity, against the Spanish we have sworn eternal hatred. But if ever you should find yourself in such a situation, present this card, and instead of hanging you they'll take you in their arms." I happily took the precious card, with its gift for saving my life in some emergency, for I could not know what might happen to me.

Still, despite the pleasures I found at Durango, thanks to the library and *el amigo Salvarez*, I was starting to tire of it. The sedentary existence did not suit my temperament.

THAT CELESTIAL PARADISE, AVILEZ: 1866

It was already the spring of 1866, the start of the rainy season—diluvial rains, preceded and accompanied by terrifying thunderclaps that shook the houses and cracked the windowpanes. Our comrades in the First Battalion had left long ago, together with the men shifted into the Ninety-fifth, to rejoin their battalion in the Chihuahua region. But our battalion, the Second of the Seventh [regiment], was at another location, and it was felt that our numbers were not great enough for us to go as well without risk of being slaughtered en route. For that we would have to await the arrival at Durango of our irregulars. Each regiment had one such company made up of the hardiest walkers, fearless men, who ranged about day and night reconnoitering the various terrains and providing links among different detachments of the regiment, which were often situated hundreds of leagues apart. One day that company finally reached Durango, with orders to take us to Avilez, where our Second Battalion was then located. We left immediately with the irregulars, who never stopped to rest.

I don't know how many leagues lie between Durango and Avilez, but it took us about fifteen days to cover the distance. It is true that we went a zigzag route because of the streams. In that country, the riverbeds serve as roadways in the dry season, but in the rainy season they turn into wild torrents, and the vast plains into lakes and ponds. The company had its own guide, as we did. But theirs spoke French, and he was also in charge of supplies for the column. Though I don't believe his supplies cost him much. Evenings, on reaching the layover, he would lasso an ox or two and have them bled and cut up by the company butchers. In the cities, villages, and haciendas, he procured us sugar, coffee, bread, if there was any, or corn tortillas, *aguardiente* or mescal, and other local foodstuffs. It was all billed to *el emperador Maximiliano*, whom these people never saw. The accounts were worked out later, between the company commander and that excellent supplier/guide. The fellow must have made himself a nice fortune working his two trades at once: traitor and thief. But the fortune was not much use to him in the end, for he was among the first men [whom the republicans] hanged after we left the country.

We finally reached Avilez—*Hacienda de Florez*, in the words of a Spanish song composed by our commander of the Second Battalion, who like to consider himself a poet, doubtless because his name was de Musset. The *hacienda* is set on the most beautiful, richest site to be found anywhere on this globe. All about were enormous prairies, woodlands, virgin forest, natural fruits of all sorts, even grapevines, which I never saw anywhere else in Mexico. Two great watercourses flowed by, one right through the village and the other a kilometer away. And the whole of this vast, rich countryside belonged to Don Florez,

one of the most powerful *señores* in Mexico, a man who had ded-
icated all his powers and talent to fighting the invaders, and as
such was condemned to death, though not executed. I was
even told that he came over to France to talk to the Emperor,
describing the dreadful position of the Imperial Army in
Mexico, to the misery of that country and to France's shame.

The irregular company stayed a day at Avilez, awaiting the
commander's report to take to the colonel. I was put with the
Second Company. There each company was assigned to a particular cabin, in which the men had constructed, two by two,
a kind of leaf bed. The day after our arrival, when we were settled in, we went to see the river that ran about a kilometer
below Avilez, and which at the time was a wild torrent dragging clumps of earth and trees along its silty yellow waters. We
bathed there nonetheless, not in the torrent itself, of course,
but on the surrounding meadow, where the water spread out
in a tranquil, less muddy sheet. When we got back, the irregulars were gone. There had been a request for candidates for
corporal, their names to be appended to the commander's
report to the colonel, and one of the men who arrived with
me had told the sergeant major that I used to be a non-
commissioned officer. The major went into my knapsack for
my service booklet, and, when he saw my service history, he
put me at the top of the list of corporal candidates. When I
heard that, I tried to protest, but it was too late: the list was
gone. Anyhow, the position of corporal-in-training would not
change my rank, and I would have some time before the
irregular company returned to Avilez, or before the regiment
was fully back together; the campaign might be over by then.

Meanwhile, we were not too miserable in that earthly paradise of Avilez, even though we were surrounded by enemies—like everywhere else, in fact, since each day the sentinel
watching from the village bell tower would signal us about a

few horsemen in red—the Garibaldi uniform—calvacading around the village. We often went after them, but in vain. Our poet-commander was like a god there. Imagine—chief officer of such a beautiful, vast countryside, with full powers—applied by force, of course, otherwise he would have had none at all. He would strut through the village or hacienda with his aide-de-camp, the captain adjutant-major trying to copy him, like an old peacock who's lost his feathers but is determined anyhow to flare his tail. People always said Alfred de Musset was mad, but a mad genius; our commander de Musset was also a madman, but a vain, stupid, nasty madman. To entertain himself and annoy the two or three important clergymen in the village, who were his vassals, he would give evening musicales beneath the arcades of the village hall. He had formed a choir with a half-dozen cutups from the battalion. Each time, as a finale, he would have them sing his "Spanish song"; the thing was just a series of rhythmic lines, in rather bad rhyme, with no sense, or sequence, or meaning, which he had set to an aria from the opera *Fra Diavolo*. The message of the song was that he loved everything about Mexico: *"Me gusto Tampico, Pueblo y Mexico. Me gusto Durango y su lindo rio; sus bellas almedas y sus senoritas. Me gusto Avilez, hacienda de Florez, luego maravillo, tal un paraiso."* There were another twenty couplets on all the places in Mexico where everything was so fine and so beautiful. And the poet-commander was right: for those gentlemen, a lovelier existence anywhere would be impossible to imagine.

GORGEOUS ORGIES

Even the inventors of paradise never imagined pleasures such as those robber barons found out there, an endless variety of pleasures. In the big cities, bullfights by day, and by night, the theater or singing and dancing parties with all kinds of bacchic and Borgia-esque orgies. The famous M. Loisillon,* in his letters to Madame Cotu, a lady-in-waiting to the Empress Eugénie, would describe all the gorgeous orgies he attended in Mexico City, where he was an officer at "Emperor" Bazaine's headquarters.† And all at the expense of the poor Mexicans.

Outside the big cities, they had their hunting and fishing, and bullfights in the open fields—better than the fights in the arenas, where all one saw was blood, with men and horses eviscerated and trampling their own guts. When they decided to visit some interesting site—a virgin forest, a river, a lake, a volcano—they would muster an escort of troops and order full packs on their backs on the pretext of carrying out some expedition. The *señores* were on horseback, in white cloaks and broad *sombreros* to shield their precious bodies from the burning rays of the tropical sun. A herd of mules would follow behind them, bearing loads of all sorts of solid and liquid provisions. When it was time for lunch they would stop, and if there was no shade from the sun's rays or shelter from the rain, they would have their servants set up tents, and beneath them they would sip absinthe and lunch on several good cold meat dishes—hare, duck, turkey and other delicacies; they would have coffee and juggle oranges, while the troops roasted in the sun or soaked in the rain and gnawed at a chunk of dry biscuit as hard as stone. And that horrible contrast, that display of misery and suffering before their eyes, only doubled their pleasure.

SOCIAL QUESTIONS

On our outings around Avilez, I reflected a good deal on the very troubled social questions of our time, for here was a

---

*Author of *Letters on the Mexican Expedition*, 1890.

†Achille Bazaine was commander of the French Expeditionary Force in Mexico.

country so vast and rich with almost no population, while back in Finistère, the most arid terrain, every island and islet, nearly naked of vegetation, is crowded with inhabitants one on top of another, three-quarters of them sunk in servitude, abjection, and poverty. And yet there are deputies from Finistère urging the baby-makers on with various dispensations to produce as many as possible—say, seven each at a minimum. In Mexico, on the contrary, procreation is little encouraged. At home, with the support of the Civil Code, the sixth and the ninth of God's Commandments are considered by priests to be the most damnable sins, and by the Civil Code to be crimes, whereas in Mexico these needs, these demands of nature, are considered to be pardonable; young girls there respond to their leanings and nature's calls very early, thereby losing their strength and their reproductive capacity before their time, which in any case does not last very long; at twenty-five they are already old and out of service. On the other hand, infant mortality is, if not encouraged, at least highly desirable in every Mexican family. All are eager to have one or several angels up in heaven; their intervention guarantees the family members a place there themselves later on. So it is a great joy for a household when a child dies. They keep the body in the house for several days, surrounded with flowers and perfumes. Other families come to seek favors from the new angel, and they beg permission to take the body home with them for a while. Later it is accompanied to the cemetery by a procession playing fiddles and dancing and singing merry tunes.

History reports that the mothers of young Aztec children sacrificed to the god Tlaloc to bring rain were cheerful and happy, especially when their children cried hard before and during the slaying, because that meant the rain would be abundant and beneficial. In our day, too, mothers of Indian children are very cheerful and very happy when their children are sacrificed to the god of the Jews—now also become the god of western Aryans by virtue of the Holy Bird—for they believe they thus provide heaven with angels who will one day reach down their little hands and lift their mothers up to heaven as well. The Indians of the haciendas and the pueblitos are also the most fortunate race on earth living under the feudal regime; they need worry about nothing but eating, drinking, and playing. They grow a bit of corn and a few vegetables here and there on the haciendas, but without much labor or expense, for those fields can yield two harvests a year without need of manure or other improvement. Just some elementary tilling with the most primitive tools is enough. But there will come a time, perhaps very soon, when the Americans, their neighbors, will move into the country with steam and electric power to exploit the very rich soil. And then those poor Mexican Indians will be forced to disappear, as their brothers to the North did at the invasive advance of the Yankees.

We stayed some three months in those parts, visiting Don Florez's grand estates, living at his expense. The rainy season was drawing to an end. We finally left Avilez on a fine day in the afternoon. The notables of the area looked sad as they watched us go. They probably knew they would pay a high price for their friendship to us, their weakness, and their cowardice before the enemy.

THE ENEMY WAS UPON US

We were supposed to cross to the right bank of the river, but it was difficult. We tried at different points, in vain. The officers, even with their horses, could not cross. We finally reached a vast plain where the waters increased in width and thus decreased in depth; there we were able to cross by stepping this way and that like ducks. If a good landscape artist had been there to sketch that crossing, he would have made the most wonderful painting of the kind ever seen. The Hebrews, they say, crossed the Red Sea on dry foot, thanks to their god Jehovah separating the waters for them. That god, or his son, should certainly have done as much for us, since we were there for his sake, for his ministers and his monks— to restore to their full powers his beloved children, routed by the wicked republicans. But no, our feet were not dry, and neither were our heads. We were soaked with water to the waist, and streaming with sweat to the brow, for marching that way, carrying packs through water, is without a doubt the hardest march there can be.

Late in the day we reached a village called Saucedat where we met up with the First Battalion of our regiment. This one was under the command of "old man La Maïs," so called because, as a German, he always used the feminine form where the masculine was called for, and he would tell his orderly: *"Co, Chosef, stijll corn ["la" for "le" maïs] fuhr mein horace she is hunger."*

There was only one sergeant with this company, and when people learned that I was a former non-com, I was promptly named warrant officer to assist him. This sergeant was a good man, not nasty in the least. I soon came to be an equal partner with him as if I were his equal in rank. We stayed at Saucedat for two weeks, our battalion alone; the other continued its advance toward Durango.

We were left on the front line facing the enemy, the real one this time. These were no longer gangs of thieves, and arsonists that we were dealing with; this was the Republican Army, which was coming from behind us as well. After two weeks, we set out once more for Durango. But when we had got within a few days' march of the capital, we turned back to Saucedat; in fact, our own company, together with the light infantrymen, went three stops farther on, and we reached a hacienda just as their Independence Day celebration was going on. There were bullfights, contests, dancing, fireworks, and general carousing. I took the occasion to talk with some of the revelers, to try to find out the state of political affairs, for I no longer understood anything about these marches and countermarches. But those poor Indians had no idea either; they had been told we were gone for good, and some Mexican officers had even come the night before to tell them the French were done for in Mexico. So they were quite surprised to see us back. However, we only stayed there a few days, and then returned to Saucedat to join our battalion. But the battalion went back down for several days, leaving us behind again, the two last companies. This intrigued me more and more. And there was no way to find anything out. Our officers knew no more than we did; they just had orders to stay there pending new orders and to keep a sharp watch, for the enemy was close upon us. In fact, by day, from high on the house terraces, we could see horsemen riding up to the city walls, and every evening came the announcement that we would be attacked during the night, but though we spent the night on alert and without sleep, the enemy never did come.

We spent some three weeks that way, imprisoned and barricaded in a corral. Finally one afternoon we were told to prepare to leave that night. And we did quit Saucedat in the middle of the night, clandestinely, with no ado. The next evening we were already far away, for we had marched half the night and the whole day. Despite that, the enemy was still on our heels and we had to spend the night on watch. And it was that way every day until we rejoined our battalion, which was waiting for us a few days' march from Durango. I was eager to arrive there for I would surely learn, from the newspaper *El Telegrafo* and from my learned friend, if he was still there, just what our situation was.

SO WE WERE RUN OUT

And so, as soon as we were there and settled in a convent, I hurried to the cabin of my old friend whom, fortunately, I found writing crouched over his books and journals, the only furnishings in the place. He recognized me instantly, despite the red braid on my sleeves, and came in delight to greet me, stroking my shoulder with his right hand, a Mexican's warmest gesture of friendship. Then he told me it was all over for us French, that we were now on our way home. And when I asked if it had all been negotiated, he said the Mexicans had nothing to negotiate with France, or rather with the Emperor of the French, except to demand damages and compensation for the vandalism, the robberies, and the crimes his generals had committed in Mexico. But they were going to ask nothing. They felt that this thug and murderer, and the whole of France along with him, would be punished enough by the shame and horror of so many crimes, and by losing the friendship of two great free nations, the North Americans and the Mexicans, who had honored and been utterly devoted to France until she committed those enormous, dreadful crimes. So, no negotiation.

The Emperor had simply been told by the United States to withdraw his troops from Mexico immediately. The Americans, who had just spent four years fighting for freedom, would not stand for the imbecile tyrant of France coming to impose chains on a people who were both friend and next-door neighbor to them. They had stationed sixty thousand men along the Mexican borders, ready to march in case the Emperor should refuse to comply immediately with their ultimatum. The Emperor, who had no notion what was happening over there, had sent General Castelneau with full powers to carry out the American orders to rid Mexico of the

French army presence.* "No," *el amigo Salvarez* said, "no treaties here, and no agreements; your criminal Bazaine and his murdering, thieving thug generals are invited pure and simple to get out of the country that they have disrupted and ruined. And they will leave hounded out by the contempt and jeers of the people. And worse yet, all the French nationals who had been living in Mexico, most of them rich and well-respected before that ignoble and criminal intervention, must go as well, and leave their fortunes behind; for the republicans, exasperated by so many atrocities committed here by Bazaine and his henchmen, will take revenge on your compatriots and on all the Mexicans who betrayed their own country by collaborating with Bazaine or that other wretch Maximilian, so-called Emperor of Mexico. The poor imbecile would do well to pack his bags and go fast too, and before the rest of you do, because an hour after the troops leave he'll be hanged. Now your scum de Morny† and his crony Jeker,‡ the two main instigators of all these crimes, can just go starve. They forced your sorry lord of an emperor to send an army over here to rob us of our millions to fill their own coffers. And indeed we have been robbed, by the hundreds of millions, but most of that went into the [private] coffers of Marquez, Forey, Saligny, Bazaine, and other great thugs and thieves. Let de Morny and Jeker get their share from those fellows. 'Thieves and scum are made for each other,' the saying goes."

Now I finally knew the ending. I knew why we were going

---

*Henri de Castelnau was assigned to evacuate the French troops. 30,000 sailed from Vera Cruz in early March 1867.

†Charles-Auguste de Morny, Napoleon III's half-brother, was Interior Minister and President of the legislature from 1854–1865; he incited the government to intervene in Mexico.

‡Jean-Baptiste Jecker: a French banker in Mexico, who plotted to bring about the intervention. He was shot by the Paris Communards in 1870.

away and why the liberals were pursuing us. With no peace treaty yet concluded, the liberals were still pursuing us as the enemy, and with all the more confidence because they knew they had the support of sixty thousand Americans, the same people who had issued the order for us to clear out fast. So we were being run out, the way marauding herds are run out—with whips and whistles. And some writers can be found, even among people who were there, to glorify that expedition which was nothing but an expedition of vandals, bandits, arsonists, and murderers. The notorious Dupin,[*] whose very name set the Mexicans trembling with fear and horror, committed more crimes in that country all by himself than [the legendary felons] Mandrin and Cartouche together ever committed in France. The Abbé Dominick, one such writer, called this expedition "magnificent" because the Emperor had declared that he was waging the war to reestablish order in Mexico, to give power to the bishops and freedom to the Jesuits and the thieving monks whom the republic had run out. There were writers in Spain, too, who had hailed the crimes and horrors committed there by Hernando Cortez and his bandits. Great bandits, deceivers, great murderers of men can always find writers to glorify them, to wreathe them in incense and deify them. The only gods that are ever proposed, or imposed, for the adoration of ignorant, benumbed populations are bloodthirsty monsters or cannibals. Most men who have written about that incredible Mexican expedition neither saw nor understood anything of what went on there. I later saw accounts of the expedition by a man named Loisillon. The fellow was a cavalry commander, but he was attaché to Bazaine's headquar-

---

[*]Charles du Pin (1814–1871), a mercenary in the Mexican army, later a colonel under Bazaine. He became leader of a band of soldier-brigands who sowed terror in Mexico.

ters and never left Mexico City except for a pleasure trip around Guanajuato and Guadalajara with that famous Prince Bibesco about whom there was so much talk out there; a self-described prince but mad as a hatter. And Loisillon boasted of being the friend of this madman, whose madness was apparently contagious. The stories he told about the campaign are clear proof that he had lost his mind, and the friend who had Loisillon's *Memoirs* printed posthumously in Paris did him a very bad turn.

The accounts by this lunatic, in fact the most contradictory of them, barely touch on anything but himself, the Mexico City orgies he attended together with clerical-party figures, whom he nonetheless called "corrupt," constant recriminations against the people who gave out promotions and decorations, who never gave him as many as he deserved. When he thought to discuss issues of the place—the war, policies of Bazaine, or Maximilian, or others—he could express nothing but coarse stupidities, each coarser than the last, and all of them contradictory. His accounts were addressed to a lady in Napoleon's court. And the friend who had these strange tales published said, in a preface as nonsensical as the accounts, that Loisillon's memoirs would be the best document to consult on matters Mexican, and the best guide for writing their history. *Ah! ma Doue Beniguet!*

We stayed for some time at Durango, which allowed me to go often to talk with *l'amigo Salvarez*, who knew the background of all these terrible matters and could foresee the approaching dénouement. At Durango, the French had put together a battalion of volunteers they termed "imperial troops": some French officers, noncoms, and corporals were assigned to it for training the volunteers, who had only joined up because they were paid a few piastres and promised more of them. My friend shrugged his shoulders when he saw it. He said that any Frenchmen who had gone into the battalion were simply training men to get shot, if they had the bad luck to stay on after their regiments left. He said Juarez' army was near at hand and merely awaiting our departure to enter Durango.

Finally, departure day arrived. Our company was posted on the Cerro de los Remedios. It is an old volcano, on whose summit stands a church to a saint whose specialty is healing people stung by scorpions—thus the name "Remedy Mountain," for in Mexico, because of the influence of the monks and the Jesuits, doctors and pharmacists are useless. The saints fill all their functions, at a nice profit.

As we were strapping on our packs to come down the mountain, we were very surprised—I especially—to see a company of that above-mentioned battalion of volunteers, with the Frenchmen commanding it, arrive to replace us. Reaching the square, we found our regiment set to leave. My *amigo Salvarez* came to say an *ultimo adios*, telling me that he would soon be following us and that we could meet again in Mexico City. The whole population of Durango was there to see us off, but with no demonstration. The non-commissioned officers and corporals who had enlisted in Maximilian's "imperial" battalion came up very sorrowfully to shake the hands of their comrades; they could sense that they were going to find themselves in a bad situation. We set out, but late on the third day those same French officers, sub-officers and corporals arrived in our camp, panting and exhausted. They had ridden day and night to catch up with us. The Republican Army had entered Durango, and those supposed "volunteers for Maximilian" had instantly run to greet the Mexican force with cries of "Long Live the Republic!" leaving their French officers flat. The officers managed to get out, with the non-coms and corporals, while the enthusiastic populace was busy greeting their national army. Poor Maximilian, if he had seen that spectacle, he would have rushed to get out as well. A few kilometers out of Durango, our fleeing Frenchmen came across a half-dozen men hanging from trees, among whom they recognized the city police commissioner. Knowing the fate that awaited them [from the approaching republicans], the victims had tried to escape to our army, the only one that could afford them a little protection for the time they were under its wing—all those sorry wretches who had betrayed their country.

IN MEXICO CITY

We took the same route back to Mexico City that we had taken to go up to Durango, except that this time there were no detours for expeditions to Jalpa, Tabasco, and Via Nueva. We crossed the Tropic [of Cancer] at Sombrerette again; but the sun was no longer there, it had gone off on its annual trip to the other tropic, of Capricorn. For this was at the turn of the year 1866 to 1867. In the course of that long march, we had lost two soldiers from our company, and we buried them in two small villages, with the whole company in attendance. Two others had deserted, and had probably met their deaths as well. If they had deserted in the early days, when the liberals were appealing to all the French with magnificent promises, they would have been welcomed. Now it was too late. Querétaro was the last big town before Mexico City; we stopped for a week there—the town that attained to a somber celebrity shortly afterwards from the death of poor Emperor Maximilian. When we reached the capital, it was overflowing with soldiers—French, Belgian, Austrian, and *margouillas*, (gray lizards), the name given those so-called "imperial" soldiers. But Bazaine still held the capital under his tyrannical civil and military laws; he had an army of undercover police, armed with sabers, daggers, and revolvers running wild through the town, day and night, sowing terror, particularly among the barkeeps, whom these thug-policemen would force to pay heavy fines, often without the slightest grounds. Emperor Maximilian meant nothing there. Meantime, our despot Bazaine, Loisillon's god, was ordering all the cannon of the citadel sawed in half, the gun-carriages destroyed, the cartridge-packs dismantled with the capsules set aside, and the gunpowder scattered into the water. And in a letter to his woman friend in Paris, Loisillon said that this Bazaine—so intelligent and adroit and self-confident—had solid and sensible ideas and would be the best guide for Maximilian; that with Bazaine plus a good army, Maximilian could in ten years become absolute ruler of Mexico, and would be in a position to reimburse France for all her expenses. The poor lunatic. Loisillon was perfectly suited to be the close friend of that idiot Prince Bibesco, who wrote as many foolish things about the Mexican campaign as Loisillon did himself.

One day, I was commanding the demolition work at the citadel, the men taking apart the cartridge-packs, when the poor lord Maximilian rode his horse past the doorway where I stood. On glancing inside and seeing so many soldiers at work, he asked me in rather poor French "what those soldiers were doing inside there." I told him frankly what they were doing. He went off without saying more, but saluting me as if I were his superior. And that made it so—I was more than he was. I was a corporal fulfilling the functions of a sergeant whereas he was only a nobody. However, seeing that this idiot intended to stay on after us, one day I took up a sheet of paper to write to him, laying out his situation now here in Mexico, and the still worse one he would find himself in when the French Army left. My Durango friend had made very clear all the political and other questions concerning his country, and along the road back I had met more good liberals, no longer afraid to speak, who confirmed everything he had told me. I do not know if this emperor of straw ever saw my letter, for these wretched kings and emperors are always surrounded by legions of courtiers who are not eager to have their masters know anything true about what goes on in their kingdoms. A few days later, though, Maximilian secretly left Mexico City and went to Orizaba. But there he was stopped, and he returned to the capital. Many people, among those who knew something of that miserable war, wondered what notion or what influence or what madness made Maximilian return to Mexico City just when the French army was about to quit the place forever. Yet it was not so hard to explain. All the churchmen who had rallied to Bazaine and to Maximilian, who had betrayed and sold out their own country to these two, now saw themselves doomed, and they determined that, at the least, the man to whom they had sold out their fatherland should stay there to die with them. They did not have much difficulty persuading this poor ignorant fellow that with Bazaine gone he would now truly be Emperor of Mexico; that the deeply religious Mexican populace listens exclusively to the voice of their clergy, and would proclaim him unanimously and enthusiastically as soon as they had been delivered from the tyrant Bazaine. And the poor idiot believed them, and let himself be persuaded. Back in the capital, and when the last French troops had left, they showed him an army, "the Imperial Army" that he had only to lead against the Republican forces and they would instantly scatter or, if he chose, surrender to [him], their Catholic emperor, Mexico's savior. And, intoxicated with praise and blinded by ignorance about everything, the fool climbed onto his horse and led his *margouillas* to Querétaro— where he was abruptly abandoned by his entire Imperial Army.

All the Mexicans went over to Juarez, shouting *"Viva la*

República! Viva Juarez!" Left alone with his aides-de-camp, His Imperial Majesty was seized, tried, condemned to death, and shot. It all happened just as *mi amigo Salvarez* had foretold, except that instead of hanging him, Juarez paid *El Emperador* the honor of shooting him. Thus ended the Emperor and the ephemeral Empire of Mexico. *Sic transit gloria mundi.* The Empress Carlota went mad. And that was the end of that Mexican campaign so highly praised from the start by Badinguet's courtiers, senators, and deputies, and which they considered to be "the grandest idea of the reign." That scene in Querétaro took place, of course, only after our departure, and, in fact, we learned of it only when we had got home to France.

THE LAST OF THE MEXICAN BULLETS

We were the last to quit the Mexican capital, the ducal realm of our rascal Bazaine, whom the republicans would have been happy to shoot as well. But the criminal was, as Loisillon said, "very intelligent, very adroit, and he knew how to get around obstacles when he couldn't surmount them with his great confidence." All the same, it must have been hard for him to leave the beautiful capital city which, as Duke of Mexico, he owned, where he had remarried—a stupendously rich countess, and where he had dallied and danced for three years. We were told he was on the journey with us, though we never saw him. He must have stayed hidden away in some carriage with his treasure. We left Mexico City again by the same route, and we arrived at Passo del Mache, where we had spent our first night on Mexican soil.

We were again the last, the rear guard, which in a retreat is the position of honor. There at Passo del Mache the honor was receiving the last bullets the Mexicans fired at the French Army in that country. As we sat eating our evening meal, shots rang out in the forest across from us and several shells landed in the middle of the camp. We took up our weapons and we were put into position, ready to form a square in case of attack. But after emptying their guns the red cavalrymen apparently left, for we heard nothing more. Though, we did remain on alert all night. From the Passo del Mache we marched on to Cameron, the site of the most terrible and most glorious feat of arms in the whole campaign. There a train picked us up and took us on to Vera Cruz. As we drew away from Cameron, we saw red cavalry in the woodland along the line; they bade us a last farewell by firing a few blunderbuss shots after the train. An hour later, the Mexican Republic was delivered of the presence of *los esclavos y bandidos de Napoleon tercero, el assassino* (the slaves and bandits of the murderer Napoleon III).

Indeed, upon arriving in Vera Cruz, we moved immediately from the train onto the barge to take us to the *Souverain*, the largest ship France possessed at the time. I had thus gone through Vera Cruz twice without seeing anything of the city except the wharf. Bazaine was also on board, we heard, but he hid away just as he had on the journey from Mexico City. That shameful and piteous retreat, those kicks in the rear from the Americans and the Mexican liberals, had probably made him ill. When we arrived on board the *Souverain*, another great transport ship, the *Magenta*, was setting forth loaded with troops like ours. The Gulf of Mexico was terribly rough, the sea was heaving great rolling mountains, and behind them the *Magenta* was lost to our view as if it had gone under. We soon set out ourselves. The enormous mass of the *Souverain*, its belly full of iron, flesh, and bone, had difficulty getting under way in those liquid mountains. At first I thought this colossal nine-story structure, taller than the Mexico City Cathedral, was built to defy the fury of the waves. But I was wrong, I soon saw that great mass being knocked about by the enormous swells to starboard and port, to bow and stern, tossed up to the crest of the waves like an empty coconut shell. And that went on for two nights and two days. The masts were lowered all the way to give the huge structure some equilibrium. It was sailing under steam now, at least the engine was laboring, but I believe the vast structure was barely advancing, the power of the engine being inadequate to move such a mass unless she could use the sails as well. We were moving north, though, and thus following a route opposite from the one by which we had entered the Gulf of Mexico. We sailed between Cuba's south coast and the Yucatan peninsula; on the way home we passed between the north coast of Cuba and the Florida peninsula. There, once again we crossed the Tropic of Cancer. The sea finally grew calm, and the ship could hoist the masts and sails again and resume normal progress toward Havana. There we stopped to take on provisions, and in those twenty-four hours I had the pleasure *de hablar* again, for the last time, the beautiful language of Cervantes and of Quixote de la Mancha, with the women who clustered around our ship to sell us those lovely succulent, nourishing fruits of the tropics.

After Havana, we never touched land again until Lisbon, where, for some reason, the *Souverain* halted for only a few hours. Then we came to Gibraltar, and dropped anchor at some cliffs cut into terraces and studded with stones and cannon from top to bottom. It would not do to approach those cliffs without asking John Bull's permission. The governor of these rocks came on deck to review our seamen and us as well, and—more important, certainly—to greet the Duke and Duchess of Mexico, and the little one too, for we had heard that Madame the Duchess had borne a child en route, in fact, right in the middle of the storm! What a fine birth for a great hero's son! He should have been baptized the Tempest's

Child. That day everyone saw Bazaine's macabre figure, which we had not seen since Mexico City. The English governor's visit did not last long, fortunately for the Marshal Duke, who was surely not very eager to discuss his sorry Mexican adventures. The band only had time to play the two British rigadoons, "Off to Syria" and "Got Salve the Quin." From Gibraltar to Toulon, we had a taste of another little storm, during which a poor sailor was killed stone dead, hit in the head by a hoist and knocked from the top of the main mast onto the deck. He was a family man, and a collection was taken on board for his widow and children. Disembarking at Toulon, we went and camped at the very spot where we'd embarked for the Italian campaign eight years before; then the next day, our packs on our backs, we set out for Aix along the same road we had taken to go to Italy.

I STARTED TELLING STORIES

Our regimental base was at Aix. There were twice the number of troops at that base as in the battle forces returning from Mexico. In fact, those men almost all dispersed in short order, many took their final discharge, others went on midterm or extended leave. The regiment was replenished with young recruits from the base. There was a devil of a to-and-fro for a week. In fact, I was standing in as a sub-deputy sergeant and still obliged to run my squad, which was now made up exclusively of young recruits new to the regiment. I had so much work, confusion, and trouble during that week that I fell ill from it. I even went to the clinic to ask the doctor for a few days of bed rest. But the doctor apparently found me sicker than I thought I was, because instead of giving me two or three days' bed rest, he put me into the hospital.

It was both a military and civilian hospital, run by nuns,

like all the hospitals in France at the time; there has been much talk about these nurses, from various standpoints. Some people think them excellent, others very bad. I found myself in their care on three or four occasions during my military career, and I declare that I never had reason to complain of them; quite the contrary. I preferred seeing one of those girls at my bedside to some arrogant, brutal doctor. At Aix, there were two of them caring for the military men, one older and one young, both charming girls with whom you could get on nicely, even laugh and joke if it was done gently and politely. They did wear crosses and rosaries, true, but the way other women wear earrings and bracelets. They mumbled prayers morning and night, but the way other girls hum love songs. They took a particular interest in me when I told them I was an atheist free-thinker. They had never seen one. They had heard tell of them, though, and they thought an atheist must be some fearsome monster. But when they saw that this atheist was a humble little fellow—shy, polite, affable, mild, not affected or hypocritical—they grew more and more interested in my odd person. All the more since I was a Breton from Catholic Brittany. I very much enjoyed chatting with them, as well, for I saw that they had not completely lost their human personalities, which usually does happen to all the clericocos who enter into the bosom of the Church, given that the church leaders teach them to link everything, consecrate everything, to God, and nothing, absolutely nothing, to humankind. Mainly, those two girls were beautiful. And physical beauty makes for moral beauty as well. There were many soldiers in that hospital, a half-dozen non-commissioned officers: sergeants, quartermasters, sergeant majors. Three or four of them made officer later on, which allowed me to note yet again what poor lumber goes into constructing big military leaders. It would be impossible to find men more stupid, more ignorant, more cretinous than those non-coms, all of them products of the same schools, incidentally—the schools of the *fratres ignaries jesuitorum,* whose mission is to instruct children for the purpose not of making them into men and citizens, but of making them into slaves and cretins. These future officers infuriated me so, with their unbelievably stupid discussions and arguments, that to kill time, and to entertain myself and the men on the ward who asked me to, I started telling stories, beginning with some of the Breton tales, the kinds I described at the start of this account.

Once I began, I could not stop. Every night at bedtime, from all corners of the dormitory, men would shout, "Go on, corporal! You've got to finish last night's story. I have a nice cup of tea for you here when you get thirsty!" And that's how it went night after night.

When I had gone through the Breton tales and legends I knew by heart, I was forced to make up new stories out of whole cloth. That showed me how easy it is to fabricate some sort of novel. Victor Hugo, one of the great novelists, was said to write a book in a week, and at the time people thought that was miraculous. I even read his famous *Bugh Jargal,* which resembles so many other novels, tales, or legends. As for me, there at the hospital, they'd give me only twenty-four hours to invent something—a story or a legend, same thing. But my audience, which included those future officers, proved that I was good at inventing. True, those listeners did not know I was making the stories up. The only thing that surprised them was seeing that, as they believed, my brain was a bottomless well of tales and novels and legends, myths and stories.

We were not too bored in that pleasant hospital, at least in our military ward, where there were really not many seriously ill patients. Most of them, notably the non-coms, were there

because of the *male mulierum cupidus venusis*,* a disease supposed to have been brought into France by the Neapolitans or
by Christopher Columbus's sailors. It was very much in vogue
in the regiment at the time, and one which many old troop-
ers carefully kept active so they could go to the hospital when
they had enough of the service. I stayed nearly a month in that
nice place, and I could have stayed longer still if I'd wanted.
But I had been promoted again. Right while I was in the hospital, I was made a corporal of light infantry, a rank that had
suited me wonderfully during my first term of service. I could
not stay on at the hospital without getting myself a bad name
with my new colleagues, whom I did not know yet. I was
assigned to the Third Light Infantry Battalion, stationed in
Avignon. So to Avignon I went on the same day I left the
hospital.

THE BRETON AND THE CORSICAN GET ALONG FINE

I took the train to Aix and that evening I joined my new company, which was billeted in the Palace of the Popes. The
evening roll call was done, the soldiers were already in bed. A
man from my company, who was on duty at the Palace gate,
escorted me to the dormitory and announced me, the new
corporal. Immediately from the far end of the hall there came
a loud voice, sounding stern and official:
"All right, corporals—up and out to the canteen to welcome
our new colleague."

Everyone answered at once from all over the vast hall: "Yes,
yes, here we come!"

And the men of the Eighth Squad called out, "Over here,
corporal, your bed's all ready."

---

*"A disease caught from women when a man is too avid for Venus": syphilis.

They had known I was to arrive that day or the next. Soon I was surrounded by my seven new colleagues, and we went down to the canteen. The one who had ordered the others up called for a giant Italian punch for all of us.

I knew none of these new colleagues. Of the seven present, six were former non-coms like myself, and all six were Corsican. The other, the young one, was from Normandy. The six former non-coms had done what I did; they took their discharges after the seven years' term. Two of them had even served fourteen years. But finding no means of livelihood elsewhere, they re-enlisted. So this gathering was a kind of non-com reception. We drank punch after punch, chatting all the while about all sorts of things. But soon the Corsicans fell to speaking Italian, and they were quite startled to see that I continued the conversation with them as if they hadn't switched languages. Only the poor Normandy boy could no longer follow. . . .

The old Corsican and I came to be real friends. The Breton and the Corsican got on extremely well. We were both philosophy-minded, a rare pair to find together in the army. We could talk and argue on many topics. For, having no need to worry over his future, freed from any vainglory and ambition, and with his natural good sense and reason kept intact amid the brain-dulling conditions of the job, the man had begun studying, reasoning, and reflecting. Unfortunately he had been to school, and school always starts by teaching children wrong things, lies, wrong information, and wrong moral values. And all those wrong notions put into young minds stay graven there for good. The Jesuits who still run our schools—to the great delight of those who exploit ignorance—know this very well, and they will not change the educational system. And therefore my new friend, who considered himself educated, was educated only in wrong knowledge. He had some acquaintance with general history as set out by Bossuet, of

French history as concocted by Loriquet, of Napoleon's history as told by the man himself or by his friends and admirers. And he had taken for fact all the errors, the lies, the falsehoods promulgated in the books that these exploiters of mankind put together; he had taken for heroes and gods all those thieves and murderers who are simply monsters. In a word, *mio amico* Orticoni—that was his name—lacked a critical mind.

So we would go for long walks in the countryside around Avignon, talking, arguing, philosophizing in two languages, sometimes in Italian and sometimes in French. And occasionally, when we had a little money to spare, we would go and play some billiards or chess, for *mio amico* loved noble games, games of knowledge and art—both are needed to play them.

PROMOTED TO SERGEANT

It was now the first of January, 1868. And suddenly *l'amico* Orticoni and I were told that we had been promoted to sergeant. "Fine," says Orticoni, "it's the two philosophers." He snatches up my tunic and his own and carries them off to the tailor to sew on gold stripes in place of the wool ones. An hour later, we left the area with our new colleagues to wish our officers a happy new year, since now we too bore the title of officers, lower-grade. And that evening we attended a colossal punch-party given by the regimental officers for their non-coms. There in Aix, all the non-coms in a battalion were billeted in the same hall. So Orticoni and I found ourselves together again, for I was assigned to the Second and he to the Third [companies] of the Third Battalion. We joined a great roomful of non-coms, a collection of all types of characters . . .

There were men from every country, every trade, and every religion, which often gave rise to quite venomous discussions—quarrels, rather—with all those fine barrack-room epithets that make up a whole separate language the *Académie française* knows nothing about, and neither do Messers. Ramolot and Ronchonot, despite their reputation as the most advanced experts in military lexicography.

However, we also had a barrack-room chief, the oldest ranking soldier, of course. He was also, or at least claimed to be, a Freemason—that is to say, "fearless and faultless," as he said himself, and for the most part people believed it. He was responsible for cleanliness and good order in the barracks, and he demanded and got obedience, with no back talk, for many men feared he would challenge them to a duel, which he invariably did in response to an insult. Some of the usual foulmouthed, stupid, tedious squabbles would occur between Jews, Protestants, and Catholics. But the disputants did not get very far, for from his corner, the chief, the Freemason, would call in his loud, commanding voice, "Will you shut the fuck up with your crap gods . . ."

And if anyone protested he would say instantly: "If you don't like it, you know, the foils are right here, and they're not here for stringing beads."

My friend Orticoni and I never joined in those vulgar idiotic squabbles. The *amico* owned a chess set, and if we had to stay in the barracks on weekly duty or some such, we would entertain ourselves at the noble game the other men understood nothing about. When we were free, we would walk over the countryside, talking philosophy as we went, and at night we would go to play a game of billiards.

THE HERMIT BEE-LOVER

One day, walking and talking philosophy on the footpaths outside Aix, we found ourselves at a little fenced farmyard with a sign on the gate in large letters:

MARCELLIN, Apiculturist.

"What kind of work is that?" asked Orticoni.

"That," I said, "is the practice of bee-keeping."

But as we talked at the gate, Monsieur the Beekeeper, who was walking about beneath the trees of his bee farm, appeared and very politely invited us to come into his hermitage—for that is what it truly was, although inhabited by several million winged denizens. He showed us his apiary, a new design. It was a long shed inside which the hives sat on racks one above another. The bees entered and left their respective hives through slits cut into the shed wall, each slit opening directly into a hive. They all had glass panes at the rear through which the beekeeper could observe the interior state of the hive without disturbing the bees and without inconvenience to himself. The hives were square and made of white spruce-wood. He would set the hives one on top of another, and when both were full he would lift away the upper one and put an empty one beneath the other. It was very simple and convenient. He never risked being stung by his bees. He did not need to kill off those good workers, smother them, as is done almost everywhere, in order to harvest their output.

When we had seen everything, he took us into his *bastide*, a little cottage with only the one floor but lacking nothing for comfort. He served us drinks of all sorts of liqueurs he had made out of honey and fruits. We ate honey cakes as well—in his house as in the house of the Nordic gods, everything was made of honey. He had written a brochure describing his system, which for two and a half francs he would send to anyone who asked for it. He also went around to the chateaus in the area to give practical training to any of the gentry who wanted to take up bee-keeping as a hobby. In the end, my friend and I concluded that this man must surely be the happiest person in the world, and Orticoni promptly declared that he would adopt the system as soon as he finished his military service. I said as much myself. But, unfortunately, I saw that a system of such skillful, intensive cultivation was only practicable in warm climates, where the bees could gather pollen almost year round. In Brittany, the honey season is just a few weeks long, late July and early August, and if the weather is bad during those few weeks the year's [labor] comes to naught. Still, a meticulous beekeeper could earn five or six francs a year per hive, so with a hundred of them, he could live like a lord. From that day on, we talked constantly about bees and about our plans for the future. The hermit-beekeeper's fine independent existence made us envious. Orticoni already had a brother in Corsica, he said, who lived like that, not from bees but from chickens and rabbits—an old philosopher like himself, who cared not a whit for the grandeurs and vainglories of this world. We went back several more times to visit the hermit bee-lover, and we were always made welcome.

TO MY OLD BRITTANY I SHALL RETURN

At that time, the Emperor began dismantling his army, to the great delight of the Prussians, who were in the process of building theirs up. He decided to do away with the elite companies, the grenadiers and light infantry, which did such valuable service in battle and were a spur to illiterate rank-and-file soldiers, whose sole ambition was to become grenadiers or light infantrymen themselves. A sergeant or corporal could be given no more gratifying honor than an assignment to those elite companies. So the announcement of the decree caused great consternation throughout the regiments. At the same time, old soldiers who had served more than fourteen years were refused re-enlistment. It was felt that fourteen years of good service must have used up a man's powers, and Castellane didn't want another seven years from them. The bastard said a good soldier should be worn out too by the time he'd worn out a greatcoat made to last seven years. My friend

Orticoni, who was finishing up his third hitch, said: "I'm in a fine fix—twenty-one years in the army and now I'll have to go begging for my bread."

"What about the bees?" I said.

"Yes, sure, that's true. Living like our friend the beekeeper isn't bad. But it still takes money to get started."

"Your brother who makes a living from his chickens and rabbits—he'll help you set up as a beekeeper near him. That shouldn't cost too much, starting off small, which is the best way to pull it off. As for me, I'll be discharged in a few months, and I have my plan all set. Where I come from, there's a certain uninhabited spot—at least up to now, the only inhabitants were wolves, foxes, boars, stags, badgers, hares, rabbits, all sorts of birds, and then there were elves, too, and *corrigans,* wood sprites and water sprites. The original ones, the wolves, boars and stags, are gone now, but the small game are still there with their fur and feathers, and there's a stream, too, where you can get salmon, trout, and eels. Way back in that place full of woods and bramble and rock . . . that's where I mean to go set up my hermitage. It seems to me that with my modest tastes and my way of thinking, I could live in peace there. And if not, I'll still have the supreme last resort; I'll take the road to Nirvana, into the nothingness I came from. There's room there for everyone. I won't ask a thing more of anybody.

"The first time I went back home, when I was twenty-six and in good form, healthy, vigorous, and eager to work, I had found no means of employment anywhere, so it would be pointless to go asking for it now after fourteen years of army service and as many campaigns. I would gladly have returned to Mexico, where I could have found a dozen different jobs to choose from, but we have committed so many misdeeds and crimes in that country that the word 'Frenchman' is and will forever be as much accursed as the word 'Spaniard.' I have a friend there, a rich, learned man who would certainly welcome me with open arms, but he could not keep other people from damning me as a Frenchman. So it's back to my old Brittany I'll go, and I'll settle in amid that tangle of brush and rocks they call the Stang-Odet—the Odet River valley—where I spent my childhood. The *stang* is something like your Corsican *maquis*—it's terrain where nonjuring priests* hid out during the revolution's Reign of Terror." The *amico filosofo* nodded approval, and we went off to play a game of billiards.

"LONG LIVE THE EMPEROR!"

We had orders to resume the journey, this time with no halt until the camp at Châlons, where we arrived just in time to start the grand maneuvers; a nice rest! The Emperor arrived there as well, a few days after us. It was exactly ten years earlier that I had seen him there. But back then he was making a triumphal tour, had just shown off his lovely Spanish Lady to the Bretons and the Normans, and was on his way to Rheims to get the holy flask, the little vial of celestial oil, poured over his criminal head. At that time, when his coiffeur had spent an hour or two massaging and putting-over the lines on his face, he was at least presentable. But alas, these days, there was no way to smooth out or fill in the foul markings of that mournful mask. Seeing him pass by us, I really did think it was a mask, and among the ugliest and most grotesque that could be. It reminded me of the face of Quasimodo, that character in Victor Hugo whose face horrified even himself. The lovely Eugénie was not traveling with the Emperor this time; only the imperial prince followed behind his grotesque papa like Sancho Panza following Don Quixote.

As he progressed before the encampments, the soldiers, at least some, would shout as per order and upon command:

---

*Priests who refused the secularizing laws of 1793.

"Long Live the Emperor, Long Live the Empress, Long Live the Imperial Prince!" . . . and even those plaintive-sounding cheers were liberally sprinkled with other shouts, more vulgar expressions that could sound almost the same—they ended in "ore" and "ress" and "ereal."

In the course of that year, the Châlons camp was trying out various new maneuvers, which were real child's play, and must have brought smiles to the lips of the foreign officers who came from all over the world to observe them. I nearly got myself killed by my own rifle. Those famous "chassepot" guns[*] had been assembled hastily, and never even tested. The barrel on mine was visibly warped; I pointed it out to my captain, who said it was nothing. But the first shot I fired, the barrel burst in two and the recoil was so strong that I fell over backwards, my four paws in the air. They thought I was dead, but I got off with a contusion on the shoulder that exempted me from the maneuvers, which I no longer needed since I was soon to be discharged for the second and last time. It was pointless to imagine staying on in the army for the rest of my career. Every day I was seeing soldiers and non-coms leaving after fourteen years' service, men who were no longer wanted. They were considered too worn out. I saw a sergeant major who had served for twenty-one years and in eighteen different campaigns. The poor old fellow was weeping as he left. He would now have to go begging for his bread, after giving all his time, his youth, his capacities to his nation. I could not help weeping with him—not over my own fate which, however clearly laid out, was just as sad as his, but over the injustices, the iniquities, and the crimes to which the exploited poor are always and everywhere subjected to, by a mob of scoundrels and trash who deck themselves out in many-colored robes, in helmet and plumed hats, in gold and silver embroideries,

---

[*]11-caliber rifles with a range of 1,200 meters.

and take themselves titles of *majesty, holiness, eminence, lordship* in order to fleece, bleed, and slaughter the poor.

I finished out my fourteen years of service to the day, on the 11th of September 1868. My colleagues asked what I would be doing next, after fourteen years of army service and as many campaigns. I told them I was going to become a hermit, in a place similar in every respect to the mountains they had seen out in Crimea, the Kordambels; a river runs through them, the Chornaiya, that looks like the Odet that runs through our mountains at home, which the French call "Stangall" and the Bretons call "Stang-Odet." The soldiers didn't believe a word of it, of course, and that hardly mattered. Anyhow, I was discharged on the 10th, and that very evening I took the train at Mourmelon. My good old friend Orticoni came with me to the station, where we arrived with two hours to spare, two hours spent comfortably chatting and drinking for the last time. I was not weeping, like the old sergeant major I mentioned above. On the contrary, I was singing, for I felt free now, and I would not be obliged, as he said he was, to go begging my bread right away. With the money I had waiting in army credit and in the savings bank, I could put together about two thousand five hundred francs, which would easily allow me to live for two thousand five hundred days, or seven years, if I should find no other livelihood. With joy and hope, I said a last *addio al carissimo amico Orticoni*, paraphrasing lines from Dante: "*Me voi con ogne speranza, en mia povera Bretagnia*" (I go with every hope to my poor Brittany.) I promised to write him as soon as I was settled in my hermitage. But I was figuring without fate, that blind and irresistible force that reigns over all things in this little earthly world. As the Mohammedans say, it's futile for man to seek out his destiny, for his destiny will seek him out. On my way through Paris, I decided to stop over for twenty-four hours to gaze once more on that enormous human anthill before entering into life in the wild.

III

THE FARMER

1868–1882

THE PRODIGAL RICH MAN

I reached Quimper on a Saturday, just on the eve of the great festival of Kerdévot. On leaving the train I looked up an old porter like that good fellow Robic, the old man who had piloted me into the army fourteen years earlier. I asked if he knew the tavern keeper LeGac, and whether he was still alive.

"Yes," he answered. "He's still got his tavern."

"Well," I said, "help me carry my trunk there, and you won't regret your trouble."

For I had bought a trunk at the Châlons base, and stuffed it with clothes and all sorts of gear, enough to last me a good long while. This LeGac was a distant uncle of mine; he did not quite recognize me, but when I told him whose son I was—Déguignet's—acquaintance was quickly established. He knew my other old uncle very well, the former gendarme whose house I hoped to stay at while I prepared to settle in the Odet Valley, the Stang-Odet, near where he lived. Once the acquaintance was established with the uncle, the aunt, and the children, I stood the old porter to a drink, as much as he wanted, and gave him another fifty sous for his ten-minute labor.

"*O fei vat!*" * said the aunt, when she saw me hand the porter two silver coins. "You must be very rich!"

"Oh, yes, auntie, right now I am rich, and since I spent a long time holding out my empty hand in these parts, now I'd like to hold it out full to the needy."

The aunt had one daughter left to marry off, and immediately offered her to me. But a farmer from Le Guélennec, over in Ergué-Gabéric—where my gendarme Uncle Le Quéré lived—who had come to the Quimper market, recognized me in the tavern and offered to drive me and all my baggage right out to Uncle Le Quéré's door. So I left with him, to the great despair of Uncle and Aunt LeGac and even, I do believe, of the young cousin, who all thought I must be a millionaire. This old farmer, at whose place I had often begged in the past, and where I had been a farmhand, drove me in his cart to the old gendarme, who had built a little house on the road out of Le Guélennec; he lived there with his sister—my aunt and godmother both—managing with his small pension, a little garden, and a cow.

The two old people were somewhat surprised to see me turn up without warning. They had left off thinking of me, it was so many years since they had had any word. But they had no time to express their astonishment, for the villagers who saw me coming through, and among whom I had still other relatives, soon crowded into the cottage. The old grower who had brought me there went off, spreading the news that he had just driven little Jean-Marie Déguignet, the onetime beggar-boy, to the gendarme Quéré's house with a trunk and a sack full of gold and silver, not to mention pockets crammed with twenty-franc coins. The rumor ran rapidly through the village. And so all those folks came to see. In that large village,

---

*Roughly, "Good heavens!"

where there were more poor people than rich, many brought
their little children along, in the obvious hope of picking up
a few sous from the rich cousin or uncle—for by now I was
everybody's cousin or uncle. Those youngsters were very
happy that night: I gave out all the sous I had with me. I knew
what a pleasure it was to be given sous; well, I took still greater
pleasure in giving them. I was happy to play the prodigal rich
man at least once in my life.

When the gogglers had gone, I told my uncle and my godmother my plans to settle by myself in the Stang-Odet, and to
live there as a hermit with bees, hens, and rabbits. But these
oldsters were a couple of Bretons. Now, Bretons are often
described as great believers, but they never believe a thing
except the unbelievable. My two oldsters started laughing, of
course, for they assumed I was talking the way Bretons usually
talk—teasing, sarcastic, and ironical.

THE GREAT *PARDON* OF KERDÉVOT

The next day, Sunday, was the big Kerdévot religious festival.*
I set out early in the morning to make the rounds of the commune, going first to the houses of old people I knew, then to
the mayor's, to tell him I was coming to live here. Everywhere
I was well received, much better than in the past when I went
door to door at these same farms with my hand outstretched,
mumbling my *Paters* and *Ave Marias*. I was even invited to dine
with the mayor, the grand dinner for the Kerdévot *Pardon*,
with the important figures of the district. In Breton there is a
proverb that goes: "*Daou, tri sort amzer n'eus in den neket hanet
neil ous i ben.*" (Man goes through two or three kinds of time,

---

*The great *Pardon* of Kerdevot, on the second Sunday of September, is the
most heavily attended of that region of Finistère.

all of them quite different.) That is not true for everyone. I know many people here whose existence has hardly varied at all. But for me, that day at the mayor's house was a great change. In the past, I would have stood at the doorstep mumbling prayers as I waited for a crêpe, or a bit of black bread, or a pinch of buckwheat or oat flour, and now I was sitting at the head of the table in the place of honor. And there were old men and women there who readily recalled the contrast, of course to my great credit and praise, though uttered with a glint of irony because Bretons cannot speak any other way. To their mind, sincerity and forthrightness are vices.

After dining copiously at the mayor's house, I went to look in on the *pardon*, and found that nothing had changed. At the entrance I saw again the same cripples, the same paralytics lining the road, loudly demanding the pity of passersby in jeremiac and "jalimic" [*sic*] tones, on crutches, missing arms or legs, some displaying hideous, horrible wounds that they often maintained on purpose to excite compassion, others afflicted with half a dozen little ragamuffins, artistically arrayed in order of size on beds of straw or fern fronds. And it was in the name of God and of Mary his mother, Notre-Dame de Kerdévot, that all these wretches were imploring charity, and in the name of those same fictions they got it—mankind had nothing to do with it. It was not "alms" these wretches were being given; it was funds invested at high interest, for the donors were supposed to get a hundred times the value back in graces and indulgences, as it is told in the Gospel: "And Timothy said: the rich man who gives is also building a future treasure invested on a solid base."

The general look of this great *pardon* was much as I had known it in the past. The esplanade was entirely covered with drinking stalls and long white tents, which were filled with people drinking *camots* and *demi-camots**—blackish water mixed with the worst-quality brandy. I still saw men and women moving around the chapel, some standing, others crawling on their knees. But now I could note that despite the epithets laid on Bretons as to their ignorance and fanaticism, I had seen other peoples still more ignorant and fanatical, just as often among various sorts of Christians as among Mohammedans. I had seen Russian muzhiks crawling on their knees to reach the Holy Sepulchre in Jerusalem, supposedly following Christ's Via Dolorosa, and burning their foreheads, breasts, and other body parts with candle stubs lighted from the fire of the Holy Spirit. In Mexico, I had seen women crawling on their knees, skirts lifted, behind the carriage of some potbellied bishop, and on one Holy Friday I had seen a reenactment of every scene of the Passion with some poor fool offering himself up to torments as if he were Jesus Christ. The insanities of religion can go no further. At Kerdévot, though, I noticed that miracles were in shorter supply, there were not so many sacks of grain, so many sheep, oxen, or heifers, as I had seen in the past being offered up from people cured by miracles and from those who hoped to be. This is probably because despite her many offspring, the Lady cannot manage too many commercial establishments at once. Here in Brittany she had run several successively, probably thanks to her mother, their prime patron,† but one after another they all went into decline, especially ever since the Great Industrialist [Mary] transferred her operational headquarters to the Pyrenees.‡ Anyway, I did walk through and observe the

---

*From the Breton word *mikamo,* a blend of coffee and brandy.

†Saint Anne, mother of Mary, is patron saint of Brittany.

‡To Lourdes, where in 1858 young Bernadette Soubirous saw visions of the Virgin. The site became a major center of Catholic pilgrimage.

whole festival, despite appeals from all sides, for already the legend of the stupendously wealthy non-commissioned officer, broadcast by the old Le Guélennec farmer the night before, was widely known, and people stared after me with curiosity.

But I did not linger long talking with the ones who stopped me, and this gave the legend still greater substance. One of the richer peasants in the commune seemed to be jealous of me, and showed his feelings by asking harshly, in a roughneck's crude French, where I'd stolen my sergeant's stripes from, because he had done seven years' service too and he hadn't even made corporal, despite having ten times my talent and abilities. But it was clear that he was an ass, and I pretended not to hear or understand him; for with such people any explanation or reasoning is futile. The only way to convince them that you are their better is to knock them down and plant your foot on their throat.

Finally, despite the many invitations offered me, I managed to slip away from that infernal scene, and I set out for Le Guélennec over familiar fields and trails, more convinced than ever that I could no longer be happy anywhere but off alone in the Stang-Odet, which I was eager to go explore, to find the site for my retreat. The old man and the godmother were startled to see me turn up so early at the house, they had not even expected me that day. We talked a long while again in the evening, and I was very surprised to see that this former gendarme, who had served for thirty years, twenty of them in Paris, had remained completely Breton. He had held on to all the ideas and superstitions of his birthplace. He had forgotten nothing and learned nothing, except for constructing two additional fetishes for himself: the Brumaire man and the December man.* You could not hold a reasonable conversa-

------

*Napoleon I and Napoleon III.

tion with him on any subject at all but the Paris streets he had tramped for twenty years, and the poachers in the Côtes-du-Nord where he had wound up his flatfoot career.

I SHALL SET UP AN APIARY

When I described my plan to go live in the Stang-Odet, my uncle told me the *stang* was still, and more than ever, haunted by ghosts and *corrigans,* and that the old *groac'h* (the ugly fairy) still ruled there. He said he had seen her many times. She was a tall woman, her body pure white, with a crown of holly on her head. He had seen the *corrigans* too, those evil little gnomes who loved to work all kinds of mischief on nighttime travelers unlucky enough to pass nearby the places where they dwelt or frolicked. Earlier, I told the story of those goblins and sprites that my father also saw regularly. Of course, my godmother had seen them all too, and other things besides. She asked whether I had visited the priest. When I told her that I meant to have no more to do with priests, not that one nor any others, she moaned in sorrow and called on the Virgin Mary and her sweet Jesus to help her save the poor wandering godson. With my father and mother long since gone, the old woman believed it her duty to watch over me, for she knew all her prayers and her catechism: the Breton catechism says that in the absence of parents, the godfather and godmother are responsible for their godchild's Christian upbringing and spiritual welfare. The woman began running again and again through the evening prayers, in which she made a point of including a *Pater* and a *Mater* for her godson's conversion. Throughout that night, I considered how impossible it would be for me to live among these people. Better to return to Mexico at the risk of getting myself killed, if I could not settle in the Stang-Odet far from any contact with my miserable compatriots.

And so the next day, I set out early to walk the gorges and cliffs I had walked so often as a boy. But I saw that the Odet valley had undergone great changes. Lumber merchants had come into the country with mechanical saws, and had found a way to take the centuries-old oak trees out of those gorges we had thought were inaccessible. Still, enough woods, thorn, and bramble remained. I went first to Griffonez, one of the big farms that bordered on the Stang-Odet and owned the largest part of it—the steepest, wildest, most inaccessible part.

This was the area where those resistant Breton priests went to hide during the Terror [of 1793], in a place called Bec Ar Grip, where there is nothing but rocks, chasms, and precipices. I made my way to the cave where the terrified priests had taken refuge for fear of Guillotin's machine, which at the time was more powerful than their all-powerful god. In that spacious cave, which is still called Toul ar Veleien (the Priest's Hole) a person can live comfortably and well, and be safe from unwanted visits, for it takes boldness, skill, and agility to find one's way there. It would even take knowing Ali Baba's secret words. Unfortunately, there is neither water nor wood there, and not an inch of arable land.

So I left the Toul ar Veleien to look for a better location. There is no shortage of space, actually, for those titanic gorges are some sixteen kilometers long, with what the Castilians would call *el lindo Odet* (the beautiful Odet) flowing swift and turbulent along the bottom. Everywhere on the walls of these *stangs* there are caves, natural dwelling-places for the supernatural beings, the *corrigans*. I felt true happiness ranging alone and free through this wild country, the witness of my younger years, where I used to gather firewood and acorns to feed the pigs, and bird's nests, hazelnuts, and *luz* (blueberries), and wild blackberries too. I had already seen several quite likely sites by the time I finally stopped at a spot called

Loch Tano. There was a little spring murmuring among the crags, and it was surrounded by a vast forest of oak, walnut, holly, birch, bramble, and thornwood. Wild native fruits were everywhere, the same fruits that must have fed our earliest ancestors before they invented tools to till the earth. I quickly made my plans: I would build a cottage, by myself and in my own way—there were stones and wood aplenty; and then I would set up a covered apiary for a hundred hives, row above row. But I would start with just thirty, which would cost me about three hundred francs. Then I would see. I expected I could also clear a few acres of land to plant vegetables. That way I would have work to do all year round, on top of hunting and fishing, for I could see that the fish and small game had not all vanished yet. My bees would give me four months of work, from early June when swarming usually starts to the end of September, the time for selling and for processing the honey and the wax. During the winter I could till the land, hunt, and fish, and then I would also have hives to build. Not moveable, crafted hives like the ones I had seen down in Aix, at our friend the expert beekeeper's; I was sure that such hives only make sense in specially favored territory where the bees can gather nectar nearly year-round so it is possible to do intensive, scientific apiculture. But here, where the bees can find honey only in midsummer, in July and early August, small straw hives are sufficient, and they are easy to make and to handle. I planned, in fact, to bring certain improvements to the system, as experience showed me what was useful and advantageous. Everything in this world can be improved, given that the creator made nothing perfect himself. The straw hives are actually the best homes for the bees. When well constructed, such hives protect them from the winter cold and the great heats of summer. I could certainly build a few out of wood planks with glass panes at the rear, like the ones I had seen in Aix, but it would be just for pleasure—to let me observe the interior workings of the colony, so curious and amazing to watch.

On the topic of those little creatures, Bretons have, and I believe will always have, the most erroneous ideas, as, by the way, they have on a good many other creatures and things. Peasants—my father for one—who have been raising bees their whole life long know nothing about how these insects construct the fine internal architecture of their homes, nor how they reproduce. The best and most experienced of Breton beekeepers will tell you that those are secrets no one knows and no one will ever know. There is a legend, like so many in Brittany, that says it is absolutely forbidden for any beekeeper to seek to discover the secrets of the bees' labors. He must not even wonder about such questions, or he will be severely punished, as many have already been punished, according to the legend. My father, an old experienced beekeeper, used to say—and everyone believed him—that bees that swarmed in the week after the holy days of Corpus Christi or the Blessed Sacrament all built replicas of the Blessed Sacrament on the inside of their hives, even though he had certainly never seen such a thing himself except in his dreams. Just as he insisted that if the mother bee, or queen, should die, she could be replaced by a sprig of rye dipped in pig excrement.

Pondering all these things and sucking on wild blackberries, I climbed down to the edge of the stream and sat down, my feet dangling above the limpid, tumbling waters of the *lindo* Odet, which reminded me of various other watercourses I had seen as I roamed the world, particularly the Charnoïa in Crimea. Watching the water flow, I smoked a cigarette and fell asleep. I needed it, for by then I had scarcely closed my eyes for several nights. As I slept, my spirit, ever restless, set off on a jour-

ney. In that short moment it roamed over all the events of my
wandering life, from the day, the first I remember, when I
nearly died of scratches and terror in a field of brush and
thorn not far from here, right up to my return today, then the
spirit came back into me and woke me up. As I woke, I seemed
to hear a bugle call to arms, for I thought I was in Jalpa, a town
in Crimea, where I once spent a gloomy night on the banks of
a stream like the Odet. But I soon came to myself and recognized my situation. Night had fallen, probably long since. The
moon glowed faintly on the treetops. The time was right for
the night prowlers—the hares, rabbits, badgers, otters, and
the gnomes and fairies. I could not keep from thinking of
those last creatures of the night, so permanently does a man
harbor in his head the earliest notions people put there. Now,
my own head had been crammed with legends, with ghosts and
goblins, fairies and gnomes, and now here I was, smack in the
world of those night denizens, and just at the hour when they
turn to their nocturnal labors and frolics. It was no good shaking my head or telling myself it was really too stupid to dwell
on such foolishness; those primitive ideas from my childish
brain persisted. Of course, those imaginary beings did not
frighten me now. If I had been in the same situation at the age
of twelve, I would have run out of there with my eyes shut and
my hair standing straight up on my head like the needles of an
angry porcupine, and silently praying *Our fathers* and *Ave
Marias* to Our Lady of Kerdévot, imploring her to come protect me against all those evil night creatures. Fortunately, I
knew roughly where I was, having so often tramped these *stangs*
in the past. I knew that somewhere nearby was a path leading
from the stream halfway up the slope to a kind of cart trail that
ran into Le Guélennec. Eventually I found the fairly tortuous
path, and I climbed it up to the cart road; then I reached the
Vuern spring, the lovely spring I had so often dreamed about

when I was dying of thirst out there in the deserts of Africa and Mexico. That spring gave the finest, best water you could ever find. I was not thirsty just then, but I had to taste the wonderful water anyhow; then I sat on a rock beside it to smoke a cigarette. Below the spring, there was a laundry trough that was haunted by the night-washerwomen *(couerezet noz)*, evil women who loved playing all kinds of tricks on any mortal woman unfortunate enough to wander into their presence at night. And not far from there was a great plateau where the *corrigans* or gnomes also came to play at night. To judge by its shape, I believe the flat area must have been a Roman camp that Breton archeologists have missed. This was also the meeting-place for the night-screamers (*hoper noz*); these are children who died unbaptized, and who must wander the world until the Last Judgment.

All these beings come out of the superstitious, fear-ridden mentality of the Bretons, who always tend to see supernatural beings everywhere. The sight of a white rock at night, a holly trunk crowned with thorns, a hare, a rabbit; the echo of voices that, especially in these *stangs,* resound with astonishing power and sharpness; an owl's cries that sound like the cries of peasants on harvest days or drunk; the cry of the tufted owl that is a perfect enunciation of the Breton word *pot* (boy); this probably contributed greatly to the creation of the supernatural beings of Lower Brittany, many of whom have no counterpart among other superstitious peoples. While I sat there, beside that good and graceful spring that might have caught Narcissus' reflection despite his wishes, I saw dawn break behind the mountain.

Thereupon, I hurried back to my uncle's house. He was already up when I arrived. As he and the godmother were surprised to see me coming in at that hour, I gave them a thorough account of how I had spent my day and my night. They did not believe a word of it except that, if I really did go into the Stang-Odet, I could have been taken captive by those fairies or *corrigans* I seemed to think were a joke. Then my godmother scolded me for not staying at the house, where many people had come to see me, even some *bas vanel.* The *bas vanel* are old wives whose task is to match and marry up young people. It's a pleasant trade, and very lucrative too for those who are good at it. But I told my godmother that I was terribly sorry, I was obliged to go into Quimper again today, right away; I had to cash a check for twelve hundred francs, and see how much there was in my account at the savings bank. I told the good woman to let the *bas vanel* know they would be wasting their time with me; I was planning to marry the Stang-Odet Fairy. I downed a milk soup and left for Quimper, to my godmother's great displeasure.

SHE WAS A DAUGHTER OF KERNOAS

Yet along the way, I could not help thinking of what my godmother had said about the *bas vanel,* and I had a presentiment of some unavoidable misfortune, having to do with my weakness of will and my kind heart. When it comes to my political and religious opinions and ideas, I would go to the scaffold or the stake rather than cede an inch or retract a single point; I am convinced that my opinions and ideas are the only ones which, if put into practice, could provide the human race the greatest possible well-being, in brotherhood, truth, and justice, for its brief journey on this globe. But when it comes to helping or rendering service to anyone, even my worst enemy, I never say no. And that is the source of all my misfortunes. In my military career, I would never have been cited for any penalties if I had not tried to help out some friend or colleague. In civilian life, all my miseries and misfortunes come from having done some service for anyone who asked it—miseries and misfortunes hugely aggravated by the absolute irreducible tenacity of my political and religious beliefs. On my way to Quimper that day, I could already foresee the misfortunes hanging over my head. And after I had made such fine plans for the Stang-Odet.

At a place called Penker Bronnec, I came to three different paths that all led into Quimper. Alfred de Musset tells us that Hercules once had to choose among three paths where three goddesses—Fortune, Sensuality, and Virtue—beckoned to him. In the end he elected to follow Virtue, who looked the loveliest to him. Here there were no goddesses; I gave a quick glance at the three paths and without a pause took the one on the left. It is unnecessary, says the Mohammedan, to go seeking out your destiny, for your destiny will seek you out. That day, though, I do believe that I was seeking mine—unless I have two different destinies, one ahead of me and one behind. This path ran through the Stang-à-Leur, a major meeting ground for elves, then through Kerzudal and Lézébel, and ended up at the high road from Coray to Quimper. A kilometer before Quimper, at a spot called Poul ar Raniquet, I came upon an old fellow, a woman, and a young boy unloading a cask of cider. Seeing that they were having some trouble, I went over spontaneously to offer a hand. I recognized the woman, and she soon recognized me, too.

She was a daughter of Kernoas, a large estate bordering Le Guélennec and the Stang-Odet. She had married a man named Rospart, from one of the richest families in Kerfeunteun. They had farmed the Kernoas estate as tenants for several years, until two minor children, who were to succeed to the estate, should come of age. One of the two took over the property when he reached his majority, and the Rosparts were obliged to look elsewhere. They found a farm to let at Toulven in Ergué-Armel, next door to Ergué-Gabéric. And she—the Widow Rospart—lived there still; her husband had died two years earlier. By the look of the cart and team she was using to deliver a cask of her cider to a tavern keeper in Poul ar Raniquet, I gathered that she must be in dire straits—she, the daughter of one of the richest landowners of Ergué-Gabéric, the prettiest and strongest girl of her time. After a few toasts at the tavern she invited me to come back with her to see the farm at Toulven; her sixteen-year-old son, who was driving for her, took me by the hand, and the old tavern keeper, a friend of theirs, urged me to visit as well. Impossible to resist. We all climbed into the old wagon, dragged by two poor skinny oxen and an old horse that could barely stand up.

At the farm, they had no food to offer me but some leftover oat mush already moldy. The meat-locker was bare, and although it was nearly Michaelmas, harvest season, there was not one potato or vegetable on the farm, not a single grain in the silo, for the little wheat that had been harvested was sold immediately. On the other hand, there was all the cider you could want. The cider apples were abundant that year, and a large group of workers had come for the day to harvest them—a *grande journée*. That was why the widow had gone to deliver a cask of cider to the tavern keeper, so she could buy something to feed the apple pickers. When I had eaten a bit of the reheated mush and drunk cider aplenty, I asked to have a look at the apple pickers. They were in the big orchard, twenty meters from the house. When I arrived there, at the center of the orchard I saw a band of young folks, boys and girls, who were indeed picking apples, but picking them to throw at one another, having a grand time, then, glancing off to the side, I saw three characters smoking and chatting around a big pitcher of cider. The youngest one, who was the widow's sole servant, recognized me.

He was a former colleague of mine from my begging days; he had done a stint in the artillery and learned a few dozen French words there—and what French! One of the two others had also served, under Louis-Philippe and under the 1848 Republic; and with never a word of preamble, under the influence of the strong cider, he started right off in execrable French reciting all his campaigns. The only thing I could catch from his garbled recitation that might have been true was his story that he was at Lyons in a light infantry company when, one day during blank-ammunition exercises, someone shot a bullet-extractor that hit Marshal Castellane's hat. He even said that the soldier who had shot the thing was his bunkmate. The other listener, who was so drunk he couldn't see straight, was a day laborer at a brick factory nearby. As I talked—or rather, as I listened, in irritation—to these two cider drunks, the young folks were still idly lolling and whispering at a distance; they were probably wondering who the devil this could be, this sergeant with his three medals. But the widow's servant, the artilleryman now acting as apple carrier, went over to tell them who I was. At the same time, though, someone else came into the orchard, a gentleman, this one, with a quiet, serious manner, before whom the three drinkers bowed. Louis-Philippe's veteran soldier poured him some cider and ordered the others back to work, for he was supervising the project. He said a few words about me to the gentleman and then he too went off, shouting to the young folks to hurry, for the day was getting on.

I was left alone with the gentleman, who spoke quite good French; he told me right away that he was the steward for M. Malherbe de la Boissière, the owner of Toulven, of which the chateau was right next door, its turrets visible through the trees. He gave me to understand that he himself was the real master at Toulven, as the count paid no attention and saw nothing on his own. Then, when he came to speak of the

Widow Rospart and her sorry situation, he spoke the way a mayor might: he said, "We let the Widow Rospart stay on here when we should have dismissed her two years ago, because we hoped that she would work out an advantageous marriage for her elder daughter, who's certainly the strongest and prettiest girl in the district. There have been three or four candidates so far, but they were idlers and drunks."

Then he questioned me on what I meant to do in the area. With my usual candor, I told him my plans to settle in the Stang-Odet. He laughed; then, turning serious, he said, "But why not come here? This is practically a hermitage here, with the sea surrounding it on all sides; the farm leasehold is very cheap, and if the place got a sensible manager who knew agriculture, he'd make his fortune."

The former Philippist walked past us, on his way back from taking a load of apples to the threshing yard, and the agent said to him, "Look, Rospart, here's the man we need for Marie-Yvonne and for running the farm."

"Yes, yes," the old man stammered. "I had the same idea right off when I saw the sergeant turn up here."

This Rospart was the widow's first cousin. He was a farmer too, nearby. He started singing the praises of everything at Toulven—of Monsieur and Madame Malherbe, of this steward and his wife, of his cousin the widow and particularly of the widow's daughter, of the other tenant farmers, himself included. In fact everything was fine, wonderful, here on the Toulven peninsula. This old fellow who'd been answering "yes, yes" to the agent without quite knowing what he was saying, now understood exactly. So he dropped his sack and invited us to come to the house to have a drink and chat with the widow. There, the business was quickly settled among the three of them, with no need for a word from me. But as the proverb says, "He who does not speak, consents."

The agent wanted to take me over to the chateau to show me to his lord and lady, who alone had the right to give the widow whatever son-in-law they wanted. I had the strength of will to refuse to go, a fairly unusual thing for me.

"Considering," I said, "that from my standpoint, nothing is decided. You're mistaken about me. I'm not the man you need here."

But it was no good, I was the man they needed because the sterward had said so. Meanwhile, night had fallen, supper was ready, and the harvesters had come in. I wanted to leave, but it was impossible, I had to stay to eat and watch the games, *ar c'hoariou*, that are indispensable for finishing off any *grande journeé* properly. It was like what happens in the elegant world, where a grand banquet would finish off the Opera or the Comédie Française. Old Rospart took his niece Marie-Yvonne by the arm and shoved her toward me, telling her, "Look, niece, here's your new good friend—who's gonna be my nephew, right, sergeant?"

The girl, who knew that she would not be allowed to choose a husband to suit herself, answered, in that sardonic style peculiar to Bretons, that I was just the man she had always dreamed about, the reason she hadn't married before this was that she'd been waiting for me. We had not yet finished eating when all the servants from the chateau, the agent leading them, came in to watch the games, and also to see Marie-Yvonne's "fiancé," for the man had already described me to his lords and masters and told them that the thing was arranged.

The games finally began, those vulgar, stupid games, always the same, the *basculades* (sic), the women, who always go first, shoving and toppling the men, and then the men doing the same to the women. Then the young folks, and even some elders, started performing what they call feats of skill, but which are actually feats of unskill—crude, stupid, and dangerous.

But, well, these are the only amusements that backward places can offer, and the participants get more real enjoyment from them than blasé rich folk do from their theaters or their great balls with full orchestras. As for me, I withdrew with the steward to the far end of the table to chat, leaving the players to their games. At the end, though, Philippe's ex-trooper, still the most adroit and nimblest of the bunch, in what was perhaps a calculated move suddenly challenged me directly, and I leapt up onto the table and did a dangerous rear-flip to the ground; then I took off walking on my hands with my legs in the air and finished with another two dangerous leaps, one on my hands and the other in the air. I returned to my seat beside the agent. Everyone stood there gaping. The old trooper did finally say that he'd made a mistake daring me, and that he could see he had met his master. Then they asked me to do some of the magic tricks much in fashion at the time.* I knew all those disappearing and sleight-of-hand tricks—there are plenty of such performers in the army—so I did a few things, some sleight-of-hand and disappearances, and ended with the famous great vanishing act the Chinese supposedly invented and the Davenport brothers used to promote spiritualism; the trick of it was only discovered in Paris, in the City of Light, by Robert Houdin, the great conjurer. The feat involves having one's wrists bound with a strong cord wrapped several times around and secured by a Gordian knot, so that the cleverest man in the world looking at someone tied up that way would never think he could escape, at least not with his wrists freed, unless someone should cut the cord. . .

I proposed to do it, and they went to fetch the rope and cord. The steward, who was not drunk and who naturally

---

*In Breton, *troioù fuzik*, from the French *physique*—physics, which in Breton has the sense of "magic."

thought himself the cleverest man in the place, set about binding my wrists together, declaring that I would never manage to get them free unless someone cut the cord. When he had finished, he took the rope, slipped it between my wrists and around the cord, and grasped its two ends. The man was at least twice as strong as I was, but I told him that if he could pull me two feet out of position I would declare myself stupider than Mary Magdalene's boyfriend.

"Oh," says he, "I'll pull you all the way over to the chateau."

"Let's go, then," I said.

He started pulling, but instantly tumbled onto his back, all four hooves in the air, with the rope and the cord dangling from his fists, while I showed the others my wrists unbound but bearing the marks of the cord, so tight had it been. They all examined the rope and the cord, nothing was broken or cut or unknotted. Therefore it could only be the devil—or Paulic, as he's called in Breton—who snatched me free. Bretons, as I have already pointed out, give the Devil credit for anything at all unusual that they cannot explain otherwise.

Once I had executed that final feat, which left everyone quite amazed, I took advantage of the chance to slip away. Anyhow, some groups of young folk who lived a distance away had already left. When I reached the outer road, I heard a group walking ahead of me discussing the incredible evening they had just spent. They were talking about me, of course, and about the devil, about Paulic, who must be my aide and my inseparable companion, whom I must have made a compact with. But I did not want to go on listening to these poor ignorant people. I skirted them to move ahead, without their noticing me, and I hurried along the Quimper high road, my brain boiling.

If at the time I had had some means of noting down all the ideas and feelings coursing through my brain, I would have made them into a poem the likes of which has never yet been seen. I thought about everything I had just seen that evening, which was a delirium of delight for all those poor ignorant folks, for the widow herself, and for her [five] children who were on the verge of having to go beg for their bread unless, as the agent told me, some person of good will could be found to come to their aid. For there was nothing, absolutely nothing left on that wretched farm, and Michaelmas was approaching, and they would have to pay the landowner eight hundred francs rent. Where to find it? There was not one potato, not one grain in the barn, and the harvest was already over. There was one small haystack, of the good local hay, but I learned later at my expense that it had long since been sold, and the money withdrawn and eaten up. If at Michaelmas the owner sold off the cattle and the paltry farm equipment, he would possibly get his money's worth, counting in the cider apples. But then the buyer of the haystack would have lost his money, and the widow and her children would be reduced to escaping to Quimper, where all the failed farmers take refuge.

Walking toward Le Guélennec along footpath and field, I pondered on that, and on other things as well, for fifty thousand thoughts were clashing about in my boiling brain. At times I seemed to hear Marie-Yvonne's voice calling to me: "Jean-Marie, Jean-Marie, *me gar a c'hanoc'h a greis ma c'halon.* (Jean-Marie, I love you from the bottom of my heart.) Do you remember, Jean-Marie, when you used to come to Kernoas? How my mother would give you food and drink when you were dying of hunger and poverty at Le Guélennec? She would give you clogs when you were barefoot and clothes to cover you. Oh, you ingrate, now you flee from us because we're penniless." Then I thought I heard the word "coward" echo in my ears. That painful word, which journalists use so excessively these days without their targets taking the slightest offense, but a word which has never been applied to me, I declare here and now that if anyone is luckless enough to apply it to me he won't get to do it twice. Coward—I did feel I was guilty of cowardice, sneaking away from those poor souls who were reaching out to me, leaving them not a word of hope. But then other thoughts came to send the first flying in an instant. Going to Toulven would require me to make the greatest sacrifice a man can make: the sacrifice of my fortune, my freedom, and my life, just when I was preparing to go enjoy in peace all of nature's favors. And who would even comprehend what a sacrifice it was? A Breton has no idea of such things.

I was being called upon to save that poor family, that was clear. But was I capable of saving them? Wasn't it just as likely that I would sink with them instead? And then my whole sacrifice would only have gone to make me ridiculous, the object of every kind of scorn, of sarcastic jokes from every peasant in the canton. And besides, I wouldn't be the only one to suffer afterwards, for I would probably have offspring, and through those children I would suffer ten times as much as for myself. I would blame myself, and those children would have the right to blame me too, for being stupider than other animals—stupider than birds, who take care to prepare nests for their little ones before creating them. There were people younger than I in Le Guélennec who were burdened with children, all of them in want. I knew perfectly well that the priests and the rich, all and always of one mind, were quite happy to see poor wretches manufacture children. Baptisms, marriages, and burials bring in big money for the priests, especially Breton priests. And for the rich exploiters and parasites, the more beggars there are, the larger the pool to choose from for their cheap labor, and their pleasures in this world are all the greater for the spectacle of poverty and suffering around them.

MY DREAMS OF FREEDOM WERE OVER

Eventually, as I mulled thousands and thousands of thoughts on human misery, on my situation, and on everything I had seen at Toulven, I got back to the little cottage in Le Guélennec. The two old folks naturally asked where I was coming from so late, for by then it was two o'clock in the morning. I told them in detail what had happened to me. That was enough. They immediately asked what answer I'd given to such a fine proposition. None, I told them, and I had even left without saying goodbye.

"Well now, well now," said my godmother. *"Setu aman eun den drol vat.* (Aren't you a strange fellow.) Why wouldn't you be pleased to marry into that family? It's one of the richest ones here, in this commune and in Kerfeunteun both. The widow's older brother owns the next estate, he's chief councilman of the commune, and the nephew, the proprietor at Kernoas, he's married to the daughter of the former mayor, who's the richest and most respected man in the commune! And the relatives on the father's side are all landowners or rich tenant farmers in Kerfeunteun. And you would refuse— you, the former beggar boy who begged for your bread at the door of all those people—you'd refuse to go into their family as master of your own household?"

"It may well be," I told my godmother, "that the Toulven widow still has very rich relatives, but she isn't rich herself, she's about to be put off the place for inability to pay her rent."

"Yes," said the old gendarme, "because the girl's father, old Rospart, was a bit of a drunk and not much of a worker, and because since his death his widow never found a foreman who was capable of managing the farm. But you—you know agriculture and you know business, you'll bring things back up soon enough."

"Yes, yes," the old lady said again. "You mustn't miss this great chance."

The two old people went on with their pleas and exhortations, and probably kept it up long after I had fallen asleep and into completely contradictory dreams, some cheerful and consoling, others dark and disconcerting.

When I woke in the morning, my nightshirt damp with sweat, it was already broad daylight, and there was no one in the house. I found some milk soup on the hook in the hearth. I ate it and then took a walk through the garden to look at the old gendarme's horticultural projects. It wasn't too bad, there was a bit of everything in the little garden: cabbages, potatoes, carrots, turnips, parsnips, currant bushes, and strawberries, even flowers. When I had finished my inspection, my godmother appeared; she was coming from Guélennec Izella, she said, where she had gone to see René Le Péron, the elder brother of the Toulven widow, whose estate was just minutes from there. She had informed him of my impending marriage to his niece.

"He's very pleased," she told me, "for he heard you had a lot of money."

"But where's Uncle?"

"Why, you know very well where, for heaven's sake—he went to Toulven to settle the matter promptly. You told him yourself this morning to go!"

And then I remembered that, indeed, in the course of that dreadful sleep, and in the midst of my dreams, someone spoke to me, and unconsciously I answered him. It was Uncle, asking if I agreed to accept the excellent propositions I'd been offered, and in my sleep I had said yes. It was all over now, my dreams of freedom and peaceful contentment in the Stang-Odet, unless something should halt the forward march of events. . . .

So now that I saw I was embarking on a new existence, I took up my role bravely and philosophically, intending to fulfill my duties there as elsewhere, and leave it to Mr. Destiny to take care of the rest. But I had to go to Quimper to cash my money order and finally to see how much cash I could put together, for I would soon have need of it. This time when I arrived at the triple fork in the road, I took the one on the right, the one I should have taken the day before. In Quimper, when I had completed my errands, I went to visit Uncle Le Gac, whose house I had stayed at when I returned to Quimper from the Châlons army camp. This elderly fellow, the first cousin of the old gendarme, was completely stupefied from alcohol; all he did now was ramble. Impossible to hold a conversation with him, if he ever had been capable of that. His wife, on the other hand, was a very good conversationalist, or chatterer. When I told her the story of what happened to me the day before, and the likely consequences, she began twisting about, crossing her arms and gazing at me with pity, all the while giving me a long speech that was the opposite of my godmother's, who thought the proposed union was magnificent and highly honorable, whereas Aunt Le Gac thought it unworthy of me. Why would a noncommissioned officer, now turned a proper gentleman, go and marry a rough peasant girl, when here in town I could find young ladies who were well educated and well bred, for instance her own daughter Octavia, the cream of the Quimper girls? And young Octavia, who was present, felt that her mother was not at all excessive. The two of them were making scornful faces about the rough peasant girl. I was obliged to stay for dinner, a dinner during which I was further obliged to hear the litany of recriminations from mother and daughter, along with the father's alcoholic ramblings. Finally, after dinner, I made my escape from the tiresome chattering, and returned to Le Guélennec by the middle road, crossing over field and meadow.

My godmother was surprised to see me back so early this time. But when I showed her a sack full of yellow coins, she understood that I had done well not to linger outdoors at night. The poor woman rejoiced at the sight of those coins; she had never seen so many. Yet there were only twelve hundred francs there; I was supposed to draw another thirteen hundred. I told my godmother that this would have been enough for me to settle in my hermitage in the Stang-Odet, but for Toulven it was not enough, and I even held out some hope that the lord of Toulven, the absolute master in the choice of a son-in-law to assign to the widow, would reject me because my fortune was so small. I had even decided that when I had heard the outcome of the old gendarme's mission, I would write the gentleman, giving him clear, honest details on my person, on my financial situation, and on my political and religious views. In order that no one should be misled, I would declare myself to all the interested parties. By means of such frank and honest declarations I was still hoping I might readily escape the chain to which people were planning to rivet me. Never would these Catholic, monarchist noblemen, these supporters of divine right, want as their tenant-farmer, right next door to their seigneurial home, a man who was a republican, a freethinker with the utmost contempt for all the villainous, monstrous divinities that charlatans and rascals have created to exploit men's idiocy and cravenness. Surely, when they heard such statements, the widow and her daughter and all the relatives would be terrified, would curse me and damn me and send me straight to hell. I discussed all this with my godmother, who didn't understand a bit of it. She had only one thing in mind now, and understood nothing but that: to see her godson become the farmer at Toulven and marry into one of the richest families hereabouts. Finally Uncle came in too, three sheets to the wind, beaming with delight and singing the song about the police captain and the flatfoot cop. He had settled everything with the widow, the daughter, old uncle Rospart, the steward, and finally with the lord and lady themselves. Everyone was pleased. But the chatelains did want to see me. It was arranged that I would go there the next day, not merely to show my physical self to the lords of the manor, but also to tour the grounds, the obligatory tour before a betrothal, which is usually the occasion for a special meal. The old gendarme had also stopped by Guélennec Isella to see the widow's brother, and it was decided that he and his only son would come along with us. The son was also ready for marriage, but they could not find a wife rich enough for him. I decided to let myself be led like a sheep right to the end. I've already said as much: in life's ordinary matters, when I am convinced that it is for the best, I have never been able to resist. But in political and social matters, I have never given over to anyone else's lead.

BETROTHAL MEATS

So the next day we went to Toulven with the Pérons, father and son. The elder Péron was a child of Kernoas like his sister, the widow at Toulven, but instead of staying on at that estate as was his right, he had bought the Guélennec Izella property and left Kernoas to another of his sisters. That woman died, though, leaving two minor children, and her husband also died some time later. Marie-Anne, the present Toulven widow, married then and took over the property on behalf of the minors. One of them died young, and the whole Kernoas property went to the other, and when he came of age, having found a very rich wife, he took over the estate and put his aunt out. She then went to Toulven, where her husband Rospart died two years later, leaving her with five young children.

Old Péron was the most silent man I ever knew in my life. He never spoke, although he was neither deaf nor mute. And no one had ever seen him laugh or cry. He expressed his feelings and opinions only by a faint growl of "Hum," such that you could not tell if he was saying yes or no. But his son, known as Big Jean, talked far too much. That one inherited his tongue from his mother, long since dead. But like most Bretons, he only spoke in ambiguous ironies, in sarcasms and mockery, extremely tasteless and stupidly wounding. So I found it impossible to chat reasonably with these two traveling companions, alongside whom I looked like a little schoolmaster, for I was dressed in gentleman's garb. With the remains of my discharge pay, when I had decided to go live in the Stang-Odet, I had bought some civilian clothes, and I had a whole trunkful of them, never worn. Anyhow, we reached Toulven a little late, for we had stopped at several inns along the way; my companions might not know how to hurry but they did know how to drink.

The dinner, the betrothal spread, had been ready for some time, and people were starting to worry that the intended would not come. So we had to sit down at the table as soon as we arrived. Rospart, Philippe's old veteran trooper who acted as master of the house, took me by the hand and pushed me to the head of the table, the seat of honor, already calling me his nephew. The dinner was noisy and very merry for all these guests, the brandy and cider having set all their tongues wagging except old Péron's, which never loosened. As for me, it was all very tiresome because my own tongue was for the moment like old Péron's—it had nothing to say. And, besides, what sort of remark could it ever stick into such conversations, or rather such eternal Breton drivel, where clumsiness vied with stupidity? So people kept saying, "The fiancé, there—he's not saying a word." No of course not, I wasn't saying a word because I had nothing to say in that muddle of inanity and foolishness. I was certainly ridiculous in my silence, but I thought I would be even more so if I got mixed up in that foul-mouthed talk.

Fortunately, the steward M. Pierre had come to see if I'd arrived. I therefore got up from the table and started talking with the gentleman. He told me that M. and Mme. Malherbe very much wanted to see me. When he had put away several bowls of cider, it was decided that we would go to the chateau right now with him—M. Pierre the steward or general facto-tum. He was the coachman, gardener, porter, and game-keeper, and on top of all those jobs he had another as well, I later learned, one he excelled at: spy. We set out with M. Pierre, the Uncle Rospart, my gendarme uncle, and the Péron son, that is, everyone who could speak a little French. For the seigneurs did not know a word of Breton. When we got to the chateau, the steward as a matter of course led us into the kitchen, the reception hall for peasants, and Monsieur [Malherbe] de la Boissière soon entered. He was a very large man, but his look and his ways told me immediately that he was not a great man. I saw that this was a former student of the Jesuits, a man of no ability, who nonetheless considered him-self superior to the farmers who kept him fed. He spoke first to Rospart, one of his tenant farmers, then to my Uncle Quéré, who had visited him the night before. Looking at that face, which displayed every aspect of his soul, I said to myself that this marriage business was certainly going to stop short here and now; for since I had not had time to write to the Jesuitical gentleman as I had planned, I immediately resolved to tell him, aloud and before witnesses, all my negative cre-dentials; they would keep him from accepting me as his farmer. When he had spoken awhile with the two old men, and asked who Big Jean was, he came up to me: "So you're

Déguignet, the former sergeant. But do you know anything about agriculture?"

"Yes, monsieur, I do, " I replied. "It is the only work I did before entering the army, and I spent two years at the Kermahonec agriculture school in Kerfeunteun, where they do practical training, and where I was a kind of teacher myself—not among the least important ones, since I taught the students how to manage livestock, which is the most important skill in agriculture. But despite all that, I am not the appropriate man here for several reasons, the first, and the most important in the present case for the widow, her daughter, and yourself, is that I have no money. Altogether I have only two thousand five hundred francs."

But there they stopped me: the gentleman and all the others spoke up at once, saying that was more than enough, it wasn't money that was needed, it was a man, a good farmer. Fine, I thought, they've beat me on the first point, let's see about the others. So I began describing to the gentleman, bluntly, forthrightly, and honestly, my political and religious views, which I knew to be categorically opposed to the views of all Bretons. But the two old uncles and Big Jean himself, though they barely understood what I was saying, broke in every other minute, telling Monsieur in their working-class French that he should pay no attention to this ex-soldier's talk, that soldiers are all like that, teasing and fooling. I could not make out exactly what the gentleman, in his Catholic brain, was weighing between the serious, forthright, and honest account from a former non-commissioned officer on the one hand, and, on the other, the silly, vulgar remarks of my interrupters; finally, though, he said—in a hypocritical, Jesuit way—that when it came to political and religious opinion, everyone was free. But he was speaking with that rhetorical tactic called "paralipsis," in which one says the very opposite of what one thinks.

Meanwhile, the lady of the house came in as well to have a look at her new farmer's face. A woman as tall as her husband, but more refined and haughtier, whose head I sensed was filled mainly with the pride of the so-called "noble" race. She had been present for the last part of my declaration, and she shared the opinion of her husband and everyone else: she thought I was just the man they needed. And despite her natural pride-fulness and despite the distance she established between her-self and me, she made some effort to be pleasant, and even went so far as to flatter me and then give me a thoroughly idyl-lic little "speech" on the pleasures of Toulven as a place where everyone lived in harmony and happiness, and where I would be happiest of all because I would have as my partner the loveliest girl in this little paradise on earth; happier even than she and her husband, the seigneurs of this paradise, since I spoke Breton. Finally, after that poetical apologia from the lady, the session came to an end, not without a glass of the good wine she had ordered uncorked for us.

Once outdoors, my escorts could not congratulate me enough on my incredible success with these great noblemen. The lady had given me the eye, said Uncle Rospart in his trooper French; she was already jealous of Marie-Yvonne. With her there, I'd be able to do anything I wanted at Toulven, I'd be king of the peninsula; and the two other men went even further than Uncle Rospart. And when we got back to the farm and my guides had reported my great success at the chateau, and I saw Marie-Yvonne looking radiant with joy, love, and beauty, could I possibly resist all that? But old Saint Anthony himself could not have resisted if Pluto's wife, the lovely Persephone, had deployed such seduction on him.

Now we had to drink another toast to the health of the landowners, and of the "fiancés," too, since the arrangement was fairly well set; then, finally, we went to do the obligatory tour *(ar vueladen)*. That took very little time, actually, for there was nothing to show but the fields and meadows with nothing left in them, and that the fields and meadows were all centered around the farmhouse. Going through the barnyard and the threshing floor, the men were forced to acknowledge that there was very little there, that the farm tools were extremely primitive and in poor condition, but as they say in Breton, *"gant fall ve gret, mes ebket n'er quet vit ober* ('bad' you can work with; with 'nothing' you can't do a thing)." It is an adage that contradicts the theological teaching that God accomplished everything with nothing. Walking through the fields, the two old fellows kept kicking at molehills, saying that the land was prime quality, that it just needed working by an intelligent man; then they talked about the moon, for like all Bretons the two uncles believed in Phoebus' influence over everything on earth and especially on things agricultural. The two moon lovers were thoroughly versed in all that, they knew which phase was best for sowing which seeds, and they kept saying that a farmer who did not know those rules or refused to follow them would never get anywhere. I would have been happy to give these two selenites a scientific argument on their erroneous thinking, but as the proverb says, talking science to donkeys is a waste of time. With these two fellows I would not only be wasting my time, I would be at serious risk of setting off obscene and idiotic protests. I left the two "lunatics" to their rambling chatter and began looking over a large stretch of marshland covered with spiny reeds and briar, called "red prairie," doubtless for that reason. But old Rospart came over to me, saying that this plot was worthless, it was only used to pasture the livestock during the summer when the fields and meadows were growing crops. I answered him immediately: "Well, now: if I come here, I can assure you that this will soon be the best plot on the whole farm."

The moon lover laughed, of course, shaking his head, and the others did the same. The tour being over, it was time to eat and drink some more; then we agreed to go on Saturday, two days later, to the town hall and the curé to post the banns.

THE SACRIFICE IS TO TAKE PLACE IN A FEW DAYS

On Saturday, then, everyone gathered at Quimper, for we had to go first to the notary, since I was to take over the management of the farm. And I was to assume responsibility not only for the eldest daughter but also for her four minor siblings and her mother the widow; and I was also to give the widow fifteen hundred francs whenever she decided to ask for it, and four hundred to each of the minor children as they came of age. That was the arrangement arrived at among the widow Rospart, her cousin, her neighbor, and the children's guardians, who had been told that I was very rich and would therefore not look too closely. And indeed I did not; I was agreeing to take on five people, dress them, feed them, and pay them a total of three thousand one hundred francs for an establishment worth less than a thousand. But I had decided to give over on everything, never voicing a single opinion on the financial matters, although those are the only questions dealt with in these marriages involving smallholders or tenant farmers. Not love, not feelings, not the moral outlook or the personal tastes of the future couple, none of those count: financial matters above all.

Anyhow, when the business was completed with the notary, we proceeded to Ergué-Armel. I expected to stop first at the town hall, but my escorts said we must start with the parish priest.

So we went, not to the curé's house but to the sacristy where the sacred accounts were kept, and until recently the town [civil] accounts as well, for the town hall and the sacristy were one single entity. There, we dealt with the drunken old priest, already tipsy, and nasty like most of the Breton clergy. Before the session ended, there was a moment when I thought the whole thing was going to stop right there. For in Brittany it is customary for the priest to ask the future couple to recite a few sections of the catechism, which everyone has long since forgotten. The old drunk first turned to me, asking if I knew my catechism in Breton, of course. Seeing that I was dealing with an insolent brute, I answered: "Yes, of course I know my catechism in Breton, and in several other languages as well. But don't expect me to reel off that nonsense for you."

I got no further, for at those words the drunk recoiled as if he'd been bit by a snake, and started bellowing like a madman. He was holding the paper on which he had scribbled our two names, and he made as if to tear it to pieces.

"Go ahead, tear it up," I said, "and tear up your robe, too, like old Caïaphas."

I would have gone on, but in an instant the document was torn to bits and the maniac went to lunge at me and throw me out. But Big Jean Péron, who was friendly with all the priests in the area—he had been a choirboy and was still the church cantor—stopped him and brought him back to some degree of sanity; he explained that I was an ex-soldier and that soldiers are all like that when they come out of the army, but after a while they turn back into Bretons, and good Catholics like before, and "Cousin Déguignet" was sure to do the same.

"Yes, yes," said the two moon-lovers: "that's for sure. We know all about that, we're old soldiers too."

"He's going to have to do like everyone else," said the old drunk. "He's got to submit to the commandments of the Church or he won't be married."

With that, he took up his pen again and wrote out the names of the future pair afresh.

I had no wish to prolong that stupid session, so I did not reply, and I went out of the sacristy, leaving my escorts behind to arrange things with the man of God, of the god Bacchus. I went over to the town hall. The others came along eventually, too, and said everything had worked out with the priest; they had assured him that Déguignet would certainly submit to all the rules and commandments of the Church, like everyone else.

"You're wrong," I told them. "I must tell you once and for all the same thing I said at Toulven to Monsieur and Madame Malherbe de la Boissière, and at the farm to the persons most involved, that I will never compromise on my political and religious views. In politics, I am a republican of the most advanced sort, and in religion a freethinker, a philosophic friend to humankind—the real humankind—and the declared enemy of all gods, who are only imaginary creatures, and of priests, who are only charlatans and knaves; do you understand? Because I insist on openly declaring all my faults, and Bretons consider such political and religious views to be great faults, although they are the finest qualities of true citizens. I do not want anyone to reproach me later for deceiving and stealing my way into this position."

But just try talking seriously, forthrightly, and honestly to Bretons! That is exactly when they take you for a yarn spinner, a joker. And that was how they interpreted my forthright, honest statements. Those believers in falsehood, those unbelievers in truth, all began laughing or grinning again, except of course for old Péron, and they led me over to the town registry.

Our business there did not take long. The secretary, who was the schoolmaster, gave me just a small lecture on what papers I would have to present on the day of the [civil] marriage ceremony. For Breton peasants, this marriage before the mayor, the only one recognized and regulated by law, means very little, since it involves neither God, nor priest,

nor song, nor ceremony, nor a fee. The entire ceremony consists of a reading of eight lines from the Civil Code, of which
the new couple understands nothing and cares less.

We left the town hall and went to the inn where the wedding feast was to be held. It was decided that the feast would
take place on the third Tuesday from then, and would go on
for three days, for several of the bride's guests would be
unable to come all on the same day. When all the arrangements were made, we went our separate ways. The old gendarme, I, and the two Pérons had still to go on to
Ergué-Gabéric to deliver to the priest and the mayor the two
documents we were given by the Ergué-Armel priest and reg-
istrar, for I had to publish the banns in the commune where
I lived as well. Now all I had left to do was pick up my papers,
for I had no invitations to issue, knowing full well that any
such would be pointless. In the Quimper area, it is the custom
for each invited guest to pay his share and a little more
besides, for, also according to custom, he should be giving the
newlyweds a little money; so poor people cannot attend such
weddings. And I had only poor relatives, and in any case the
peasants in that area never go to the weddings of people who
haven't come to theirs, except for neighbors who have certain
reciprocal obligations with the groom's parents. I fit none of
those categories. I had never been to any wedding, and I had
neither neighbors nor friends with obligations toward me,
after my fourteen years away.

But even without invitations to send, I had a good deal of
difficulty with my documents. And, indeed, when I had collected all the papers I needed, it turned out that I had three
different names. My military name, the one the mayor of
Guengat had handed me when I left for the service was
"Duguines," the one I had just been given at the registry was
"Déguignet," and my father's name on his marriage certificate

was "Le Déguignet." The clerk at my own town hall told me that it was impossible for me to marry with all those names.

"Well," I said, "I foresaw all sorts of obstacles that might block this marriage, but here's one I didn't think of, and this could be the one to do it."

Meanwhile, after consulting various articles of the Civil Code, the clerk told me I could marry after all if I agreed to take my father's name, "Le Déguignet," a name my father himself never knew, at least until he married. On one of my trips to the Ergué-Armel town hall, I encountered the curé at his garden gate, and he told me in commanding tones: "Well, I expect you to come to confession, at least here or in your own parish, otherwise I won't marry you."

I had not seen any of those priests yet. However, I would have to go and ask them the charges for publishing the banns. Coming into town, I had stopped to see a cousin of the Toulven widow, a woman who kept an inn I had visited with the Pérons the evening we made the arrangements. She said, "Well! you haven't been in once since then. You certainly know that betrothed couples are required to go at least once to hear their marriage banns read out at the church and take confession. For heaven's sake, people are saying all sorts of things about you, and you're going to get an earful later from the vicar, because you'll be picking up your documents from him—the rector's away."

"No," I told her, "I haven't been in town since then, I've had no time. And if I had come in, it wouldn't have been to go to Mass or confession. And as to your vicar's sermon, it doesn't scare me."

The woman made me coffee anyway, meanwhile lecturing me in advance of the vicar's own lecture—and perhaps even his thrashing, for she said he was a rough customer and a skilled boxer, that he fought the toughest fellows in the commune, even Big Jean who was the toughest of them all. But she did add that however tough they are, peasants don't fight a priest, even if he is the puniest man in the world; priests are so learned about all matters. Bretons do believe that priests know everything there is to know, not only about this world, which they think constitutes the entire universe, but also about the mythical worlds of Paradise and Hell. Whereas these priests, all of them sons of peasants, are the most ignorant of men, having been made stupid in the church schools and going on to complete their stupidification at seminary, studying *theostupidology*.

A peasant came into the inn from the church and told us that the vicar was in the sacristy with the parish treasurer. I knew the man, one of the richest peasants in the area, at whose house I had often begged for bread and where I had even worked, with my father, as a wretched little day laborer at five sous a day. He was also a priest manqué. The time had come to go see the terrible vicar. The old innkeeper said she wished she could be there to hear the sermon I'd be getting. I told her she could probably find out about it from the treasurer, who was a customer of hers. At the sacristy it was immediately clear that the two chums were already discussing me. Someone had probably told them that I was in town. Indeed, no sooner did I appear, very polite, hat in hand, than without giving me time to say a word the vicar stood up abruptly and said *"Cetu ma aman al lapous* (Here's the bird now.)"

The word *lapous* is used in many ways in Breton. It is applied to grand speechifiers, jokers, blowhards, flatterers, charmers in the phrase *lapous brao* or *lapous kaêr;* but it is also applied to knaves, thieves, rascals, and all sorts of scoundrels. And I knew that the vicar classed me with that last category. Nonetheless, I kept my calm in the face of the crude insult, stoically awaiting the rest of the sermon I had been warned of.

So, given my calm silence, which he probably took for fear and humility, the boxing vicar went right on. After calling me a "fine bird," a wolf, a Protestant, a Freemason, and a heretic, he told me I was a wheedler, a confidence man, a swindler, a man without shame or modesty, burrowing my way like that into a fine upright family to poison it from within. He broke off, for rage was strangling the words in his throat. The whole time, the treasurer was watching me steadily. As he never saw me move a hair, he assumed I was crushed, undone, terrified by the scarcely priestly rant from this man of God. However, when I saw the young lout stop, unable to wrench more insults from his gullet, I told him: "Monsieur the vicar, I see that you do not know, or you forget, the principles of the gospel which it is your mission to teach. The sermon you have just given bears little resemblance to the Sermon on the Mount."

But I could get no further, for the enraged boxer yelped in a strangled voice: "What? You come here to teach me the gospel—me!—*paour kez asen* (you poor ass!)"—and at that he made to lunge at me.

But the treasurer stopped him, telling him to let me talk a bit since I was talking politely.

"Yes indeed," I said, "I am polite, often far too polite, especially with insulters like your vicar. But since you permit me to talk, you who are in charge here, I have a few words to say to this insolent youngster. You have doubtless been informed that M. Déguignet Jean-Marie will never again make confession to any priest, nor kneel before the images of their god or their saints. However, one confession I will make to you, standing upright—a forthright, honest, and sincere confession. Monsieur the treasurer will not contradict me, I'm sure. He knows that I belong to a family that is one of the poorest in the commune but also one of the most respectable; he often saw me begging at his door in the days when I walked this whole area house to house, barefoot and ragged, to gather the wherewithal to feed myself and my little brothers and sisters. He saw me working at his place, with my father, on the days I was not begging alms. He saw me when I was a farmhand and when I was a cowherd, and he knows very well that no one ever had reason to complain of me. While I was away on military service, when I learned that my father had died and knowing that my mother was in deepest want, I found a way—it was unheard of—to send her money by drawing against my advance and my salary, and by taking on certain paid jobs. I left this place knowing nothing but what I learned tending cows at Kermahonec for Olive, the professor of agriculture. I returned wearing sergeant's stripes and speaking four languages fluently. I decided that I had done enough service and slavery, and being totally sober and free of ambition, I was planning to withdraw completely from the world—when chance, with a hand from relatives and friends, suddenly intervened to push me toward Toulven. There, at the spectacle of poverty overwhelming a family who in times past used to comfort me in my own miseries, my heart was touched—for I do have a heart, Monsieur the vicar; urged from all sides to go to their aid, and convinced that I could save them, at the cost of my own freedom and repose, I agreed. I promised to sacrifice everything to save that family, everything but my freedom of conscience—for I also do have a conscience, Monsieur the vicar. I have said this everywhere, I have declared it formally to those persons most concerned in the matter, to the seigneurs of Toulven who are presently the absolute masters of the Widow Rospart's fate and that of her children. For I will not go there as a deceiver or a hypocrite. The sacrifice will take place in a few days, unless some obstacle foreseen or unforeseen should block it. The curé Roumigou, who is supposed to consecrate the sacrifice, tells me that he will not do so, since I refuse to sacrifice my freedom of conscience as well.

However, he said that before he makes a final decision he will await your opinion, since I reside in this parish, and my family is here as well."

Through the course of this declaration, which I made as succinctly and swiftly as possible, the insolent and irascible tonsure-head tried several times to stop me, but the treasurer silenced him with a wave of his hand. At the end, I asked the vicar for the wedding banns certificate, telling him to note on it his least favorable opinions and observations about me, for those opinions and observations would decide the curé at Ergué-Armel whether or not to marry me in the church, the only marriage ceremony that Bretons believe valid. He finally sat down to scribble out a document, trembling with rage and choking back all the furious, vulgar abuse that was strangling him. But he dared not go too far in the presence of the treasurer, the richest and most respected man in the commune, who had the power to bring the young maniac to reason. When he finished writing, he sealed the document; he did not want me to know what he was telling his colleague at Ergué-Armel. I tossed ten francs on the table for him and took the document; then I shook the treasurer's hand and I left, with a final disdainful glance at the insolent fellow in the cassock.

The innkeeper was waiting anxiously for me. As I had been gone a long time, she thought the terrible vicar had forced me, by the power of word and fist, to kneel down before him and confess my sins. But before I had time to tell her about the conversation, the treasurer came in and took it on himself to describe it. He told her that in the battle at the sacristy, the loser was clearly the vicar, who could not contain himself for rage, and that if he, the treasurer, had not been present it would certainly have been not a battle of words but a battle of fists.

"And," I told him, "I'm afraid your nasty vicar would have been beaten there too, for all his fighting skills. I was gymnastics coach in the army, I've done singlestick, clubs, fencing, boxing, and kickboxing—and aside from fencing, none of them have I ever used for anything but play. I would not have been displeased to put them to a different use on that insolent tonsure."

"*O Intron Varia Kerzeot béniguet!* (Oh my blessed Lady Mary of Kerdévot!)," cried my future mother-in-law's cousin. "You would have dared to strike *un Den Doue* (a man of God)!"

"Yes, madame, if that man of God, vomited up by the demons, had laid a hand on me as he wanted to, he might just be lying on his bed right now with his ribs and his kidneys in a bad state."

"*A Guerc'hez vari,*" she kept saying, clasping her hands. "Look what you've turned into now! You used to be so gentle, so humble, such a good Catholic, like the rest of your family."

"I am still the same, madame—still gentle, humble, obedient, and obliging. It's just that my conscience requires me to denounce, repudiate, and despise people who exploit mankind, especially political and religious charlatans, knaves, and imposters. I offer proof of my gentleness, my kindness, and my obedience by obeying the voice that calls me out to Toulven to save your cousin and her children, against all my own best interests—personal, material, and intellectual."

The treasurer, who was one of the big yarn spinners and wags in the commune, seemed to enjoy listening to my words, but without attaching any significance to my views, assuming that this was just a style of talk, a business of bluffing—the way he did himself, attaching no greater significance to his own words than he did to other people's; he said that if I intended to live among Breton people I would just have to do as they do.

I hurried off to show the letter from the fighting vicar to the drunken curé at Ergué-Armel. On the way between the two towns I met a well-dressed peasant who said abruptly: "You're Déguignet, right?"

"Yes, I am—Jean-Marie Déguignet."

"Well, you're a thief! You stole my girlfriend Marie-Yvonne. She belonged to me, that girl."

Barely controlling myself with this vulgar bully, I told him that Marie-Yvonne hadn't been stolen yet by anyone, that he was free to go get her if she belonged to him. Thinking, as all Bretons do, that I was mocking him, he flung another vulgar insult, untranslatable into French, and made as if to attack me. This time my philosophy and my stoicism lost their equilibrium: with a punch and a kick, both at once, I sent him spinning into the ditch and went on my way. A moment later I heard him shouting after me that he was going to go tell the mayor and the police.

"Hurry up, then—we can go together, I'm on my way to town!"

But he did not seem to be hurrying, so I left him behind. In town, I learned that the fellow was a miller who had a little money that he was fast eating his way through; he had indeed gone to Toulven to ask for the hand of Marie-Yvonne Rospart, but the seigneurs of the chateau, informed that the gentleman was a lazy drunk and a brawler, refused him. He did not come into town, this sorry character, on whom I had the honor for the first time in my life of utilizing the skills of boxing and kickboxing, and I never heard of him again. On reaching town, I went straight to the curé's house to give him the letter. But to spare him the trouble of showing me the door, I stayed outside after handing his servant the paper. A moment later the drunk came to the door, the letter in his hand, saying,

"But you're a veritable demon! Right in the sacristy, before the crucified body of your lord and master, you insult the vicar with abuse and blasphemies! That's absolutely dreadful! And you think I'm going to marry you to the Toulven girl?"

"Pardon me," said I to the good curé, "you already told me that, but you must tell it to the landowners of Toulven, to the widow, to her daughter, and to the other interested relatives. As to the insults, abuses, and blasphemies uttered in the Ergué-Gabéric sacristy, it was the vicar himself who uttered them, and if the parish treasurer had not been present, he would have added blows and kicks to those filthy insults."

"So," said he, in a fury, "you're saying the vicar of Ergué-Gabéric is a liar?"

"Precisely," I said, "and he is merely conforming to the Christian principles, the art of lying, lying forever and always, *ad majorem dei gloriam* (for the greater glory of God)."

Then I really thought he would rip off his cassock and roll up his sleeves. I left with a shrug and went to look in at the inn where the meal was to be held, the great two-day-long wedding banquet. People there were somewhat uneasy, for word had come from the parish side that there would be no feast because the priest refused to marry me. But from the Toulven side, where the most interested parties were, the word was that it would take place. The tavernkeeper, who stood to gain handsomely from the banquet, asked why I didn't just give in to the priest, why not go to confession, it's so simple and it doesn't cost a thing.

"For the rest of you," I told him, "I know it's nothing. But for me it is the most serious thing in the world, because it is a matter of lying and deceit; lying to my conscience and deceiving everyone, including God himself if he should exist. No—no hypocrisy, no lies, and no betrayal. I gave my word to go to Toulven, but to go as the person I am. If I'm not wanted that way, let them give back my pledge and that's the end of it. I'll go right now to see them again, for this business has got to end one way or another."

But at Toulven, I found everyone still in the same frame of mind, waiting impatiently for the great day. I met with the seigneurs' steward, and told him there would be difficulties with the priest.

"The curé?" he said. "But he is a protégé of the chateau, he's a dinner companion and a good man. Don't you worry about it, no, no. Monsieur and Madame have accepted you and await you with impatience, therefore the priest will marry you no matter what, even if you were the devil incarnate."

It was just as I had thought. In Brittany, the priests and the nobility are always in league. Since they all live off the blood and sweat of the people, they must work together to bleed them and sweat them as much as possible. And here, the priests have the advantage over the nobility these days, since in the business of exploiting ignorance they are past masters, paid and protected by the laws and the government.

Now there seemed no further obstacle to the execution of the sacrifice, for it was agreed that the civil ceremony would take place on Sunday, and it was already Friday.

The next day, Saturday, I had to go into Quimper again to buy the all-important ring, *ar c'habest* (bridle), one of the most important items in a Breton marriage, especially for the woman, for once she has put the ring on her finger she considers the business over and done with. And in this purchase, her old parents find all sorts of portents; they can see deep into the fiancé's character as he discusses the choice of ring and its cost with his fiancée, the parents, and the jeweler. For my part, all I did in this matter, as in all other matters, was follow other people's lead. The girl could make her own choice, with the help of the old women. She started by looking at silver rings, for though they were rich, none of the older women had ever had gold rings. But the jeweler, seeing that the payer was a gentleman who seemed not to be watching too closely, hurriedly placed gold rings before them, saying that this was the latest fashion. It occurred to me that the fashion would not be a bad one if it were also the fashion to marry only people able to buy gold and silver rings, and able to provide such guarantees as the capacity to raise a half-dozen children in the best possible circumstances, and provide them with the means to buy their own gold rings and to keep stepping along the path of progress.

When the jeweler laid out the gold rings before the fiancée, she looked over at me with a laugh as if to ask what I thought. Poor girl, all she could think about just then was having nice things and being well turned out on her wedding day to draw everyone's admiration. So she did what the richest people of the time did, she took a gold ring *and* a silver one, which I paid for at the asking price, without a murmur, which was unheard of: a Breton paying for something without quibbling. It is also the current fashion for the fiancée to buy her fiancé something. In the past this would be a long silk ribbon to decorate his hat; now it is silver tassels for the two ends of the broad velvet hatband of the wealthy Breton peasant. But for me the new bride had to buy nothing, since I would be marrying in a regular city suit, with no stripes or ribbons.

The following morning, Sunday, I went to the town of Ergué-Armel alone to meet the mother and daughter, who were waiting to go with me for the civil marriage; only Uncle Rospart, the widow's cousin, was with them. As I have already said, Breton peasants attach no importance at all to the civil ceremony, even though it is the most important act in a man's life, as it determines all the rest of his days. We went to the town hall, stopping at the inn to pick up four people, at random, to act as witnesses. Before the mayor, a poor ignorant peasant, the solemnities were accomplished in utterly low-grade fashion, with laughter and jeers, Breton-style hoots and all sorts of vulgar joking. The mayor wore his sash over his everyday clothes and tried to recite a few words, which he translated as best he could, from Articles 212, 213, and 214 of the Civil Code, but nobody understood a word he said.

On the way back to the inn to pay monsieur the mayor a little something for his trouble, and the witnesses too, I said to Marie-Yvonne, "Well, my poor girl, now we're bound together forever."

"Oh, not yet!" she maintained still, laughing like a madwoman. "We've got to go to the church first."

I knew that. This solemn act was seen by Marie-Yvonne and all the others, including the mayor himself, as nothing more than a game for children playing wedding. Like so many beliefs, this one was so profoundly rooted among the Breton peasants that nothing could rip it out. And the priests take great care, besides, to keep the idea alive as best they can, for the sake of their cash-boxes. Their catechism says that the only legitimate marriage is the one performed according to the laws of the Church. They have invented a Breton proverb for the young folk, saying that the church's permission is required to put the male chemise next to the female; the *rochet* beside the *hinvich* in Breton.

THE WEDDING FEAST LASTED TWO DAYS

On the next Tuesday, which was October 6, 1868, the wedding took place at the church, followed by two days of feasting. I simply put on one of the suits I'd bought at Mourmelon and had intended to take along with me to my hermitage life in the Stang-Odet. And we set out, the old gendarme and I, for the town of Ergué-Armel, like any two people going for a walk. My godmother would have come along with us, but she was waiting for some cousins whom she had gone in person to invite to the wedding celebration of her godson, the former beggar-boy, who was about to marry into one of the richest families in the region. As we walked unhurriedly toward town, several wagons rolled past us on the Benodet road carrying Marie-Yvonne. When we arrived, the town was already full of people. More guests arrived than were expected, and all the local people from round about came out of curiosity, to see what might happen between the curé and the groom, for that cassock-wearing drunkard had gone right on telling everyone that he would refuse to marry me. So as soon as I arrived, the old women, Marie-Yvonne's aunts and cousins, came up to me in tears, saying that would be really sad, heartbreaking, a wedding celebration without the priest's blessing!

"Don't cry," I said, "This wedding will be blessed just like any other." And seeing that some of the women were already under the influence of the banquet wine, I told them: "I'm the one giving the orders here today, and your curé will obey, you'll see."

And indeed, a few moments later the bells began to peal, calling us to the church, and the faces grew calm. But it still remained to be seen how things would go at the church, for that morning the drunken liar was still saying he would refuse to marry me. So the little Ergué-Armel church filled up swiftly with rubberneckers. When I arrived with my wife, the rascal was already at the altar, set to mumble his *oremuses*, to call upon the God of Abraham, Isaac, and Jacob—that is, the cruel god Jehovah, the god of bandits, satyrs, and assassins—to come and bless our union. *Deus Abraham, Deus Isaac et Deus Jacob vobiscum sit et ipse conjungat vos empleat que benedictionem suam in vobis. Alleluia, alleluia sacramentum hoc magnum est in christo et in eclesia* (Praise, Praise the Lord, this mystery of marriage is great before Christ and the Church; for Christ and for the people of the Church.) It might well be a mystery, since the Gospels say that the union of a pigeon and Mary Joachim, produced a sheep—the *Agnus Dei*; but for Reason guided by Science, there are no more mysteries.[*] I listened impassively to the old satyr as, in his kitchen Latin, he called down the blessing of the Jews' god onto the heads of a freethinker and

---

[*]Joachim, Mary's father; thus, her maiden name, according to the author.

an unthinking Catholic. I could see no one but the officiator and his assistants, who stood facing me, but I was certain that all eyes were fastened on me, watching to see what attitude I would adopt and what gestures I would make in the course of the ceremony. But they saw nothing unusual, only a peasant dressed up as a petit-bourgeois, who throughout all the holy monkey-business budged no more than old Saint Allour, the parish's patron saint, next to whom I was standing.

When it was all over, we had to go into the sacristy with witnesses to sign the sacred document and pay the charges, six francs plus a tip; the latter is optional, but the biggest is always the best received by those representatives of Him who always said that the rich and the moneyed gentry [*sic*] would never enter into his kingdom. With those tips, the gifts, and the collection plate, our Breton priests make ten thousand francs' income in poor communes. As I walked out of the church, I was literally besieged by a legion of beggars. Fortunately, I had stuffed my pockets with coins, and had soon distributed them with a free hand. I recalled that in the past, I, too, used to chase after *en dud ne'vez* (newlyweds) asking for change. But back then we had a special routine for stopping newlyweds and fairly forcing them to give us a few sous or liards. At the time, we had no such things as charabancs to ride in. Newlyweds and the rest of the wedding party would go to town on horseback, the man in the saddle with his lady riding on the rump behind him. We beggars, we penny-seekers along the way, would go to the narrowest part of the road and string a sturdy rope across their path, and when the *mab ne'vez* or the *Merc'h nevez* arrived, we would shout: *arc'hant craon pe ar verc'h an traon!* (Half a crown or the bride comes down!)* The coins would fall, and we'd lower the rope. Sometimes some sharp horseman would dash his horse forward to try breaking the

---

*Literally, "the new son" and "the new daughter," designating the newlyweds.

rope. But that was a crime, a sacrilege—refusing to give *gueneen an drugare* (lucky money) to the poor, God's true children; it was a crime that could draw bad luck down on to the new couple. So the bold fellow who had rushed the rope would hastily find some old man and stop him, saying, *Malevurus, petra zonjes te?* (You, poor fellow, so what do you think?) But the custom is abandoned now, like many others. No matter how tenacious and stubborn they are, the Bretons still eventually abandon their old customs as they do their old costumes. There is one thing they do, though, that will never disappear as long as the race endures, and that is caustic mockery. On that point, I notice some progress day by day now that children go to school.

As planned, the celebration went on for two days, which was not entirely pleasant for me. I made some futile efforts to seem cheerful and pleased. As I find it impossible to disguise anything about my character, my sentiments, my opinions, I can honestly say that rather than happy and pleased, I felt myself the most unfortunate of men. I could already feel the weight of the double or triple chain I had welded myself to, which I could bear only by deploying all my powers of abnegation, my philosophy as a Stoic. And to cap the miseries of those feast days, late on the second day, when we were to leave for the farm, the horse that was meant to take us there had vanished. It was a fine prank some nasty fellows played on newlyweds. No matter, we started off anyhow, a party of half a dozen, dragging the cart with its load of brandy bottles in a basket and one poor little girl, the youngest of the family, who had long been ill from her privations and miseries; but she yearned to come to the final day of her sister's celebration, and it was the last one she would ever see, for three days later we buried her.* The wedding journey had an odd, comical

---

*Marie-Renée Rospart was six years old.

quality to it. Fortunately, it was nighttime, so no one saw us, although it certainly deserved to be seen and noted, some painter could have made a magnificent canvas of it. On reaching the farm, the first thing we saw was the horse, standing at his stable door for what had probably been a long while, with no one paying him any mind. There was a servant at the house, an old soldier; but the fellow had attended the first day of the feast and had still not sobered up.

The house was crowded, in fact, with old folks and young, come to attend the bedding of the newlyweds, *àr zouben dar lez.* This is another old Breton custom, one of the most vulgar and most grotesque, most stupid and immoral in the eyes of anyone at all civilized, but one that Bretons see as just innocent fun. And that is the bad thing about our much-vaunted civilization—everywhere it produces people who are bored and boring, irritating and irritated. That night, everyone was having a fine time, with no holds barred, no worries, and not a glance for the poor child we had tossed dying onto her bed as she came off the cart. Everyone was laughing, dancing, drinking and eating and singing, tumbling and fumbling and nuzzling as unself-consciously as any other animal. I myself, the only half-civilized creature there, stood about like an imbecile, with no idea what to do or say. I withdrew to the bedside of the poor dying girl to ask if she was in much pain. And the poor child, near death as she was, again asked me why I wasn't enjoying myself like everyone else. She wanted to see me do magic tricks again like the ones she saw the first time I came to Toulven. Poor child, with death breathing hotly on her, she was still thinking about the pleasures of this world, and I—full of life, vigor, and health—I was pondering its sorrows.

However, the moment was coming when I would have to undress and climb into bed with my wife, in front of this whole mad drunken crowd, and undergo all sorts of teasing, vulgar innuendo, vile talk. But I knew that my usual stoicism would not suffice to withstand it. So I took advantage of a moment of general uproar to slip out the back door and into the woods a hundred yards from the house. My heart was bursting and my head ready to split. The cool forest air did me good. In the woods there were several lanes, and I followed the one where my legs took me; it led to the beach at the edge of the sea, which happened to be at high tide just then. I threw off my overcoat and my hat and started plunging my head into the water several times. The drenching restored me; my thoughts, near confusion, returned to their natural course. Reflective, I began to follow along the shore, breathing great lungfuls of the fresh salty air with its scents of seaweed.

Walking between sea and wood, I came upon another gate, and a different broad lane. This one was an actual lawn, already covered with autumn leaves. Thinking that it too must lead back to the farm, I followed it. But soon I reached a fork where it split into three branches. There I stopped, and I listened, to see if I could hear the hullabaloo that must still be going on at the farm; hearing nothing, I turned about and went back down to the sea to rejoin the path I had come by. But now that my nerves had relaxed, my brain calmed, a kind of general lassitude set in, on that soft lawn covered with grasses and leaves. I sat down to smoke a cigar; I still had a few in my pocket from a pack I had bought for the guests. But I had not slept for several nights, and before I finished my cigar I fell into the arms of Lord Morpheus, one of King Sleep's ministers. And immediately my *spiritus*, my immaterial being which never rests, set out upon a journey through the world, to revisit all the countries I had seen. In Mexico, it found *el amigo* Don Salvarez, the philosophical savant, and told him all its adventures since leaving Mexico. The good citizen of the Americas did not blame the spirit, but sincerely lamented that it had got itself entangled in chains when it might have lived free. I also saw *l'amico* Orticoni, who seemed truly to pity my fate; he had thought I was already living in my solitude, free and happy with my bees. Then from one dream to the next I moved back to my present situation. I saw myself lying there as if lashed to that lawn, unable to move, while my young wife, still a virgin, sang and danced with the fellows at the farm. And then, to carry out the *ar zouben dar lez* (milk-soup ceremony) some other man would have to go to bed with the new bride for lack of the husband, who might possibly have done what the well-known Saint Alexis did.[*]

I finally managed to wake up, just at the moment when rosy-fingered dawn appeared on the horizon. I went back to the sea to bathe my head, then set out on the farm road I had come by. Everyone was sleeping now, except for the servant, who, bowl in hand, was heading for the cellar to quench his thirst. He told me people had been looking everywhere for me. But they were not worried, for such things still happen rather often, the new husband or wife runs off to hide at the very moment, to avoid the grotesque farces of the *zouben d'ar lez*. I followed the servant down to the cellar, where the sterward also appeared, on the pretext of asking after me. Then other neighbors, Uncle Rospart first among them, came in on the same pretext, but really to have some cider and a little liquor to drink, for the cider was good and there were still several bottles of good brandy in the house; and soon the partying took up again. After the men, the women came along too. But when they had drunk and eaten their fill, they all set out for home, assuring me of their warm friendship and of their help if ever I should need it.

A FEW HOURS OF SUPREME HAPPINESS

When everyone had left, and I saw that I could do no work that day, I proposed to my wife a walk by the shore to show her

---

[*]Late fourth-century solitary who fled his father's house in horror at marriage.

where I had spent the night. The weather was magnificent, and it was a pity not to take advantage of it to thresh a little buckwheat that had been harvested, the only crop the farm had; but for now I had shaken off all such concerns, in order to devote myself entirely to my young wife, whom I hadn't had time even to look squarely in the face. In cities, young people court for months and years before marrying, so by the time they marry their love is already old and worn. That was not the case for us, we had had no time for flirtation, to *fritañ ar qarantez*, as the Breton expression goes. Now, though, we had the right to do so. We were united by civil law, and sanctified by the Church, and as it is told in Genesis, we were henceforward to make but one and the same flesh.

The wood that borders the Toulven farm is very large and thick; it is called the boxwood forest. It still belonged to the former owner of Toulven, the present owner's uncle, who had sold off all the rest of the land but kept the woods and gardens for his lifetime. This aged bachelor, who still lived in an old manor house adjoining our farmstead, had been a first-class bon vivant; while he was rich, he had made Toulven a real lover's paradise. The wood where I was taking my young wife to stroll for the first time still bore the traces of it. Everywhere one looked there were bowers and groves, pavilions surrounded and nearly hidden by all sorts of exotic plantings. When we had walked by the sea and I had shown Marie-Yvonne where I spent the night, she led me into the middle of the wood to a large pavilion that was approached like the famous labyrinth, by circling it several times, looking hard for the entrance. Inside this love nest there were divans all around. On the ceiling a few remnants of painting were still visible; one could even make out the mythological subjects that Papa Antoine, as he was now called, used to love but, they say, loved better in flesh and bone than in paint, and still loved nowadays, even though he was eighty-four years old.

Contemplating this place, all the mythology, Bible stories, and legends came back to me, and all the celebrated loves in history and novels, from the story of Adam and Eve up to modern-day flirtage [*sic*]. And there we were, in the midst of this wood, in this love nest, far from prying eyes. Two people full of life and health and sap—she nineteen years old, a sturdy beautiful peasant girl, still a virgin, and I, thirty-nine, in my prime and not yet spoiled or contaminated by bestial loves, as are many men by that age. So we were in the best possible situation for surrendering to real love, to that supreme happiness all creatures have a right to. I could not offer my young Breton girl the idyllic, romantic lovemaking of a Romeo; she would not have understood it. Though there must be some appeal to such lovemaking, since it leads so many young people to suicide in hopes of going on to love one another in the next world. There in that pavilion, which had witnessed the senile lovemaking of old Papa Antoine, we made love as nature's children, like birds in springtime when nature wakens and urges them to love.

> All creatures form an eternal chain, and
> Unthinking, hand along the torch of love
> Each one hastily takes the immortal torch
> And gives it over in turn
> At least you will once have seen the gleam of a Sublime
>   light
> It will have marked your life for a moment
> As you fall you will carry with you into the Abyss
> Its dazzlement.

Yes, when two beings come together thus for the first time, two young and vigorous beings urged toward one another by similar feelings and similar overflowing needs, the moment is truly sublime. One must have felt it to understand it; must have felt it in the all the same conditions as Marie-Yvonne and I, for that sublime happiness cannot be expressed in any language. Mohammed said that in his Paradise such happiness is constant and eternal, so his Paradise is better than the one his colleague Jesus offers, where that sublime, supreme happiness is forbidden. Our miserable priests make it a sin, and a capital sin at that. They do not allow their flocks to enjoy that happiness "except in marriage only," and with certain restrictions even there. These men who, like their God, do not marry, the better to use and abuse this delight without assuming any of its consequences—except for the bodily rot they bring on themselves by self-abuse—and, except for prison, when publicly caught [in the act of] abusing children. We were able to give over to that supreme happiness without fear, without constraint, without false shame, with all the gifts that Mother Nature had granted us. Never had that sublime happiness been better tasted nor better shared than it was by the two of us, as true children of nature, with all our powers and ripeness, in the blending and fusion of our two beings that were now and henceforward one and the same flesh, as is written:

> *O giorno memorabile de tanti filici*
> *anima mia si ricorda ojedi*
> ["O memorable day of my delights—my soul recalls it
> still today . . ."]

Yes, for those few hours of supreme happiness, I have forgiven Marie-Yvonne all the sorrows that have crushed me since.

MY "NEW-FANGLED WAYS"

But after those more than heavenly delights, I had to consider the reality of my situation, the responsibility I had just undertaken. Looking about me everywhere on the farm, I saw nothing but ruin and poverty. The poor little girl was dead, surely dead from poverty. Her two other sisters were sick as well, from lack of healthy food and sanitation.

There was nothing to eat, for man or beast. There was only cider to drink. I would have to begin by procuring food. I bought a fat pig and a cartload of potatoes; lard, potatoes, and black bread is one of the Breton peasant's most valued meals. I also had to pay the yearly rent to the proprietor, whose greatest concern in my regard was that I should pay him, since I had declared that I had money; actually he didn't care a fig about how, now he had me bound by the lease and it was up to me to work things out. I had come up with a scheme that would have put me on my feet in the first year, if I had been allowed to do what I wanted. I would have liked to sell off everything on that poor farm: the cattle first, since there was nothing to feed them through the winter, and all the farm equipment—old carts and harrows and plows, terribly primitive, heavy, clumsy equipment. And then I would have bought new things that suited me better, as they were needed; and cows, when I had food for them.

And then I would have preferred to do no planting [the first year], at least no autumn planting, given that there was no manure and no land properly prepared for planting. But that scheme, which to my mind was a masterpiece of wisdom and foresight, was impossible to execute. People would have thought me insane, and might have carted me off to the asylum; there was one in the next commune to Kerfeunteun, full of peasants because it is also a huge agricultural enterprise, and once a good farmer goes into that place, insane or not, he never gets out. And besides, the landowner, who never gave a thought to his tenant farmers beyond extracting money out of them, would not have allowed me to strip his farm like that, the cattle and the equipment being his principal surety, and over which Articles 1766 and 2107 of the Civil Code gave him all rights. I was therefore obliged, despite myself, to keep within the usual custom for the moment, merely replacing the draft animals, who could no longer stand up, with others who could walk and work, and modifying the crude, heavy tools into more manageable, lighter ones. I began my "newfangled ways" by cleaning out the barnyard, which was full of filthy pools and could not be crossed in rainy periods; it was certainly a major source of the illnesses that reigned constantly on the farm. I say "newfangled ways" because everything I was to do there, no matter how much it might be in the best interests of all, would be called that: *kichou névez.*

After the barnyard, the house needed disinfecting. In that house, as in all the old Breton farmsteads, there was a great stone trough fitted into the wall, facing and very close to the dining table. Into that trough were tossed all the leavings from meals, spoiled milk, dishwater, and other household garbage. All those materials were in constant acetic, putrid fermentation, poisoning the household air. I knew it would be a rough business to get rid of this foul sewer, *ar veol,* a thing Breton women consider to be the most important feature of the house. So war was now declared between me and the whole family, including my wife, and I would have to keep the family going by myself or founder in routine and destitution along with it.

For this important operation I chose a Sunday, when my wife and her mother had gone into town to High Mass. With help from the old manservant and my brother-in-law, I threw the contents of the foul trough onto the dunghill, and after cleaning it thoroughly I plastered it over. Then I had them move all the cooking vessels from around the sewer into a corner at the far end of the house, where a special installation was set up. Then in their place, across from the table, I set a new cupboard and a tall pendulum clock I had bought, which certainly looked far better there than that *ar véol*, that poisonous and poisoning trough. The house was completely transformed; it looked like a parlor now.

But for me the story was not finished. I was sure that when the women returned, I was in for some terrible tongue-lashings, which were often more terrible than knife-slashings, especially the ones that came from the mother-in-law, who had a remarkable talent for hurting people around her without losing her composure. But I had made a stoical resolve never to enter into any discussion, or rather dispute, with her, nor with the rest of them. Trying to discuss or argue with ignorant people, fools, and fanatics wastes time, and risks bringing on trouble. When the two women came in, a little late because they had met up with some other biddies to discuss the famous son-in-law who was the talk of the town, they stopped short, confused by the new cupboard and the clock; they thought they might have come into the wrong house, for they had had a few drinks with the other biddies. I went out to round up the cows in the field, telling my brother-in-law to explain to the women, when they had got over their astonishment, my reasons for doing this, which were the same reasons I had disinfected the farmyard. They raised a ruckus, especially about the sewer-trough. They even said they were going to take out the two handsome new pieces of furniture and reopen the rot-basin. But they did nothing of the kind, because every day and every minute I pulled another *kij névez* (newfangled trick) on them, so that they had no time to spend on the last one. I had books, and good ones too, in several languages, languages that I knew; I subscribed to an agriculture newspaper, and whenever I heard the mother-in-law attacking my new ideas as she did every two minutes, I would pick up my paper or book and let her tongue run on as if I didn't hear or couldn't understand.

Anyhow, in a short time the farm had an entirely different look, indoors and out. All the crude tools had been transformed or replaced, the areas around the house cleaned up and made healthy. My wife's relatives and friends, who came visiting out of curiosity to see what that strange fellow was up to—that fine son-in-law at Toulven causing so much talk in the area—would compliment me on all these changes. But these compliments to me did not please the mother-in-law; she would rather see me muddling along and stagnating in the old routine and rot; she would rather see me go into town every Saturday and to Mass every Sunday, and come back to the house at night liquored up, singing and waving my arms the way her husband used to do, instead of staying home, working the farm, and tending my cattle. What riled her above all was to see me reading my books and my newspapers, and writing. She said agriculture wasn't done with books, nor with pens. However, when she went too far with her stinging insinuations, for the woman only spoke by insinuation; when she scolded me too bitterly for my religious and political views, I would tell her to remember what I had made a clear point of declaring to everyone, to the interested parties in this situation, before I entered into it.

THE GOOD MOTHER-IN-LAW WOULD GRUMBLE

Knowing that on this farm, dairy cows were the only way to make a living, I immediately turned my attention to that area. For good milk cows, you need good pasturage in summer and good hay in winter, with a strong fodder-root system. Therefore all my efforts went to the meadows, to preparing the soil by deep tilling in order to sow or plant forage roots in the spring. But I put the greatest effort into the aforementioned marshland, the biggest piece of terrain on the farm, which was called "the red meadow" because there was nothing on it but pools of red water, thorn bush, reeds, moss, and briar, and which the people hadn't even wanted to show me when I had my official tour, saying that the marshland was worthless. And even then I had already considered it to be the best plot on the farm. Through that whole first winter, when other work was not too demanding, we would go and work there. First I had deep channels dug to drain the red, stagnant water. But whenever we went to work in the red meadow, the good mother-in-law would grumble, saying that we were wasting our time over nothing. But my brother-in-law, who was beginning to trust me, would tell the old woman: "*Malesgast!* (Son of a gun)! We absolutely won't be wasting all our time." And in fact, in that marsh, which connected to the sea by a brook, we found enormous eels that could have made us a good deal of money. But whatever we could not eat ourselves I gave to the neighbors and to the seigneurs at the chateau. When the channels were finished and the red meadow drained, I had workers clear the thorn, the reeds, and the briar, and then level the ground. The material dredged out of the ditches, which was only vegetable matter—peat with thorns, briar, and heath—was dried, heaped up, and burned, which gave me a good supply of ash to spread on the field. All of that was done during the winter, and thus with no loss of time, as the old woman would say—she was always going on about our wasting our time. She even found something to criticize in the ash, she said it could have been put to some worthwhile use, whereas there on the red meadow it would serve no purpose. By the end of April, though, that meadow was no longer red; it could now be called "the green meadow." Indeed, from the addition of the ash, there sprang up a thick cover of all sorts of clover, bird's foot trefoil, and heavy fescue grasses. It was like a miracle, and in fact that was how the neighbors understood it—not a heavenly miracle, of course, since I denied the Nazareth miracle-man, but a miracle of Satan, who according to the Bretons works a hundred times as many as the miracle-maker of Gennesareth, for he is the one they credit with any great fortune and any unexpected good luck befalling people. The red meadow suddenly transformed into a green one could only be the doing of my ally Satan. And the old mother-in-law even said that the clovers and other grasses from that field would not be good for the cattle. But there again the old woman was disappointed, because by the end of May, I was able to start feeding them that good fodder, and then I could begin the milk and butter sales that I knew were the sole practical means of drawing [any income] from the farm. By using this fodder in the stable, I would produce the manure I so needed to build up the exhausted soils.

The devil came to my aid in another circumstance that year as well. I had been told it was impossible to grow buckwheat on the farm, as the soil was so badly infested by the notorious parasite plant that is the despair of all Breton growers, what they call *olc'houenen* (wild mustard). Its seeds live on forever in the soil, and grow so vigorously in freshly cultivated earth that they exhaust and crowd out the cultivated crops. The field where I wanted to sow buckwheat happened to be right next to the red meadow, and was said to have the worst infestation of the wild mustard. I had turned up the soil very early in the winter, and then again in the spring I gave it another harrowing, which destroyed a heavy crop of the parasite plant already sprouting. Then after that harrowing, and a rolling, it grew in again just as thickly. The old woman laughed maliciously, seeing me struggle with this awful enemy, which she was sure would get the better of me unless the devil came to my aid again. And the good devil must have done, because by the end of June, the old woman, along with the astonished neighbors, could see the most gorgeous field of buckwheat in the whole neighborhood, with not a single yellow weed in it. It was another miracle by Paulic, the devil. In fact it was a double miracle, for the jealous old woman had predicted that I would never get buckwheat to grow there, first because of the wild mustard and second because of the way I had done the sowing, that is, I had prepared the soil and sowed the seed exactly opposite from the way other people did, from the old tradition.

This showed me that if the human brain is poisoned when it is young, it will understand nothing later on, even the simplest things. I tried to tell some farmers how easy it was to keep this much-feared parasite plant from damaging the cereal crops in any way. The seeds of the yellow mustard only sprout when they are brought all the way up to the surface of the soil, and if they have already sprouted, just a light crosswise harrowing on a sunny day will be enough to destroy them completely. Buckwheat can then be sown over the surface, but in covering the seed you must harrow only very lightly, to avoid bringing more of the parasite seeds up to the surface. That's the whole secret, and it doesn't cost a thing. But our local farmers do not understand it, like so many other equally simple secrets, and thus every year they lose time and money needlessly.

So now I had already worked two great miracles, both at almost the same time and one after the other: a wild meadow considered worthless transformed into a clover field, and the finest field of buckwheat on land where I was not supposed to harvest anything but wild mustard weed, useless *olc'houenen*. But I still had a good many miracles left to work, for like the god of the Jews and Christians, I needed to create everything from nothing.

One thing still troubled me terribly, seeing my wife obliged to buy vegetables in Quimper when she went to the market. I had promised her that our business would soon change—that instead of going to town to buy vegetables she would be going there to sell them. There were two plots of land that were neglected because they were too small and irregularly shaped to be worked with the plow. I made two fine kitchen gardens out of them. In the spring these gardens gave the women white cabbage, carrots, onions, early potatoes, peas, and all the salad they wanted, which these people had never tasted but which they found delicious during their hard labors at harvest time. These good vegetables were my own personal project; nobody worked that garden but me—labor and care that I did on Sundays, holidays, and evenings after the day was finished in the fields. I had built a shack nearby, and in it I would take my siesta, smoke my cigarette, read my paper. I had also put up a half-dozen beehives there, just for amusement, for I was sure that the area was not suited to apiculture. When someone told the lovely jealous mother-in-law that the "red meadow" had suddenly turned green, she scowled as if to say that someone was trying to pull her leg but she was too old and too experienced in agricultural matters to be fooled. And when she was told that the buckwheat field was superb and hadn't a twig of *olc'houenen* in it, she didn't believe that either. However, she did not dare go to look, for fear of finding herself face to face with reality, which would have made her sick; especially about that worthless red meadow that she had offered to rent to the first taker for twenty-five francs a year, and here I would be earning at least six hundred francs from it that first year without spending a sou.

So I was pleased with myself. I could see now that, but for a catastrophe, I would not fail in my undertaking, despite the terrible struggle I was having to wage against everybody; even against my own wife, and especially her old mother, who instead of backing my efforts did everything they could to thwart them; never approving of anything I did, because I did not do it the way other people did it. And yet day after day they received compliments from people who would come to view the farm; and, in town, when they began selling milk and butter, products they had never sold before and which customers were soon competing for, once the products became known. Soon, in the Rue Neuve neighborhood, people talked of nothing else but the Toulven milk and butter, which until then were unknown on the market.

But I had only myself to look to for contentment and satisfaction, and that sense of pleasure in working and living, for there was no one else to tell about those feelings; I was less fortunate than other domestic animals, for they do find a way, through all kinds of movements and sounds, to express their feelings.

HIS LITTLE GOD LOCKED UP IN A BOX

That autumn, I did find two or three occasions for expressing my feelings such as I had always declared them. The Breton priests customarily solicit alms on the farms every year, after the harvest, when they know that the barns and cupboards are more or less full. The curé sends out two people prominent in the commune. I happened to be at home when the men came in announcing that they were collecting alms for Saint Allour, the patron saint of the parish. I told them right away that this Saint Allour had never existed, and, even if he had, he no longer needed any bread or money, and that this work they were doing was the most shameful, despicable work possible: to have the audacity to go asking for grain and money from poor people who themselves didn't have enough bread to feed their children, and asking it for a rascal bachelor to whom the ignorant and stupid villagers give over ten thousand francs a year. That is not mendicancy, or collection. It is a vicious swindle, like everything else those tonsured rascals do. There is nothing they do, and nothing they can do in their godly profession, that doesn't fall directly under Article 405 of the Penal Code, if it were properly followed and applied to their case. I said all that to the two alms-collectors to explain my refusal, meanwhile pouring them glasses of cider.

A few days later, I went into town with a wagonful of wood, and on the Bénodet road I ran into the curé, who was carrying the Good Lord, the viaticum, to a sick person; a man walked ahead of him with a lantern on a pole. On such errands, these god-peddlers are used to having people— grand and humble, rich and poor—prostrate themselves as they pass by. I felt no need to prostrate myself before that tonsured drunk, nor before the little god he kept in a box. Seeing this, the god-porter bore down on me, a raised cudgel in one hand and the other pointing to the box hanging at his neck that contained the soul and body of his lord in the form of a wafer; he was shouting through his foaming mouth, "If you refuse to salute the priest, at least salute the sovereign master he is carrying."

Instantly I answered sharply, "I pity him, that sovereign master, and you too; you may not respect the people who feed you with their blood and their sweat, but do not attack them on the high road the way bandits attack travelers."

He went on his way, still brandishing his club, raging and foaming. That quasi-tragicomic scene had several witnesses: my manservant who was driving my cart; the lantern-bearer, who was the local road-mender and barkeep, Dordu du Moulin des Landes, one of the nastiest gossips in the commune, forever trying to cheat people but too clumsy to pull it off; and other passersby who had stopped to watch. But there was one very significant witness: the deputy mayor of the commune, who had kept hidden behind the hedge across the road, in a field he owned. I saw him only on my way back, at an inn where we stopped to drink a mug of cider, my servant and I. The deputy mayor had just been describing the event; he had never seen the like in his life, he said. For a moment he had been frightened, he said, and that was why he had stayed hidden. Because the priest just might bring charges, said the honorable deputy mayor.

"Yes, I know," I said, "that these charlatans and imposters who used to make up their own laws—civil, military, and religious, retaining all rights and powers for their side—now forbid us under threat of fines and prison from disturbing them in the slightest in the pursuit of their activities. But that's not the case here, because I'm the one who was disturbed and impeded in the pursuit of *my* activities as farmer, merchant, and wagoneer—activities that are far more useful, worthy, and honorable than his, which are nothing but charlatanism, imposture, and scurrilous mischief."

The incident caused a good deal of talk, and would have given rise to some terrible legend if it had occurred a few years earlier. Still, the whole thing did finally convince people that I was not, as they thought, a bluffer and a wag; that I do match my actions to my words.

MY FARMING FOLLIES

I continued to make improvements on my farm, despite resistance from the women, both mother and daughter. Day by day, as she aged, the old woman grew grouchier, more cantankerous, and supremely nasty. She had collected within her own person all the vices that got loose from Pandora's box; she would have made a good Catherine de Medicis or Queen Elizabeth, if need be. My wife, now that she had all the money she wanted, never missed a party or celebration, where she mingled with rich farmers' wives whom she tried to match in magnificence; little by little, she abandoned all the house-hold concerns and activities.

The gendarme uncle, whom I've mentioned, came to live with us, having nowhere to go after the death of his sister, my godmother; that was a burden for me, and one more enemy. With his Breton stubbornness, his ignorance in all matters, of course, the man also deplored everything I was doing. One year, especially, he had a good long spell of criticizing his idiot nephew's growing methods.

I had one newly cleared plot that had so far only grown buckwheat and therefore had not been infested with weeds. It was light soil, and rather deep, so I intended to put in carrots, one of the best winter fodders for dairy cows, and good for horses and pigs as well. I had prepared the soil well, and had given it a good dose of manure. In the spring, I sowed my carrots early. I had fashioned a tool that was half hiller, half hoe, which I used to plant my potatoes, hoe them, hill them, and pull them out; now I used that same tool to sow my carrots in rows. The old cop, when he saw that, nearly split his insides laughing, but it was a hollow, sickly, bitter laughter—now the nephew was no longer just an ignorant oaf, he was raving mad. The old man left the field thumping his club on the ground and the bushes, and went to tell the ladies about my crazy idea. Not only was I planting carrots with a "plow," as he called my peerless tool; I was also planting them at the new moon, which was absolutely contrary to common sense, which showed a complete ignorance of every agricultural principle. Never seen anything like it. He had plenty of time to grumble, too, for carrots take a long time to come up. Two weeks later, he was telling the women and the servants that something should absolutely be sown or planted in that field, as it was so well tilled and fertilized, as for the carrots, they'd never see a single one. Meanwhile, my carrots were coming up nicely, and when the rows showed clearly I gave them a light hoeing by hand. But the old cop told the servants and the women that they were wasting their time again: those weren't carrots, they were weeds brought in with the manure. After that first hoeing, the carrots shot up visibly. I cultivated between the rows a second time with my peerless tool, which I could turn as I liked into a plow, a hiller, a hoe, or a harrow. When the carrots had reached finger size, since they were crowded, I thinned them out progressively by pulling a few each day to feed to the young calves and the pigs, mixed with dishwater and spoiled milk. The young animals enjoyed that mightily, and even grew plump. My codger uncle really could no longer deny that those were carrots, fine yellow and white carrots, true fodder carrots. The poor old lunatic simply did not know what to say anymore. The women, who had sided with him at first, were making fun of him now, and the servants coming in from the field with cartloads of carrots would show them off to him and sneer. From then on, the old uncle fell silent, and when toward the end of August he was shown carrots of a length and thickness never before seen in the area, he left and went into Quimper to stay with another nephew—to everyone's great satisfaction, in fact, except perhaps for the old harpy, who no longer had anyone to tell her about the agricultural insanities of her over-kind and over-patient son-in-law.

LONG LIVE THE REPUBLIC! DOWN WITH THE PRIESTS!

In the current campaign, I shall do all I can to help the candidates who call themselves republicans; for the other ones, the noblemen and the Jesuits, would certainly drag us backwards four or five centuries, back to the good old days when peasants and workers were considered and valued at seventeen grades lower than draught animals and dogs; the struggle had begun.* The government had chosen the system of voting by local district; it was hoping this would yield an easier and more thorough victory for its candidates, who in each district were chosen from among the most prominent, the best known, the richest and the most influential of the Jesuitico-clerico-monarchist party. Their chosen candidate for our district was a big industrialist, a millionaire many times over, clerical and monarchist to his fingertips, with support from the whole administration, the nobility, the priests, and his fellow industrialists. The other, the republican opposition candidate, was just a poor lawyer who actually did have support from a few millionaires who were monarchist but anticlerical.

The friends and protectors of the official candidate had arranged for the distribution of brochures in French and in Breton, in which the Republic and the republicans were disparaged and damned in every way. The poor republican candidate was caricatured and called all sorts of names: a devil, a wolf, a fox, and an ass. The Jesuits and clericals, although confident of winning, nevertheless thought it worthwhile to draw in the peasants and workers any way they could. They sent their agents out into the countryside, pockets stuffed with hundred-sous coins, to spread readymade speeches and patter, brochures and newspapers, cigars and *guin ardent* (brandy). The landowners called together their tenant farmers and their workers and treated them to what used to be called full *rastels* (troughs); that is, all they could eat and drink. Our chatelain had called his people in too on the evening before the vote. After the *rastel,* he told them to turn

---

*In the legislative elections of February 1876, Louis Hémon, a lawyer and a republican, was challenging the incumbent Augustin Dumarnay, who favored a constitutional monarchy.

up the next morning at an inn near the town, where more *guin ardent* would be handed out, along with ballot slips, and the master would then lead them all together in serried ranks to the polling place. But most of those who had gone for refreshment at the chateau came to my house afterwards, to ask me for ballot slips in the name of the republican candidate. I gave them out, recommending that they fold them up tight and hide them in their undershirts or up their sleeves, for Monsieur Malherbe might easily search them before giving out his own marked ballots the next day.

The next morning I was in town early, at the inn designated by our Lord Malherbe. There I found most of the men who had come by my house the night before; they had already drunk to M. Malherbe's health. They all told me, "Don't worry, Jean-Marie, we're having a dance with the lordship's half-crowns—they don't dance very often—but we'll dance with his ballots later on, too."

"Don't talk too loud," I told them. "We'll see tonight."

When I saw the count's carriage arriving, I moved off so he would not see me with his group. He climbed out of his carriage, offered more drinks to people who wanted them, then lined them up on the road and handed each of them a tightly folded ballot slip. He did not search them. The distribution completed, he took command on their right, and conducted them to the voting place, walking behind to keep them from taking other ballot slips on the way. All the other landowners were arriving too with their own bands of fifty or sixty. I did see several voters, though, who like me were determined to preserve their independence. These were new republicans, converted since witnessing the actions of this fine so-called "moral" government. These men were saying, as I was, that the aristocrats and Jesuits and their like were going to have some disappointments when the day was over, since they were counting on near-unanimity from the voters in our commune. In fact, the former bonapartist mayor, the principal agent for the monarchist clergy, never left the doorway of the town hall for a moment, and as each of the landowners arrived with his flock, the fellow would tell them they could rest easy, people were all voting as one for the official candidate; the gentlemen would shake his hand and smile. I, too, was standing by the town hall doorway, and I was smiling as well, for the majority of the voters, as they left the voting place with their leader to return to the inn to drink and eat again at the expense of Monsieur the Count, were signaling me by finger or wink to say "Fine, we've taken the old guy for a ride."

One of the count's group, a man I knew to be a spy and a traitor, came to take me along to the inn to eat and drink to the health of the chatelain, who was very pleased with his people, the man said. But I refused. The count had long since already offered me more than food and drink, and when his promises had no effect on me, he had turned to threats, but the threats were no more effective than the promises. That being the situation, I was not invited to the Saturday night *rastel*, nor to the post-ballot gathering on Sunday morning. Monsieur saw that all was fruitless with me.

Then, just before the ballot urn was to be opened, a carriage arrived from Quimper bearing the most prominent figure in the commune, a man who owned several estates there, an old bachelor and millionaire who had become a republican because he disliked priests. He was the one who, through his personal influence and the influence of his gold, had urged and persuaded the peasants and workers to vote for the republican candidate. Stepping down from the carriage, he came over to me, knowing that he was talking to the main republican in the area. He asked how the day had gone. I told him in an ironic tone, and rather loudly so that the former mayor should hear me: "Well, Monsieur Eugène, according to our former mayor, the day has gone very badly for us—so badly that it could mean we'll be sent off to Devil's Island in a few days, you and I especially. Actually," I said with a laugh, "we'll hear for sure in a moment."

The tally was about to begin. We entered the hall, which was already full of excited, anxious voters. Monsieur Eugène Le Bastard de Kerguelen was appointed to take the ballots from the box. Suddenly from all sides of the hall sounded cries of "Long Live the Republic!" which terrified the former mayor and nearly made him fall over, for those were not the cries he was expecting; the [beadles] standing with him turned all crimson. What did it mean? But in a loud, authoritative voice, Monsieur Eugène called for silence, and the moment was truly solemn. However, the first ballot slips to emerge bore the name of the candidate of the clerical party, and those faces grew calm. But then only republican ballots appeared, and the shouts of "Long Live the Republic" started again, together with a few "Down with the priests!" The tally did not take long, for there were only two candidates and five hundred voters. When the ballots were all pulled out and counted, there were four hundred fifty for the republican, and only thirty-four for the clericals' candidate.[*]

The shouting and stamping was indescribable. The former mayor could not believe his eyes, despite the evidence, for Monsieur Eugène had carefully set down before him all the ballots as he unfolded them. The [beadles] walked out, wailing like calves, saying that all was lost for them. These poor fellows, who had run throughout the whole commune distributing reactionary brochures, newspapers, and broadsides, and telling voters that all the republicans would soon be sent off to Devil's

---

[*]218 Hémon, 3,458 Dumarnay.

Island, believed that the victorious republicans would do the same to them. But they did have one hope left: other villages had probably not voted like Ergué-Armel. The devil Déguignet, to whom they attributed this incredible defeat, had not been to every commune. And I thought that myself. So when it was all over in our district, I decided to go to Quimper.

A rich local landowner who was a nearby neighbor of mine, and who now called himself a republican as well, came with me. When we drew close to the prefecture, where all the Quimper voters were gathered waiting for telegrams to shout their acclamation—"Long live the Republic! Long live the commune of Ergué-Armel! Long Live Hémon!" we learned that our candidate, Hémon, had actually defeated his clerical opponent by a large majority.[*] And before leaving Quimper— where we stayed rather late, detained as we were by friends— we learned that all but two of the republican candidates in the department had won in the first round. So I thought we could be confident about the rest of France, since the republicans had won such a victory in a department in Brittany, the most Catholic place in the world, and where administration and clergy pressure had been so heavy on the voters.

[Déguignet's role in the local republican victory infuriated his landlords.]

I stood condemned from that day on, and when my lease ended the landlords would not forget it. But I had five years left to go, and perhaps things would change between now and then.

In any case, the monarchists, clericalists, and Jesuits, who were beaten, even though they held all the power in their hands, were forced to submit to the will of the people, at least

---

[*]5,218 Hémon, 3,458 Dumarnay.

for the moment. And Mac-Mahon, their leader and the President of the Republic, who had promised to go all the way, was obliged to do a somersault. The three hundred sixty-three deputies he had put out of the chamber came back, with others as well, and they told the man who had run away from [the battlefields of] Froeschviller and Sedan he now had one choice: either submit to the people, or submit his resignation.* The conqueror of Paris resigned. He was replaced by Jules Grévy, and then the real Republic was proclaimed—people were even calling it the *democratic* republic. But the unfortunate fact was that among the representatives of that democratic republic, there was not a single democrat. Democracy means government of the people by the people: *Civitas in qua populi potestas summa est,* yet in our democratic republic, the people—the true people—had no true representative. What they did have among their representatives were glib talkers, sophists, and phrasemakers who knew how to lull people with the magic powder of rhetoric, promising them bread and butter, even a chicken in every pot, like the wily Gascon† and his crafty [minister] Sully. In fact, that is how peoples are governed everywhere and always. The governing figures, the politicians in power, send to the populace the kitchen smoke and aromas, and meanwhile they eat up the stew with their own friends and relations. If that republican chamber of deputies had been made up of democrats, they would have begun by doing to the Jesuits and the reactionaries what those people had sworn to do to republicans if they won: they would ship off the biggest reactionaries to Devil's Island, where they had promised to send all us republicans;

---

*In 1877, Mac-Mahon named a Royalist cabinet and dissolved the Chamber of Deputies; new elections again returned a Republican majority.

†King Henry IV of Navarre.

and send all the Jesuits and other churchmen off to seek their own true kingdom, which, according to their Gospels and their own claims, is not of this world.

HEAVEN'S FIRE

In 1879, I suffered an illness that took me within inches of the grave. One Saturday, when I had mostly recovered, my wife went into town with her old mother. The servants were out in the fields cutting buckwheat. The weather was very fine, and I decided to leave my bed and have a look at my fields and animals, which I had not seen for a long time. I spent more than two hours on my rounds. When I came home, the house was in flames. Workers, who were digging pottery clay two hundred meters behind the house, had seen the smoke and come running, but too late. The entire house was reduced to ashes, and, knowing I was ill, the workers thought that I myself had been consumed in the house. When my wife and her mother returned, intoxicated, they began screaming curses on me: it was my doing, I with my blasphemies against the priests and against God himself, I had drawn heaven's fire down on the house. God was finally taking revenge on the rebel. As usual, I did not answer the women's abuse. I thought that the fire may not have come from heaven, but it could well have come from those people who are always talking about heaven, about God and about paradise, in their fierce hatred of a man who stood up to them on all matters, including the matter of death; for during my illness, those men of God had tried every means to get to me, with no success.

However, when the inside of the house was cleared, a hatchet was found near the spot where the great cupboard had stood. I told the servants that this hatchet had certainly not fallen out of the sky; before he set the fire, the arsonist must have used it to break into the cupboard for the money he expected to find there.

The gendarmes came to investigate, to find out how the fire started. But when they were told that a hatchet had been found beside the cupboard, they were convinced it was a crime, and they looked for the criminal; they actually found him. It was an old beggar, or rather an old robber, a man of the Church, of course. Several neighbors had seen him coming toward our farm with an empty sack and leaving with a full one. But the old thief was a friend of the priest, and the priest was the friend of the public prosecutor, and, of course, nobody bothered the criminal. Great scoundrels always manage. Like my women-folk, the priest merely said that it was heaven's fire sent to punish me, and everyone believed him. I did learn, though, that there were not only enemies surrounding me, for the next day, neighbors came bringing us linens, kitchen equipment, clothing, and other small things. They even came in wagons from very far away, bringing whole bolts of cloth, and grain, and lard. Even the seigneurs at the chateau, my mortal enemies, gave us many things; most importantly, they gave us the essentials—shelter and beds. Papa Antoine's old manor, adjoining our house, had not burned down (although the seigneurs probably wished it had, for they hated that old house as well because its now-deceased owner, their uncle, had been their sworn enemy). In the house-sale held after old Antoine de la Hubaudière died, the beds had been spared, for they were built into the walls and fixed there. So we were put up in his old manor, where we found the beds all ready for us; the mistress had sent over sheets and blankets.

Fortunately, I had paid my rent some weeks before the crime. The criminal, who had first broken into the cupboard, would have expected to find a hefty sum there, as it was close to Michaelmas, the season when tenant farmers pull together their every sou to send to the landowner. So, having lost none of my cattle, nor my heavy farm equipment, I was able to go on, to the great disappointment of my enemies, who thought that I would never recover from the blow. They thought my rent was unpaid and that the landowner, being my enemy as well, would not miss the chance to force a sale of the cattle and the equipment to collect his money. They were mistaken once again. But the time was approaching where their cannibalistic, wild-animal instincts would be gratified. For I had only two years to go on my lease, and everything led me to expect that it would not be renewed, despite all the fine promises made to me when the seigneurs first lured me on to the farm, promises they renewed several times more until 1877, until the day when the dame came to believe that by means of some kind of hellish power, I had unquestionably turned white ballots into red ballots inside the election urn.

I HAVE FATTENED YOU FOR FIFTEEN YEARS . . . AND NOW YOU PUT ME OUT

The final year arrived. At Michaelmas, when I went to pay my next-to-last rent, I told the count that it was time to let me know whether or not the lease would be renewed. The would-be gentleman replied hypocritically that it was not likely we could come to terms.

"I expected that," I told him. "So much for your 'gentleman's word,' which we're told people could rely on in the old days. I haven't failed you from my side. I have devoted all my attention, my labor, and my sweat to your land, I have fattened you for the past fifteen years, and raised the value of the land as I did so. And now you put me out, breaking your promises, keeping for yourself everything my labor and sweat have produced here, while I with my wife and children, will have to go back to begging for our bread. Oh, I know why. You were not satisfied with having my hands to feed you; you also insisted on having my conscience subjugated to your will and your whims. I told you frankly that I would come here to commit my body to labor and slavery, but that I meant to retain my full moral freedom and my freedom of conscience. I shall never sell those freedoms, not to you or to anyone."

After that heartfelt and necessary little rebuke, to which the craven gentleman had no reply, I departed, leaving on the table the glass of wine the man had poured me in exchange for the thousand francs I had just given him, money that came from my labor and sweat.

So now it was over. Another fifteen years of my life wasted. After working so hard to improve that farm, now I had to leave it, at the point when I could have begun to live there in some ease, drawing on the fruits of my advances in physical improvements and in income. After spending fifteen years fattening these noblemen—as vain as they were useless in this world—I would undoubtedly have to return to beg for my bread as I did in my early days. Then I was begging for my father and mother; now I would have to beg for my children. There were a half-dozen neighboring farms to let at the time, but all of them belonged to local aristocrats, which is to say, to friends of our seigneurs at Toulven. So it would be useless for me to apply, especially as there were several other people applying as well. My wife was pleased with that, actually all she wanted was to go live in town, where she saw so many women—countrywomen like herself—living without lifting a finger. Still, several times over the course of the year, the house servants at the chateau would tell me to go see the seigneur, that he wanted to talk to me. But I always told them that I had no need whatever of M. Malherbe; if he needed me, he knew where to find me. I told them, as I had told that so-called gentleman himself, that their lord and master was just a traitor and a coward and other things too, knowing that it would be reported back to him. Despite that, and although a number of people had already asked to lease the farm, he had not leased it yet, thinking that I would throw myself at his feet in tears, and plead for the favor of toiling and sweating for him for another fifteen years.

Jean—my friend Jean—often came by, too, to ask me why I did not go to see M. Malherbe, that he was still awaiting a new request from me before letting his farm. I told Jean, as I had others, that never would I ask twice for something; it was already painful enough when a man is forced to ask once, especially for something he has a right to, if there were any real justice. But, in France, there is no justice for workers. Workers, laborers, proletarians are not recognized in the Civil Code. Those codes are written for the rich.

This is poverty, my children: while writing the word "rich," my hand hit the inkwell, which fell against my jug and broke, and since I haven't the means to buy another one, I continue to write with my pencil.

Meanwhile, the farm at Toulven was leased, thanks to a cousin of ours—the son-in-law of that fine fellow Rospart from Keruella—who described it to a cousin of his on the other side, some poor bugger who could not have held on there for two years if he hadn't found the land already cleared and improved, and straw, hay, and an abundance of good fertilizer; I had done all the labor and he was going to reap all the rewards. As for me, it was the end of August and I still had no idea where to go. My wife was absolutely determined to live in Quimper. She had found a tavern she visited each time she went to town. The barkeep there was overwhelmed with debts, and hoped to pay them off by selling us his material at double or triple its worth, knowing that we had no experience in the business. My wife was no longer good for much since she had taken to drink, and yet she was determined to choose the trade she was certainly least suited for. It was not where I wanted to go.

I had considered buying a boat with the few sous I would have left from selling my farm equipment, my livestock, and my harvest, and from what I would recover from the landowner or the incoming tenant for the surplus hay, straw, and manure I was leaving on the property. With such a boat, I expected I could still earn a living as plenty of others do, transporting sand from the bay into Quimper. It is a difficult trade, but I have always preferred difficult, laborious trades to any that require the use of hypocrisy, vile behavior, deceit, and cravenness.

THE RUMOR OF MY DEATH REACHED TOULVEN BEFORE I DID

Unfortunately, in the interim, another accident befell me that nearly carried me off to the cemetery. In my haste to rush my grain and other goods to town before Michaelmas (I often went in twice daily), on one of the final days I was coming home quite late when I saw a woman neighbor with a load on her head and another under her arm. I tried to stop my horse to let her climb into my wagon. But the horse had a very hard mouth, and he could not be stopped. So I went to jump to the ground. Unfortunately my foot slipped on the shaft and I fell backward on to the road, right under the wheel, which rolled across all my ribs and broke them and the clavicle of my left shoulder. I had not felt a thing and yet I was dead, at least so said everyone there; even a doctor, passing by on his way back from Fouesnant, said, like everyone else, that it was certainly all up for me. Meanwhile, my horse had gone on his way and was stopped at the bar called *Ti ar Briant*. The barkeep there, alerted to my disaster, brought back the wagon in which he had laid some straw, and with the help of two or three others he loaded my corpse into it—for to them as to everyone else, it was only a corpse now.

Back at his bar, though, he stopped the wagon at the door, for his wife had said she wanted to put a white sheet over poor Déguignet's corpse. But as the woman was arranging the sheet over me, I woke, and in a voice choked with the blood flooding into my lungs and gullet I told her to give me something to drink, quickly. At the sound of my voice, she uttered a scream, leapt terrified down from the wagon, and ran into the house. Meanwhile, her husband had heard my voice too, and he came to ask what I wanted to drink.

"Anything!" I said. "But quickly, I beg you!" for I felt I was about to choke, this time for good.

He ran and brought me a full glass of brandy, and without looking to see what it was, I swallowed it in one gulp. The shock was harsh, and I thought this was truly the end now, but after a few minutes I managed to breathe. I was saved for the moment. They wanted me to stay there, they would go fetch a doctor, but I refused. I told the man to take me home, dead or alive. He obeyed, and at the same time someone else went to Quimper for a doctor, who arrived at my house just as they were lifting me out of the wagon. The house was already full of people, for the rumor of my death had reached Toulven before I did. Monsieur and Madame Malherbe were there themselves. The doctor palpated me and frowned unhappily; he walked over to the count shrugging his shoulders. I did hear him say that I had only a few hours left to live. All my ribs were broken as well as the left clavicle, and the blood had collected around my heart; it would certainly stifle me before long. He did absolutely nothing for me, doubtless judging that it was useless. Throughout this time, the seigneur and his lady were staring at me, their poor victim. If this miserable pair could have read my eyes just then, they would have understood clearly what those eyes were telling them; to some degree they did understand, certainly, for I saw that the dame had tears in her eyes, and the seigneur had bowed down his head. My eyes were saying, "Treacherous, craven wretches, are you satisfied now? Is your revenge complete enough, your criminal idiotic revenge? I now leave you the last drop of the blood you have drunk so much of over these fifteen years. And when you see my corpse go down into the earth, and when you see my wife and my children forced to beg for their bread, you will taste all the pleasures of the gods."

They finally left, ordering their servants to stay and witness my last moments. Jean, my poor friend Jean, stayed all night by my bedside, weeping like a child watching his father die.

But the night went by and I was still alive, so I asked one of my servants to go tell the doctor that I had not died and to come see me again. He came quickly, probably quite amazed to find me still living. This time, after palpating my ribs and shoulder again, he proceeded to set them as best he could, then he wrapped my whole body into a broad stiff canvas and affixed my left arm to my chest; finally, he crucified me, so to speak, on my bed, unable to move anything but my right hand. The seigneurs had come back to witness all these procedures, during which I had not once cried out in pain, which utterly amazed the doctor. When he had finished, he told the chatelains that I could be given whatever I wanted to drink and to eat, for to his mind I had no chance of living longer than four days, as my heart and lungs were drowning in blood; as soon as the blood should begin to spoil, fever would overtake me and that would be the end of me, forever this time.

The fourth day, as the doctor warned, did indeed look like

my last. Her ladyship, without saying a word, had sent her coachman to fetch the vicar. She apparently thought that by having that young tonsured rogue give me extreme unction she would be expiating all her crimes toward me. But her little vicar arrived too late—happily for him, for otherwise I would have spit in his face; but by then I could no longer talk, or spit, or even move. Nevertheless, I could hear him mumbling his confession-booth slogans, telling me about Christ, heaven, and forgiveness. I was thinking—because although I had lost speech and nearly breath, I hadn't yet lost all consciousness—that if there was anyone who needed forgiving, it was that noble lady, the Fury from the chateau, who was standing a little way off with tears in her eyes, and the noble seigneur, the betrayer and coward, who stood hidden behind the bed. The lady had brought all the finest burial material from the chateau: white cloth, great tapers in silver candelabras, even holy water in a vessel that was also silver. Everyone was weeping around me, women, children, and strangers. However, the tonsured conjurer, the Catholic prestidigitator, seemed rather amused. These people know nothing about emotions, or about human feeling; they are always busy singing while others weep. When he had finally done with all his monkey business, he tried to persuade me to swallow his little wafer, which he said contained Christ's body, blood, and soul; but there he was thwarted, because he could not make me unclench my teeth, so his Christ's body stayed outside mine, it melted between my lips and my teeth. But as far as he was concerned, the deed was done, and the spectators, who saw nothing, also thought that all had gone well, that in a few minutes my soul would rise straight to heaven—this poor soul that the canton's tonsured troublemakers had long ago consigned to eternal flames.

When the man in black had left, doubtless delighted at having extreme-uncted an atheist, and even more delighted to think how in two days he would be collecting a nice fee for chanting the *dies irae* and the *requiem aeternam* over my corpse, the gentleman traitor took my right hand in his and held it for a while, staring into my eyes; then he laid that hand over my heart and left with his head bowed, probably thinking it was all over. However, I was not dead: I could see and hear. I remained in that state until about midnight, with no one quite sure whether I was dead or alive. Then I managed to unclench my teeth and slightly move my right hand, to signal that my feet were cold. Someone immediately heated a large brick and put it on the soles of my feet. A moment later, I felt myself return to life—I felt the blood running back into my lower extremities, which showed they were not completely congealed.

The next day I was able to speak, to the great stupefaction of the lady, who came very early in the morning to see me, having heard from the servants that I hadn't yet died. Of course, that noblewoman did not fail to credit the miracle (for it *was* a miracle, she said) to the presence in my house of her little vicar with his savior God, and to take credit for that herself, since it was by her order that Christ and his minister had come there. So she was gratified in another way too—she may have persecuted me unto death, but here she had given me back my life. Now she put at my disposal the best her chateau could offer: meat, broth, old wine, and all sorts of liqueurs. She visited me every day thereafter, always accompanied by the maidservant bringing something, always delicacies to drink or eat. The mayor, my friend and the best man I have known here, also came to see me, with other friends.* This good man, who would split himself in four to do a friend a favor, was at a loss to know what to do for me; he wanted to have me moved to the hospice, where he thought I would be better cared for, and at the commune's expense. But that was impossible in my condition. And the seigneurs who had so

---

*Louis Le Couturier, mayor of Ergué-Armel from 1881 to 1886.

persecuted, betrayed, and robbed me would not have permitted that now. As wicked and vindictive as they were, they now acknowledged their misdeeds, their criminal vengefulness, toward a man who had fattened them for fifteen years with his toil and his sweat; they now bent all their concern and attention on me, probably with the idea of expiating their crimes thus. And I was improving day by day, my ribs were mending, and so was my left clavicle. But I was to stay on my back and immobile as a mummy for six more weeks.

FORTY-EIGHT YEARS OLD AND HALF-CRIPPLED

Meanwhile, Michaelmas came and went. My wife, who was free during this time, had leased the bar in Quimper at twice its value, and paid the outgoing barkeep fourteen hundred francs for his fittings and an old billiard table which later proved to be worth only two hundred. The poor woman knew absolutely nothing about such things, and besides, she had already fallen to the next level of alcoholic illness; just one level lower could mean death, and that was not a long time off, for she had chosen the best [means] to get there.

The sale of my own cultivating equipment, cattle, furniture, grain, and other objects was handled by a notary, who used to be the notary for the chateau but was no longer. And that day, the aforementioned cousin from Keruella, the one who had brought in another relative to take my place, did his best to keep the prices down, disparaging every animal as it came up for sale as well as the wagons, the plows, and other implements, so as to buy them cheaply himself and resell them later. He bought the horse that way, after belittling it to everyone, and resold it at a profit of two hundred francs—to M. Malherbe himself, who was absolutely determined to have that very good horse, doubtless to keep a tender memento of

the best tenant farmer he ever had. And that rascal of a
cousin—the most crooked, treasonous, and cowardly you
could find—was still saying later to anyone who might be
interested that if it weren't for him the sale would never have
brought so much. Well, that miserable rascal is the man most
highly respected by the chateau, by the seigneurs and the
tonsured schemers, even though he robs and cheats them all,
just as he robs and cheats everyone who has dealings with him.
That's one fellow who will never be put off his farm for showing too much firmness in his political and religious views.
After the sale, the same notary came again with another
expert to redo an evaluation of the farmstead itself—what
they call here the "assessment of *stut*."*

That day I had the strange experience of watching, from
my bed of pain, a scene between the notary and the
landowner that was like the prologue and epilogue of a
tragedy in which I played the role of victim, the notary that of
the avenger, and the landowner the role of the prosecuted
and repentant criminal. Indeed, this notary had already come
several times in the past to appraise the farm, where, he said,
he never used to see anything but untended fields overrun
with brambles and bracken, meadows covered with moss and
reeds, hedgerows in bad condition and ungated fields, the
threshing floor and the barnyard empty of hay or straw or
manure. Now, though, he found all the fields producing well,
the hedgerows in good repair with gates where they were
called for, prairies green with clover and high-quality grasses,
the threshing floor loaded with stacks of hay and straw, and
the barnyard full of top-grade manure. This notary was of the
same political persuasion as our so-called gentleman, but he

---

*"Assessment of *stut*": literally, of manure, fertilizer. This old juridical term
concerns appraisal of the assets and productivity of a property.

had knowledge, appreciation, and respect for work and for services rendered; he reproached my landlord quite bitterly for his conduct toward me; his reproaches were seconded and supported by the other expert, and the seigneur Malherbe could make no answer except for stuttered words and gasps, for the notary was pointing right at his victim.

But, meanwhile, another silent character in this scene was just as dumbfounded by the notary, who played his avenger role to the hilt: it was the incoming farmer, when the two experts told him he owed the outgoing tenant eight hundred francs immediately for the stocks of hay, straw, and manure. The fellow, who was not rich, nor very knowledgeable about agricultural matters, replied that he found the price awfully high. But the experts explained that on the contrary, that was the lowest price possible, because if, when I first arrived on the farm, I, Déguignet, had asked for an appraisal done the way it is done these days (that is, with the hay, straw, and manure valued at current market price), it would be not eight hundred francs he owed me but easily three thousand francs, or even more. But that made no difference because the poor bugger didn't have a sou with him, and the dear cousin who had brought him in, telling him he wouldn't have to pay a thing at the outset, had no eight hundred francs to lend him, either. And the landowner announced that this was not his concern. Finally, the experts, who were somewhat responsible to me for that sum, told the new farmer that he must, without fail, deposit eight hundred francs the next day at the notary's office, or his property would be seized. At this talk of seizure, some odd expressions crossed the landowner's face, as he no doubt thought "Well, this is a fine start for my new tenant, who came so highly recommended." The notary did, however, finally get a deposit of eight hundred francs, I don't know how. Eight hundred francs which I collected from him later on, the only money left to me from my fifteen years' worth of toil and sweat, because the rest—the money from the sale itself—my wife squandered before I ever got to Quimper, buying the bar equipment and the liquor license, and furnishing the new household, which she set up like a rich person's and paid for, as she did for everything else, at twice its worth.

The doctor had said I was absolutely not to move from my bed for another two months, on pain of certain death this time, for my barely healed ribs would break at the least movement, and this time it would be the last straw for me. Fortunately, I was in a small iron bed brought over from the chateau the day the doctor came to patch me up, and the lady, after consulting with him, ordered that, until I was well enough to leave, the incoming farmer, or rather his wife, must allow me full use of that whole end of the house, where my old shrew of a mother-in-law was to stay on and take care of me. But the shrew did not have to do much for me, for everything was brought me from the chateau; I lacked for nothing, they even gave me old wine sixty years in the bottle. The lady also brought me books and newspapers—she who used to wince when she saw me reading my agricultural paper. Ah! truly, that onetime Fury, turned gentle as a ewe these days, was trying with all these late-day indulgences and attentions to make me forget her abominable crimes. I would have liked to forget those crimes, as well as others inflicted on me, but to do so would be an insult to truth and reason.

I was doing a lot of thinking now on my bed at Toulven, knowing that my wife was stupidly squandering all the money from the sale; I was sure that in her hands it would not last six months, even if her alcoholic insanity let her live that long. It was clearly all over now, and I cursed death for not keeping hold of me when she had me twice in her grip, for that would have spared me from being present down to the last moment of the long cruel tragedy that began at Toulven and would end in the Quimper hospice. What could I do now? I did not know if my ribs, which had all been broken, would allow me to make the slightest physical effort without breaking again; and my arm, which was still bound to my chest, would probably no longer be any use at all. If this latest misfortune had not befallen me, things might perhaps have turned out better, for I would never have gone into tavernkeeping, the trade least suited to me and even less to my wife. I still had two possible means to earn some sort of living: I could keep my horse and buggy and do odd jobs and errands; or I could buy a boat and haul sand. In my present condition, though, that was out of the question. But I kept coming back to my old stoic philosophy. I had already known so many miseries and misfortunes that one more should not frighten me, even though I was hardly in condition now to struggle against them, except by my strength of spirit.

Finally, after two weeks, I wanted to leave Toulven for good, this place where I had so labored and sweated to feed and enrich terrible people. And once again, pressing her belated kindness to an extreme, the lady offered the use of either their pleasure boat to take me by water or their carriage to take me by land. But this time I refused everything: my physical strength, and my moral strength too, had largely recovered from the frailty these seigneurs had so abused to make me accept favors from them that in any other circumstances I would have rejected indignantly. I told them all this and more in a farewell letter I sent the day of my departure. A friend came to fetch me with his buggy and drove me safely to Quimper, where it was clear to me on arrival that all my forebodings would soon come true.

The house was fully and opulently furnished, and the bar was stocked with all sorts of beverages, half of which held no interest for these drinkers. I could not say a thing, it was point-less. Besides, I was still ordered to keep to my bed for another two weeks. During this time, people—hangers-on male and female—would visit me every day in groups, not actually to inquire about my health, which mattered little to them, but to drink and eat; which my wife, always vain and grand, and always between two cups, was quick to serve up in good meas-ure. Those good folk repaid her with praise for her fine fur-nishings and her richly fitted tavern, and that satisfied her.

After two weeks, though, I began to leave my bed and walk about the house. I freed my left arm, which had been strapped to my right shoulder for so long that it hung inert along my body. I thought it was gone for good. However, it recovered lit-tle by little, and after a few days I was again able to use it a bit, and hoped I might still do something if I found something to do. My good friend [Couturier], the mayor of Ergué-Armel, often came to see me. He also saw that we would not last in that sorry business for long; he knew my wife's condition. One day, he said I should apply for a tobacco license and open a shop; since I had done so much military service and lost my livelihood and my future supporting the Republic, they wouldn't reject me, he thought, in his naivety and good-ness, this good man who would certainly have given me two licenses if it were up to him. I pointed out that the people whose job it was to give out tobacco licenses were precisely the people who hated democracy most bitterly, so citing my "serv-ices to the Republic" as a recommendation would be enough to get my application tossed right into the wastebasket.

"Apply anyhow," he said. "I'll do what I can to support your application, and I'll mention it to our deputy—after all, you were put out of Toulven for supporting his election. And I'll talk to the prefect."

"Ah, if all those people were to take up my case the way you are doing," I told him, "then I might actually get a tobacco license."

Nonetheless, I did make out an application then and there, and my friend took it in hand, telling me he would see to the rest.

Meanwhile, all I could do was sit in that miserable tavern doing nothing, except for listening to squabbles, abuse, and insults from drunkards and from my own wife, who was never sober anymore, day or night. But what could I do? Where could I find work? I remembered very well how in 1861, when I was first discharged at age twenty-six, I looked everywhere for a job or some kind of work, from Quimper to Brest, and never did find any, and how I was forced to go back into the army, or else—as I considered doing for a moment—throw myself into the sea from the top of the Recouvrance Bridge. How would I find work now that I was forty-eight years old and half-crippled?

IV

---◄○►---

PERSECUTED

1882–1905

THE NATIONAL INSURANCE COMPANY

Then an old insurance salesman, familiar with my situation and knowing I ardently longed for something to do, proposed that I travel for him, saying I could earn something while I took myself on a little journey; he did not offer me an actual position, merely a certain percentage of any policies I might sell for him. It was not much—that is, nothing for me, for this was one more job I was not suited for: a salesman's job that would call for declaiming bantering, and enough arm-waving to dislocate them and my tongue, and all to drag a contract out of peasants who are always suspicious (and with good reason), for they are so often fleeced by so many rascals taking advantage of their ignorance and credulity. Still, seeing that I hadn't found any other work, and was on the verge of falling ill again out of boredom and heartache, I decided to go on the road, if only to distance myself for a few days from that veritable prison, for it had become impossible for me to stay put any longer without seeking a breath of free, invigorating country air. I would be earning no less than I did at home, and food would not cost me much.

So one morning I went off to the insurance agent's office to

ask him for some instruction on how to operate. After giving me
the necessary information, he handed me a packet of
brochures and company business cards that mentioned millions and billions of francs, probably cited to inspire confidence among customers. I had brought fifty francs from home;
I had left three or four hundred francs at the house, which, I
knew, would not last long in the hands of a poor madwoman.
The agent told me that the area where I was most likely to do
business was around Concarneau, especially in the large commune of Trégunc. I departed immediately for the area, pleased
to leave my sorry prison behind me, glad to forget for at least a
few days the cares and heartaches beginning to overwhelm me.
As I traveled through my old commune, I stopped at a bar kept
by a woman who had once been a housemaid at my Toulven
farm. This woman knew what a sad state I was in since my wife
had fallen into drink. When I told her I was on my way to
Trégunc to try to sell some insurance but wasn't very hopeful,
she said that I could begin by selling one policy, at least, right
there in her tavern: for some time now she had been meaning
to buy insurance. So I made a good start in the very first house
I entered. That gave me a bit of heart. I said to myself that perhaps the work was not as hard or as thankless as I first thought.

I had left Quimper, certainly, with no further expectation
than to breathe a little free air, far from the miseries surrounding me, and the old agent had also made it quite clear
that he hadn't much confidence in me. No matter; after starting off with my former maidservant, I went straight to
Trégunc, and reached there as night fell. I asked for dinner
and a bed at a tavern: a big crowd was there, celebrating Holy
Monday—this was a Monday. As I was not dressed in the local
manner, I was immediately seen as an outsider. But there were
two people there who were already settled in the town, a
cartwright and a weaver who also came from the Quimper
region; they saw by my clothes that I came from their home

territory, and invited me to have a drink with them.* When I
told them why I had come to Trégunc, the weaver, who was
also a gravedigger, said that if I liked, he would come along
with me and point out the different farmsteads—he knew
them all—and help me if I needed it in my work as a "traveling salesman." He would join me for forty sous a day, roughly
what he earned at his own work. I accepted his proposal
gladly, for he seemed like a good fellow and a good conversationalist, a prime quality for this trade.

My man did not fail me the following morning; he arrived
very early at the tavern where I had slept, a stout staff in his
hand. I bought him a good breakfast, copiously washed down
with strong coffee to get him going, and we set out. He
planned to start our rounds where he customarily started himself, when as a gravedigger he would go about collecting
tithes. We reached the first place early in the day; the farmer
was not even up yet. My guide took it on himself to explain
why we were there. The man asked me what company I represented, and I showed him the cards from "The National."

"It's a rich company," he said, when he had laboriously
made out the millions and billions noted on the cards. "But
the company really does exist, I hope?"

"Yes, absolutely," I answered, "for fifty years now, and it's
known worldwide."

"I asked," he said, "because some time back there was a
man here, very richly dressed, who wrote policies for several
farms and collected the first year's premium and the contract
fees in advance, but, when the customers tried to find the
company, the only place it existed was on the papers he'd
given them." This man himself hadn't been taken, but nearly
had, he told us.

---

*Déguignet dressed in the clothing of the Glazig region, where Quimper
lay; *glazik* derives from the Breton word for blue.

As I went about the area later, people did show me several insurance policies with no name on them, or just the heading "Fire Insurance Company," and then at the bottom an illegible signature. These poor folks had been victims of a clever swindler, the sort there are so many of everywhere.

Our farmer got up; he went to fetch us some cider and as we drank, after asking for full explanations of the insurance, he agreed to take a policy; he even went to call in a neighbor who took one as well, right then and there. But we had to go over to his place to inspect his buildings, his farm equipment, his furniture. At his house we had more good cider to drink, fried lard to eat, and coffee again to finish up. We stayed there a long time, for the cider and the very powerful coffee had loosened all our tongues. The gravedigger, who knew all these people, was completely at home there; it was nearly noon when we left that farm. But I had not wasted my time: I had earned fifty francs for myself. So it was a good start, and that encouraged me and made me a little bolder. My guide took me to another farm where we were again very nicely received, and where I sold another substantial policy. I told my guide that was enough for the first day. We went back to town, and I bought him a hefty Pernod and invited him to supper; then I paid him his day's fee with a fifty centimes' tip, and we made an appointment for the next day. He was sure not to miss it, for he felt as I did that the work was not bad.

The second day was even a little better than the first. And that was roughly the case every day until Friday. On Friday morning, the gravedigger told me he had to "go to paradise"—*ar Barados*, which is the name of a village quite far from the town. I went with him. I thought I would be losing the day anyhow, and that would be no great misfortune since all the other days had been fruitful. But it turned out that this fine paradise, where there were two big farms, was not insured. My guide had no trouble bringing the two farmers to see the advantage in taking insurance with a solid company. And so I did sell the two policies, again at a meal, as we sat drinking and eating and even laughing and joking, especially about the village's name. Said the gravedigger, "The Good Lord and His saints, the virgins and the angels, they can sleep easy now: Paradise is insured!" And when it was all done, the two good peasants argued over which of them would take us back to town, for they both wanted to come. They finally had to draw straws for the honor. I said to my guide, who also came from near Quimper, "It's just unbelievable that these people here belong to the same race as the ones in Quimper. Here they're polite, gentle, good-natured, and the people from around Quimper and farther out are savage, coarse, angry, and insolent—they'd sooner throw a stranger out the door than invite him in to sit down."

"I know that," the guide said. "That's why I don't want to go back."

The next day, Saturday, I had to return to Quimper, for my briefcase was full and I needed to hear what my employer would have to say; he had probably forgotten all about me, for secretly he must have believed I would do no business. When I left my guide behind in Trégunc I told him I might be back that same evening on the mail coach, if nothing kept me.

I brought the postman home with me, to my tavern; but barely had we stepped inside than I saw the old insurance agent come in too, holding out his two hands to me: "My compliments!" he said, "I hear you did some fine business out there."

"How do you know that?" I asked him.

"In our office we know everything that might concern us. Come right over to the office," he told me, "the chief is expecting you!"

I left with him, telling the postman that I would probably go back with him that evening. This time, the chief offered me his hand with a smile, and when he had examined the contents of my briefcase, he complimented me warmly. Never had any agent done so much in so short a time, he said. Now he was happy to give me money, but I had no need of it yet; I had not used up even half of my fifty francs, and as for taking money and carrying it home to my wife, I might just as well toss it into the river. That poor woman had not even noticed that I was back.

So I left Quimper again that evening with the postman, who helped me earn another good day on our way through Beuzec-Conq: he arranged for me to sell two policies there. We reached Trégunc very late. The next morning, the gravedigger came to my lodgings to see if I was back. When he learned I was there, he was very pleased, and he invited me to go home with him for the noon meal, after high Mass.

After dinner, we took a walk around the town and I wrote another three policies—in very bad weather, for snow began to fall, and I told my guide that the next day we would have a forced day off. That did not keep him from coming by the next morning, and very early, although the snow was already very deep and more was falling. No matter, the gravedigger wanted to set out anyhow. He said there was a large village near town where we were sure to do some good business that morning, because several farms in the village were uninsured, and we would find all the farmers gathered at one of them: there had been a big party the night before, and with Breton peasants there is never a party without a morning-after party, which in Breton is called *dilost ar fricot*. I was forced to follow my guide; indeed, I was no more worried than he was about the walk or about the snow. I'd seen plenty of both. As the gravedigger had said, we did find all the farmers of the large village, Lanvintin, gathered together and already busy drinking and eating. No sooner did we enter they invited us to sit down with them at the table, never even asking what we were doing there in such weather.

(

Here we were among the prominent figures of the district. There were municipal councillors who immediately began to converse with me in French, proud to show me that the peasants of this remote place did actually know the language. Thus we were divided into two groups. My aide, who did not know a word of French, laughed and joked with the non-French-speaking Bretons, for he was quite a wag, a type often found among Bretons and particularly among such churchgoers; whereas I had more serious talk with all the men who more or less spoke French. Meanwhile, though, in the course of his joking, the gravedigger had told people what we were there for. The conversation shifted immediately, and because among them were several uninsured farmers, they asked me to explain about fire insurance policies, what they cost, and what indemnities were guaranteed in case of accident. I showed the cards and schedules to those who could read, and soon after, all I had to do was write, for now they all wanted insurance. I should mention that the haste of these Trégunc farmers to take out insurance was a response to a huge fire that a few days earlier had burned up all the furnishings, the house, the stable, grain stores, and cattle of a rich farmer near town, and now he was completely ruined, for he had carried no insurance. So on the spot I wrote four big policies, drinking and eating all the while. And in the end, they urged us to stay the night, for they said we could never manage the journey back to town what with the snow, and also the drink we had been steadily putting away since morning. We went back to town nonetheless, but with much difficulty, and a couple of dozen tumbles in the snow. I had to take the gravedigger right to his house, for he no longer knew where he was. I laid three francs on the table for his wife, telling her that her husband could sleep late the next day, till noon at least, and I would pay him for the whole day. But the good fellow had no such intention; the next morning he arrived at the tavern before I was even up, saying we had to start walking again. He would take me to another large village, not too far away, where we would surely do more business.

I wrote only two policies, but that was enough, I thought. The weather had turned fine again, and we were able to journey about throughout the whole week, during which I wrote several more [contracts]. As I had the previous week, on Saturday I returned to Quimper on the mail coach, and when I went to the office and unloaded my case, the old agent told me, "For sure, you're a sorcerer, just as people told me."

"It's not over yet, though," I said. "I haven't gotten to half of Trégunc yet, and after that, my assistant down there says he'll take me to some other communes nearby where he has a large acquaintance."

Indeed, I had promised the gravedigger that I would be back with the mail coach the same night, or, at the latest, the next day. But, alas, when I got to my house, it was clear that the whole thing was finished. My wife had deteriorated from moderate insanity to raging madness; she had to be put in restraints, and two days later the doctor told me she must be taken to the hospice, or she was sure to commit some desperate act.

DELIRIUM TREMENS

Now I was forced to stay at home, for the maidservant had left in fear of being killed by the poor madwoman, and the old mother-in-law could do no more than see to the children. The old agent and the chief himself often came by to urge me to return to Trégunc. In vain I told them it was now impossible; they kept coming back. The chief now offered me a fixed salary on top of what I would earn in commissions by traveling. All of that was wonderful, and it might have been a way to earn an honest living; but impossible, fate had nailed me down in my hell.

My wife stayed in the hospice for only two weeks, and emerged supposedly cured; but the cure only seemed real. In fact, a few days later she fell back into what is called the last stage of *delirium tremens,* and then she quietly died, like a candle with the last thread of its wick burning out.

Now I was left alone with four children, the eldest only ten years old, and what was our situation?* Since she had been keeping this wretched bar, my wife had done nothing but spend. All the money went out and not a sou came in, and there were still liquor supplies to pay for. Her old harridan mother fled to stay with another daughter, who had fallen into roughly the same state as her elder sister. But my former maidservant, the one who had run off in fear of my wife, came back to tend the children, whom she loved and who loved her. As a barkeep, I did not have much to do, since I sold practically nothing; the customers had long since abandoned the place. The previous tavern keeper had a wife somewhat like my own, better at driving customers away than at drawing them in. And my wife had also been poor at attracting them, so that I could consider the place null. Nonetheless, I had to be present or else close up shop.

There was an old billiard table there which my wife had kept, but the balls were chipped and the tips of the cues were missing. Besides, the game is barely known among Bretons. After a while, though, as people saw me alone in the place, a few began to stop in. Among my new customers, some did know billiards and asked to play, but it was impossible. Still, these enthusiasts were absolutely determined to play at my place because they would be undisturbed there, and eventually they did find themselves some second-hand balls in good condition. Despite the difficulties, the billiard table was refurbished and I soon had several enthusiasts, apprentice-boys who could not go to the grand cafés, where in any case they would never be allowed to play. Knowing the game myself, I

---

*Jean-Marie, born August 5, 1873; Marie-Renée born December 14, 1875; Jean-René, born December 6, 1879; Yves, born March 22, 1881. Louis-Auguste and Corentin-François both died young.

was able to give lessons, for I had to do something to kill time. I could not go on without using my limbs or my mind, as I see so many people do. With no footing, with no hope for the future, I resolved to let events guide me.

MY TOBACCO SHOP

The good Monsieur Couturier, the kindly mayor of my previous hamlet, often came to visit me, and he was the only person who truly pitied my fate, because that man had a really human heart that suffered over the misfortunes of others more than his own. He would always ask me if my tobacco license had arrived yet.

"Alas, no, my friend," I would say each time; "I don't even think about it. I do believe I'll be dead before it does."

"No, no," he'd say. "You'll get it, I assure you, be patient, take heart."

Patience and heart—I'd always had enough of those my whole life, otherwise I would long since have returned into the nothingness I came from. However, one morning as I was cleaning my bar, in comes a gentleman in a tall hat asking the whereabouts of a Monsieur Déguignet.

"I am Déguignet," I said.

"Well, I've brought you your tobacco-agency license."

I thanked the gentleman, whom I did not know, and I tried to offer him a drink, but he must have found my lowly bar too humble for him; he refused and went on his way.

I believe I have already written this: There is not a happier, more contented man in the world than I am, any time I receive a few gestures of acknowledgment and understanding from other men, or even from women. A greeting, a smile, a handclasp from respectable people are enough to make my heart rejoice, and I'm ready to pardon the wicked for the sake of those few good-hearted folk. But this time it was more than a smile, more than a handclasp I was given: it was life itself, an existence for me and my children. I had only three children left to me, three boys. The owner of the house I lived in had taken my daughter, a child of seven, assuring me that she would be responsible for her, that I need not fear she would be unhappy. I let her go, for I could not say she would not be unhappy with me.

[The license authorized Déguignet to sell tobacco in the village of Pluguffan. —L.A.]

A few days later, the prefect called me into his office and told me that he wanted me to run my tobacco shop myself.

"Certainly," I told him, "I would like nothing better than to be able to go there and stay. Unfortunately, though, this license is for a location in the most reactionary, clergy-ridden commune in all of Finistère. Not only will I have trouble finding a shop to rent in Pluguffan, but no one will come in to buy tobacco from me. It will be explicitly forbidden by the priests, on pain of eternal damnation."

"Still, try to work it out," he told me. "If you can't live there, you'll be given a better location."

So there I was again back in difficulty after the surge of joy I'd felt, for my children's sake more than for myself. For finding a place in that clerical township, thoroughly dominated by monarchists and priests, would be hard if not impossible for me to do. I was known there, as I was in nearly every commune in the Quimper district, as a red republican, a Freemason, a Protestant, a priest-eater, and so forth. No one would ever rent me a house; he would be instantly excommunicated. And even if I should find a place to rent, no one would come to buy tobacco or anything else from me, especially since Pluguffan was right outside the city of Quimper, where the peasants could get their provisions instead. And, moreover, I had another problem as well: How could I set up a tobacco shop?

For when I paid off all the debts my wife had contracted, and paid my rent, I would have nothing left, if indeed I weren't actually still in debt.

The woman presently managing the Pluguffan tobacco shop came to see me as soon as she learned I was the new license-holder, saying I should lease it to her, that she had run it for fifteen years, that I would not find anyone else in the village capable of managing it. I told her to wait a while, I would see later. But after her came the clerks from the Tobacco Bureau, friends of hers, who also urged me to work out an arrangement with the woman, saying I would not find anyone else. They told me I should not even consider going over to run it myself. I told them that the prefect had ordered me to do exactly that.

"Well then," they said, "the prefect will have to build you a shop, because for sure you won't find one to rent."

And the two clerks, who went out to Pluguffan every week, came by regularly to tell me that I absolutely must let my license to that woman. Since I kept asking for more time to decide, they reached the point of threatening me, saying they would speak to the Bureau director if I refused to obey, for now I was answerable to the Bureau and had to obey it or give up my tobacco license. The two agents, a couple of clericocos very close to the tobacco-shop woman and the local priests, were trying to frighten me, but they had the wrong man.

In the end, I found a friend in that commune, a former non-commissioned officer like myself—the man who had taken over my job with the insurance company—who said he would find me a place in Pluguffan that would be quite suitable for my tobacco shop. He knew a fellow who owned a house there but lived in Quimper. One evening he brought over the man, who agreed to rent me his house for two hundred francs a year. The fellow told me frankly that he was asking twice the price he presently got for the house, but in order to rent to me he would have to evict three small tenants presently in the place, and then he would have repairs to make, apart from the fact that he ran the risk of being excommunicated by the fearsome curé in the parish, and that it would be difficult to rent out his house afterwards, once the devil had lived there. Having no choice in the matter, I had to accept the man's terms; he did promise me, though, that later on he would lower my rent.

I immediately signed a 3-6-9 [year] lease, sight unseen. Meanwhile the two rascals from the Bureau, who knew nothing about the arrangement, kept coming by, sometimes cajoling and sometimes threatening me. In the end, I told them that I had rented a house there, and that by next Michaelmas I would start running my tobacco shop personally. They thought I was twitting them, and in a fury said they would go see about that, for it seemed impossible to them. They must have "seen," because they never came by again. But for me, still, it wasn't enough to have found a shop. I would have to figure out how to set up there. I would never have enough money for that. I thought of my friend Couturier who had arranged for me to obtain the license; he would certainly help me again to set up shop, but I felt it would be too much to ask of him.

THE FINE LADY

At that time I often read a newspaper from Lorient lent me by a friend. This paper, which was concerned with working men and women, offered free employment listings. One day it occurred to me to advertise there for a housemaid or clerk to help manage a rural tobacco shop, together with a widower. Three days later, some forty letters arrived from all over Brittany, Rennes to Brest.

"*Ah ma doue!* (Oh, my lord!)," I said to myself. "I see I'm not the only unfortunate in the world! . . . Here are forty girls or women in Brittany, without jobs and perhaps without food, and that's just among women who read the papers; how many more are there, then—perhaps one out of every hundred?"

I went through all the letters, most of them from girls eighteen to twenty-five years old, and found three from childless widows. Among those was one who gave me lengthy information on her earlier life and even about her present circumstances. She had been left without a job in Lorient, having chosen not to go to England with her former employers. I wrote a letter to that woman, giving her all my particulars in turn, and describing frankly, as was my custom, the impoverished condition I was in at present, and the still worse one I expected to be in come Michaelmas. I was sure that after reading such piteous information, I would get no further response. I was wrong, for that very evening, I received a telegram from the widow saying she would be at my house the next day.

And indeed, the next morning at ten o'clock, a lady entered my house whom I could never have imagined to be a housemaid or cook or clerk, for she looked more like a grand countess or marquise. She was a sturdy woman, with the very face of the Republic—an open, cheerful face.* If she had the manner, the walk, and even the speech of a grand lady, it all came naturally to her; it was clear that she was quite unaffected. When we had got acquainted, I told her that it was unbelievable that a grand fine lady like her should want to come work as a maid for a poor peasant like me, and live among mountain savages to do it. She answered that she was a former peasant girl herself, and had tilled the earth as a farmer's wife; after her husband's death she sold everything and went into service as a chambermaid and then as a cook for aristocratic households, but she had had her fill of aristocrats and especially of big cities; and since I had said that I was going to be living in the countryside, she would

---

*The French Republic is most often represented by the image of a handsome woman in revolutionary dress, called Marianne.

be very pleased to go there with me, with no conditions attached. She was to be free to leave after a while if she did not like it; similarly, I would be free to dismiss her if I was not satisfied, without either of us having any claim on the other. Then she told me that she was rich enough now to live independently if she chose, besides which her father, now ninety years old, would be leaving her a sizeable estate he owned at Arcis-sur-Aube, near Troyes.

As she talked, the fine lady had taken off her fashionable hat and her silken dress and, putting on a white apron, began to make a meal as if she were in her own house. And when the children came home from school, they were very surprised to see such a grand lady there, serving them a dinner the likes of which they had never eaten. She stayed in the house until the evening train out of Quimper at eight-thirty. Before she left, she assured me that I could count on her. When I knew exactly what day I would be going to Pluguffan, I would have only to tell her and she would arrive there at the same time as me, or at latest the following day. Knowing my sorry financial situation, she even tried to leave me some money to take care of initial expenses. But I did not want to take it.

After the departure of that curious lady, I thought long and hard. All my life I have trusted in people even though I have always and everywhere been duped and betrayed by them. This woman had spoken to me so openly that it was impossible to doubt her word, she had shown me references, all excellent, from all the great houses where she had worked; she had shown me her birth certificate, her marriage contract, and deeds for the property of her father, whose only child she was now, since her brother, a lieutenant of infantry in Africa, had recently died. What more could she do to convince me of her honesty and her loyalty? And yet the perfidies of women kept running though my memory, whose workings are unfathomable. All the legends about early women are the same.

Everywhere, women brought ruin on the human species, tricked men by their treacherous ways. In Jewish legend, which became Christian legend as well, Eve tricked Adam; in Greek legend, Pandora, whom the gods had endowed with every physical and moral virtue, used them to corrupt men through every vice. This fine lady, Louise Thorey, also seemed to have all the virtues of that first woman from the Greeks, but might she not also use them to dupe men? A problem for me. In any case, I was determined to let things happen as they might. The fact is, Michaelmas was not very far off.

THE BIG DAY

It was the big day, the opening day. I would finally see whether, despite threats from the tonsure troops, anyone would dare to come buy tobacco from the Protestant, the Freemason, the Red Republican, the devil's henchman, and the other names those black rascals hung on me to scare off the good Catholics. Having got everything ready the night before, I was curious to go to early Mass and see what the priest would say. But the rogue saw me walk into the church, just as he was leaving the sacristy to begin his magic tricks. I thought he might take advantage of the circumstance to point me out to his sheep, saying, "There's the devil, watch out for him, he says he's selling tobacco but instead he'll sell you black ashes from hell!" But no. I believe the devil had frightened him, for he said not a word about me. Which really surprised the congregation. For they all thought that he was going to deliver a major sermon on me, especially today, this solemn day on which my life and death might depend. I do not know what the curé thought during his Mass, especially seeing me practically in front of him whenever he turned around toward his sheep to launch a *dominis vobiscum* or an *orate fratres*; I imagine he was thinking something very different from his *oremuses*.

When the Mass ended, I walked out, and finding there in the square my friend the man who kept the bar on the road to the station, and then the two farmers who had fetched me from Quimper, and a few others as well, I invited them all to come home for a drop. The lady and my older son tended the tobacco counter. Myself, I was left free to welcome customers, and serve them a nice brimming glass as they arrived. The first to come told other people that there were drinks to be had at the tobacco shop. So others came in by groups, the ones drawing along others, and I actually think a couple of them came in several times. After the busiest moment had passed, a few I knew stayed on to chat with me. They were all surprised that the priest had said nothing at the Mass.

"For sure," they were saying, "you must have cast a spell on him, because everybody expected him to deliver a terrible great sermon about you."

"It could well be," I said, "that I scared him, but one way or another he must have said a very odd Mass this morning. He didn't give a sermon—maybe later at High Mass he will, to lay a curse on people who came here for tobacco this morning."

However, though many men had already come in, several of them doubtlessly drawn by the bait of the free drinks, not one woman did. But that night I learned why not. I had gone to early Mass, so Louise, the fine lady, told me that she planned to go to High Mass. "Well," I said, "seeing me there this morning, the old man couldn't do a thing but stammer his Mass; when the other one sees you, the young priest, he won't manage to say anything at all. And the mayor's wife,* the Countess de Longray, and her sister, and their daughters, who will probably be there too—what are those women going to think, seeing an unknown lady like you?"

---

*Madame Émilie Hamon de Kervers, wife of Stanislas Delécluse de Longraye, mayor of Pluguffan from 1869 to 1919.

She said she had seen plenty of countesses and marquises and even princesses in her life, and she wasn't afraid of the Pluguffan countesses. So she went to High Mass and took a seat among the peasant women, towering over them with her height, her silken garments, and her jewelry. Everyone's eyes were on her throughout the Mass. The men turned around to look at her, and the young vicar saying Mass must have been fairly uncomfortable too, looking at that extraordinary woman, beside whom the mayor's wife, her daughters, and other ladies present as well looked like mere little ragpickers. The curé did preach a sermon, as he does every Sunday at High Mass, but he still said nothing about the tobacco shop, which completely disconcerted the woman who had been running it before, the close friend of the churchmen; she was counting on them to keep me from making a living at Pluguffan.

After the Mass and to some degree all day long, many more men came to buy tobacco, but still no women. Toward evening, though, various people came in to tell me that the old dear, the former tobacco agent, or shopkeeper, had been selling tobacco all day as usual. Then I understood why the women had not come in. I could bring suit against that nasty church-hen, but I told the customers who came in with the news that I would show the people of Pluguffan that the man they were calling the devil was neither as nasty nor as low as all those rascally priests and their stupid, nasty sheep. I would forgive the old dear this time, but she'd better not do it again or it would cost her dearly.

The town clerk himself came to buy tobacco from us—he, a close friend of the vicarage, cantor in the church, and vestry treasurer. The man wanted to impress us with all his titles and also with his command of French, which, he said, he knew enormously well. But the fine lady, whom he was addressing in particular, showed him very quickly and very politely that she too knew French. Then he tried to boast of knowing Latin too, since he'd been trained as a priest. But there again he was quickly shown up, by this poor peasant who never went to any school. He said then, "Oh, my word! Some smart folks in this tobacco shop—damn, damn, I never would have believed it!"

He then began to speak Breton, a language he knew better than French and Latin. As the town clerk, and since he said he was chief of the commune—*Mest ar bars**—I offered him a coffee; he accepted eagerly, and then he left with thanks, saying he would be seeing us often, for he was a heavy smoker. When he had gone, I told Louise, "Good, so we've had the vestry treasurer and parish leader come in on the first day; we can expect the curé himself tomorrow."

Whatever the reason, and despite old dear and her sister church-hens, I sold eighty-five francs worth of tobacco that first day. It should be said that out in the countryside, the peasants buy nearly all their tobacco supplies on Sunday. Still, I wasn't dissatisfied with the day's work, for there was a big difference between selling nothing, as predicted, and selling eighty-five francs' worth. The next day, liquors we had ordered arrived, and the incredulous vendor, who had laughed when I told him the fine lady was my maid, was convinced this time. Here I was a shopkeeper-barkeep again, the trade I detested most. But I had high hopes, if the lady stayed on with me, of spending as little time as possible in the shop, the more so since in those country towns there is not much business except for Sundays and holidays. I would look for other occupations outdoors, even breaking stones if I found any to break. But I found something better, and without much looking.

*Parish leader.

SO THINGS WENT ALONG RATHER NICELY

Near our house there was a small abandoned field that had not been cultivated for a very long time. I went to find the owner, to see if he was willing to rent it to me. As it happened, this landowner was one of the few republicans in the commune. We worked it out directly. He rented me the field for fifty francs a year, for me to cultivate as I saw fit. Now I was happy, I had found what I most desired. I set about the work immediately; I wanted the field cleared before springtime, so as to plant potatoes first and then other vegetables. One day, I was working there when Louise came to fetch me, saying that I was wanted at the house. When I got there I saw that it was the two clerks, the ones who had done their best to keep me from coming to Pluguffan. One of them, the old dear's close friend, had rooted about everywhere and found a bottle of wine on the floor in a corner, one I had forgotten there when I first put the [household] wine into bottles. The fellow still hated me because he had not managed to keep me out of town; he tried to start a quarrel with me over that wretched bottle, and even made some threat [to report me for liquor on the premises of a tobacco shop]. When they left, Louise asked me if I was afraid of those people, since I had not answered them back.

"Oh, no," I said. "But why bother answering thugs and rascals like them? I'll give them an answer soon enough, another way."

And, indeed, because the prefect had told me to keep him informed of my situation when I had got settled in my new tobacco shop, I took the occasion to tell him about the department clerks' stupid grudge against me, ever since the day I was granted the tobacco license. Two weeks later the rascal, my persecutor, stopped coming to Pluguffan, and his replacement told me later that he had been first transferred, then dismissed. Now the clerks were friendly and polite with me. So things went along rather nicely.

When the former manager finished selling off the tobacco she had kept illegally, the women of the town also began coming in to buy tobacco from us. The mayor himself and his brother-in-law, the two local aristocrats, would come in every Sunday, and each would buy twelve or fifteen packs at fifty centimes. I worked every day on my field, while the fine lady took care of the house. She cooked very well for us, even too well for us poor peasants used to living on potatoes and black bread; she mended the children's clothes, and even made them new ones. Twice a week, she brought in a woman to do the wash.

That woman later made trouble for us. She too was a sanctimonious church-hen, a hypocrite, a spy, one of the most vicious gossips among the many vicious gossips in the commune.

By spring, my field was ready, and I planted early potatoes first, then others, and eventually peas, string beans, carrots, turnips, and greens. I had also put in several varieties of cabbage, early- and late-yielding. By the end of May, this field, once covered with brambles and prickly scrub, was transformed into a fine kitchen garden, to the point where people would stop to look at it; and the nuns who lived in the house across the way would come to see it and even buy vegetables from me, though they had their own garden. But their garden no longer produced anything, for they were trying to cultivate it without using manure. These good sisters had the same idea as George Sand, who said she would happily have become a farmer if soil didn't require manure. The mother superior often came to watch me work, and to admire my beautiful vegetables. She would ask how I managed to get such good things out of land that used to yield nothing, and that nobody cared for. I told her it was the labor, primarily, and then the effect of manure that made the vegetables grow so well. Manure, I said, nourishes plants first and ultimately nourishes animals, man especially. Nature gave vegetables a prettier role than animals: animals turn the loveliest products of nature and industry into manure and rot, whereas vegetables turn that manure and rot into fine roots, into shoots, into leaves, into flowers, fruits, and grains. The good sister, whom I came know well, listened to me with interest, but it disturbed her that I did not believe in God. Never had she heard that there might be anyone on earth who did not believe in God.

"But what God," I asked her, "would you have me believe in?"

"Well, Jesus Christ of course, my poor man—the only Son of God, Creator of heaven and earth and of all that exists here below and on high."

"What? God's only Son? but I see in Genesis, the first of your holy scriptures, that this God who's called "the Eternal" had..."

[Here follow many pages on the Bible.]

THERE PROBABLY NEVER WILL BE A WOMAN WITHOUT VICE OR FAULT

Meanwhile, I could never speak to the fine lady about her ways or about running the house, for it was largely to her that I owed my current situation. When I had to go into town to buy my tobacco stocks and other things, I would always find the necessary money available. Often, she would even tell me that if I needed more, I had only to take it from her cupboard, or even from mine, where she had put more rolls of gold coins and bundles of banknotes. What could I say? I let things go on that way, philosophically, as if they would continue forever. So far I had never discovered any blameworthy vice in that extraordinary woman, whom everyone, especially the poor folk, had come to speak well of. Still, there never was and probably never will be a woman without vice or fault. The greatest Christian saints even said that woman consisted of nothing else but vices and faults. The famous Saint Jerome said that woman was just a sheep with all the devil's vices. The old rascal said this in his old age, because in his youth he had indulged too much in women and had grown disgusted with them. Saint Thomas said that woman was an accidental being, an incomplete thing. Saint John of Damascus called woman a monster, a donkey, a dreadful tapeworm lodged in man's heart. Saint John Chrysostom said that she was the source of evil, the author of sin, the soul's perdition, and the portal to hell. Saint Gregory said she had no sense of the good, and Erasmus called her an incompetent and ferocious animal, the cause of all our miseries. Such are the views on woman—on all women—held by those great saints, who must have had some tangles in the heavens above with the female saints. I myself never had many dealings with women, but all those I have had something to do with, I have found to have vices—more vices than virtues, alas!

So it was to be expected that the fine lady, Louise Thorey, should have some too, like all Eve's daughters, who were further corrupted by the sons of God (see Genesis 6:1). I would doubtless have discovered her great vice much earlier if I had been a keen observer of souls; but I am as deficient in that art as in the arts of lying and deceiving. So Louise had to display her great vice, or fault, quite openly in order for me to see it. I say "fault" in the singular, for she only had time to show me that one. There were probably others in reserve, for women are skilled at dissembling for long periods. I know something about that because my mother-in-law, who was riddled—as St. Jerome said—with vices and faults and who displayed them by the hundreds, managed to hide the worst of them from me for fifteen years.

Being busy all week long with my garden work and on Sundays with serving customers till one or two o'clock in the afternoon, I went for a walk one evening with the schoolmaster, who was rather bored in that cheerless little village. We would go to the railroad station and play a game of cards with the stationmaster, either in his place or in the bar next door. And on the way home we would stop in to see my friend who kept a bar along the road from the station to the village. Now, in those bars there were often two girls who would join us at cards. My housekeeper's maid often came by to fetch her husband, who spent his Sundays there; she saw us playing cards with the girls, and reported it to Louise, her mistress—in the Breton style of course, bantering, but this was a woman unfamiliar with Breton ways, who took seriously what she was being told. Occasionally, too, we would stop in our village at a bar kept by another girl, the best-run bar in the town. Louise knew that too. One night when I came home she said, "You've been to see your pretty girls again, right?"

"What pretty girls?" I said, "I've been making my usual rounds with the schoolmaster."

"Yes, yes," she retorted, "your usual rounds—I know all about them: first, you go see the girl at the railroad station, then the one at Moisan's place, and then the girl who tends the bar in the village here. People say you're going to marry one of them."

As she spoke, she paled, trembled, and fell back onto a chair, saying in strangled tones, "My god, my god, I'm doomed to be unlucky everywhere I go," and she fainted.

I stood watching her for a moment, stunned; then, not knowing exactly what to do, I took a flask of vinegar and put it to her nose. After a few minutes she regained consciousness, and as soon as she could rouse herself, went to bed without saying a word. The next morning, she did not get up. I was obliged to stay in the shop; toward eleven o'clock, though, she came downstairs. Then she told me about her sickness, and asked my forgiveness: jealousy, a sickness she inherited from her mother, who died of it young, and which she herself had nearly died of more than once during her husband's lifetime. Even in the lordly households where she worked, she said, whenever she saw the male servants laugh and joke with the other women she had to go off and hide to keep from falling into a fit.

However, she had thought that among peasants, out in the countryside, this terrible disorder would not affect her. I told her that it was indeed rather odd, that the disorder should hound her so far as to me, a poor Breton peasant of the sixth order, and all the more as she knew that I would never be marrying again—I'd had enough of it, even a bit too much, from my first marriage—and as she herself had sworn after her husband's death never to do it a second time. No matter, all that [reasoning] could not heal her sickness, which was hereditary and incurable. She did promise me, though, to do her very best to get over it. But alas, in vain; for after that first attack, whenever she saw me chat with any woman at all, young or old, or learned that I had gone for a walk with the schoolmaster, she would fall ill again, only to apologize again the next day. I eventually stopped paying attention to her nervous attacks, and no longer responded to the nonsense she always talked when they took her.

When she bothered me too much, though, I would tell her that she was free in my house, that she could stay or to go if she was not comfortable there. Her maid, the laundress who knew about her sickness but took it for a mere quirk, enjoyed provoking it by constant remarks about the local barmaid, a girl called "Stumpy" because both her arms were slightly deformed. The laundress always laughed and joked as she talked, half in French, half in Breton, but Louise, who understood very little Breton, took everything amiss. Around then, as it happened, "Stumpy" was preparing to marry a local youth. The laundress told her mistress about the marriage, but she told it so oddly that the credulous Louise understood that I was to be the groom, for the maid had mentioned that the groom was named "Jean-Marie," and that could only mean me, according to Louise, who was still devoured by that horrible jealousy. She could not help speaking of it to me again. This time, though, I emphatically sent her packing, with the famous expression of the famous General Cambronne ["*Merde!*"], together with a few others no less emphatic, and I went off to my labors, leaving her to moan and writhe. Thereafter we went on for some time with no new incident.

But then one day I left early for Quimper to pick up tobacco supplies. A few moments after my departure, "Stumpy" walked past our house, on her way to Quimper as well. Seeing her go by, Louise asked a neighbor, "And where is Stumpy off to, all dressed up?" The neighbor told her as best she could that the girl was going to Quimper for her wedding, and the laundry-maid came up just then and said the same thing, with a laugh as always. Louise, however, did not laugh. Because I had left for town especially early that morning, it must be for my marriage to Stumpy. This time she lost her head, and without further questions she ran to the school to send my older boy back to the house; then she fetched a cart from the next farm and, with the help of the farmer and his servant, packed and loaded her trunks; and before noon the fine lady was on the road to Quimper, to the great astonishment of the neighbors, whom she had not answered by so much as a word when they wondered at her precipitous departure. For my part, when I went to pick up tobacco, I almost always returned by train to shorten the distance I would have to carry my sometimes-heavy load. That day I had got off the train and, reaching Moisan's bar halfway home from the station, stopped to rest and smoke a cigarette. But a moment later, I saw my second son, who knew my usual route home, come to tell me that Louise had gone, leaving everything topsy-turvy in the house, and that his brother wanted me to come right home. I left immediately, not too surprised at the news. There were several women at my house, talking with my son about the development. These women, the village gossips, wanted to see how I would take it. They must have expected me to weep and moan. They were quickly disabused, for I told them that the fine lady had done well to leave that way—it spared me the trouble of putting her out, which I had been considering for some time. Still, despite everything, I was not entirely easy, for I did not know in what state she had left the tobacco shop. In the cash box I found only six francs. I had a good supply of tobacco to sell, true, but would I have enough money to go back for more in a week? I was not certain.

Not knowing where she had gone, I wrote her father, to find out whether she was at his house, and telling him that Louise had gone off abruptly while I was away from the house and had left my affairs in disorder. The good man replied that his daughter had not come home to him, but that he would soon learn where she was, and begged me not to pursue his poor Louise for any wrong she might have done me—to wait another few days till he should have news of her.

"Do not break my heart in my old age," he said in closing, "on the subject of my only child. My daughter will indemnify you, I am sure, for the harm she has done you."

A week later, I received a letter from Louise, enclosing two hundred francs, the sum, she said, she believed she owed me! I could not say. She was in Troyes. She mentioned Stumpy again, saying I had betrayed her with that idiotic peasant girl—which showed that she was still under the influence of her terrible nightmare and had taken seriously the silly jokes of the Pluguffan chatterboxes. She told me that if it weren't for that, she might never have left Pluguffan, for she had been negotiating with an old landowner to buy some land from him and build a house on it, as much for me as for herself. And that was true; the man confirmed it later. Finally, in her letter she said she had been reluctant to leave me. I was sure that if I wanted her to return, I had only to write her a nice letter explaining away all those old wives' tales she had let herself be taken in by. But for what? She would have come back still sick with her incurable illness.

THIS BLOW COULD ONLY HAVE COME FROM THE PARISH

But how was I to manage now? For there was no question I had to stay in the house: one cannot close the door to a tobacco shop. I did not want any more maids. I do not take long to make a decision: since I could no longer cultivate my field, I gave it back to its owner. I was leaving him a field in good condition where there had been a neglected and unproductive tract. I also gave up the bar, which brought me more trouble than income. Until then, I never knew how much the tobacco shop brought in, since Louise had not kept any accounts; she said putting figures down on paper was pointless. I had often heard—from people who ran tobacco shops for long periods— that tobacco made no money. However, a friend in Quimper, who had been keeping his shop for a long time and from whom I used to buy pipes, cigarette papers, and other such things, would tell me that tobacco shops do actually turn a nice profit; it is customary to say they don't, and he himself told other people that, but with me he had nothing to hide. Anyhow, I would soon find out, for from now on our family of four would have to live off the tobacco income alone. It would not take long to see, actually; just one week would be enough to show us, since we sold about the same amount every week. I did a careful calculation and saw that in fact I would be left with seventeen- or eighteen-francs' profit per week, exactly what my friend had said I should. With that we could live and pay the rent, which the proprietor had reduced by fifty francs, since he knew he was charging over twice the value of the house. I still had a great many potatoes too, which would keep us alive for a long while. My elder son, who was twelve years old and had got his school certificate, could help me on Sundays, and stay at the shop whenever I had to leave to fetch tobacco supplies.

Yet the new priest, a thief and a scoundrel like his predecessor, the pig Le Mao, who was dead of excess and rot, found it odd that I could go on living as I did in my tobacco shop with three children. He thought, as did many other people, that the fine lady had been supporting us; now, with her gone, the rascal expected I would have to lease out my tobacco shop and leave, too. But when he saw that I was staying on, he looked for some other way to force me out. He made a deal with the owner of my house, covering him for any losses, of course.

My three-year lease was to end on the coming Michaelmas, and the owner sent a bailiff with an eviction order for us to quit the place on September 29, 1887. I suspected strongly that this blow could only have come from the parish house, and since that vile tonsure-top had managed to persuade my landlord, who no longer lived in Pluguffan, to evict me, he would surely arrange with all the other landlords in town not to rent me a shop. However, the baker, who was supposed to be one of my great friends, would soon be proprietor of a house he planned to build alongside the cemetery; he told me he would build another small house off the larger one and rent it to me for my tobacco shop. That suited me very well, and we made an informal arrangement. I could count on him, he said; no priest or anyone else would ever stop him from renting me that maisonnette. I trusted him and I slept easy as to the future.

I AM RUN OUT OF PLUGUFFAN

But Michaelmas was drawing near. The baker's house and the attached cottage he promised me were completed. One night the baker and his wife came to my house to buy up my tavern equipment, for they intended to set up a bar in their new house. We quickly came to an agreement. I let them have the stuff at half price, as a friend, since we would be living together from now on in the same house, so to speak: there was a connecting door between the two—a doorway built expressly to allow the customers to step from the tobacco shop to the tavern. They even said I could move into the cottage early, before Michaelmas, since it was ready.

Everything was going well up to that point, and I was starting preparations to take over my new shop, when one evening a woman came to my house to tell me the baker could not give me his cottage after all. I did not need to ask why. I was sure that this new blow also came from the priest Guédès, that Jesuit, hypocrite, crook, and low life. He had managed to turn the baker against me just as he had turned my landlord, with threats, promises, and gifts. What would I do now, just before Michaelmas? It would be futile to look for another shop in this town. I did go to see the baker, though, to ask him the reason for the turnabout. The timorous, cowardly fellow tried to run out when he saw me enter his shop; whatever I asked him, he kept answering, "What do you want, that's just how it is, it's not my doing."

"Whose is it, then?" I said. "The priest's, right? Because the rascal threatened you with hellfire, and probably greased your palm besides, and because you're a traitor and a coward. You're committing the vilest, the most cowardly crime a man could commit; you're putting me and my children out on the street with no roof over our heads and with no livelihood. I know the priest will pardon you for this crime, and he'll even grant you all sorts of plenary indulgences."

I went out and left the wretch in a collapse, unable to say a word.

My lease had been made only verbally, like all small leases in these parts. The Civil Code, that idiotic code, does say that both written and verbal leases can be valid. But it goes on to say that testimony from a witness does not constitute proof of a verbal lease, even though witness testimony is acceptable proof in all sorts of other matters less important than a lease. The party denying the lease can be required to swear an oath, though, and I could claim that last recourse; but before he came into court, the cowardly baker would probably consult his priest, and that priest would tell him to deny the agreement, meanwhile raising his right hand before the image of the treacherous renegade Jesus, since it was for His honor and greater glory that they were forcing me out of Pluguffan. *Ad majorem dei gloriam.*

I therefore merely wrote the prefect to tell him that I would be unable to go on running my tobacco bureau myself, and why. In his answer he told me to try to find some "expedient" to live on for a while, until the next distribution of tobacco licenses; then I would be given a different, better one.

Find some expedient to live on, the good prefect was saying! I had no other expedient but subletting my license, if I could find a taker, and going back to Quimper to live in some attic! That was what I did; for fortunately, and contrary to my expectations, everyone in town wanted to take over my business, outbidding each other for it. The old dear did not come herself to make her offer, but she sent someone else to do it for her. The baker who had built a locale expressly for this business would also have been very glad to have it, but he understood it was useless to come and ask for it. I knew now how much the license was worth, since all four of us had been living on it alone for a year. But I did not want to charge too much, for fear of being reproached later; I preferred to be reproached for the opposite reason, and I was, several times, afterwards—not by the people who won it, of course, but by those who had wanted it. I let it to a widow who had her own house at the center of town, for thirty francs a month, payable monthly. Then I returned to Quimper and found a garret to rent at Bourg-les-Bourgs, on the edge of town. . . .

Now, counting what remained from the tobacco shop sale,

I had nearly four hundred francs. With that and the widow's monthly thirty francs, we could live for at least a while. My children went back to school in Quimper, where they had begun. Myself, I cooked their meals and mended their clothes.

Knowing I had no work, an old friend, a baler to whom I often used to sell hay, sometimes called on me to help him bale several tons of hay. It is independent work, which only requires a degree of purely physical skill. And farmers always welcome balers, particularly the best of them, no matter what roughnecks they are, better yet if they are the sort of roughnecks that everyone fears. There was a big grower at Bourg-Les-Bourgs whom I thought of asking for work, but I could see that the man had ten candidates for every job, and those workmen would have held it against me, for I had a tobacco license and I should not deprive other men of a job. I thought of asking for a post as customs agent from the mayor, who was also on the township council and a senator; I had done a good deal of work for him in the past, neglecting my own interests. But there again, I would have been sent packing by the deputy-mayor, who stood in for the mayor. The man was a wine merchant, and needed some help; a friend of mine had suggested the deputy hire me, but he answered that I would not do, he needed a clerk who could read and write and do a letter in French. If I asked for a customs post he would have given the same answer. So I stayed at home, in my garret, mending my children's clothes and cooking their meals, and occasionally going to bale a few tons of hay or straw when the friend came to fetch me. Meanwhile, my elder son finally found a job as scribe with a notary, at a salary of fifteen francs a month, which gave us forty-five francs, a month's wage for an ordinary laborer here. We did not risk dying of hunger on that income, together with the few sous I contributed now and again.

TAKING MY CHILDREN

I stayed three years in the garret in Bourg-Les-Bourgs. Then I came back to live at Poul ar Raniquet, at the other end of Quimper, but within the territory of my old township, Ergué-Armel; it was the very place where, on my way back from the army, I had met by chance—or by fate—the Rospart woman who became my mother-in-law . . . never law-abiding, never motherly, always very nasty, hateful, and vindictive unto death. We were still living in a garret, but a much better garret than the previous one, and less costly. The old scoundrel Le Gall, the local curé, was still in place. That monster, who did not have even a human face, had first suggested to his Pluguffan colleague—the one who had died like a pig—the best way of forcing us to starve to death, me and my children; and then again to the successor Guédès, the hypocrite crook who got me evicted with his filthy tricks.

The monster's fierce hatred had not yet died out, if indeed hatred in those tonsured scum ever can die out. Those villains hound their victims not only throughout their lives but after death too. This lowlife inquired about us, of course, and learned that we were living very nicely in our garret. My elder son was still working in the notary's office, and the other two children were at school in Quimper. This state of affairs pained the blackguard's heart. What?—here I was run out of Toulven after being persecuted there for fifteen years, then persecuted for another three years in Pluguffan and run out of there, too, and yet I still wasn't dead—not of poverty, or heartache, or despair? I really must be harboring the devil in me, was the belief of that skirt-wearing scoundrel. So he would have to try some other tactic. This new one consisted of taking my children from me, now that they were all cleaned up and capable of earning a living. With the help of the old shrew mother-in-law, who was now living with her other daughter, it would be a simple matter.

The older boy, who was now earning forty-five francs a month, was a good choice. My dead wife's sister, his godmother, now penniless from drinking, lured her godson into her house to help her feed her children. The two others, the old Fury placed with relatives, to tend the cows. It was all done undercover, in secret, without a word to me. Those crooks thought I would fight back, make a huge ruckus, to such a point that I would end by getting myself jailed; I would lose my tobacco license, and that would be the end of me. However, those scum were wrong again. They did not know that Déguignet was a stoic philosopher, "quite as invulnerable to temptation as to pain, beyond the reach of vices and misfortunes both; recognizing only virtue as a true good, only remorse as real ill." Now, I was not remorseful, for my conscience had no grounds to reproach me—except perhaps for sacrificing myself too much for others' sake, without my sacrifices producing the results I hoped.

But I considered the laws of nature, and felt I was properly in line with them. I had created children, and had raised them with a good father's care and concern. They were all sound of health, and able to provide for themselves. Oh, yes, there was one wrong I did blame myself for, a wrong which many unlucky folk commit unthinkingly. I knew I had committed a grave fault in bringing creatures into this world before I was sure there would be a place for them, and was sure I could give them the means to survive here. That was the sole wrong I blame myself for. But if my children never become too unhappy, perhaps they will forgive me for it. I, who as soon as I could walk had to go out begging my bread, for myself and for my brothers and sisters, have never blamed my father for that, nor my mother for giving me birth in such sorry circumstances, and despite all the miseries and persecutions I have suffered, I do not resent them for bringing me into the world.

Now, alone in my garret, I pondered a good many matters,

for what can a person do in a garret but reflect? Despite having little reason to boast of any kindnesses toward me from the human race, I would have liked to do it a few more good turns before leaving it forever. I would have liked to find some impoverished farmer to hire me to tend his livestock, a job I knew very well. If I should find such a one, I could certainly give good value to whomever might take me on, and it would not cost him much; I would only ask to be fed, lodged, and kept clean. Along with caring properly for his livestock, I could advise him on agriculture and even establish some accounting systems—these farmers haven't the slightest notion of accounting, and therefore no idea of how or where profits and losses occur. But what farmer would take me? None, probably; first off, the rascally tonsure-tops in his commune would forbid him to hire me, or risk damnation to body and soul. And, besides, what farmer would let me handle his livestock differently from the way he does it himself, and would be willing to listen to my advice, given that the most ignorant among them thinks himself to be the greatest expert, and constantly declares that no real farmer needs study or theory, that experience and tradition are quite enough? If his animals don't do well, if his harvests are skimpy, that's not his fault; it's the fault of the weather. If the grain and the animals sell poorly, it's the government's fault. With farmers of that sort, I knew it would be almost impossible for me to find a position, no matter if I offered to work on the most favorable terms. Therefore, despite my wishes, I gave up on that idea. But I still could not simply sit back like a Buddhist *bonze* contemplating my navel, or like a Tibetan lama on his pierced throne, or like Simon Stylites perched on his column; my physical faculties and my intellectual need to be busy would not permit it. Since I could not find a material occupation, I could at least find myself some intellectual ones that would also provide a little activity to my whole body.

AND I BEGAN TO WRITE THE STORY OF MY LIFE

I decided to take up the little instrument I am using at this very moment, this little pen, which they say is sometimes more dangerous than a sword, and I began to write the story of my life, in utter frankness, with no literary claims, and here and there interpolating my political and religious views, and my moral, social, economic, and philosophical ideas. It could certainly be said that I was wasting my time. To those who say such, or might say it, I say not. Louis Courier's father scolded his son[*] for wasting his time studying Greek and Latin. Louis answered that he did not consider any time wasted that provided him satisfaction and pleasure; if his studies produced no more than that, they would be enough. That is my response to those who will feel I have wasted my time writing this story of my life. And even if these pages bring me nothing for my material needs and satisfactions, I believe they are bound to bring something to other people, just as my physical labors over a lifetime benefited many others without bringing me anything myself.

I said in the first volume of these writings that a literary fellow who read them took away the first twenty-four notebooks, saying that he would have them published under my name, initially in a magazine and then in book form; he said it would be a shame to let such fine work be lost.[†] He even paid me a hundred francs' advance, assuring me that I would soon be receiving hundreds more, as publication proceeded. I trusted him, as I have always trusted people who promised me something, despite the fact that I have been duped and swindled every time, everywhere, and will be as long as I live. I knew the

---

[*]Courier: Pamphleteer, 1772–1825.

[†]Anatole Le Braz (1859–1926), noted writer on folk tales and traditions of Lower Brittany, especially *The Death Legend among Armorican Bretons*. See editor's preface for remarks on him.

man only by name, having read some very mediocre works he had published, in particular some Breton legends he had collected here and there from the mouths of old women and aging sailors for the price of a few drops of *guin ardent*: legends he completely distorted and mutilated. He also calls himself a poet—"a charming poet," added some of his colleagues. He is also president of a gang of Breton monarchist clericals, secretary of the Celtic studies society, and a teacher at the Quimper lycée besides. Apparently his teaching tasks are not very demanding, since he finds time for so many other activities. I learned only some months after I gave him my manuscripts that once again I had fallen in with a rascal of the sort I had so often met up with in my life: a Jesuit, a hypocrite, swindler, poltroon, and thief by the name of Le Braz Anatole, a worthy follower of Loyola and of Loriquet.

One day, to find out how far he had got with the publication of my manuscripts, I went to his house. But the rascal saw me coming, and told his maidservant to turn me away on the pretext that he was ill, even though I could hear him upstairs laughing, probably at his too-naive victim. So I understood that, once again, I had run into a rogue, but a new sort for me, which I would never have expected to be dealing with. How could I ever have imagined that my literary labors would some day interest an important writer, and even excite his envy to the extent of causing him to commit a heinous crime so that he might seize them for himself?

Back in my hole, I set to reflecting on the extraordinary adventure of my life. How in the world could my works so excite the interest of this dastardly Jesuit? He had told me he would get them printed immediately, even that he had already come to an agreement with his publisher; and that the hundred francs he gave me were an advance payment from that publisher. But my writings spoke against him—against all his ideas and his views, against the Jesuits who had been his teachers and were still his friends; against the tonsure-tops of every order who were also friends of his; against all the exploiters, robbers, and thieves; against those numberless babblers in the legislative and academic and other forums: against the scribblers in newspapers and pamphlets—all of them hypocrites, liars, who dupe and poison the people by their daily hypocrisy and lies. So it was possible that this Jesuit stole my manuscripts only in order to burn them, for fear that they might fall into other hands; or to hide them, till the day when he changes his own views and ideas—for all these chattering hypocrites do change opinions and ideas the way they change shirts; they shift with every favorable wind, the winds that blow money and put gold in their cashboxes. In any case, I don't believe he has had them printed yet. Whatever the case, I have rewritten what he stole from me, and before I've completely finished, I will have a nice page or two on him and his friends, the Breton monarchisto-nationalisto-clericocos he presides over.

I stayed another two years at Poul ar Raniquet, in my garret, amusing myself with scribbling down my life story; and when I tired of writing, I would go for a walk along the river and sometimes try to pull a few fish out of it, but in vain. These little streams and brooks of Ergué-Gabéric used to have as many fish as the Garonne, but they are completely depleted these days. The same is true of the game; there is nothing left at all. Yet in the past, the people of the Armorican peninsula had only that to live on, fishing and hunting, as they did not farm the land. Still, several landowners are beginning efforts to replenish their waters and their game preserves; they have posted signs around their estates: No Fishing, No Hunting, No Trespassing.

MY SON IS BURIED

But I did leave Poul ar Raniquet, where I was living in a garret too large for me alone, and which I found too costly for my meager income. I came to settle in town in the place where I still live, a hole six cubic meters in size. So I have a little more than half the space that experts say a man needs if he is to have air enough to live; in their view, it takes eleven cubic meters. But I don't believe in experts; most of them are only fools and idiots. They prove it every day: I see here, as I have seen elsewhere, families of ten and twelve living in little holes, on top of one another, with less then a cubic meter of air each. They live miserably, that I agree, but more for lack of food and clothing than for lack of air. However, the idiot experts would never set foot, let alone a nose, in those holes; they would be too afraid of being asphyxiated. Since I have been living here in this hole, smaller than Diogenes' barrel (though M. Courrier says the barrel was just an earthen jug), I have continued to write when the weather permits. But often in summer I'm broiled by the sun up there, no way could I work; and in winter, I'm frozen, and unable to make myself a fire for two good reasons: first, there is no fireplace, and second, I haven't the means to buy fuel. *Sic est vitam pauperes in hace mundo.* (Such is the life of the poor in this world.)

The old shrew, my mother-in-law, one of the principal authors of my misfortunes and miseries, is dead now, she who because of my atheism told me *guelde rafac'h eun devez benac, pa viot taoled en tan da rosti* (you'll see some day, when you're flung into the flames to be roasted). Poor old lady, not satisfied with doing me all the harm she could manage in this world, she still wanted those triple and quintuple evils to last me an eternity.

My second son died, too, in the time I have been living in

this hole—died in the hospice, of course, where so many penniless wretches go to die. That is where we end after a lifetime of work for hire, of labor and poverty, providing our poor bruised and emaciated bodies to those who exploit the human body, to the doctors and medical students who use them as pieces of anatomy to practice poisoning and killing their patients, according to all the traditions of the craft, just as their brethren the priestlings at the seminary practice exploiting souls, according to all the Jesuitical traditions. The two skills walk arm in arm, and the victims of either never come to complain of being mistreated, duped, and robbed. When my son died, I was ill myself, ill of cold and poverty. Nonetheless, on the day of the burial, I could still take up my pen and, shaking and shivering on my cot of fern fronds, I wrote this verse-letter to the cowardly Malherbe de la Boixière, tormentor and murderer:

Exult, knave! another of your victims fallen,
At nineteen years,
After a hundred horrid torments and tears.
You must be glad, and pleased with your crimes,
For this is the fifth of us they caused to die.
But take heart, hangman: still three of us remain;
Call in your henchmen to finish the job:
We are the sheep to you the wolves.
This poor victim died at the hospice
where one day we all shall go to die, we poor.
There shall we suffer our final pain
For the sake of you miserable, ignoble,
    fortunate ones.
His burial I did not attend,
I, the sorrowing sire of the poor victim son. No,
I stayed at home on my meager cot, shivering with cold
    and shaking at the crime,
For had I been there, my fatherly gut

Would have risen up in indignation
    and, on that corpse descending into the mud,
    sworn an oath, coward, for your eternal damnation!
You know Déguignet; you know that never before
In his life has he failed to do as he swore.
Thus, hangman, shall you pay your due:
On my son's ashes will I immolate you.
For, knave, you understand full well
That seeing such crimes unfold
It is surpassing hard to keep sane,
To master one's heart and its surges
To stifle anger and indignation.
But no, betrayer! I leave you to live with your crimes.
One day you may feel remorse, thinking—
If you do think—of those poor lost victims. Then,
    rather than a single death you shall suffer ten,
And feel as a weight on your heart the blood of the
    innocents
You have sacrificed to your fierce hatreds,
As you seek to punish the father by killing his children.
Coward, you deserve the most atrocious tortures.
I must cease my writing, for I tremble with horror
As I think of the cowardice, the dumb loathing
In which you all are steeped—Scum! and villains!
Stinking detritus of the human race!
You, Seigneur Malherbe, known as la Boixière,
You, ignoble nobleman, murderer and brigand,
You, vile beast cowering in your burrow,
You, infamous hangman:
Be you damned forevermore.

This I wrote the night my son was buried, he the fifth victim of those miserable cowards, robbers, and murderers. Malherbe had that letter the next day, and he would probably have had a visit from me as well if I had been capable of walking, but I was kept home by a dreadful pain in my side. I would have gone to his house, or to the house of that disgusting tonsure-top Le Gall, who bore just as much guilt for those murders. And there, what might have happened I cannot say—whether I would have killed him or been killed myself; perhaps both. For us poor, exploited, robbed slaves, there is no other justice possible. And such justice is permitted, even commanded, by Holy Scripture, the same text all those tonsured villains and their henchmen feed and profit from. The Scripture says that the liar, the swindler, the false witness may be killed by the very persons they have wronged. A tooth for a tooth, an eye for an eye, a hand for a hand, a foot for a foot, a burn for a burn, a wound for a wound, a bruise for a bruise, a life for a life (Exodus 21:24 and thereafter).

THE ERGUÉ-GABÉRIC PAPER MILL

I read somewhere that the famous billionaire Jay Gould once told his workers who had gone on strike once not to do it a second time or he would immediately replace them all by steelworkers who never strike and who work day and night with never a complaint. Well, *tonnerre de Brest!*

Right here in the heart of Brittany there is an industrialist who aims to carry out the American billionaire's dream. I spoke earlier of the paper mill in Ergué-Gabéric, tucked away deep in the Stang-Odet valley; I was there at its beginnings.* In the past, the mill used to employ all the workers in the area, male and female, young and old. Well, these days there is almost no one left there, although it produces ten times the amount of paper. Two or three years ago a man who had worked in the place was visiting my neighbor the wigmaker

---

*The Bolloré family owned the Odet paper mill from 1861. It employed some 200 workers before World War I.

and remarked that the day before, another ten workers had had their arms chopped off at one stroke!

"What," exclaimed a client who did not fully grasp the irony, "Ten arms at once? By one machine?"

"Yes, that's right—by one machine. A new machine that came in from Le Creusot the other day, that does the work of ten men all by itself, and consequently the boss has laid off ten workers. And that's not the end of it—more of those machines are coming, until all the workers are replaced by machines."

And indeed, that seems very likely to happen. I have gone by there since, and where I used to see a veritable human anthill, I no longer saw anyone. If I had not known the factory since it began, I might have thought I was standing before one of those enchanted palaces of oriental fable. I could see machines turning everywhere—outside, up above, down below, to right and left. High up I saw mounds of shapeless things being swallowed into great troughs where they were ground up into a mash; from there the material moved along into other troughs; then all that rotted material, bleached pale, ran into pipes that poured it out onto a steam-heated flat surface. There the pale mash turned instantly into paper; it glided through several rollers turning in opposite directions, and emerged twenty meters farther along, to be taken up by other machines that sliced it into the desired format. But however hard I looked, I could not see a person, at first because of the steam. However, when my eyes finally managed to pierce the steam, I made out three or four men standing with their arms crossed on their chests as Breton peasants do. They stood there like ghosts, staring at the machines and not moving, not speaking. First of all, speaking is impossible in the roar of those machines. Finally I stepped outside the vast enchanted palace, marveling at human genius, but also saddened to think how such genius is working counter to the goal it should aim toward—that is, distributing the world's good fortune among all people equally—but aims instead toward piling wealth and happiness upon a few privileged persons only, and thrusting away further and further the millions of disinherited wretches whose arms—their sole resource in this world—whose arms the machines chop off daily, as that displaced workman said. And those men of genius, those inventors of arm-chopping machines, collect praise, encouragements, congratulations, patents, medals, and pensions, just like the men who produce the deceitful writings that most thoroughly swindle, dupe, stupefy, pacify, and soothe the pain of the poor wretches . . . who stand impassive, placid, inert, their empty stomachs in shreds, before those machines that turn day and night for the profit of a few trillionaires, machines whose perpetual motion seems to laugh and to mock at the poor flesh-and-blood machines standing there, watching them turn, and starving to death. Meanwhile, you hear all those workers crying out against the machines, which will certainly put them all out on the street in the end. You even sometimes hear a few self-proclaimed economists, all of whose cost-cutting "economies" come from these machines, saying deep inside their offices that these machines might well become a danger—but then they go on to say that we can't block the march of technology, or we risk falling back into the Dark Ages.

THANKLESS CHILD

After this long lifetime of poverty, slavery, and persecution, I have just been dealt yet another blow that has nearly put an end to my long career of tribulation. I have told how, after my wife's death, I was left with four very young children, and my only resource a meager little tobacco shop. And even that, the tonsured scum prevented me from making what I might of it, by forbidding the local owners to rent me any shop in Pluguffan. Nonetheless, I managed anyhow to raise my children to the age where they could earn their own livings. And that was when their maternal relatives, who until then had never showed any interest in them, came and took them from me—stole them, rather. However, the eldest one, who was in the army at the time, wrote me a letter one day asking forgiveness for his cowardly behavior in the past. This poor old philosopher father, always quicker to forgive than to condemn, not only granted the thankless child his forgiveness, but sent the boy another five francs, depriving himself of food by so doing. From that day on, my ungrateful son has always refused to have anything to do with me. He came through the neighborhood on his way home from the army without stopping to see me. He clerks for a notary in Pont-l'Abbé and comes to Quimper every week without ever speaking to me. However, one day I received a very insolent letter in which the wretch told me that he was planning to be married, and that according to Article 159 of the Civil Code I must give consent to the marriage whether I want to or not. I did not reply to the insolent letter, hoping he would come to my house to invite me to the wedding and we would work it out then. The following Saturday, he did in fact come to Quimper. I saw him leaving the railway station, but when he caught sight of me he turned on his heel and hid behind the wall. Two hours later, a notary came to my house, up into my little cubbyhole, accompanied by a clerk and two witnesses called "instrumentals," to notify me on behalf of that ungrateful son of an act described as respectful, but which was to me the most disrespectful, odious act that could possibly be directed at a decent man. And it was also an act of revolt against the rights of a father, whom he had nothing to reproach—except for having been too kind to him, except for suffering in silence for ten years the effects of his ingratitude. And now he was even inflicting this ultimate outrage, and publicly. So despite my stoicism, I could not help but spring into fury beneath the whiplash of this monstrous outrage erupting unforeseen to drive me insane. And when the notary and his "instrumentals" left, I went outside and made for the railway station, my head swirling, thinking that I would find the miserable son there. But he did not come. He must now have understood what a crime he had just committed, and that even if I forgave him all the others, I could never forgive him this one.

But my last act of stoicism is not the least interesting among so many I was forced to endure. On the day of my son's wedding, I dared to go to Pont-L'Abbé—on foot, in heavy wooden clogs, and in abominable weather, in hopes of seeing the woman I should have been embracing that day and calling "daughter," my daughter-in-law. But I arrived too late; the religious ceremony was over and the newlyweds and their guests were already at the banquet. So for two sous I bought a little bread and went off to eat it a kilometer outside the town in an old quarry along the Plomeur road, while my children were dining on roast and drinking wine. But when I had eaten my bit of dry bread and rested a little, I decided to go back to the tavern where the wedding meal was going on. I bought myself a mug of cider downstairs and listened to the wedding party talking and laughing upstairs. Before leaving, I gave the barmaid a slip of paper to carry upstairs, not wanting to disturb the party; if my son had seen me he would have trembled with fear, for he is so cowardly that he is an ingrate, a traitor, and a liar. I do not know what other parent would have behaved as I did in such circumstances. Neither history nor legends mention any such event except for the one with Jesus' mother, whose son did not invite her to the Wedding at Cana, nor to the other weddings her thieving vagabond son celebrated every day. And when the mother did appear with her other children at those weddings, she was abused and grossly insulted and chased off by that bandit, who refused to acknowledge her as his mother. But I did not want to do as Mrs. Joseph did, not because I feared being abused or insulted or being run out by my ungrateful, cowardly son, but because I did not want to disrupt his guests, among whom I would have been an intruder. Despite my exhaustion and a foot injury from my clog, I chose instead to walk back to Quimper, where I arrived at nightfall, very tired, limping, as drenched as a soup, and with some regret for having made such a useless trip. And I did not sleep a minute all night long; I thought back over my whole life and wondered what harm I might possibly have done to mankind that would cause it to persecute me so until my last days, and through my own children. I could find nothing to reproach myself for. But from another viewpoint, I did see how my children, taught by their mother's relatives, could reproach me for everything. Those relatives—ignorant, hypocritical, stupid, lying, and evil—told them that if their father had been a man like other men, they would be rich today.

A man like other men—I had often heard that. I do know that I am not a man like other men, since I have never met one who resembles me. That is probably due to the accident that befell me at age nine when I was tending the bees—the accident that fractured my skull and left an opening in my left temple, which since then has allowed me to see things as they are, and also gave me the will and the firmness to tell them as I saw them, that is, differently from everyone else, at least from the people I know. As Boileau said, I call everything by its true name: a cat a cat and a priest a scoundrel. But that's just the problem. Because Bretons say: *ar wiryone neket mad da lavaret.* (The truth is not a good thing to tell.) The French say, "Not every truth is good to tell." Certainly not. In fact, *no* truth is good to tell; I know that better than anyone, since my whole life long I have been a victim, and suffered cruelly, for having always told the truth.

THAT GREAT BRETON REGIONALIST UNION

The well-known "Breton Regionalist" organization is completely made up of aristocrats and clergymen; it has no use for paupers in its ranks—they smell too bad. Such poor folk they leave in the hands of the local priests and other exploiters, who give back a share of the products they harvest from those who are exploited. But the regionalists, under their president the Jesuit and thief Le Braz, go to some pains to keep the herd of exploitees in hand by working—and by urging their underlings, the little curés and little schoolmasters to work—to maintain the Breton language and old ways among the children, young and old. For these scoundrels know that as long as the Bretons can be held to those primitive ways, and as long as they can read only Breton books, all of which are religious, the people will remain in a state of dullness, passivity, and idiocy—which is to say, in the best possible state for exploitation from every angle. One of those clowns from the great Union of Breton Regionalists told his colleagues last year at Vannes, at their celebration honoring Dutchess Queen Anne of Brittany:*

> I am certain that our work together will give rise to a most fruitful enterprise, but that will require one crucial condition, that you put into real practice the "Union" in your title, and that you dedicate all your efforts to defending Brittany's interest and to preserving her traditions, her language, her beliefs, her arts, her literature, and her unique industries.

That's exactly it, you gentlemen regionalists, you monarchisto-Jesuitico-clericoco-Breton regionalists: your goal

---

*Duchess Anne of Bretagne: Brittany was bound to France during her reign in 1488. A pact in 1532 guaranteed autonomy to the province, but it was finally absorbed into the French Republic during the Revolution of 1789.

would be to lock the poor people of Brittany into their primitive old traditions, their barbaric language, their foolish beliefs, so that through their art and your "unique industry" you can go on forever exploiting them, sucking from them as much juice as possible.

"We are not prophets," said another of those regionalist jokers. "We are Bretons like you, but we say to you, that if you will it, you and others, Brittany will live again."

Yes, indeed, Brittany will live again—in its dukes, counts, marquises, and the other aristocrats who used to go hunting Bretons for fun.

IT IS THE TWENTIETH CENTURY AND I AM STILL ALIVE

January 1, 1901:

It is the twentieth century and I am still alive. Born July 19, 1834, I shall soon be sixty-seven years old. It may be too long to live when one no longer serves any purpose. True, many people who have never served any purpose are even older than I am, and they bear their old age without moaning, and without bemoaning the people who put up with them. In fact, these people, and I know several hereabouts, no longer think; if they ever did think, now their moral outlooks, their spirits, their intelligence no longer matter, if ever they did matter over the course of their existence. Their life today is just a thoroughly animal, or even vegetal, life; their reason, their feelings, go no further than those of such animate or inanimate creatures. Still they are relatively happy creatures, those who are not too tormented by physical ailments.

THESE STUPID PROLETARIANS

Now the dockworkers of Brest and Lorient are starting to agitate, too, like the miners.* They say it is time to take action, they are starting to understand what I have been writing for a long time; that complaints and petitions mean nothing, that the politicians pay no attention to such things. Now they understand, as I always said, that it is necessary to take action by violence. But will they do it? I doubt it. Certainly the thing would not be difficult, they have numbers, strength, reason, and justice on their side. But one or two groups would not be enough; they would have to come to an agreement and all march together. In twenty-four hours, they could toss all the bourgeois capitalists into the sea, along with the deputies, the senators, the archbishops' sons, the monks, and the other thieves and parasites. Perhaps, finally, poverty will force them to act, for the poverty is growing dreadful. The dockworkers who have steady work every day say they cannot live and raise their children on their wages; and the other laborers, who half the time have no work at all, earn only thirty sous a day when they do and have broods of children to feed. If they do not wake up this winter, which is expected to be a harsh one, they will certainly die of hunger while the big scoundrels wallow in superabundance and in orgies—for particularly in winter, the hardest winters, when the workers shiver with cold and die of hunger, is when those heartless, ruthless rogues go about indulging their greatest pleasures. They have thick clothes and furs to shield them from the cold, and bright rooms heated to 54 degrees; winter is when they hold their great balls, their theater, their nights of song and music, wild dinners and suppers at fifty and sixty francs a head. Meanwhile the proletarians, who provide them with all those pleasures, dine and sup at ten centimes a head,

---

*The arsenal workers' union was organized in 1900; from 1901 on, Brest was the scene of massive protests against the maritime prefect.

and lie down on straw mats, in damp, cold holes. But those proletarians certainly deserve what they get, because of their ignorance, their servility, their lack of courage. Populations get the
governments they deserve, the saying goes, and these stupid
proletarians too have the masters they deserve.

I was saying earlier that the winter would be hard for the
wretches without bread, without work, without clothing, and
without lodging. But for me too; I'm the first to crawl into my
narrow, damp hole, with no fire or bed and only tatters to cover
my old body, bruised, worn, and emaciated. Today, though, I
went to the town hall to request a certificate that I must submit
every year to the indirect-tax bureau for my tobacco shop. There
I came upon two clerks who told me that my situation was not
so bad. No, of course not, my situation is not so bad, when all
around me I see hundreds of people much worse off; if I were
a complete dolt, with never a thought or a reflection, I would
probably be the happiest creature in the world, for I have bread
to eat and a hole to hide in. But I do think, I do reflect; and I
ponder the miseries and torments of my fellow sufferers, and the
villainies, the cheating, the crimes and injustices they are subjected to by the thieves and thugs who have the impudence, the
cynicism, the gall to call themselves the peoples' governors, representatives, protectors, when what they are is the peoples' masters and murderers. I suffer ten times more from these miseries
and horrors than I do from my own personal misfortunes.

But the bad weather goes on, after the freeze comes glacial
rain, and I suffer dreadfully here in my hole. Should I continue
to live this life of misery, or end it? I often consider ending it.

A MONTH WITH NO FOOD

And now yet another humiliation—not an enormous one, it's
true—has befallen me, and others will doubtless befall me till

the end of my days, unless they go on befalling me after that as well.

I have lived in this box for ten years, and for ten years I have bought my food from a crêpe-and-grocery shop almost directly downstairs. This crêpe-maker was a typical peasant woman in kind and in nature, like the others whose physiognomy and psychology I have described. My own nature, and my style, is not to disparage, insult, or slander, but rather to analyze, to show things and persons as they are or at least as I see them through my studies and observations. Like many of her kind, this woman has several bad features, the least of which are a quick temper, pridefulness, ignorance, thoughtlessness, hypocrisy, and slander. She never talks without slandering someone, meanwhile crediting herself with every possible and impossible virtue. Her husband, a good fellow who is an angel of candor and know-nothingism [*sic*]—if he hasn't lost his job ten times over, it's no fault of his wife's.

Well, on Christmas night I went out after supper with the husband. I even played a game of piquet with him in a tavern. But since his friends were not mine, I left him there and returned home. Apparently the fellow stayed on very late, so the next morning, when I went to the shop to buy something for my lunch, the poor oaf was getting a dressing-down, and taking it without a word, which was his habit in such cases. But the shrew was not satisfied with beating her man about with obscenities; she tried to attack me too by ricochet, in a hypocritical, roundabout way, of course.

The day after New Year's, on some silly pretext, the good shrew again mentioned Christmas night, still hypocritically trying to involve me in the business. So I left without a word, and since then I have not entered the shop. But the worst thing for me is that on New Year's Day I had paid the woman all my money in advance for my food, so that now I shall have to live the whole month like Doctor Succi, who went a month without eating, they say. Because, as I have said before, I am an extremely sensitive and scrupulous person, I do not dare ask people for anything, lest I be refused. I shall not have to submit totally to Succi's diet, though: the baker from whom I get bread from time to time will be selling me a bit extra this month, which may surprise him; and the woman at the tavern where I have bought all my drink over these ten years will also give me a few more liters of cider than usual. With bread and cider a person can easily live for a month. Prisoners used to have only bread and water, and bad bread at that, and yet they lived, sometimes for long years, on that diet, and in worse hygienic conditions than I, besides; in my hole, cramped as it is, I can let in air as much as I like, sometimes even more than I like. And I have my freedom; I can go off walking on the roads, in the game preserves, in the fields, and in the meadows along the water, and I can store up oxygen, the very foundation of animal life, which the plants cede to us while keeping for themselves carbonic acid, which means life to them.

In any case, it is now January tenth, and I am doing very well except for a slight grippe, for want of clothing to protect me from the cold and the damp. Another twenty days and my little ordeal will be over. The worst part of the ordeal, while it is not so bad as Tantalus's, is being deprived of coffee in the morning, or at least of that nice drop of hot water made black by chicory and a pinch of coffee. But I hope that in three more weeks I will make up for it.

"PISTIGOÙ"

The pleasures of the pre-Lent carnival days have come to an end. I believe they were fairly merry here, to judge by the shouting and singing I could hear from my hole, where for the past six days I have been confined by pains in my side, a malady common among Bretons, who call the trouble *pistigoù*. Such ailments, incidentally, may come from bad weather or from a natural predisposition in the race—by which I mean the race of the poor. For the rich, here as elsewhere, are spared such ailments, and many others to which we poor folk are unavoidably condemned by excessive labor and privations that are even more excessive, since we lack for everything, food, clothes, and housing.

I RESOLVE TO KILL MYSELF

I have just received an order from my landlord evicting me from my hole, where I have lived for ten years, on the grounds that my neighbors are complaining of lice which, it seems, go from my hole into their room, although these good little beasties, whom I have known for sixty years, never do abandon the back of whatever poor wretch they were born on. True, I myself have had the company all my life of these rather inoffensive little bugs—more inoffensive than fleas or bedbugs, and I would just as soon have these good beasties. They are right in that there is certainly more valor in living with bedbugs, or scabies, or scrofula, or syphilis, or tuberculosis and other microbes, which are all more trouble and more disgusting than lice. But, about this order, I don't know what I will do. According to the landlord, I must leave my hole at the end of the month, and today is the sixth. But he tells me that the principal cause of my eviction is one of my neighbors, and it could happen that this person leaves before I do. I have just spent the evening with several friends—for despite everything, I still do have some. It may have been the last good evening of my life, for I am, so to speak, condemned to die; we are all of us condemned to die, yes, but I am condemned to die in a few days, one way or another. I mentioned elsewhere that I should long ago have murdered Malherbe de la Boixière, the primary maker of my

miseries, or Cambourg, the second, then I should have killed
Le Gall, the curé of Ergué-Armel, Le Mao, curé of Pluguffan
and his successor Guédès, and then I should have done in
Elias, the former baker, and Baron at the prefecture.

And now I would also be within my rights to kill that poor
idiot cripple Losac'h, who is presently sending me to my death.
But is it actually revenge to kill a criminal by a single blow? I
think not. It would even be doing any scoundrel a great favor
to kill him that way, for his soul—presuming he has one—
would happily be rid of so vile a body. So the best revenge is still
to rid oneself of a life that has become useless and burden-
some, and leave one's persecutors to their own fates. Most of
mine, as I have said, died miserable deaths, and the ones still
alive are in sorry situations that are worse than death.

Well now, this time it is a result of too many persecutions, and
especially of the injury my landlord did me in turning me out
unexpectedly after I have been living in this place for twelve
years and always paid my rent in advance; and finally of the
horrible insult from a police officer, the wickedest and stu-
pidest of all those officers, who are as ignorant and wicked
toward poor devils as they are prostrate and cowardly toward
great scoundrels. In the face of so much wickedness and skul-
duggery, my sensitive heart and spirit can no longer go on,
and instead of killing one of these bastards, I resolved to kill
myself. I gave away all I owned to an old rag-and-bone merchant for a few sous, and bought two sous' worth of coal.
Then I wrote the following letter to the Police Commissioner:

Dear Commissioner:

I am about to die, murdered by your officer Le Quillec
and by Mathurin Lozac'h. But even before this, for a
long while now, half-killed by my many persecutors,

particularly Malherbe de la Boixière, Cambourg, the priests Le Gall, Le Mao, and Guédès, Hélias of Pluguffan, Baron of the Prefecture; and Déguignet junior, a notary's clerk. I ask you to kindly have my body removed tomorrow. In my room you will find books, manuscripts, and many letters; you may do with them what you like. I beg your pardon for any trouble I shall be causing you. Farewell.

Déguignet

Having prepared everything for my departure, I went off again quite merrily to have a few drinks with friends. I waited till midnight to ignite my coal; then I lay down philosophically with my head beside the stove. I went quickly to sleep, thinking that it was forever. What happened during my slumber, which was meant to be eternal, I cannot understand, for in the morning I awoke but was unable to move my arms or legs. Turning my eyes, though, I saw that the candle I left lighted had gone out, and so had the coal, though it had not all burned. However, after about an hour, and more by strength of will than by my depleted natural strength, I was able to rise, first on my knees and hands; then, eventually, by clamping one hand to the edge of my cot I managed to stand up. I examined the door, which was still firmly shut, with stuffing all around its edges; so was the casement window. Seeing that nearly half the coal was left, I stoked the stove again and lit the fire. This time I was sure I would not escape, as I had already died once and was barely half-resuscitated.

And indeed, in five minutes I did lose consciousness. But, oh, what destiny dogs my life!—how much later I do not know, I awoke again, this time in the arms of two police officers who seemed to be showering me with equal amounts of concern and insult. And then a moment later, when they eventually revived me completely, I also heard the stupid, derisive voice of the commissioner, ordering his officers to shake me hard and wash my face. Then when they had rubbed and shaken me enough, they dragged me into the street and made me walk half around the town to the hospital, where I have been for the past week with no idea what they plan to do with me. The doctor tells me nothing. But he saw my manuscripts, which the commissioner transported here with my books, and he asked me if he could consult them; he even says he has begun reading them and finds them very interesting. But what will he do with them? I have no idea, just as I have no idea what he means to do with me, myself. If he keeps me here for another month and a half, I might perhaps find some way to live a while longer. But if he decides to put me out before that, it will be all over, since I no longer have any housing or clothing or money. It is actually not bad here in this hospital, which is so much disparaged by the very people who could not live without it.

DECLARED A MADMAN, IDIOT, FOOL

As for me, I have never been so nicely housed or better fed in my life; and if the doctor, who is also one of the municipal councilors who have supervisory rights here, wanted to keep me, I would happily stay. I see a good many old fellows here who have not done much over the course of their lives, and who are put in here to finish out their days. The worst nuisance is that there is no one to talk to; there are only laborers, peasants, paupers, poachers, all of them more or less ignorant and dull-witted. So I have taken up my pen again to go on tracing the story of my life, since against my will, that life refuses to quit my old body, it is clear that the "vital principle," as they say, is bolted firmly somewhere inside this aged carcass. I have actually put together a few verses on the subject, which I shall transcribe here. I even mean to show them to the doctor, the one who has declared me mad, afflicted with persecution mania, as if I were the one persecuting and not the persecuted. The French language has a number of these odd definitions.

Here I lie stranded on a hospital bed.
It must be writ in the book of fate,
That I should endure the greatest miseries,
That I must go through every horror

That here below might crush mankind,
Horrors so well told by David in his psalms.
And it is not over; I have still to drink
From other bitter cups. Another purgatory

Awaits me near at hand, in another asylum,
To be declared mad, idiot, imbecile
Worthy to join this company of the deranged,
Of alcoholics and of epileptics.

Science insists, before its decrees
Must I bow my head, silence my faculties;
They exist no more, for science makes them null,
And I revert to childhood.

Modern science or the Goddess Phreno
Decrees that back to the cradle I go,
'Tis well I still retain the philosophy
That all my life has served me so kindly.

Yet what shall I do in these mournful halls
Where madness is queen in tawdry finery?
This place must be like the inferno,
That Dante describes in some crude linery.

Here too one could write his same words:
"Abandon hope, all ye who enter here."
What will become of me here in this pandemonium?
Am I to go mad as well?

If I believe I have tumbled into madness
As ever-infallible science declares,
Am I to sing, crawl about on my knees,
Weep, laugh, leap, like the other lunatics?

Send packing all my faculties
And trample to oblivion all my past works.
Thus long ago in the Elysian Fields
Did the souls of brave men, plunged into forgetfulness,

Taste the greatest joys and delights,
No longer recalling the world of suffering.
But despite my efforts, I shall never be able
To forget who I am, or who I was.

I might sing with these madmen of Armorica,
Yet Echo will repeat: *te cantas in dolor.*
Madmen are we all, said Boileau long ago,
And the learned Lombroso affirms it today

Affirms by the laws of phrenology
That all humankind is touched by madness.
History gives no assurance otherwise,
Nothing but madness there, under the name of glory.

Madness and fury, ferocity and hatred
This the whole history of the human animal.
It could be sketched in one quick instant,
Just dipping a thick brush in mud and blood.

Not too far back in the history of France
We have seen Frenchmen, all fallen mad,

Writers and generals, citizens, judges,
Calling each other frauds, villains, scoundrels.

And by their minds gone perverse, all these grand maniacs
Filled up the universe with their vast insanity.
But all these madmen, succumbing to rage,
Each believing he alone has inherited wisdom,

They put a few paupers under lock and key,
and announce that those, only those, men are mad.
If there were somewhere, in some corner of the heavens,
A God like we are told—great, strong, and generous,
He would long ago have tugged from its orbit

And ground to dust this accursed earth.
Never could he have stood for so many crimes,
Nor watched the streaming blood from the victims.

But I was nearly forgetting that I am insane,
Ruled out of humankind and society
For having determined, as a Stoic,
to quit this poor world, have no more to do with it,

For that I am adjudged afflicted
With persecution mania. Yes, all my life
I have bitterly suffered persecutions
By scum, charlatans, and knaves.

If suffering silently is termed mania,
Then I am surely mad, madder than madness.
They should long ago have locked me up
With the imbeciles, the idiots, and the deranged.

But rather than mad, I was more a coward,
I ought to have taken a dagger or a heavy ax,
And gone in justice to tear out the entrails
From those stupid, ignoble, vile torturers.

And fed them to my poor children,
Reduced to poverty by these tyrannical monsters.
Many of those monsters are already dead
And have surely been rewarded already on high.

By Him who told them in his last farewells,
"Whatsoever ye do shall be kindly seen in heaven,
Whatsoever ye shall do here below on earth
We shall applaud ye, I and my noble Father."

I could easily cite all those tyrants and torturers.
I will cite at least the main ones
The first, a priest, named Roumigou,
Was an alcoholic, a worthless ignoble thug.

Then Cambourg, and Malherbe known as La Boixière,
Ignoble gentleman, traitor, coward, fraud, and counterfeiter
Le Mao and then Guédès and the cowardly LeGall,
Deserve all to be thrown to the infernal furnaces.

And the deceitful, knavish, triple-coward milord clerk
And hundreds and hundreds more, for they are legion.
All of them truly have the great persecution mania
The mania *to* persecute and the mania for deceit.

And it is I who suffer for all those scum,
Those pitiless, mindless, heartless, gutless scum.
They have seized my body [is made captive] but not my spirit;
My mind is free, free both day and night.

[Eleven more stanzas follow]

THE DECREE EXPELLING THE NUNS

But now I have finally regained my freedom. Tomorrow morning I leave the hospital after an imprisonment, or internment, of nearly four months. The doctor says that he has never told anyone about the supposed persecution mania, and he says that I am within my rights to sue the newspaper that published the story. I do believe I should sue the paper for damages, for the moral and material prejudice it has brought down on me. Yes, if there were justice for us poor slaves and pariahs, but we all know very well that there is not. No matter, I will try anyhow. So here I am, free, or at least relatively free. For absolute freedom does not exist in this world, no more for the rich than for the poor.

I went to Pluguffan to see the man now running my tobacco shop. Things are very bad in that unfortunate commune, which is almost entirely in the hands of the nobles and the clericals. These groups rebelled against the decree expelling the Sisters of the Holy Spirit who run the girls' school, and forced their farmers and day laborers to take up arms to defend the good sisters.* That started a hatred, a fierce hatred, between the ignorant wretches on both sides. But the fanatics defending the nuns are far more numerous, so the others must hold their tongues; and now they are being boycotted by the clerical party. Their people may not go near those poor pestilent republicans, or buy from their shops, even though here as elsewhere these great clerical partisans are very quick to cry "Up with Liberty!" My manager told me he had lost a great many customers since the revolt began. The schoolmaster was cursed, insulted, and stoned by these "friends of Liberty." And every day I hear people, even republicans, saying that the government is wrong to run out the nuns and monks who, they say, do no one any harm.

In any case, the decrees are now being put into effect in our department, after three weeks of feverish expectation. The process began with Quimper, Kerfeunteun, and Ergué-

---

*In 1902, the anti-clerical republican national government decreed the expulsion of religious communities and the prohibition of the use of Breton for church services; this provoked violent response in Brittany.

Gabéric. Everything went off without incident, even though all
the gendarmes, police, and a few companies of infantry had
been brought in. Mostly women and children stood before the
nuns' establishments, shouting "Long Live Liberty, Long Live
the Sisters!" Of thirty-eight establishments ordered closed,
thirty-five still have townfolk guarding the sisters night and day
for the past three weeks. And the senators, deputies, town
councilors circulate daily throughout these areas, encourag-
ing resistance among the poor fanaticized peasants. And those
louts abandon their farms, their fields, and their harvests to
come and obey the great scoundrels, who mock and laugh at
them. For while the idiot peasants lose worktime and suffer
hunger and heat or rain out in the public squares, the clever
senators and deputies and their consorts go about from one
mansion to the next carousing and stuffing their bellies. But
why do they not all join together, all those senators, deputies,
councilors, county and town politicians, nobles, priests,
monks, and burghers, all of them fervent Catholics, and
declare Brittany's secession from France? Then they could
do anything they choose here, the way the nobility used to do
in the past. They would find a *populo* of workers and peasants
who are more ignorant, more stupid, and more cowardly than
they were back in the noblemen's time. For I do not believe
that ever in any period, in any country, have the proletarians,
peasants, slaves, or serfs been as ignorant, as dull-witted, and
as cowardly as those I see nowadays.

This Celtic race is, in any case, doomed to die out like all
ancient races grown morally and physically degenerate. Long
ago, living in the forests, lacking mind or morality, the race did
at least have physical energy and strength. No more now. All it
has left nowadays is the language to babble, squabble, banter,
and lie, overwhelming with its stupidities and idiocies any poor
devils who still have a few milligrams of sense. Their physical

energy has degenerated so much that now, despite the efforts
of their pastors, mayors, deputies, and senators to urge them
to actual revolt against governmental decrees, these leaders
only manage to herd them together, like herding a flock of
sheep, to bawl out in chorus the way they mumble psalms in
church: "Long Live the Sisters . . . Long Live Liberty. . . ." And
that's all. It takes a mere twenty gendarmes to disperse a mob
of four thousand of these degenerate Bretons, whereas twenty
of their ancestors, flailing their *pen-bas* cudgels, would have
scattered and laid low four thousand gendarmes. And, anyhow,
the deputies, senators, councillors, and priests urging the peasants on to revolt are even greater cowards than they are. When
the masters have worked these poor ignoramuses up into a
fanatical fit, when they have made them swear to spill their
blood defending the nuns, the minute the authorities arrive
with some gendarmes and a few soldier-boys, these gentlemen
start preaching calm, and go very politely up to the authorities
and hand over the school keys. What a farce! And the peasants
are foolish enough to listen to these parliamentary blowhards
and clowns, and to leave their crops to wither as they go off to
stand guard over a few old maids in white wimples, and spend
money and catch colds while they're at it.

With that sort of system, the government these monarchisto-
clericocos rant against can rest easy. And it can fearlessly order
the expulsion of all the male and female religious communities,
and all the shaven monks, along with the people who support
them. But it should make sure to confiscate their enormous
holdings, which they stole from the poor idiots around them.
Let us rid humankind—real humankind—of all these
scoundrels, swindlers, liars, idlers, infectious parasites, vampires,
bloodsuckers, deceivers, and thieves. Clericalism has been called
the enemy for a very long time now, well, then let us run the
enemy out! Oh yes indeed: clericalism, deism, theism, and poly-
theism are the most dreadful enemies of the human race. . . .

Down by Lesneven, in the communes of Saint-Méen, Folgoat, and Ploudaniel, the [clericalist] deputies and senators Gayraud, Pichon, and Cuverville have been keeping the peasants up day and night with the same speeches or sermons, about the good Sisters and the heroic resistance all must put up against the forces who would come and rob them of "these angels of charity and goodness," as Admiral de Cuverville calls them—a resistance which must press on to the bitter end. And the peasants swear they will all die rather than let the good angels get stolen away. Yes, for nearly a month now these clowns, these chattering representatives, have kept the peasants up guarding the nuns, building barricades, digging trenches, carving their *pen-bas* cudgels, and shouting and swearing to die in defense of their good angels; and now I read that the nuns in those three terrible communes were ousted yesterday, August 18th, by the same process as everywhere else. The defenders were all called on to shed their own blood, but instead they shed buckets of excrement on the government officials and gendarmes— excrement that should have smelled beautifully, actually, since it had been produced by angels. Nothing kept the Abbé Gayraud from giving another long speech, or sermon, after the authorities and the gendarmes left, thanking the poor dumb peasants for their long and energetic resistance and ended by saying, "We are persecuted because we wish to serve God and to obey His laws, because we love the Church and wish to be faithful to its Commandments. A handful of Freemasons seek to dominate the country and tyrannize us: we shall fight to defend our religious faith, and to safeguard our children's souls . . . Long live Christ! Long live Our Lady! Long live the Good Sisters! Long live France! Long live Liberty! And again, thank you, and farewell!"

Farewell, said the clever Abbé-deputy, yes, farewell, and in four years the scoundrel will be back to tell them a fresh bunch of lies in order to capture their votes so he can dupe them for another four years.

A SHORT TREATISE ON BEEKEEPING

I have never felt regrets over my past life, as I consider the past to be null and void. However, I could not forget my project to go live as a hermit in that marvelous primitive wilderness, where I would have spent my life amid my friends the bees in peace, far from the turmoil, the roar, the assaults, and treachery, the vileness and the horrors of the civilized world, into whose machinery fate thrust me just as I was on the verge of leaving it all behind. Yes, whenever I go into those *stangs*, wild and yet so picturesque and filled with natural wonders, I linger a long while gazing at the place I chose for my hermitage, which is still in the same state and doubtless will remain so till the end of time, unless some seismic cataclysm comes to change the face of those deep gorges. I spend silent delicious hours there, thinking and dreaming about the matters of that small world where so many millions and billions of creatures appear and disappear as you watch, and leave no trace nor memory of their passage. That is still the place where I spend the best moments of my life, watching the waters of the Odet bound from one crag to the next, and contemplating those enormous boulders hanging hundreds of meters above the stream, those rough wild marvels that testify to an immense cataclysm, perhaps the one that sent the great continent of Atlantis plunging beneath the waters several thousand years ago, and put a deep sea, the deepest of all seas, between America and Europe.

. . . I mean to submit a short treatise on the art of beekeeping to a Breton "regionalist" organization, although that will be quite difficult. Writing a scientific and artistic treatise in a barbaric old language like Breton is nearly impossible, because the main elements are lacking: the words. As he was writing his famous "Divine Comedy," Dante complained that he was unable to express himself as he would have liked, and as the subject demanded, in a language that was still in its cradle: *lingua chi chiami mama a babo* (baby talk). Our ancient Breton tongue, perhaps one of the oldest, is nonetheless still in its cradle, and it will probably die there. These regionalists and their collaborators the priests are complaining loudly these days because the government has forbidden the use of Breton in sermons and catechism—these people, three-quarters of whom don't know a word of Breton. Ah, if that ban had come from the pope, how they would have cheered it! Especially the priests, who have trouble giving their sermons in Breton, the more so because as they move from one canton to another they must change their speech, if they can, and it is not always easy. So everywhere they are ridiculed by the peasants, who don't understand a word of their patois, which is half distorted French, a quarter kitchen Latin, and a quarter some unintelligible kind of Breton. Oh yes! At bottom, these priests would love to see a complete abolition of this Celtic jargon, with its thirty-six gibberish dialects, all of them largely unintelligible even for the most learned Celt-specialists.* What is even more amusing is that the Bishop of Quimper and Léon, who knows not a word of all these barbaric old idioms, knocks himself out to defend them. Oh, of course, the reason the old crucibled-and-mitered fellow car-

---

*Like all languages, Breton has its dialects. The division of Lower Brittany into four archbishoprics promoted the emergence of different written forms. The dialect differences are invoked to disparage the language by its enemies, and the argument is taken up by the anticlerical press. In his military career, Déguignet had occasion to witness the same kind of difficulties in communication among French-speakers from various regions. This question of the dialects and patois in nineteenth-century France is discussed by the American historian Eugene Weber, in *La fin des terroirs*: Fayard, 1991. (*Peasants into Frenchmen.*)

ries on this way is not solely to defend an ancient tongue that he doesn't know. It is because what he does know is that as long as the Bretons preserve their various gibberishes, they will be incapable of moving ahead into the light, the light that these black charlatans are determined always to conceal from the populace; for they know that if the *populo* should discover it, that would be the end of priests once and for all, *finis te deum et omni prebendes.**

Well, in any case, I began to write—in Breton—the little treatise on beekeeping, but like the curés in their sermons, I am forced to use a good many French words, and even Latin words, because apiculture comes from the Latin *apis* (bee), and *cultor* (husbandman). And all the materials that bees need for fabricating little larvae, and all the transformations these larvae undergo to become bees, are expressed by Latin and Greek words. It is true that in their contest announcement, these non-Breton-speaking Bretonists told poets and other writers that in their poems and prose they should do their best to enrich the Breton language and raise the intellectual level of Bretons. That's all very well. Enriching the language is an easy matter, I enrich it nicely and necessarily in my little apiculture treatise. But when it comes to raising the Breton intellect, that is a different matter—an anatomical and anthropological matter.

Now, to write a treatise on beekeeping, one should be an actual beekeeper, not an armchair one like an armchair farmer. One must work with bees to know them, must study them closely to understand their ways and to learn how to draw from them the greatest possible benefits. Of course almost all the peasants here have a few hives on their farms. But those bees are, so to speak, left to their own devices, in ill-

---

*"Lord, thou art the goal, and all depend from thee."

made hives that are often half-rotted, crushed under loads of turf, stones, old earthenware or iron pots, and buried in grass and brambles. Besides, the superstitions that surround these daughters of Aristeus guard them against any progress in this backward countryside. Everyone knows superstitions are rife among Bretons, but on no other matter do such ideas proliferate as they do about bees. Here above all do we see Breton folk's ignorance and utter lack of any spirit of observation. If you decided to tell a Breton beekeeper that his bees never go, and cannot go, farther than two kilometers from home, you would be very quickly sent packing, called an imbecile and a dunce; he stands ready to provide you with the eyewitness testimony of sailors who have seen bees on their ships thousands of leagues from land. That has certainly been seen. But those sailors know no more about the habits of these insects than the ignorant Breton beekeepers. They may have seen bees on the open ocean, but that is precisely because the insects fear the sea as they do any great expanse of water. The bees were gathering fatty matter from the masts of the ship in dock, but the ship left port while they were busy sucking up the material that they use it to make propolis, the beeswax, to plug the cells, the *alveolae*, and seal in the honey or the larvae that will become bees. Once the vessel has gone as little as a hundred meters from land, the bees will no longer fly off and leave it, so frightened are they of water. So when those poor beekeepers assert that bees must go to sea to get water for salting the honey, that's another great one! They would also tell you that the bees must fly to the Americas to get *caotchoug* (rubber) for plugging up the alveolae of their honeycombs, because the nature of the propolis bears a strong resemblance to rubber. They do not know much about the propolis, either: what it is, where it comes from, how the bees make it, any more than they know how or from what bees manufacture wax. For they will all tell you that wax is made with pollen, the fine dust which bees collect from flowers to nourish the larvae. Never would they allow that the wax is made from honey, even if the God of the bees were to come and tell them so himself. They will also declare that a queen bee who dies in a hive can be replaced by a sprig of rye grass dipped in *coc'h pimoc'h.** And then they will say that when a hive's owner dies, that's the end of his bees, no one else will have any luck with them because for these learned apiculturists, the whole science lies in luck. No luck, no bees.

It is these superstitions and wrong ideas that keep Bretons from developing the art of apiculture, an art that is both pleasurable and lucrative, and one by which many poverty-stricken rural families could transform their purgatory into an earthly paradise. I see a good many such unfortunate families around here, who have some paltry cottage with a couple of yards of land in the mountains, or along abandoned roads, where all they have to survive on is potatoes and black bread. If those families had the slightest knowledge of the art of raising bees, they could turn their sorry home into a true Eden. I do not know what those non-Breton-speaking Bretonists will do with my little treatise on beekeeping, written in Breton as they require. However, I do know that if they were to have it printed and get it into the hands of those poor wretches I mean it for, they could do a great service. For I think that despite people's ignorance and foolish prejudices, by reading this little essay, which is practical, clear, and detailed, they would come to see reason, and would toss aside their prejudices and superstitions about bees.

Recognition from these regionalists, actually, does not matter to me. I don't write to earn money; I write to kill time and to satisfy my intellect, which always needs feeding. It's just that I would have been glad to see that little treatise come into the

---

*Pig manure.

hands of those poor ignorant, superstitious peasants, most of whom are unfortunate and poor only because of prejudice and superstition; and not into the hands of the old folks, there would be no point in that, but of young people, the ones whose skulls are not yet completely hardened into stone. They could probably derive a good deal of profit and pleasure from it.

In any case, this very day, June 6, 1903, I have sent off the little treatise to Saint-Brieuc, to someone named Vallée,* to whom we are told to direct all these essays in Breton from the Léon, Tréguer, and Cornouailles districts.†

The gentleman is apparently a noted expert on Celtic matters; he would have to be, if he can manage in all these different written dialects. I too can understand these three idioms when they are spoken, but in writing, I must wrack my brain to guess what the authors are getting at. To begin with, the Breton words they write are spelled in a way impossible to pronounce as true Breton; and then they write great numbers of words that seem closer to Chinese or Arabic than to Breton, and which the rest of us Breton-speaking Bretons have never heard of. But these writers who claim to be knowledgeable in Celtic matters may be taking these barbaric words from all the various Celtic tongues, of which there are many, since they count as Celtic peoples not only the Bretons but also the Basques, the Irish, and the Scottish, although their dialects differ among themselves as much as Russian does from French.

---

*François Vallée, grammarian, author of a fine dictionary of the Breton language, is considered the father of modern Breton (*trad ar yezh*).

†Déguignet's work was noted by the jury: "An honorable mention to Monsieur Tanguigot [*sic*] from Quimper, who has written on bees. His work is full of very interesting information but his Breton is poor, full of words from French, Latin, and even Italian." ["Kroaz ar Vretoned," n. 281, October 4, 1904.]

THE DRUNKARDS' ROOM

Earlier I mentioned those brutes who overrun the squalid trough [of an inn] called Moysan's. I said that one day, if I was pushed too far by that vilest of vile barkeeps, I might smash the miserable alcoholic's head or gut. Well, it happened. The other day, after I had spent the night outside in the rain to escape the racket and the unspeakable filth of that disgusting creature, I returned to the [bunk] room toward noon, thinking the brute would be gone. But he was there, and immediately began swearing at me, claiming that I was bothering him and keeping him from sleeping. At those remarks, the sort you hear from uncouth Bretons always blaming other people for their own worst features, my nerves snapped and I lunged at the beast, my stick in my hand. He was standing by his bed, but at the sight of my raised club he flipped backwards and smashed his head against the wall. I tried to hit at his ribs, but he was flailing with his legs and feet in the air, so I could only connect with those parts. But at the third blow, my club skidded off the tip of his raised shoe and ricocheted right onto his forehead, which instantly spurted blood. The animal began to howl, and a few people came running to find out what was going on in that filthy room, correctly called "the drunkards' and rioters' room." In a couple of words and gestures, I set out what happened. The beast was still crouched on his bed, bellowing and howling, so he was not dead despite his claim that I had killed him. I certainly could have killed him. And without a doubt, if my blow had landed directly on his skull, hard as that was, I would have split it in two, and I would not have regretted it in the least, even if I'd been sent to prison or to the scaffold for that act of justice.

I expected to be seized by the police commissioner or the gendarmes, for anything can be expected from scum. But no. The miserable fellow is fully aware that he has a bad reputation everywhere, and the man and wife who own the place also know that their filthy pigsty is just a foul hell-hole where all kinds of hoodlums, thugs, crooks, and rascals gather. So that whole fine crowd kept quiet. For my part, I simply asked for my bill, and fled that hell where there are as many demons and furies as in the Infernos of Aeneas and Dante Alighieri both. Now I am in an attic at Poul ar Raniquet, the place where thirty-four years ago I was caught in a snare, the matrimonial snare that produced all the miseries and misfortunes of my existence ever since. Now I sleep on straw, but I am a hundred times happier than I was sleeping on feathers at Moysan's.

AT THE LIBRARY

Winter is coming and it will very probably be long and harsh; I will have no other way to keep warm but to run about in my old wooden clogs. Fortunately, I will not be hampered as I run as my clothing is not heavy, even when I put it all on at once. Nor will food be a burden, since at most I can spend only sixty centimes a day on it, and the price of bread keeps going up; I will soon be unable to eat anything but black bread and potatoes. And I will not be the worst off, for many workers earn only thirty sous a day when they find a job to do, and have three, four, five children and more to feed.

In fact, as I began this twenty-fifth notebook, I wrote that, thanks to a clear conscience from a lifetime of work and probity, I would think myself the most fortunate of men if only my heart and mind were not tormented at the sight of the charlatan tricks wreaked by the scoundrel priests, and the farces that the so-called peoples' representatives play, with even more cynicism and more contempt for the people than the representatives of the nobility in times gone by.

Some time ago I went to the library, which is called the Quimper Public Library. The librarian, a friend and flunky of those charlatans and comedians, scowled meaningfully on seeing me in my peasant smock and hat, enter the sanctum sanctorum where he reigns like a god. When I told him I wanted to consult a certain work on astronomy by Flammarion, he burst into Jupiterian laughter, and with no further response than that side-splitting guffaw, he shoved me toward a dim recess saying, "Here, look, there are some good novels here, pick one; that will do you nicely." There was indeed a pile of old discarded books. I picked one up at random, hoping that if I brought it, the librarian he might be better disposed toward me and would give me something better. But that time, too, the fellow made the same face, telling me to take another volume if I liked from that pile of discards. I was brave enough to return several times but, met by those same scowls and rejections, and seeing clearly that the presence of a peasant was shaming for such a place, especially for the grand personages who frequented it and for the autocrat who reigned there, I was obliged to give up. But that episode showed me once again in what esteem the lower class is held by all those bourgeois, grown rich on the sweat of that population, and by all those charlatan priests who suck its blood from the cradle to the grave.

Now, before starting my Twenty-sixth notebook, in which I propose to discuss the question of mythology, I must patch up my poor rags, for they no longer hold together, and the cold is beginning to make itself felt. As I did once at Sevastopol, I have to patch my old green cloth coat with bits of black cloth from some trousers. Oh, well!

The soldier can laugh at his uniform rags
As long as he trusts his gun;
He'll mend his pants with a slice from his shirt
And laugh with everyone.

Unfortunately I forgot to gather ferns, the bedding that has stood me for six years to make up my cot, and upon which, despite everything, I am probably happier on than plenty of millionaire scoundrels are on their feathers.

I HAVE SEEN MY NAME SHINING AMID LITERARY LUMINARIES

Here is a letter I just received from M. Le Braz, professor at Rennes:

Port-Blanc, near Penvenan, September 15, 1904
Dear M. Déguignet,

Herewith enclosed you will find a postal order for one hundred francs, the balance of the sum of two hundred francs I contracted to pay you in exchange for possession of your manuscript memoirs, and for the rights to reproduce excerpts from them in a journal. I beg your pardon for sending you this sum only now; but it was unavailable to me earlier this month as I had expected. I was hoping to send you a copy of *La revue de Paris* containing the first pages of your memoirs, but there is nothing of yours in the current issue, and moreover, as I told you, they have not given me a precise date, so we must still wait. I shall be going to Paris in November, and if between now and then nothing has been provided to the readers, I shall urge the editor to hasten publication, so that you may have the very rightful pleasure of seeing your signature in one of our country's most highly respected periodicals. I would be pleased to hear news of you; you know my admiration for your person and how fond I am of you as one of the most significant examples of our race. May you keep your fine intellectual vitality for a good long time. I was pleased, when I came through Quimper, to see the alacrity of body and spirit you bring to your lively old age. Think of me from time to time, and trust that I shall always remain your faithful and devoted

A. Le Braz

Yes, but that dear devoted Le Braz left me with no word for five years. What did he do with my manuscripts during that time? I read in a newspaper that Le Braz Anatole donated some very interesting manuscripts to the Bibliothèque Nationale. They are probably mine; would he have copied them and given the originals to the Bibliothèque Nationale? Now he will have fragments of the copies published in some magazine, maybe *La revue de Paris* as he says, and will put them in a book later. I have no way of knowing, and when a man betrays you the way I have been betrayed by this devoted Le Braz Anatole, he cannot be counted on. Well, he sent me a hundred francs, which did me both pleasure and good. Like those other glorious promises he had made me, I hadn't counted on it. The man was taught by Jesuits, and he has kept on with all their principles; he makes daily use of the great formula: "Lie, always lie, lie over and over again"—no Jesuit makes better use of it. But he denies it, and deny it he must. In politics he has betrayed everyone, his closest friends first among them; he believes in God without being able to say what that God is or where he perches; in matters social, he knows a good deal less than the lowest *potr saout*. From here on, all he has left is his Jesuitical hoax, with which, moreover, he has sated his most fervent disciples; and my manuscripts, with which he expects to make his fortune. So be it.

But now Le Braz Anatole has sent me an issue of *La revue de Paris* in which I have the pleasure of seeing my name figure among the illustrious writers. Yes, at the top of Issue 24, December 15, [1904], I read: *Jean-Marie Déguignet: Mémoires d'un paysan bas-Breton.* Heavens, at the risk of disconcerting my Mentor, I tell him that I feel no more joy over this than I did at seeing my name listed among the non-commissioned officers of the Twenty-sixth Line Infantry regiment, whereas on the same day a friend promoted along with me went nearly mad with joy. In fact, I never did have, at anytime in my life, that sort of rapture, those flushes of mad vanity. The most I could wish for right now is to find a few friends—or even enemies, who have always considered me a mere ignorant, worthless peasant—and show them that I am much more than they thought. Unfortunately, the friends and the enemies I have around here understand nothing about matters of literature, the arts, or the sciences. With a few rare exceptions, these are matters that never enter Breton brains.

And Le Braz says that he considers it the finest act of his literary career to have brought me through the grand portal into this new world called the Republic of Letters. And that he hopes to see me live a good long while yet, and enjoy my literary triumph, which will go on growing ever greater as the publication of my memoirs proceeds, and especially when they appear in book form. But I shall not see that; in any case, I have seen enough, I have seen my name shining amid literary luminaries, I had never hoped for as much. Here I owe thanks to M. Le Braz Anatole, against whom I have written much, but much of it is truths he cannot deny.

IT IS TIME TO END . . .

We have now come to the year 1905, and I am still living, I who have often visited the dark domain of the Parkae.* But those

---

*The Fates.

good goddesses, who are both just and unyielding, have always sent me back from their world, on the grounds that I had not yet completed my mission on this poor little planet. Those good maidens must have wanted me to see my name written in large letters amid literary engravings at the head of a great magazine.

I have lived for seventy-one years by now. My time was not wholly wasted, as is evident over the course of these accounts. And perhaps my aged days, which I thought useless, will yet be the best employed: my writings are already beginning to yield something, and Le Braz says that they will yield a great deal. And if they yield something now, they may do so more later on—in fifty years, a hundred years, a thousand years and more. Most of the Greek and Roman writers live on today through their writings, which are reprinted constantly, and which still sell at good prices. How much money those writings have yielded over the centuries!

But I believe it is time now to end these long memoirs, the authentic accounts of a long lifetime of tribulations. What will become of these long works? I do not know. Will they be torn up or burned? It is quite possible. Unless Le Braz comes again to fetch them and put them together with those earlier ones. He already has twenty-four of my notebooks, but they are each [only] forty pages long, whereas I have in hand another twenty-four, each a hundred pages long, as well as thirteen notebooks dealing with philosophy, politics, sociology, and even mythology.

If Le Braz does not come fetch my manuscripts before I die, they will certainly be lost.

One other thing troubles me; it is that my corpse will surely fall into the hands of the priests, since there will be no one here to fend them off. It is true that I have already protested, and I protest still, any interference with my corpse by priests, and now again I formally declare any such interference to be null and void.

Et sic transit gloria mundi. Thus will end my own fame in this world. For I will have had a little fame in my final days. But all that is only vanity, said that triple assassin Solomon, the adulterous son of the greatest murderer of his time. Vanity of vanities, all is vanity, said that incomparable orgiast-turned-sage when he could no longer do otherwise. He even boasted of being learned, the most learned of men. At least he was a freethinker, even an atheist, although the Catholics have let his ultra-stupid natterings into their liturgy. He said there was no difference between man and the other animals: "The death of the one is as the death of the other; they both have the same breath and man is no greater than the beast. All go to the same place, for all is ash and to ash returneth." Vanity of vanities, all is but vanity.

I end by wishing mankind the power, or rather the will, to become true and good human beings capable of understanding one another and getting on together in a societal life that is noble and happy. And . . . *Doue bardono d'an nanaon.**

Duguines–Déguignet
Poul Raniquet, January 6, 1905

Exactly one hundred years after "the Austerlitz Sun" [Napoleon] cast the world into shadow beneath the autocracy and tyranny of [that] cruelest of men.

The End

---

*"God forgive in the beyond" (a ritual phrase).

ABOUT THE EDITOR

Bernez Rouz, a member of the Arkae Association of Historical Research, has devoted his life to tracking down the complete set of the notebooks of Jean-Marie Déguignet, only a fraction of which had been on record for more than a century.

ABOUT THE TRANSLATOR

Linda Asher has translated some thirty works since 1960, by authors including Restif de la Bretonne, Victor Hugo, Georges Simenon, Jean-Pierre Vernant, and Milan Kundera. In 2000, Asher received the translation prize of the French-American Foundation for *The Case of Doctor Sachs* (*La maladie de Sachs*). She has won ASCAP's Deems Taylor Prize and the Scott Moncrieff Prize of the British Society of Authors, and recently was named Chevalier of the Order of Arts and Letters of the French Republic. From 1980 to 1996, Asher was a fiction editor at *The New Yorker*, with special interest in publishing foreign literature.